AN INTRODUCTION
TO NEWS REPORTING

AN INTRODUCTION TO NEWS REPORTING

A Beginning Journalist's Guide

JAN JOHNSON YOPP

University of North Carolina at Chapel Hill

BETH A. HALLER

Towson University

Boston ▪ New York ▪ San Francisco
Mexico City ▪ Montreal ▪ Toronto ▪ London ▪ Madrid ▪ Munich ▪ Paris
Hong Kong ▪ Singapore ▪ Tokyo ▪ Cape Town ▪ Sydney

Series Editor: *Molly Taylor*
Series Editorial Assistant: *Michael Kish*
Senior Marketing Manager: *Mandee Eckersley*
Editorial Production Administrator: *Anna Socrates*
Editorial Production Service: *Omegatype Typography, Inc.*
Composition Buyer: *Linda Cox*
Manufacturing Buyer: *JoAnne Sweeney*
Cover Coordinator: *Joel Gendron*
Electronic Composition: *Omegatype Typography, Inc.*

For related titles and support materials, visit our online catalog at www.ablongman.com.

Between the time Web site information is gathered and then published, it is not unusual for some sites to have closed. Also, the transcription of URLs can result in typographical errors. The publisher would appreciate notification where these errors occur so that they may be corrected in subsequent editions.

Library of Congress Cataloging-in-Publication Data
Yopp, Jan Johnson
 An introduction to news reporting : a beginning journalist's guide /
by Jan Johnson Yopp and Beth A. Haller.
  p. cm.
 Includes bibliographical references and index.
 ISBN 0-205-34218-3 (alk. paper)
  1. Reporters and reporting. I. Haller, Beth A. II. Title.

PN4781.Y67 2005
070.4'3—dc22

                                        2004044694

Printed in the United States of America

10 9 8 7 6 5 4 3 2 1   09 08 07 06 05 04

CONTENTS

PART III   COVERING YOUR BEAT

CHAPTER SIX
Covering the Basics of Local Government   94

CHAPTER SEVEN

Financing Local Government   127

CHAPTER EIGHT
Covering the Essentials of Education   154

CHAPTER TWELVE

Covering Specialty Beats 242

CHAPTER THIRTEEN

Elections and Polls 265

PART IV   RESOURCE GUIDE

CHAPTER FOURTEEN
Finding Resources   284

PREFACE

■ ■ ■ ■ ■

A graduate of an accredited journalism–mass communication program landed his first job at a six-day-a-week paper in South Carolina. He was thrilled. But within six months the newspaper had promoted him to business editor. He was lost.

Frantically he called a former professor to ask: "What do I report on the business beat? Whom do I call? Where do I go for information? What do I do?" In his college classes he had never written a business story. Weekly conversations over a month with his professor produced story ideas, and willing business resources in the community gave him leads and background information.

No program in journalism–mass communication can teach students how to cover each and every reporting assignment that might arise once they go to work. But graduates should come away with the skills to figure out how to develop source lists, how to think of stories "outside the box," as the popular saying goes, and how to develop a strategy for reporting those stories. They should know how to track down information and to write a complete, balanced, and accurate story. In addition, students should have an interest in people and events and be conditioned to look for ideas and knowledge apart from routine, daily news suppliers.

Webster's New World College Dictionary defines *report* the verb as "to give an account of, often at regular intervals; give information about (something seen, done, etc.)." For hundreds of years, reporters have given accounts about events seen, done, or heard by someone, including themselves. Their reports have been based on information in letters, government documents, other publications, news releases, or databases. Reporters add details from interviews and the events they and others have witnessed.

Every day reporters look for stories that will interest and educate their audiences or reveal more about their community or world. Granted, some stories are just there: the city council meeting, the hospital groundbreaking, or the community's rally to aid flood victims. A story idea may come from an editor, a colleague, or someone in the community. Sometimes reporters go after stories that will "scoop" or beat another reporter. Stories may be routine or in-depth pieces.

Any good reporting requires going beyond the obvious and expected and writing stories that are fresh and compelling. To write those stories, experienced reporters—whether they work for newspapers, television or radio stations, online news services, or wire services, or whether they write freelance pieces or books—have lists of reliable sources, who provide accurate, complete information. Every day reporters add to their source lists, particularly as they write about new topics, as new people pop up as experts or witnesses, or as sites appear online. Fledgling reporters do not have such lists, but over time they will. Just as the novice reporter assigned to the business beat, they have to start somewhere.

Reporters often get their start in reporting while in college. As a first assignment, an instructor may assign a campus story, such as student government budget cuts, a campus crime, or a visiting lecturer's speech. The instructor assumes that students have a head start on where to go for information if they cover campus events. As students, they should be familiar with the university community and its resources, right?

Not so for many students. Despite spending two to three years on a college campus, reporting students may be clueless where to start seeking information. Others may be reluctant to ask strangers questions. A few may not go far enough in the types of questions they ask. They may not be able to determine which information is important and which is not. That first, second, third, and even fourth reporting assignment may cause dismay.

Students—and even experienced reporters—need direction in finding story ideas, sources, and information. Students today often look no further than the Internet, seeking information from the comfort of the library or their dorm rooms. They need to be pushed away from terminals. Information before 1990 may not be cataloged on the Internet. Students must learn that much information can be found in thumbing through boxes of letters and memos or in reading microfilm copies of newspapers. Each tidbit of information leads to the next bit, and each discovery makes the report more accurate and more complete. Students need to get excited about uncovering each nugget of information and not approach reporting as a chore to be accomplished with the fewest sources possible.

One textbook cannot cover everything a reporter needs to know about any beat, partly because each state and its local governing bodies are set up differently. Sources change, as do issues. This textbook is designed to give student reporters an introduction to beat reporting and a solid start in thinking about story ideas, seeking information, knowing who the sources are, cultivating those sources, and working the beat. The text assumes that students using this book have had a basic newswriting course and know basic newswriting structure. This text is designed to be an overview of beats, the players, the issues, the sources, and the stories. Advanced reporting techniques would be covered in a separate text.

The first section reviews the tools reporters use from a consideration of news values and audiences to research and interviewing. The second section covers how to gather information ethically and legally and how to report the diversity of communities. The third section gets into the specifics of beat reporting: how to cover local government, local government finance, and topics such as public safety, education, courts, and a host of others. The final section gives students a list of Internet-based resources and shows how to create a source list pertinent to a specific county or state.

Each chapter hits the highlights of the beat, and each beat could be a book on its own. Throughout the text, students can read examples and angles beat reporters have pursued, the sources they used, and how they presented information. Experienced reporters share their insight and tips. Student reporters see how beats overlap and how reporters work together to research and write stories. Students can learn how to become information detectives and to relish the job of reporting.

This text, while geared to reporters, has information that will benefit anyone planning a career in mass communication. The tips on how to interview, for example, can help the public relations practitioner who is writing a story on the employee of the month for her company. How local government is financed can aid the graphic designer in drawing a pie chart that shows where local revenues come from. The ethics and legal chapter contains information that any mass communicator should know to maintain his or her credibility and to avoid libel or other lawsuits. The resources chapter will point seekers of information to keepers of information.

The student who became the panicked business reporter in South Carolina amassed a hefty file of stories during a year on the beat. For example, he got front-page stories when a major automobile manufacturer decided to build a multimillion-dollar plant in the county. He wrote the announcement story and subsequent stories about the types of jobs the company would bring, what the county would do with more tax revenues, how counties work behind the scenes to attract industry, and a dozen other stories. He learned how to develop the business beat, but he struggled. The struggle might have been less if he had had the benefit of this book first.

ACKNOWLEDGMENTS

The completion of any creative or scholarly work depends on the efforts of many people beyond the authors. We would like to thank the following people for their support and patience during the gestation of this manuscript. At UNC–Chapel Hill, thanks go to Dean Richard Cole, Professor Harry Amana, Professor Joseph Ferrell, Professor Robert Stevenson, Assistant Professor Chris Roush, and graduate student John Kuka. We acknowledge Towson University's Department of Mass Communication and Communication Studies for its time and resources.

Thanks to Pete Johnson and Eric Torbenson of the *Dallas Morning News* for their substantial contributions to the business chapter; Orange County (NC) Assistant District Attorney James Woodall for his assistance in the courts chapter; Bill Toohey of Baltimore County (MD) police, Leslie Miller of the Associated Press, and Mark Hilts of the FBI for their extensive help with the public safety chapter; Mike Morris of the *Sonora* (CA) *Union Democrat*, Jonathan Rockoff of the *Baltimore Sun*, and Marjorie Hampson of the Baltimore County

Public Schools for their input on the education chapter; Kathi Wolfe of Religion News Service and environmental reporter Dale Willman for assistance with the specialty beat chapter; Dr. Linda Florence Callahan of North Carolina Agricultural and Technical State University for review of the diversity chapter; and Jean Dimeo of Hanley-Wood for assistance with the research chapter. A special thanks goes to Jennifer LaFleur of the *Dallas Morning News* for detailed feedback on the research chapter, as well as the use of her math basics article.

We thank Kathy McAdams of the University of Maryland–College Park for introducing us so many years ago, which eventually led to our collaboration on this book. We thank the reviewers for Allyn & Bacon whose detailed feedback helped us polish the book: Dale Cressman, Brigham Young University; Marlin Shipman, Arkansas State University; and Kelly S. Wray, Eastern Oklahoma State College. Special thanks go to Karon Bowers, Molly Taylor, and Michael Kish at Allyn & Bacon for gently nudging this book through to completion.

And especially thanks to our family members: Kate Elliott, Meg Elliott, Diana Grumbles, Ernest Grumbles III, Gay Haller, Richard Haller, Mary Mc-Greevy, and Mike Yopp. We definitely could not have produced this book without all of you.

AN INTRODUCTION
TO NEWS REPORTING

CHAPTER 1

GETTING STARTED IN REPORTING THE NEWS

Most people think of reporters as people who work for newspapers, magazines, radio or television stations, or online sites. True. But in reality, every person is a reporter. Each day people gather, examine, sort, retain, dump, and disseminate information. People share information with one another throughout every day. The information might be as simple as a mother leaving a to-do list for her teenage daughter, a teacher outlining material to be covered on an exam, a weather forecaster noting the daily ozone level, or a college roommate giving directions to a popular nightspot. Each bit of information is relevant to each audience.

A reporter's job is to gather information and share that information with his or her readers, viewers, listeners, subscribers, Web surfers, or anyone who makes up the reporter's audience. Without information, no one has a message, and a reporter does not have a story. The reporter must gather enough information to ensure the story is complete and balanced. As much as possible, the story should be fair and report all sides of an issue. The reporter must double-check all information for accuracy.

Those in mass media must know how to gather and report information—regardless of whether they are newspaper reporters, public relations practitioners, broadcast anchors, magazine editors, advertising copywriters, online editors, freelance photographers, Web site designers, or in any number of other jobs. For all those professional communication jobs, knowing what information to get and where and how to get it is crucial. With that information, you will craft the story or message aimed at your particular audience.

To become a solid reporter, you need to build on the basic skills you learned in an introductory newswriting or media writing course. You might have already written about basic topics ranging from police to weather to obituaries. You might have written news releases or broadcast stories. You might have done basic interviewing. You know the news elements—who, what, when, where, how, and why—and the news values that guide reporters in determining types of leads and story organization.

In this chapter you will:

- Consider the role of media in covering their communities,
- Review what makes news,
- Tie news elements and news values into reporting,
- See how media cover news via beats,
- Consider the focus for local news, and
- Look at issues that affect reporters in doing their jobs.

THE ROLE OF MEDIA IN COVERING COMMUNITIES

The First Amendment of the Constitution states that "Congress shall make no law . . . abridging the freedom of speech, or of the press . . ." That language gives reporters the freedom to report information without governmental prior restraint or censorship. Over the years Congress and state legislatures have passed laws allowing greater access to government records and spelling out just which documents reporters—and the general public—can get. More about access to records is covered in Chapter 2.

But laws have also outlined when reporters can be excluded from meetings, which committees are exempted from reporter scrutiny, and other instances of restricted access to information. Court cases have also set precedents that affect reporters' access to events and data. Reporters must constantly fight for access to information if they are to cover their communities and their world accurately and completely. As a reporter, you must know the relevant laws and court cases that dictate how you gather information in the state in which you work.

Journalists and those who devour journalists' work agree that the media have a role and responsibility to educate and inform members of a democratic society. Journalists report on events, issues, and people so voters can participate at all levels of society—from voting at election time to appearing at public hearings that will determine the town's development. At the same time that audiences rely on the media to serve as watchdogs of government and to give them information to carry out their daily lives, audiences still are quick to criticize when they think the media have gone too far in gathering and releasing information.

A report by the Pew Center for People and the Press released in August 2002 revealed that 49 percent of 1,365 adults polled said they thought news organizations were highly professional. Prior to the September 11, 2001, terrorist attacks, 54 percent ranked news organizations as professional; the percentage jumped to 73 percent in November 2001, but the media's improved regard was short lived. Six months later only 30 percent said that the media cared about the people they reported on, the 2002 study showed.

At the same time respondents complained about news organizations, they realized their value. The Pew Center report noted people supported the watchdog role that news organizations performed. Almost three out of five people (59 percent) believed press scrutiny of political leaders kept them from doing things they should not. And half (49 percent) thought press criticism of the military kept the armed forces prepared.

Despite criticism, journalists must continue to seek out who, what, when, where, how, and why. They must find information, synthesize it, and publish it. They must tell audiences why the information matters. They must hold government officials and executives of publicly held and even privately owned companies accountable. Reporters must be able to adapt to new technology and new ways of disseminating information. At the same time, they must go about their daily work ethically and responsibly and within the limits of the law. Journalists do more than just a job: They fulfill roles as essential members of a democratic society.

WHAT MAKES NEWS

Webster's New World College Dictionary (2001) defines *news* as "new information about anything, information previously unknown; reports, collectively, of recent happenings . . . broadcast over radio or TV, printed in a newspaper, etc." When reporters report news, they tell audiences information, generally new information. Their reports might be the first time the information has been shared, updates of earlier reports, or expanded reports.

More and more, however, much of what is aired rehashes earlier broadcasts. Electronic news organizations with 24-hour news cycles have to fill 1,440 minutes a day. Audiences feel that they hear details over and over and over. And they do, because anchors recap or restate earlier news and insert a few new details. Print publications do not have the capacity to restate in great length. They devote their news columns to more expanded coverage and greater depth. Online sites do what television and print publications do best: keep information up-to-date and up-to-the-minute and add greater depth.

The need to fill 24-hour news cycles has led to criticism that the media push more sensational stories, not considering the true news value of a story, or hype the stories they report. Critics note that the type of news reported has changed in the last decade as television stations compete for audience attention: More news to entertain viewers appears along with story after story on crime and arrests. Reporters and fledgling journalists must be aware of these complaints and pursue newsworthy stories and angles that matter to their audiences. News elements, as reviewed in Figure 1.1, and news values should guide reporters—as should ethics and the law.

FIGURE 1.1   News Elements

Who identifies the individual, group of people, or even organization carrying out the action in the story or who is affected.

What is the action and generally is represented by the verb.

Where gives the geographic context of the story or where the action occurred. Where usually is found after the verb, but a dateline leading the story will tell where the story originated.

When is the time element. A story could have many time elements that could be used to tell the story or weave a series of events together. In most newswriting, the time element fits conveniently after the what or verb. Rarely does when start a story.

How gives details and expands what. If three construction workers are killed, readers will want to know how: They were crushed when an 80-ton concrete wall fell on them.

Why gives a reason a change or decision was made or explains the cause of an event. In the example of the construction workers just cited, readers will want to know why the wall fell.

Types of News

Regardless of what the surveys say about media credibility, reporters continue to go out every day, gather news, and write stories. Their beats or the areas they cover generate stories. Their editors might suggest a story topic. They might be part of a team of reporters and designers developing a package of articles on a particular issue or trend in their communities, such as the impact of city growth on the school system. Or unexpected events, such as a train derailment, might drive coverage.

The news might be time specific, that is, about events that happen on a routine basis. For example, media cover back-to-school events each August or September and holiday celebrations such as Memorial Day observances. Reporters know when and where governmental boards meet regularly. Court reporters know when traffic court or trials are set. The challenge to annual or routine coverage is developing a different angle, finding new ways of reporting the same story, or discovering a previously unknown source.

Reporters cover breaking news or events that happen unexpectedly. For example, a wooden porch crowded with partygoers collapses and falls three stories, killing 12 people. A university president suddenly resigns, or police arrest a fugitive sought for 20 years. Media are not prepared to cover breaking or spot news, but reporters' and editors' experience, sources, and talents allow them to get the information and produce the story under deadline pressure.

Reporters also write news features. Based on a news event, the feature aspect adds detail and information and expands on the impact. An accident in which three teenage drivers die might result in a story on the number of 16-

year-old drivers charged with driving under the influence during the last year. The story has news value because of emotional impact and the magnitude of the problem but less timeliness because the problem is ongoing. A reporter or team of reporters might investigate the trend by using public records and talking with law enforcement officials, parents, teenagers, driver education teachers, and others.

In most cases, reporters and editors determine news coverage based on their best judgment of which stories are newsworthy. To do that they consider news values.

News Values

News values, or the aspects of an event that make it worth knowing about, carry different weight for different media and also influence the approach a reporter takes on a story. News values also dictate the types of questions a reporter will need to ask.

One of the most important—if not the most important—news values for reporters is *impact*. It's the news value that makes people care about the story. People want to know how they will be affected. It answers when readers ask: "So what? So why should I be interested?" Audiences will pay attention when reporters tell how lives will be affected—for better or worse.

Impact, often technical, should be explained in clear language and in tangible terms. Reporters should place impact high and usually in the lead of a story. University students need to know changes in the undergraduate curriculum and how that will affect their course of study. Local residents need to know how much a road project will inconvenience their lives because of detours. State workers need to know how much increased health insurance premiums will affect their monthly checks. Reporters always need to ask sources about impact and to translate the effect clearly and logically.

Some students confuse impact with *magnitude*. While impact is the effect, magnitude is the size of the event: the numbers of deaths from a tornado, the number on the Richter scale that indicates the strength of an earthquake, or the turnout for the Relay for Life March to support cancer research. While impact answers "so what," magnitude can make readers raise their eyebrows in surprise or disbelief. Television reporters have the benefit of visuals to add the "oh, my" element to the story and show viewers clearly the scope of the event. Print reporters have to use words to convey magnitude. They can ask officials or experts to quantify magnitude. For example, if a volcano erupts on Hawaii, a reporter should ask how much lava flowed and use a comparison that readers can grasp. The answer might be enough lava to fill the Rose Bowl in Pasadena 10,000 times. Reporters can also support the story with still photos. Online news sites use both video and still art to illustrate the story.

Probably the most common news value is *conflict*. Reporters can find conflict in almost every story they cover. Visible and continuing conflicts such as battles in the Middle East lead the news almost every day. Lesser battles take place in town halls, between neighbors, or during contract negotiations. Someone somewhere is arguing with someone else to gain ground or keep control. Every time the city council considers the annual budget, conflict will arise over who is going to get how much money. Residents might object to proposed tax increases. University students might object to the loss of green space on campus for a parking garage. If reporters ask who is involved and who benefits or suffers, they might uncover conflict.

Timeliness relates to the news element *when*. People want up-to-the-minute, timely news. When an event happened generally is in the first sentence of a story and often is placed after the verb. People need to know when so they have a time context for the event, how recently the event happened, and even what preceded the event. If a hurricane hits the Gulf coast of Texas, readers will want to know when the hurricane made landfall. Television viewers will want to know the projected path of the storm and when it will sweep across other Texas cities.

Timeliness is a critical news value for television and online media. Television reporters can explain events as they are happening, such as embedded journalists did when they covered the U.S. invasion of Iraq in spring 2003. Online media follow with up-to-date and expanded reports. Print media tied to production schedules cannot publish newspapers or magazines as quickly as television and online sites can report the news. Newspapers and magazines will focus a lot of news hole or space on impact because they are not the most timely media anymore. When the terrorist attacks occurred the morning of September 11, 2001, however, many morning newspapers produced special afternoon editions.

Proximity tells *where* an event occurred and whether it happened nearby. The closer an event, the more interested the audience. Geographic proximity works like concentric circles: People are most interested in news of their towns, then their counties, the state, the nation, and the world. Most media focus on local news and how issues relate specifically to their circulation or viewing areas. Reporters often talk about "the local angle," or localizing a story as they look for ways to tie a story to the community, either through the location of the event, the people involved, or the impact. Later in this chapter is a more in-depth discussion of local news.

In a slightly different context, emotional proximity ties audiences to people they can relate to. Parents of children with special needs have emotional proximity because they identify with one another. Students are more interested in stories about students in another college community, even if the community is 2,000 miles away. Students can relate to the experiences of other students. A university newspaper editor might read a story about the increased tension between university and town officials in another state and wonder, "How is the relationship between our campus leaders and town officials?"

When the *who* has *prominence* or is well known, he or she figures conspicuously in the story. Celebrities such as singers or actors have prominence because they attract fans' attention. So do political figures such as the president, the governor, the mayor, or a U.S. senator because they have the power to influence laws or affect citizens' lives. When Arnold Schwarzenegger decided to run for governor of California, the story made national news. When the U.S. president gets a dog, that pet becomes news. When the principal of a local high school gets a dog, few people care.

When actress Katharine Hepburn died, media reflected on her career that spanned seven decades and won her four Oscars. Entertainment reporters noted that Hollywood would never see another actor of Hepburn's enduring talent. Television reporters could tell Hepburn's life story through clips from her films and taped interviews with the actress. Print reporters quoted individuals who knew her. People associated with or related to celebrities also have prominence and can make the headlines.

Some stories become news because of *unusualness* or *oddity*. An unusual aspect of a routine story will propel it to the front page. A wife kills her husband in their home on a military base. Not unusual, except the context: It is the fifth death in two weeks between spouses living on the base. When a rare right whale becomes entangled in fishing line, people around the country follow the story.

Unusualness carries with it a caution: Reporting on the unique aspect of an event might portray people as freakish or unnatural. Reporters must be careful to quote sources accurately and to use correct language that does not exaggerate what already might be a story that causes people to stop and stare. Reporters must keep out their opinions or phrasing that could distort the story.

People like stories about individuals' efforts to cope with life's challenges. That's where *emotional effect* or human interest comes in as a news value. People like stories about other people, and they are especially attracted to stories about children and animals. They like romance and reconciliation. Stories that bring people together or show their successes grab audience attention. People around the country followed the abduction of Salt Lake City teen Elizabeth Smart in 2002 and her return to her family nine months later. An attempted separation of conjoined twins and their subsequent deaths captured people's hearts.

In determining which stories to write, reporters must consider news values to guide their direction and focus. News values also can help in framing questions to judge importance and relevance of a story topic. How widespread will the effect of the council's action be? Is it controversial (conflict)? How soon will residents be affected (timeliness)? Do prominent citizens support or oppose the action? The story has proximity because the town council took action that will affect local residents. Magnitude could be a factor if the decision came after a public hearing swamped with 300 town residents. Reporters can use the news values and news elements to ensure that they cover a story completely. How well they cover the story will determine how and where the story is played.

TAKING WHAT IS NEWS AND REPORTING IT

Each day editors at newspapers, online sites, television stations, and other media outlets determine which stories will be aired or printed. They sit in news meetings as other editors present their top picks and lobby for their position or location in the paper, on the site, or in the broadcast. The news values just discussed, along with editors' gut instincts and experience, prior audience reaction to stories, and an attempt to balance national with local stories contribute to deciding the day's news menu. Editors also give consideration to audience needs and interests. In sorting through stories, editors think about what is important to their audiences, regardless of the medium they work for. What stories will help residents in their daily lives or affect the community's future? For some media outlets, concern for ratings factors in to which stories get aired.

Out of these news meetings surfaces general agreement on what is newsworthy. If you look at the front pages of five major dailies on any given day, you usually will find consensus on the world or national stories. A publication's philosophy of local news and even its format determine what fills out the rest of the front page or the home page. Some editors insist on a local government or education story on the front page or home page every day. Others follow a front-page format that requires a major reporting package or feature story and photo or other art every day. News of national or international importance might frame the daily feature. A newspaper might have a rule that a local story is always placed across the top of the front page. Such design factors affect editors as well as reporters.

Everyone who works at a media organization has a responsibility to come up with news. Wire editors get news from major wire services, such as The Associated Press, Reuters, or the *New York Times* News Service, because most newspapers cannot afford to hire and support national and foreign correspondents. Reporters and editors get story ideas by reading other publications, viewing TV and online newscasts, or listening to police scanners. Staff members of organizations from political to nonprofit supply news to the media via news releases, email announcements, or phone calls. For local stories, editors and reporters get ideas from what is happening in their own lives and their neighbors' lives. They cover the daily routine of local government. As noted earlier in the chapter, some news is seasonal, such as schools getting ready for the new academic year or holiday shopping trends, and other news is breaking or spot news.

Reporters play a key role in determining the day's news coverage. Reporters out in the community often pick up tips for stories. For student reporters to be successful in finding stories, one professor advised: "You must be curious enough about people's lives that as you drive down streets at night, you hope people have their curtains open so you can see how they have decorated their homes." Editors also rely on reporters to suggest stories based on the beats or topic areas they cover.

Covering the News with Beats

Many media organizations, particularly newspapers and news magazines, establish ways to make sure that all parts of the community are covered regularly and systematically. Editors assign reporters to specific areas or beats, and reporters become "experts" in the subjects or beats they cover. Among a newspaper's beats might be business, education, government, public safety including police and fire services, environment, health, and religion. Beats can be further divided into higher education and education kindergarten through twelfth grade (K–12); retail, high-tech, consumer, and other areas within business; city, county, or state government; planning and zoning and social services within the county; and on and on. A newspaper will establish beats based on its philosophy of news coverage. Most beats are local, that is, they focus on geographic areas that most directly affect audiences. A newspaper might rely on a wire service to provide coverage of the state capital 75 miles away so its staff can report solely on local news.

The size of the news staff can affect the structure of beats. Where the staff is few in numbers, reporters cannot specialize. A radio reporter might be one of only two reporters and thus be responsible for all city and county reporting. At a television station, reporters might be general assignment, that is, they have no particular beat but are assigned to any story that comes up. A newspaper might divide beats so that editors supervise certain reporters, such as a metro editor who oversees city and county government and their respective offices. A state editor would work with state political reporters, and a national editor would be responsible for staff members covering U.S. congressional offices and federal offices, including courts.

Once assigned to a beat, a reporter follows a process to learn the background and sources, no matter what the beat. A reporter new to a beat can become familiar with the beat via the following:

■ The former beat reporter who can give an assessment of best and worst sources, trends, upcoming stories, personalities, pluses, and minuses.

■ The newspaper morgue or library for stories that can give background, trends, issues, and personalities. These archives are invaluable to a new beat reporter, particularly if the former beat reporter has moved on.

■ Directories. Most beats will have prescribed contact lists, such as city government department heads and council members. For the business beat, a useful directory might come from the chamber of commerce.

■ Paper trail. Agendas, minutes of meetings, reports, and other documents can provide background. Look beyond local material. A national report on use of aspirin to prevent pancreatic cancer could benefit the local health reporter.

■ Internet sources. From professional and trade associations to journalism how-to guides, hundreds of Web sites give reporters quick information and contacts. For a court beat, a Web site might provide the names of district attorneys across the state.

■ Books on the topic. Dozens of books have been written on any beat, from the environment to politics. Often experienced reporters will share their insights, or they will write about covering a specific event, such as being an embedded journalist when the United States invaded Iraq. Health writer Jane Brody of the *New York Times* has written several books on how to stay healthy.

■ People. People are crucial to any new beat reporter and should be contacted after the reporter has done basic research to become familiar with the beat. The beat reporter should make an appointment with key people, such as the mayor, the county manager, the chief district court judge, the police chief, the fire marshal, the director of the health department, the director of the chamber of commerce—whoever oversees day-to-day operations of major agencies and organizations on the beat.

Establishing relationships is extremely important. When a good rapport exists, reporters have a better chance of getting tips about stories before events happen and getting quotes to put events in context after they happen. One long-time state political reporter encouraged new beat reporters to get to know secretaries. Once a week he would make his rounds, that is, stop by certain offices and chat with office personnel over a cup of coffee. Those folks often were his best sources to confirm information, quell rumors, or set up quick interviews with busy officials.

Some news organizations rotate reporters among beats. Their philosophy: Keep reporters from becoming too close to their sources. One newspaper had to switch a reporter who had covered police for more than 10 years. He overlooked a major story. He allowed police to persuade him that what he saw as a story was just usual police business in using undercover agents to make arrests. When editors move a reporter to a new beat, they have to allow time for the reporter to learn the players and the issues, which could affect that beat's coverage for awhile.

Although becoming familiar with any beat follows a fairly standard process, the sources, issues, and trends obviously will differ. Reporters' beats often will overlap. A business story might have health implications, such as the relocation of a pharmaceutical company to your town and its development of a drug to treat high blood pressure. Reporters must be resourceful and develop a "nose for news." Reporters' success depends on how well they cover the beat, learn the sources, and come up with story ideas. For the beginning reporter, that beat most likely will entail some aspect of local news.

Defining Local News

More and more, audiences are relying on electronic news sources such as CNN and MSNBC and online news sites such as washingtonpost.com or usatoday.com for national and international news. Studies also have shown that people are starting to use the Internet more as a news source. But national news sites do not tell readers and viewers what is happening in their backyards. Audiences expect to get information and more in-depth detail about events in their communities from their local news outlets, such as radio, television, online sites, and newspapers.

Responding to readers' needs has been extremely important for newspapers, which have been losing readers or circulation fairly consistently for the last two decades. While people go to television first and more often for news, they do see newspapers as being more credible and reliable. Newspapers' strongest opportunities to increase and retain readership also lie with local news coverage, according to a survey by the American Society of Newspaper Editors (ASNE).

Reporters, editors, and teachers have long debated the definition of *local* as it applies to reporting. Some build on the local government idea and use geography as a defining criterion for local coverage. Under this approach, local applies to anything that happens within the city or county limits, including individuals and entities such as schools, courts, police, businesses, hospitals, chambers of commerce, and community organizations.

Although such geographic division might seem logical, it might be limited. News coverage often extends beyond the town limits or the county line. For example, local governments are intricately involved with state and federal governments as well as agencies that regulate or finance local activities. Often local organizations have international ties.

Frank Denton, former editor of the *Wisconsin State Journal* in Madison, Wisconsin, edited a text, *The Local News Handbook,* that was distributed by ASNE in 1999. The book looked at factors of what it called "localness" or attributes of local news coverage that attracted readers' attention. Under *The Local News Handbook* guidelines, local news coverage could be divided into areas of interest: neighborhoods, education, kids and youth, recreation, religion and faith, and business, among others. Reporters for news organizations following that model could overlap coverage, such as education with kids and youth.

No matter how editors define local news, one reporter can cover only so much. Editors and publishers surveyed in the ASNE report said that the investment in more people is the greatest barrier to more local news coverage. Hiring more staff costs more money. Reporters must accept that the fiscal or business side of a news operation has a direct impact on the news side. Income from advertising and other sources of revenue will affect what the newsroom can do—from increasing salaries to hiring additional reporters.

At the same time that news organizations recognize the need for local news to keep readers, they face the reality that readers and viewers do not rate highly the credibility of their local media. In the 2002 Pew Center report noted earlier in the chapter, only one out of five people surveyed (21 percent) said they believed most or all of what they read in their local papers. National outlets such as the *Wall Street Journal*, named by 33 percent of respondents, and CNN (37 percent) ranked higher in credibility. Again, the lack of credibility should concern every reporter. Each story covered accurately, completely, and fairly increases a journalist's reputation and fosters relationships that will enable him or her to work accurately and efficiently.

ISSUES FACING JOURNALISTS AND OTHER COMMUNICATORS

In recent years the job of journalist has become even more difficult as the media have been criticized for too much sensationalism, particularly on the national level. Each scandal a president or chief executive officer faces, be it personal or professional, lends itself to criticism that the media uncovered and shared too much information. Deadline pressures push reporters to get information quickly and increase the potential for errors. The need to fill 24-hour news cycles has created an insatiable media desire for news as well as the seemingly endless repetition of those details and facts, as noted earlier. Any error decreases public trust and media credibility and increases criticism.

Criticism and Restrictions

Constant media criticism and suspicion continue to affect how journalists do their jobs. Beginning reporters must be aware that the environment might not be conducive to gathering information. Some sources do not trust reporters and might try to withhold information. Business organizations and chief executive officers might prohibit the release of data that could harm them. Others, such as state government officers, will take legal steps to restrict reporters' access to information, such as tightening states' open records laws. Even as more information becomes readily accessible via the Internet, restrictions are surfacing. Since September 11, 2001, federal and state open records laws have excluded from public view the response plans to terrorist attacks for organizations and agencies, including universities.

While the World Wide Web has provided faster and greater access to information, it has created problems for journalists. For example, so much information on the Web can actually slow down reporters as they sift through hundreds of Web sites to find accurate and reliable data and sources. Online information also makes it much easier to lift or plagiarize others' work intentionally or innocently.

At the same time reporters have been aided by technology, the advent of online communication has diverted some audiences away from more traditional media such as newspapers. The downturn in the economy at the turn of the twenty-first century affected media companies' profits, which had already been dampened in the 1990s from competition with new media. As a result, newspapers adopted innovative reporting methods, such as civic or public journalism, to woo readers back to their pages. Newspapers launched companion online editions to give readers Web site access to news and other information and to keep themselves marketable.

Many media managers looked at more cost-effective ways to produce news. Some have moved toward convergence, whereby media, owned by the same company or even competing media, shared some aspect of the newsgathering operation. Newspaper reporters have had to learn how to be comfortable before a broadcast camera, and others have had to write for both online and print editions.

Convergence: Here to Stay?

Reporters in some locales have had to accept management's move to convergence, or sharing of information and staffs between or even among media in a community. Usually the same company owns the media, although some media have an agreement to promote one another's content. Some media observers see convergence as a permanent fixture in U.S. media, others as just an experiment. Some say that online publications and sites represent convergence or the melding of print and electronic media. Supporters say that each medium within the convergence partnership—newspaper, radio, television, Internet—can maintain its values and basic structure but also can have the benefit of broader resources and expanded reach among audiences.

Critics see convergence primarily as a business-side proposition that could affect content quality and how thoroughly and accurately issues are reported. For example, a newspaper reporter who also has to write for the television station in a converged system might hurry to make a deadline and overlook in-depth fact checking. Or he might have overlooked detail that would add color to a print description that was not needed because of the visuals on television. Some critics say convergence will dilute a reporter's abilities because one reporter cannot be a good print journalist, television reporter, and online site writer. Convergence could also affect a reporter who starts the day at 9 A.M. for a newspaper but who must stay until 9 P.M. to provide commentary on a local radio talk show.

Convergence has been used particularly in the electronic field. Convergence can take several forms. A news reporter for a television station might give information about an event to a reporter from a sister newspaper with which it has a sharing agreement. A television station might do a promotion for a story in a sister newspaper. With shared staffs, a television reporter might write a story and then rewrite it for the station's Web site. Or a newspaper reporter might take along a tape recorder to get an audio clip for the story version he will write for the online site.

Among the early ventures into convergence were Phoenix, Arizona, and Tampa, Florida. The *Arizona Republic* and Channel 12 news, both owned by Gannett Inc., each referred readers and viewers to coverage on the other medium. The *Republic* could provide the deep content while the television story had the visuals. In addition, newspaper and television stations could refer audiences to the online site, which in turn could link readers to additional information.

Reid Ashe, former publisher of the *Tampa Tribune*, said that the benefits of convergence in its early stages have been to Internet operations first, then to television, and lastly to newspapers. In the *Tampa Tribune*–WFLA-TV agreement, Ashe noted in a 2001 speech:

> Each still had its traditional format but increased its resources. Advertising sales increased through multimedia packages. The partnership allowed the two to exploit the strengths of each medium. There was some institutional investment because we had to build trust among staff and an environment where people can experiment.

Publishers and media owners support convergence because they see shared staffs as a way to reduce newsroom expenses. In addition, the business side can sell advertising packages that include ads for all media in a certain market: newspaper, radio, television, and online. The package appeals to advertisers who would get a reduced rate to advertise in more than one medium. The package approach particularly helps online sites that have not been able to support themselves financially.

Executives considering convergence realize that logistics are just one piece of the puzzle. Combining newsrooms requires money and staff training on issues from news responsibilities to technology. One of the biggest challenges might be the culture of each medium and how to combine staffs of a certain mind-set and institutional history.

Broad acceptance of convergence might take time, persistence, and progressive attitudes. In cities where competition has existed, even between media owned by the same organization, staff have been reluctant to have to all of a sudden share their stories. Some newspaper reporters are uncomfortable appearing on air to promote a story in their publication. Adjusting to new ways is often difficult for anyone, including reporters who are steeped in a certain way of producing news. How media and reporters will accept it and what effect converged newsrooms will have on content has yet to be known.

The trend toward convergence has prompted some schools of journalism and mass communication to ensure students can write across platforms or in different media styles. A reporting student might write a news story for the local newspaper and then adapt the style for television broadcast. The same student might also have to be interviewed by a student television reporter to gain experience in electronic media. At the very least, media officials who hire students want them to know how writing styles differ and how to be comfortable with different media. Media managers want students to know what convergence is and how it could affect them. No matter where reporters work, however, they must still have the basic skills to gather information and produce stories.

Civic Journalism and Audiences

Newspapers began losing circulation in the late 1980s with the advent of more and more media: cable television channels, specialized publications, and the fledgling World Wide Web, among others. Readers voiced complaints that newspapers covered conflict and did not focus enough on community issues. As editors and managers listened, a new journalism construct emerged, one they dubbed civic journalism or public journalism.

Civic journalism has been practiced in a variety of ways at a variety of media and, in many instances, has become just another way of covering the news. In sum, civic journalism differs from traditional journalism because it brings the media into the story and often sets up the media as the facilitators of solutions. Media have used civic journalism to help solve community issues, not just report on issues in news columns or point fingers of blame from editorial pages. In most cases, media identified a community problem and brought together residents, civic leaders, and officials to identify problem areas and pose solutions.

For example, in traditional journalism a newspaper might run a series of stories about the poor condition of school buildings in the district. Using the civic journalism model, the newspaper would investigate but would also set up a series of public meetings for parents, administrators, and others to discuss ways to improve the schools. The newspaper might even put proposals on its online site and invite readers to vote on which proposal they believed would work. A civic journalism project could be less solution oriented and more informational, such as providing extensive background on candidates in an election.

Newspapers have not been the only medium to embrace civic journalism. Television stations and online sites have incorporated civic journalism–type practices into daily reporting. Some methods proved subtler than others did. Media have used various techniques to attract public comment and debate. They listed reporters' email addresses at the end of stories that carried a reporter's name or byline and solicited reader responses to stories. They provided officials' telephone numbers and email addresses. They sponsored debates or call-in programs. In recent years, Web sites have become an integral part of civic journalism projects. With interactive Web sites, viewers could select their favorite design for a riverside revitalization project or "walk" through an inmate's cell while listening to his comments about prison life.

As an outgrowth of the civic journalism movement, the Pew Charitable Trusts funded a 10-year initiative called the Pew Center for Civic Journalism. Based in Washington, DC, the center made grants to media who submitted proposals that would promote civic journalism projects. It also began an annual awards program to recognize outstanding and successful ventures into civic journalism.

One of the leaders in civic journalism has been Frank Denton, former editor of the *State Journal* in Madison, Wisconsin. The newspaper launched as one of its first efforts, "We the People," a one-time presidential election year project. It became the country's longest-running civic journalism endeavor. The paper used town hall meetings, candidate debates, and even interactive civic activities to engage voters and make them more aware of election year issues. The newspaper developed a partnership with public radio and television to broadcast "We the People" throughout the state.

"We the People" is still part of the Madison paper's coverage. Its success led to another civic journalism project to improve student performance in the city's schools. The *State Journal* received financial support from the Pew Center and also won awards for its efforts to bring local school and city officials together with parents and citizens to improve the public schools.

Dozens of newspapers and media organizations, including public television stations and online sites, have followed the *State Journal*'s lead. Some news executives and media observers believed civic journalism would become passé with the end of the Pew Center awards and grants program in 2002. But many aspects that newspapers used to carry out civic journalism projects have been adopted or become standard operating procedure at some media. Civic journalism requires financial and time commitments, and it remains to be seen how many media will continue to do in-depth civic journalism projects.

The effect of civic journalism on reporters has been mixed. Some reporters have said they believed that the in-depth coverage has created complete and accurate accounts of community shortcomings, and they have welcomed the long-term and intensive efforts of their media to effect change in their communities. But some have questioned the role of the media as a facilitator of change. Some believe that the media have been too involved as part of the solution and should have stepped out as soon as local officials and others began problem-solving efforts.

Student journalists should be familiar with civic journalism and its concepts. A mass communication student who becomes a public information officer for a local school system could be just as much a part of a civic or public journalism project as a local news reporter or online editor.

IN SUM: WHAT IT TAKES TO BE A REPORTER

Reporters' stories are only as good as their content, and content will be redundant, superficial, and lackluster unless reporters make digging for information a primary task. Reporters must be thorough, methodical, curious, and determined. They should pay attention to legal and ethical ways to get information. They also must pay attention to detail and should enjoy learning about other people, their accomplishments, and their failures. Reporters should constantly be searching for one more source, one more detail, one more quote—right up until deadline. And they must take pride in work that is accurate, fair, and complete.

GLOSSARY

Beat: A specific coverage area assigned to a reporter or reporters. It can be geographic or cover a specific topic, such as business or education.

Breaking or spot news: News that happens with no warning, that does not allow reporters to be prepared to cover the event.

Civic journalism: An effort by media to help solve community issues, not just report on issues in news columns. Uses focus groups, surveys, interactive Web sites, community meetings, and other forums. Also called public journalism.

Convergence: The sharing of information and staffs between or even among media in a community. The same company generally owns the media.

Localize: Taking information and using local sources and a local angle to make it relevant to audiences in the community; often the story appears elsewhere, such as on a wire service.

News: Information that is aired, printed, or broadcast.

News elements: Who, what, when, where, how, and why. Specific information essential to any news story.

News feature: A story that has a news peg or angle but that explores in depth all angles and many sources; the story has less timeliness than a news story.

News hole: The space allotted for news stories. In a newspaper, news hole fills in above and next to ads.

News values: Impact, magnitude, conflict, timeliness, proximity, prominence, unusualness or oddity, and human interest. Aspects of news that make information
newsworthy or carry importance to an audience.

Wire services: Organizations that provide news coverage to member media outlets
that pay to use the services' stories. Stories produced by any member media can
be placed on the wire service for use by other members with proper credit.

ACTIVITIES

1. Invite a local reporter who has covered several beats to come to class and talk
   about differences among the beats. Get tips on how to approach sources, the best
   stories he or she has written, the best sources used.

2. Invite a local editor to class. Have him or her discuss how beats are set up at the
   newspaper or television station. Find out why that beat structure is in place. Do
   gaps exist? Are some stories not covered? Why? How does the newspaper or
   television station decide what news to cover?

3. Informally interview five people you know about their perceptions of media
   credibility. Find out which media they use to get news. Which media do they
   use for breaking or spot news? For in-depth information? If they do not trust
   media, find out their reasoning for their lack of confidence. What would reporters have to do to restore confidence in media?

4. Based on your findings in Activity 3, make a list of the top three to five reasons
   why media have lost credibility. Come up with ways reporters can try to restore
   credibility through their interaction with sources and their own behavior.

5. Interview an editor or a journalism professor about convergence or civic journalism. What are his or her perceptions about either trend? What is necessary for
   a trend to become an accepted practice within the media? Can the editor or professor identify other trends that have died or been incorporated in reporting?
   Based on the interview, write a one-page summary of the interview and share
   your findings with those in other students' interviews. What are the similarities
   and differences in views?

RESOURCES AND WEB SITES

American Society of Newspaper Editors: www.asne.org
Associated Press Managing Editors: www.apme.com
Committee of Concerned Journalists: www.journalism.org
Information on a wide variety of reporting issues, including how-to's from newspaper
    trainers: www.notrain-nogain.org
A partner of *Columbia Journalism Review* with hundreds of free research
    tools for journalists: www.powerreporting.com
Public Relations Society of America: www.prsa.org
Radio-Television News Directors: www.rtnda.org
Society of Professional Journalists: www.spj.org
Your state press association

REFERENCES

Ashe, R. (2001, August). Keynote address. Association for Education in Journalism and Mass Communication. Washington, DC.

Denton, F. (1999). *The local news handbook*. Reston, VA: American Society of Newspaper Editors.

Pew Center for Civic Journalism. (2000, March). *Civic journalism is . . . true stories from America's newsrooms*. Washington, DC.

The Pew Center for the People and the Press. (2002, August 4). News media's improved image proves short-lived: The sagging stock market's big audience. http://people-press.org/reports.

The Pew Charitable Trusts. (1997). *Civic lessons: Report on four civic journalism projects funded by the Pew Center for Civic Journalism*. Washington, DC.

Webster's new world college dictionary (4th ed.). (2001). Forest City, CA: IDG Books Worldwide.

Yopp, J. J., & McAdams, K. C. (2003). *Reaching audiences: A guide to media writing*. Boston: Allyn & Bacon.

SEARCHING FOR INFORMATION: PAPER AND THE INTERNET

When reporters have an idea or angle for a story, they need to make sure the idea or angle is legitimate. They may have seen an article that appeared in a newspaper in another city and want to know whether a similar situation exists in their town. They may have a copy of a petition from residents who say the town needs more bike lanes. Their parents may be considering a move to an assisted-living community, a seemingly growing lifestyle choice in the area.

To determine whether the story has a basis or news peg, reporters must do research and find background information. They need additional information to make the story fair and complete. Often information gathering will push them in a particular or even a new direction they must follow.

Most likely, reporters will begin their search on the Internet. The wealth of information on the Internet makes news reporting both easier and more difficult these days. The ease comes from so many sources available at the touch of a keystroke. But all those sources can make research time consuming. Reporters in search of information can't rely solely on the Internet. Much information is still hidden away in letters, memos, and other documents that haven't found life on the Internet.

The backbone of good reporting efforts remains strong in-person interviews, which a computer network cannot yet provide. Once reporters have information, they add the human element and verify information through interviews. Interviews help translate statistics and add essential quotes to stories. Good communicators need to know how and where to gather information; do research via the Internet, public records, and other resources; and conduct a good interview, which is covered in Chapter 3.

In this chapter you will:

- Learn how reporters use public records to find information,
- Become familiar with types of records and access via the federal Freedom of Information Act and state open record laws,

- Evaluate information,
- Examine the value of other sources such as community groups, trade publications, news releases, and academia,
- Find out where the Internet fits in,
- Consider the benefits of computer-assisted reporting, and
- Learn how to keep track of notes and information.

USING PUBLIC RECORDS IN REPORTING

Reporters, especially beat reporters, base much of their reporting on public records. Reporters have used government documents to investigate major news stories, but access to that information has been and, in some cases, continues to be difficult.

In the mid-1960s, Congress passed the federal Freedom of Information Act that opened the doors to a wealth of information for both the public and the media. Since then states have followed with similar laws that pertain to state records. Florida has been a leader in access to documents through its legislation dubbed "Sunshine laws," referring not only to its nickname as the Sunshine State but also to bringing information out into the sunlight. The basic rule states that reporters—or any individual—should have access to any document produced and kept by a governmental agency unless the official holding the information can state a specific exemption. And legislators have listed specific information that certain officials can know and the rest of the population cannot.

The Federal Freedom of Information Act

Since 1966, when the federal Freedom of Information Act (FOIA) was passed, federal agencies have been required to provide any person with access to records not specifically exempted. The intent behind FOIA is for government to disclose its information whenever possible and to withhold only when necessary. Although the government can withhold quite a lot for public policy, personnel, or political reasons, U.S. residents still have access to more government information than do citizens of any other country. For example, reporters learned that safety problems with Valujet airliners were known before a 1996 crash that killed 110 people; that the Gulf War syndrome did exist and what caused it; that the FBI harassed and the CIA had an illegal surveillance of Dr. Martin Luther King, Jr.; and that safety problems existed at U.S. nuclear plants.

The FOIA applies to all government agencies, to independent regulatory agencies such as the Federal Communications Commission, and to presidential commissions. It applies to records such as computer printouts or photos and other materials that can be copied. Since 1996, it also has covered disclosure of the government's electronic documents such as emails. See Figure 2.1 for specific exemptions.

FIGURE 2.1   FOIA Exemptions

Exemptions permit but do not require a federal agency to withhold documents.

1. **National security.** Allows the executive branch, that is, the president, to determine how documents can be released. It provides three levels: top secret, secret, and confidential. All levels stop public disclosure of documents.

2. **"Housekeeping"—agency personnel rules and practices.** Permits government agencies to withhold documents "related solely" to internal personnel rules and practices.

3. **Statutory exemptions.** Includes documents that Congress has declared to be confidential such as statutes about the Census Bureau, tax returns, or patent applications.

4. **Confidential business information.** Protects trade secrets and commercial and financial information that businesses must provide to government agencies on a confidential basis.

5. **Agency memoranda.** Covers working documents circulated within an agency or between agencies. Historically they have been considered privileged government communications under common law. This exemption shields the deliberative policy-making process, not factual material.

6. **Personnel, medical, and similar files.** Includes private employment records such as performance evaluations and reports from disciplinary proceedings. Medical files cover any individual's medical records held by federal agencies. Similar files include documents that reveal any individual's Social Security number, welfare payments, marital status, names and addresses of people affiliated with unions, or people with Veterans Administration loans.

7. **Law enforcement investigations.** Allows government to withhold information compiled for law enforcement investigations. This exemption typically applies to ongoing investigations and proceedings, including interviews with witnesses, affidavits, and notes taken by investigating officers. To be exempted, disclosure "could reasonably be expected" to:

    7a. interfere with law enforcement proceedings or investigations
    7b. deprive a defendant of a fair trial
    7c. invade personal privacy
    7d. disclose the identity of a confidential source
    7e. reveal protected enforcement techniques
    7f. endanger someone's life

8. **Banking reports.** Covers government-held financial reports and audits from banks, trust companies, investment banking firms, and other federally regulated financial institutions.

9. **Information about wells.** Protects geological and geophysical information, including maps, concerning oil, gas, and water wells.

The FOIA does not apply to documents in the possession of the president and his advisers; Congress, its committees, and its agencies such as the Library of Congress and Copyright Office; or the federal judicial system.

However, reporters can gather information from these sources directly by attending presidential press conferences, sessions of Congress, and other open government meetings. Reporters can also make requests for information. Sample letters can be seen on the University of Missouri's Freedom of Information Center at http://foi.missouri.edu/foialett.html.

Also exempt are nine categories of documents that deal with national security, agency personnel rules and practices, exemptions covered by statutes, confidential business information, agency memoranda, personnel, medical, or similar files, law enforcement investigations, banking reports, and information on wells such as oil and natural gas. In addition to these nine exemptions, FOIA doesn't apply to federal government subcontractors who retain documents. A 1980 case said the FOIA applies only to documents that have been created or obtained by a federal agency (*Forsham v. Harris*). This ruling has created a huge problem for reporters because the trend in government has been to use more and more subcontractors.

Access to State Records

All 50 states have open records laws, most of which are similar to the federal FOIA. Beginning journalists should become familiar with the open records laws in their states so they will know what information they can access. Laws can be found through state press associations or on state government Web sites. Also, states' Web sites, as well as counties' and municipalities' Web sites, can be found easily through state and federal Web locators. Reporters may be able to access and download public records from some of the sites. Reporters need to know in what format records are kept because officials do not have to create special documents to make records available to the public or the media.

Public records held at the local or state level include the following:

■ **Campaign finances.** Candidates must submit to local and state election boards regular reports listing supporters and amounts they contributed. Candidates for higher office may have to report their income and assets as well. Election and campaign expenses are discussed in Chapter 13.

■ **Corporate records.** Private companies that do not have publicly traded stock do not have to make much information public. When any business incorporates, it must submit to the state a document that shows officers, company purpose, and holdings. The state secretary of state typically has these records. Federal laws also require annual financial filings, as noted in Chapter 9 on business reporting.

■ **Court records.** In most cases, criminal and civil court records are found in the county courthouse and are open to the public. Many court documents and disposition of cases can be accessed online. Court records are discussed in Chapter 11.

■ **Government finances.** Governments and their respective departments and agencies have to report their annual budgets and audit information. Financing local government is covered in Chapter 7.

■ **Historical materials.** The local public library or city or county museum may have historical documents stretching back before a city or county had an incorporated government.

■ **Inspections.** Inspection reports for restaurants and local food stores are filed at the local health department.

■ **Law enforcement.** Depending on the state or community, police make available a daily log of arrests or even copies of police reports on each case. Reporters generally go to the police department to check the incident reports for a specific time period. Police reporting is covered in Chapter 10.

■ **Licenses.** These cover everything from selling liquor to operating an in-home beauty salon.

■ **Meeting minutes.** Local government agencies keep minutes or transcripts of their public meetings, and many can be found online these days.

■ **Permits.** Most building projects need a permit, as do parades and public events. The permits can be found at the local municipal building or in the police department.

■ **Property and real estate.** Counties and cities keep information on each parcel of land or property, showing ownership history, value, location on the map, last selling price, and so on.

■ **Resident information.** Birth, death, marriage, and divorce totals are compiled at the local level and reported to the state. The basic information is filed at the county health department or courthouse, and the state produces a vital records document each year. Wills show financial information and are filed with the county.

In small communities, a reporter just walks into the local city hall or county courthouse to find most documents. A good relationship with personnel, such as the clerk of court or tax collector's staff, can speed the process when a reporter is digging for details. Reporters may be asked to pay a reasonable fee to cover the cost of photocopying records, based on the requirements of the particular state's open records laws.

For larger communities or state or federal governments, reporters can gather much information without leaving their desks because many more documents and records are online. For example, in the state of Maryland, a reporter can go to the Maryland Department of Assessments and Taxation Web site and search more than two million property records in the state. Each record tells the current owner and valuation of the property, the last date the property was sold, the seller's name, and the price. If reporters have the property address, map reference, property identification number, or property transfer date, they can have the information in seconds.

Publications, Community Groups, and Other Sources

When Jean Dimeo was a business reporter at the *Dallas Times Herald,* she said trade publications provided her with vital information, giving her story ideas and information about new trends in specific industries. For example, she turned to *Home Center News* (now called *Home Channel News*) for the latest information about Home Depot, which began to have a growing presence as a retailer in the Dallas area.

From building to broadcasting, every industry has representative trade publications, also known as business-to-business publications. Because these publications have such a narrow niche, they typically report first on topics that affect their industries. A reporter covering the business side of radio, television, and cable can turn to *Broadcasting & Cable* to learn issues important to that industry. A reporter covering real estate and general business will find helpful magazines in the housing and construction industry such as *Builder, Big Builder, Journal of Light Construction,* or *Custom Home.* Reporters should use these publications as a source of information and follow up with their own interviews and fact checking.

"Trade publication writers and editors usually know the industries they follow intimately, so they often are expert sources," Dimeo said (2003). "Trade magazines often publish original studies and surveys, which also provide valuable information and potential story ideas." Reporters should carefully evaluate trade publications to make sure they deliver accurate information. "Certainly, some trade magazines are schlock—they pander to advertisers and/or they aren't well written or edited," Dimeo warned. "But the ones that provide unbiased, up-to-the-minute coverage of the topics you report on can provide you with a wealth of background material and story ideas."

Dimeo is the editor of *Building Products* magazine, published by Hanley-Wood, a company that publishes the trade magazines in the building and construction industry. *Building Products* is "the only trade magazine solely devoted to the coverage of building products and materials used in building and remodeling houses, and a number of newspaper and consumer magazine editors and reporters rely on it for the latest information about these areas," she said (2003).

In addition, many industry groups, business associations, consumer groups, community groups, unions, and nonprofit watchdog groups do research. They provide reporters with story ideas, reports on trends, and perspectives on the impact of government decisions on their industry or group. For example, Environmental Defense, one of the early U.S. environmental groups, presented counterarguments from its attorneys and scientists when it disagreed with government environmental policies. In 2003 it used government data to show that a government policy of allowing businesses to adopt voluntary pollution measures to reduce greenhouse gas pollution had actually allowed emissions to increase by 14 percent. Reporters must be aware that information from associations and groups may be slanted in favor of their issue or business, but they still give balance to reporters' stories by presenting other views on a topic.

Trade and industry groups—and just about any organization—blanket the media with news releases. Each seeks "free" mention or publicity about products, services, employee promotions, mergers, and other topics. Media use news releases in several ways: as the basis for a story, a counterpoint to a story, a means to build source lists, and even copy used verbatim and dropped into news hole. The latter use often occurs in weekly or semiweekly newspapers that do not have large news staffs to pursue news stories. Just like with trade publications, reporters must recognize that news releases may carry a bias and are distributed to gain media attention. Reporters must decide just how much attention any news release warrants.

Sources from the academic world can help balance a story. Scholars and scientists connected to universities, medical schools, and graduate schools do research as part of their jobs and are supported through their jobs or through government grants. Their research appears in academic, medical, and scientific journals, most of which have strict policies for acceptance and require that the research be reviewed by a jury of peers with expertise in that topic area. For journalists, such research is considered reliable and can become the basis for stories. Academics may be neutral, but they, too, may have a bias depending on their research, their institution, and their funding source.

In addition to publishing in journals, scholars and scientists attend academic meetings where they present their findings. Science and medical reporters generally attend the American Medical Association or the American Chemical Society annual meetings, for instance, to hear about the most recent discoveries. For background research, reporters can access papers and published articles through academic databases such as Academic Search Ebsco, ERIC (Educational Resource Information Center), Medline, or Web of Science. However, some specialty databases cannot be accessed via the Web, so a reporter might have to visit a library that subscribes to a particular site.

Reporters can also track down scholars and scientists as sources through Profnet, a service of college and university public information officers in North America. It gives journalists the names of thousands of university professors, who have specialty knowledge about hundreds of topics. For example, in reporting on the space shuttle *Columbia*'s breakup over Texas in 2003, journalists could find aerospace engineering or physics professors close by to get a more local source for background information. Such a source could add perspective if the involved agency, in this example NASA, were not releasing information.

REPORTERS AND THE INTERNET

Much government, business, nonprofit, organizational, educational, and general information is available online these days. Nora Paul in *Computer-Assisted Research* (1999) says the Internet is no longer a "take-it-or-leave-it" resource in news reporting. These days, government agencies save money and paper by distributing their materials online. "If you want the press release, report, or latest statistics, you have to go to the Web," Paul says. "Journalists without access to the Internet are, increasingly, shut out of important aspects of their news coverage."

Paul adds that the Internet is just a kick start for good reporting, not a replacement. "It might help you locate that expert or track down that report you need, but . . . you will still need to interview those experts and qualify the information in that report," she notes.

In addition to aiding in interviewing, the Internet supplements—it doesn't replace—the digging through public records that has been the traditional part of reporting, Paul says in her book. "The Internet is not the whole world of information necessary for reporters, and it certainly is not a shortcut around good, thorough, traditional reporting techniques," she states. (Paul material reprinted with permission of the Poynter Institute, St. Petersburg, Florida.)

Problems exist in relying solely on the Internet for research, as noted in Figure 2.2. Because anyone can create a Web site, Web sites can even become part of the story being reported. For example, the Web site of Eric Harris, one of the students responsible for the multiple shootings at Columbine High School in Denver, Colorado, became crucial to that story's completeness. Law enforcement officials believed anyone reading that site could have picked up clues to Harris's subsequent behavior.

FIGURE 2.2 **Pitfalls of Online Research**

- Reporters have to go through a lot of sites to find what they want. Searches need to be as specific as possible.
- Information might not be accurate. Anyone can create a Web site.
- Web sites come and go. A site today may not exist tomorrow.
- Information may not be up-to-date. Check the "last updated" date on the page.
- Online information might be biased, depending on the source.
- Online information might be available only to subscribers, particularly for material stored in archives.
- The research and writing on Web sites might be poorly done or incomplete.

Search Engines and Web Sites

Journalists must adopt good reporting techniques in using the Internet because all search engines and Web sites are not created equal. Search engines are powerful tools in exploring the Internet, but using the wrong one can mean missing needed information for a story. The University of California at Berkeley Library says Google is the best search engine, as do most other libraries. Google covers more than two billion Web pages, and although no search engine is comprehensive, Google finds "the best" pages based on popularity, according to UC–Berkeley (2004). Among the library's other top choices for a search engine is AllTheWeb. A fairly recent addition to the search engine family is Dogpile.com, which advertises that it will search other search engines. Geared to students, Dogpile.com has tips on how to do a search from keywording to evaluating Web sites to avoiding plagiarism.

But search engines still miss quite a bit on the Web. "Search engine databases are selected and built by computer robot programs called spiders," according to the UC–Berkeley Library. "Although it is said they 'crawl' the Web in their hunt for pages to include, in truth they stay in one place. They find the pages for potential inclusion by following the links in the pages they already have in their database (i.e., already 'know about'). They cannot think or type a URL or use judgment to 'decide' to go look something up and see what's on the Web about it."

Search engines miss any Web pages not linked to another Web page or not registered with a search engine. UC–Berkeley's Library reports:

> Some types of pages and links are excluded from most search engines by policy. Others are excluded because search engine spiders cannot access them. Pages that are excluded are referred to as the "Invisible Web"—what you don't see in search engine results. The Invisible Web is estimated to be two to three or more times bigger than the visible Web.

The Invisible Web contains thousands of searchable databases, but the searches have to be specific to those databases. Much of what is on the Invisible Web is academic information and may not be useful for news stories. To begin to explore the Invisible Web, reporters need to access database search pages such as Direct Search, The Invisible Web Catalog, A Collection of Search Engines, and Internets. Another useful site for reporters, Search Power, has 14,000 sites of city and state guides.

Evaluating Web Site Credibility

In addition to finding "invisible" information, reporters must be able to evaluate critically the Web sites they do use. Librarians began wrestling with the evaluation of Internet information early in its origination. Two Widener University librarians, Jan Alexander and Marsha Ann Tate (1999), created a methodology to evaluate Web sites based on how librarians have always analyzed information sources. The first step, they say, is to identify the Web page type, which they have broken into categories: Advocacy, Business/Marketing, Informational, News, Personal, and Entertainment. Then the evaluator should go through a checklist of questions based on authority, accuracy, objectivity, currency, and coverage.

One journalism-specific resource for evaluating Web sites is the Miller Internet Data Integrity Scale (MIDIS) created by Steve Miller of the *New York Times*. He said journalists could use MIDIS "to determine if a Web site has valid information that can be used in news reports." Miller (1999) identified four tiers of credibility. Local, state, or federal government sites allow reporters to use information from official government sources and rank at the top in credibility.

Miller noted: "U.S. Federal Government Web sites all end in the extension .gov. That means that it is an official government site. While you might personally question the data, you are safe in quoting from it, i.e., 'according to the National Transportation Safety Board.'" The same rule applies to state and city government Web sites that also end in .gov.

Universities and people associated with them make up the next level of credible sites. Their sites generally end with the .edu extender. Miller explained: "Most (university) studies by recognized experts in a field are still reviewed by peers. Quoting from these studies is also a safe bet with attribution."

Special-interest groups comprise the third level of credible Web sites. "Special interest groups publish lots of data on the Net," Miller said. "Even though we know that these groups have a political agenda, it does not follow that their data is flawed. It's also safe to use the data since it is attributable."

He called his final level of credible Web sites a catchall, or "not the usual suspects." Among these are personal/vanity/hobby/obsession Web sites. Miller said via these Web sites reporters can find new people and new information, but they have to check the sources carefully because anyone can post anything. Because most of these sites have contact information, a reporter can research the Web site author, who actually may be an expert, as a way to check the site's authenticity. Reporters should always remember that "just because it's digital doesn't make it true," he said.

A Word about Blogs

Weblogs, known as blogs, quickly have become a force in modern journalism. Initially seen as ramblings of individuals online, they have morphed into both a form of and source of journalism. Typically, they are people's online journals, which are updated frequently, combined with information about other Web sites and information. They can range from people's daily journals of their move to a new city and the great restaurants they find to a journalist's blog about reform of the Catholic Church. The term *weblog* is believed to have been coined in 1997 and its official definition is:

> Weblogs are often-updated sites that point to articles elsewhere on the Web, often with comments, and to on-site articles. A weblog is kind of a continual tour, with a human guide whom you get to know. There are many guides to choose from, each develops an audience, and there's also camraderie and politics between the people who run weblogs: they point to each other, in all kinds of structures, graphs, loops, etc.

Ryan Pitts, online producer for SpokemanReview.com, noted in an article about journalists and blogs (2003) that a growing number of journalists are blogging to report the news. He pointed to the efficient, minute-to-minute coverage the *Virginian-Pilot* gave to the DC sniper trial by having its online news producer, Kerry Sipe, blog the trial as he watched it live on closed-circuit TV. Because no videotaping was allowed at the trial, the blog reporting was similar to having the news in real time. Sipe explained that the readers of blog news received a unique experience. They "are exposed to the mundane and the significant in the same way, just as those who are attending the trial are experiencing them," Sipe said in Pitts's report.

Readers seemed to like the immediacy of the trial blogs, Sipe reported. "The feedback from the Muhammad trial blog has been tremendous," Sipe said, citing more than 100 emails from readers who said they were following the story with him online. "Several of them have mentioned that it gives them a sense of being in the courtroom without actually having to devote full-time to the effort."

Other reporters use blogging to report on information their print publication doesn't have space to print. Health reporter Carla Johnson, of the Spokane, Washington, *Spokesman-Review,* uses blogging to add to her beat coverage, according to Pitts's overview (2003). "'Blog readers learn what I think is the most interesting, useful, or weird health story of the day,' Johnson said. 'Then they can go read the research themselves on the Web. I'm saying to them, 'Hey, take a look at this! And if you want more, click here.' There's never enough newsprint to adequately cover all the health research and policy questions. The blog gives more to those readers who want more.'"

Blogs can also give traditional reporters story ideas and other information. *Chicago Tribune* columnist Eric Zorn searches reader responses to blogs for column ideas. And many journalists reported getting additional information about the DC sniper trial from Kerry Sipe's blogs.

COMPUTER-ASSISTED REPORTING (CAR)
FOR FINDING INFORMATION

A good number of reporters believe that all reporting today involves doing research online, and, therefore, all reporting is computer-assisted reporting. But the term *computer-assisted reporting* (CAR) usually refers to a broader method of gathering and analyzing information.

In *Introduction to Computer-Assisted Reporting, a Journalist's Guide,* Professor Matt Reavy (2001) formally defines CAR as "the use of computers to gather and analyze data for the purpose of transforming the data into information used as part of a narrative to be transmitted via a medium of mass communication."

Nora Paul in *Computer-Assisted Research* (1999) defines computer-assisted reporting as one of four parts of computer-assisted journalism, which is focused on combining the use of "spreadsheet programs to analyze large sets of records and perform calculations, statistical programs to analyze complex datasets, database software to build original collections of records and mapping software to display data visually in a geographic context."

How CAR Differs from Traditional Reporting

While these formal definitions sound complex, many student journalists have used CAR or data analysis to develop stories relating to arrests and convictions, housing discrimination, and college admissions. Basically CAR reporters or specific CAR editors analyze numbers in databases rather than rely on others to provide summaries or interpretations of data. Their work can substantiate or explain aspects of a news story. For example, a reporter could look at all driving convictions of 16-year-olds in the state to determine whether they have a high incidence of alcohol-related accidents. The information could be used in a story about legislators considering additional restrictions for younger drivers. These types of analyses add a dimension to the traditional reporting techniques of interviewing and sorting through paper records.

In traditional reporting, journalists wrote stories from events that happened or tips that came their way. Then they interviewed the people involved, found documents associated with the story, and incorporated them. Finally, they wrote their stories. However, by the 1980s, some journalists began seeing that they could move past their role as just recording events and take control of the news agenda. They used computers as their tools. Computer-assisted reporting differs from traditional reporting: Instead of waiting for events to happen or tips to arrive, journalists take their watchdog role to the next level. Their stories answer bigger questions: What is the government doing versus what is it supposed to be doing, and is it succeeding in its role? What are the trends in modern society? What are the influences of businesses and large corporations in daily life?

Journalists often use FOIA and state public records laws to acquire datasets. By getting access to the huge databases that government keeps on all kinds of topics, journalists using computer-assisted reporting bypass the public relations stance on the information and analyze it themselves. Journalists using CAR either create their own database of information from public resources or analyze existing government databases.

Creating a database may seem like a daunting task, but databases are really just long lists of things. For example, the U.S. Census every 10 years is just a long list of all the people who reside in the United States and a variety of characteristics about them. Journalists can combine the census information with other information to reveal trends, such as the growing number of college-educated immigrants from India populating their community.

The power of CAR results from the ease at which today's computers can analyze huge datasets quickly. Spreadsheet and database analysis software are standard in most bundled software packages, so most journalists already have the technology they need on their office computers. One database by itself might give journalists plenty of information, but real investigative journalism begins when databases are combined. For example, a database of school bus drivers in the county combined with a database of all the people convicted of drunk driving in the state will reveal who appears on both lists. A reporter will have a great story of interest to readers other than just parents.

Even simple analyses make excellent stories. The Associated Press analyzed Federal Highway Administration data and found that more than 30 percent of the bridges on the National Highway System were either "obsolete or (had) structural problems." The analysis broke down the data by state and showed that in cities such as Washington, DC, 61 percent of bridges rated as deficient and in Pennsylvania, 43 percent as deficient. The AP investigation showed that most of the bridges were not about to collapse, but "some simply are too narrow to handle current traffic loads." As an Oregon transportation official said: "They're sort of the baby boomer bridges, all aging at the same time." The story contained important information for millions of U.S. drivers.

Considerations for CAR as a Tool in Reporting

With these kinds of important stories at their fingertips, why aren't all journalists analyzing databases and plugging numbers into spreadsheets? The (probably true) stereotype is that people go into journalism to avoid dealing with math. Basically, many journalists say they are "word people" more than "number people." That argument no longer works in the technology-drenched twenty-first century. As newspaper consultant David Cole (2000) said: "We've already moved into a time when reporters are using computers for more than just word processors. Most do a lot of their own research on the Internet; most can at least plug numbers into a spreadsheet to make sure they add up."

Journalists have to get over their math or computer phobia to attempt CAR stories. Jennifer LaFleur, computer-assisted reporting editor for the *Dallas Morning News,* said (1995) reporters can ease into CAR first by learning three basic formulas: percent of total, percent change, and per capita. (See Figure 2.3.) She said these three are crucial, "whether you're looking at hard copy reports from a government agency or analyzing data in a spreadsheet."

FIGURE 2.3   Math Basics

PERCENT OF TOTAL

The rule is the amount divided by the total (amount/total). For example, if Bob owns 10 animals and 2 of those animals are cats, 2 divided by 10 (2/10) or 20 percent of his animals are cats.

PERCENT CHANGE

You're dealing with two years' worth of data and want to figure percent change from one year to the next. Take the difference of the two years divided by the amount from the earlier year. Say we're looking at 2002–2003 data, in which 2002 had $2,345 in revenues and 2003 had $2,567 in revenues. The difference: 2,567 – 2,345 = 222. Now: 222/2,345 = 0.09, or a 9 percent increase in revenues.

PER CAPITA

Looking at occurrences by city, county, or state can be interesting, but remember to keep things on common ground. I can't compare raw numbers if the "bases" are different. That means if I am looking at the number of murders by city in the United States, Los Angeles and New York will probably come out on top, but only because they have more people. A more useful measure would be per capita murders. In this case, per capita murders would be the number of murders divided by population.

Sometimes these measures will be adjusted a little if the number of occurrences is low. Crime statistics, for example, are often reported per 100,000 people or per 10,000 people. These measures are used because hopefully the number of murders in a city is fairly low compared to the number of people. By looking at the figure per 100,000 people, it becomes easier to read: 50 murders per 100,000 people.

PER HOUSEHOLD

When you are trying to figure out if people per household is households divided by population or population divided by households, do one simple thing: Turn your per into a division sign. This means that people PER households becomes people/ households or population/households. If that doesn't work, try narrowing the field to a few items: For example, if I have two houses and 10 people, how many people per household is that? Of course, it is five per house.

Source: Jennifer LaFleur, computer-assisted reporting editor, *Dallas Morning News.*

With computer-assisted reporting it takes time to learn the in-depth computer skills on the software programs and to build a database yourself, if that is what is needed. Most CAR experts recommend that reporters start with small projects to build their skills. They can learn some of the more basic CAR skills quickly and apply them on a daily basis to beat reporting, according to the National Institute of Computer-Assisted Reporting's "CAR on the Beat" publication (Paul, 1995). "On the news desk, CAR can mean taking a quick look at a local or state budget, checking census data to add depth to a trend story, or building a simple database to examine crime patterns," the publication says. "Computer-assisted reporting doesn't only mean big projects that take months to complete. Beat reporters can use CAR techniques to enhance their day-to-day coverage, on breaking news, for short term enterprise, even for features."

Reporters using CAR also face what is known as "dirty data." The data may have glitches, and reporters may or may not be able to assess that. "In general, data is dirty; it contains typos and outright mistakes that can throw off analytical results," said Bob Steele of the Poynter Institute and Wendell Cochran of American University (1998). "Many stories journalists publish that rely on government records quite likely are grounded, at least to a certain extent, on databases that contain mistakes." For example, the Federal Election Commission's individual contribution records are known for having many typographical errors. Statistically speaking, most large databases have errors, so Steele and Cochran said reporters should be careful not to emphasize small differences; reporters should round off numbers and should emphasize similarities instead of differences.

CAR expert LaFleur added (1995) that journalists can take steps to "clean" dirty data. For example, a reporter might have to go through a database to make sure the county's name is spelled correctly throughout so that all data relevant to the county is in the analysis. She also reminded reporters that not only computer records have errors but so do traditional paper documents.

University of North Carolina journalism professor Phil Meyer, who is the "father" of computer-assisted journalism, noted three rules for avoiding trouble with statistics: Explain what's been done; apply the formulas consistently; and don't claim too much in the results. Finally, CAR can create information that even its sources didn't know existed. Journalism ethicists Steele and Cochran say:

> Journalists who use sophisticated data analysis tools to study a problem often become more knowledgeable about a subject than any other source. For example, in the late 1980s, journalists at Gannett News Service and USA TODAY designed new ways to measure the health of financial institutions. There were no other sources for this information, no Federal Reserve Board or banking industry studies to cite. Outside sources gave advice about how to construct the formulas, but in the end, it was journalists who wrote the formulas, decided which variables to include, analyzed the results and drew the conclusions. To . . . editors, that approach waves red flags [. . . because media] must be willing to explain our methodology and how we arrived at our facts. (Reprinted with permission from the Poynter Institute, St. Petersburg, Florida.)

Ethically speaking, a deceptive or unscrupulous reporter might invent or manipulate data that can't be checked with an outside source. Therefore, it is important that all reporters and editors in a newsroom be familiar with computer-assisted reporting techniques—so they can verify one another's work.

Also, CAR experts remind beginning reporters that its techniques are not just for those at huge metropolitan dailies or large-market TV news stations. "C.A.R. can be for the journalistic masses; not just for special projects or investigative monstrosities and the people who produce them. A fruitful technology training program is one that combines short-term and long-term projects and allows all reporters to partake in the glory," said Carol Napolitano (1994), who promotes the use of CAR on any news beat and has created a list of dozens of CAR story ideas for those beats.

KEEPING ORGANIZED WITH RESEARCH

Often a topic will arise that requires more than just one story. You may find you are doing more than one story or a series of stories on one subject. Series evolve when you have been covering a story that has critical points that need to be developed and followed in-depth, for example, alternative lifestyles for retirees. A series can consist of two or more stories that run on consecutive days, or an occasional story that runs periodically on a specific topic. In the latter case, for example, media may do periodic profiles or features on outstanding community members or on specific county departments.

Traditionally, when media start such a project, reporters sell or pitch the idea to an editor, or an editor may have an idea to be developed. Together they outline the parameters of the story, what they hope to accomplish, time and resources required, and at least one reason why to do it. Other reporters or editors may be called in to work on the series, and the photo or graphics department would be included to work on visual aspects of the story.

Dealing with a long story and lots of information requires staying organized. Some ways to do that include:

- Typing up notes as you do research so that information is legible when you return to it days or weeks later.
- Cataloging notes or separating them by topic, such as interviews, documents, or future sources. You may have some information cross-referenced in different files. With such separation, you can get to notes easily when you are ready to write the story.
- Keeping track of themes or any changes in the angle as you do research and interviews.
- Making a list of related factors. For example, if the high cost of burials is the topic, an aspect may be the marketing of caskets and other items in funeral homes. Related factors, such as emotions, alternatives to burials, and so forth, may be other issues to note. They could become separate stories.
- Talking periodically with editors and other members of the story team as you work.
- Using computer software that allows you to flag each graph as to a one-word topic. Then the program will sort your notes by topic area.

With interviews, the record keeping should be painstakingly followed. Reporters should date their interviews, type up the notes as soon as possible, include feelings or perceptions, add sources recommended by the interview subjects, and determine how each interview fits in with the stories outlined.

When it comes time to write a series of articles, some reporters will write the sidebar or companion stories first. For example, they might write the feature on a family's trauma in deciding funeral services after a much-loved grandmother dies. Another sidebar might be cremation as an alternative to burial. The main story would touch on these issues as a reference to the sidebars, but it would be a story with a specific news angle: Planning a funeral may cause some people to grieve as much as they would over the loss of a loved one—and particularly when the bill comes after the family has said good-bye. Burial costs have risen 35 percent in the last 10 years.

Specifically when writing the main story, reporters should make sure that the first four to six paragraphs set up the story. The story may lend itself to an anecdotal lead or a fact-filled lead. Each article within the series tells a story on its own but relates to the other articles in the package. Remember: You don't have to use everything you found out. Sometimes that's the hardest: tossing things out.

Reporters must consider editing as part of the writing. You have to go back and make sure all parts relate. A mapped format, wherein specific subheads identify topics within the story for the reader, may be the best approach. Often under a mapped format, each section will be organized in an inverted pyramid style of writing and topped with a subhead identifying the information.

After you have written the first draft, you may need to go through your notes word for word to make sure you have included everything you wanted to use. Double-check all names and other statistics. Make sure each section logically follows the other and that the lead sets up the story adequately. Have someone other than the editor read your piece; then go back and make revisions. Writing, sharing, and polishing your work are critical steps to ensure good writing and that your final product is complete and accurate.

Having a logical system for preserving notebooks, notes, and drafts of your story is essential. To complete a series, you may have many drafts, quite different from stories that you write under deadline pressure on a daily basis. Make sure that you label each version so you are always working on the latest draft. Don't forget to back up your work before you log off or each time you quit working. Computer files can be lost, a devastating experience for any writer.

GLOSSARY

Computer-assisted reporting: Using computers to analyze data sets to translate numbers so that reporters and editors can look at trends.

CHAPTER 2 SEARCHING FOR INFORMATION: PAPER AND THE INTERNET   **37**

Extender: Three letters of a Web site address that indicate the domain where the site is housed, such as .gov for government or .edu for educational institution or affiliate; can be used to determine a site's credibility.

Freedom of Information Act: Passed in 1966 and amended since then, allows any individual, including reporters, access to any government-produced or -held document unless specifically exempted; regulations govern how information should be requested and released and any reasonable cost associated with providing the information to the requesting individual or organization.

Search engine: The driver that allows anyone to look for information on the Internet; among the most popular are Google, Yahoo, and Dogpile.

Sunshine laws: State laws modeled after the federal Freedom of Information Act that allow anyone access to state records, except for those documents specifically exempted.

ACTIVITIES

1. You are the news desk researcher for your local newspaper. Your editor tells you that this year has seemed especially bad for tornadoes and their destruction. You need to do a retrospective and see whether this actually was a bad year. Your editor would also like a focus or news peg for the story. Research and outline in a memo format *six sources of information* you can use, such as the National Weather Service. Give a contact name, address, and telephone number for each and how you would use each one.

   Two of the sources MUST BE news stories.

   One of the sources must be *a person.*

   Write *10 questions* you would ask the person.

   Write 3 to 4 sentences that state the *focus* for the article or articles and why you selected that focus. Note the main points the story should cover.

2. You are to write a story about a campus issue. You select the issue. As part of the research, you can use the campus newspaper and any articles, the university's Web site, or any other news Web sites. To expand the coverage, do a search and find three other examples of a similar problem having surfaced. For example, if you are writing about tuition increases, find at least three other universities in your state or in other states that have faced recent tuition increases. Use background for your stories. Also as part of the research, go to your library and look at copies of the campus newspaper from the 1960s, 1970s, 1980s, and 1990s. Find articles on the topic you selected to give a historical perspective. Include references in your story as well as photocopies of at least three stories.

3. Select a campus leader to write a profile on. Use at least three nonpeople resources to gather background information on him or her. At least two have to be non-Internet sources, such as the individual's résumé. Once you have that information, identify three people you would interview to get more up-to-date and personal information about the individual.

RESOURCES AND WEB SITES

American Press Institute: http://americanpressinstitute.org
Committee of Concerned Journalists: www.journalism.org
Dogpile.com: www.dogpile.com. A search engine that incorporates searches of other search engines in helping users find information.
Federal Web Locator: www.infoctr.edu/fwl
The best search engines (2004, January 7): www.lib.berkeley.edu/TeachingLib/Guides/Internet/SearchEngines.html
National Institute for Computer-Assisted Reporting: www.nicar.org
Poynter Institute: www.poynter.org
State Web Locator: www.infoctr.edu/swl
What Is the INvisible Web (2004, January 7): www.lib.berkeley.edu/TeachingLib/Guides/Internet/InvisibleWeb.html#What

REFERENCES

Alexander, J., & Tate, M. A. (1999). *Web wisdom: How to evaluate and create information quality on the Web.* Mahwah, NJ: Lawrence Erlbaum.
Associated Press. (1997, November 3). One-third of nation's bridges deficient. *Baltimore Sun,* p. 3A.
Cannon, C. (2001, April). The real computer virus. *American Journalism Review,* pp. 28–35.
Cole, D. (2000, March). Back to the future. *Quill,* pp. 13–15.
Dimeo, J. (2003, January 20). Email interview.
Forsham v. Harris, 445 U.S. 169 (1980).
Herman, J. L. (1992). *Trauma and recovery.* New York: Basic Books.
Journalism's best. (1988, June). *Quill.* pp. 17–38.
LaFleur, J. (1995, May). Slice percent right. *Uplink,* 7(5).
Miller, S. (1999, September 8). Finding trusted data on the Web. www.freedomforum.org/templates/document.asp?documentID=11642.
Napolitano, C. (1994). 50 C.A.R. ideas for your beat. www.notrain-nogain.org/tech/tips/50tips.asp.
Paul, N. (1995). "CAR on the beat." Series of tipsheets written for Investigative Reporters and Editors, Columbia, MO: IRE.
Paul, N. (1999). *Computer-assisted research, A guide to tapping online information.* Chicago: Bonus Books.
Pitts, R. (2003). Snipers to Microsoft: Beat bloggers cover their turf. J-Lab: The Institute for Interactive Journalism. www.j-lab.org/beatblogs.html.
Reavy, M. (2001). *Introduction to computer-assisted reporting, a journalist's guide.* Mountain View, CA: Mayfield.
Reisner, N., & Napolitano, C. (1995). Computer assisted reporting on the beat. [NICAR handout].
Steele, B., & Cochran, W. (1998, October 19). Computer-assisted reporting challenges traditional newsgathering safeguards. The Poynter Institute. www.poynter.org/research/car/car_chal.htm.
Weblogs.com. (2002). The history of weblogs. http://newhome.weblogs.com/historyOfWeblogs.

CHAPTER 3

INTERVIEWING AS INFORMATION GATHERING

Interviewing resembles a conversation, except as a reporter, you take notes on what people say. Although it sounds easy because everyone knows how to talk, interviewing can be one of the more daunting tasks for a beginning reporter. Reporters have to use all their skills to get complete or new information during an interview that might last a few minutes, be with an uncooperative source, or occur after a disaster. Writing down full-sentence direct quotes can be difficult when someone speaks at a fast clip. Broadcast interview subjects who seemed articulate in an initial conversation might become self-conscious and begin to babble when the camera turns on.

Reporters interview people to gather and verify information, to get details, and to add quotes to stories. Interviewing takes skill and practice. Each story requires the reporter to determine whom to interview, what research is needed, what type of interview is appropriate, and how best to elicit information from sources. Even experienced reporters have to plan interviews carefully so they can get accurate and complete information and necessary detail and description. Reporters also try to elicit solid direct quotes from sources during the interview. Quotes make a story lively, add color, increase clarity, and add balance.

Often as the reporter you will have to build rapport with a complete stranger in a matter of minutes to get the information, quotes, or sound bite you need. Other dynamics might be at work as well. The interview subjects might dislike reporters, they might be in the midst of a traumatic event, they might have an unspoken agenda about what they want to get into the story, or they might just be "regular people" who are uncomfortable because they have never been interviewed. Whatever the situation, reporters have to be flexible and able to think on their feet when conducting interviews.

In this chapter you will:

- Learn the required homework to prepare for an interview,
- Refine formulating questions,
- Improve your note taking when conducting an interview,

- Learn how to elicit and use good quotes,
- Get tips to establish rapport with sources,
- Become skilled on what to do when difficult moments arise,
- Review the types of interviews,
- Consider the unique needs of broadcast interviews, and
- Consider how to select the best sound bite.

DOING YOUR HOMEWORK

Research is critical to a good interview. Research enables a reporter to find the best sources, craft questions, and be as prepared as possible. Reporters facing deadlines want to interview the best and most appropriate sources so they do not waste time questioning a weak link. Sources want reporters to have some knowledge of the subject or of them so they do not waste time reviewing basic information. Research gives reporters tips on the best time and place to interview someone—and even how that individual reacts during interviews. Good research enables reporters to establish rapport once they connect with their sources and to ensure they ask questions that will provide complete and accurate information.

Whom to Interview

Some important research considerations are: "Have I found the right source for the story? Am I talking to the same government officials all reporters talk to? Is this person most directly connected to the story?" In asking such questions, you evaluate your decision to use a particular source. The NewsLab, which advises TV newsrooms, recommends the following checklist to see whether you have found the best source:

> How does this source know what he or she knows? (Is this person in a position to know these things—either personally or professionally?) How can I confirm this information through other sources, through documents? How representative is my source's point of view? (Is this just one person who complains loudly about the landlord because he or she has a personal problem? Or is this the most articulate voice speaking for an entire group that has serious, legitimate problems?) Has this source been reliable and credible in the past? Am I only using this source because it's the easy way to go? Because I know I'll get a good sound bite? What is the source's motive for providing information? (Is this person trying to make himself look good, or to make his boss look bad? Why is he or she talking to me in the first place?) Am I being manipulated or spun by this source? (Courtesy of Deborah Potter, Newslab.)

If reporters are seeking experts on a topic, they can ask filter questions when they first contact the source to determine the individual's knowledge or credibility. A filter question would be "How long have you worked on the project?" or simply "Is microbiology your field of expertise?" Reporters should also ask sources for the names of additional experts in the field. Often sources will name coresearchers or leading experts or even critics of their work.

Learning the Subject

Once you have chosen your sources, research will help you prepare for the interview. Advance research has become easier with the Internet and news databases such as Lexis-Nexis, as noted in Chapter 2. Reporters can use many of the sources outlined in Chapter 2 to get information for stories as well as to help them prepare for interviews. But they might find they need to use sources to assess the need for the story and the extent that the topic or individual has been covered.

With Lexis-Nexis, a reporter can find articles about a subject or source that have appeared in major media since 1980. Before Lexis-Nexis, reporters usually had access only to the news clippings in their own organizations' libraries. Now they can get many of the English-speaking world's news clippings. Resources range from ABC News transcripts to the weekly *Zimbabwe Standard*. However, a note of caution when using Lexis-Nexis: Whole chains of newspapers are pulling out of the database in an effort to force researchers to use their fee-based archives. For example, the Tribune Company, which owns the *Chicago Tribune*, the *Los Angeles Times*, and the *Baltimore Sun*, decided to pull its publications from Lexis-Nexis, except for the six months prior to the most recent publication date. Researchers who want older stories will have to subscribe to have access or read microfilm in a public or university library.

Just as a reminder, among other news and research databases are ABI/Inform for business and trade press information; Academic Search Premier or ERIC/Ebsco for trade and academic information; Biography Resource Center, Dow Jones Interactive, or the *Wall Street Journal* for business information; or Web of Knowledge for academic citations. These resources might be in some newsrooms, but most are available in college libraries. Other background materials can be gathered from corporate, government, or organizational Web sites.

Of course, reporters should use their media organizations' libraries and clip files, particularly if they are researching and writing a local story. Other reporters might have written about the topic or individual. They can give updates or even support angles that have not been covered, as well as provide sources they might have interviewed but not used in earlier stories.

These resources will help a reporter prepare for an interview in a number of ways. First, they can tell the reporter how much media attention the story's subject or source has already gotten in the local community. If the topic has already been covered thoroughly by other media, the reporter can use that information to shift the story's topic to one less covered or possibly a new angle.

Second, research helps reporters become general experts. Third, research gives reporters the basis for formulating questions and shows them what they do not need to ask and what they might need to confirm.

When getting background information, reporters should be careful. Just because a story has been published or posted on a reputable Web site does not mean all its facts are correct. For example, the media misreported that Mexican President Vicente Fox was a "Harvard man" over and over because they relied on news articles in Lexis-Nexis that were incorrect. In fact, President Fox attended only a six-week seminar at Harvard as a young business executive. When formulating questions, it's always best to have the source confirm even routine facts at some point during the interview.

Setting Up the Interview

Once a reporter has identified the topic and the right sources, the next step, of course, is to get an interview. Often you might have to go through a secretary or a public relations person to arrange a time. Whether talking to the source directly or to the intermediary, be sure to specify the amount of time you will need.

Some ground rules might need to be clarified before the interview. For example, the chief executive officer of a troubled company might want a public relations person to sit in on the interview. Or the executive might want the entire interview to be just for background information. In establishing ground rules, do not agree to pay for an interview. Only in very rare situations should you consider paying for information, and you should have the approval of your editor.

To add detail to the story, select a comfortable place for the interview, preferably at the source's office, workplace, or home. The source might be more at ease in familiar surroundings, and you can use furniture, family photographs, or other items as a way to initiate a conversation and start building rapport. Knickknacks or collectibles can add interesting bits to stories, for example, the CEO who carves decoys.

Meeting in an office avoids uncomfortable situations that can arise if interviews happen during meals. Reporters do not want to get into battles with sources about who will pay for dinner. If a source does not want to meet where he or she works, select a neutral place and keep all food to a soda or a cup of coffee. Reporters should not accept gifts or expensive meals from sources to avoid the perception or expectation that a favorable story will be written.

If you call to set up an interview, be prepared to conduct the interview right then. The source might get on the telephone and say that now is the best time. Reporters should always be ready to ask questions; sources might be out of town or unavailable a few hours later.

QUESTIONS AND NOTE TAKING

Based on research, journalists should write in advance of the interview a list of questions they want the source to answer. Even experienced reporters make lists or at least notes of the points they want to cover. The list can help keep an interview focused and the source on topic. Reporters can use the list at the end of the interview to make sure they have hit all the topics.

Eliciting Good Quotes

In planning the questions, reporters include open-ended questions that require the source to give a lengthy or expansive answer. Within that lengthy answer, the reporter might pick up nuggets for more specific questions. For example, for a profile of a local Olympic hopeful, a reporter could ask: "Explain your average daily training regime and other activities from the time you awake until you sleep at night." As the athlete is detailing the hours of her day, the reporter will listen for unique aspects of her regime that would be noteworthy for the story. Maybe she spends an hour Salsa dancing for a flexibility warm-up even though she is a volleyball player. When the source mentions a unique topic, the reporter can probe with more questions at that time.

Reporters also ask closed-ended or yes–no, approve–disapprove questions. The responses hardly make good quotes, but a reporter might be looking just for affirmation. To get an explanation, reporters can follow the closed-ended question with a simple "Why" or "Why not?"

Good questions elicit solid quotes, provide background information, clarify statistics or other data, get reaction to a situation or person, or guide the source to reveal previously unknown information. While reporters typically have a structured list of questions they need answered, they should not be rigidly tied to them. As noted in the example of the Olympic hopeful, reporters must remain flexible if other information crops up during the conversation. They must also be open to a new slant on the topic.

Good reporters also aren't afraid to ask for clarification if they don't understand something. Sources who are specialists on a particular topic might launch into jargon, and a dedicated journalist asks for a translation into layman's language.

Reporters should also allow sources to give information they feel is important. Wrap up an interview with "Are there any points you would like to make that we have not covered?" or "What would you like readers (or viewers) to know about you and your work?"

Quotes can make or break a story. Print stories without quotes seem dry and lifeless. Broadcast stories without sound bites have no punch. (See the section on broadcast quotes at the end of this chapter.) Journalists must make every effort to obtain meaningful and vibrant quotes.

The more a source talks the more chance for good quotes. That's why most reporters, when doing in-person interviews, like to spend time with the subject and will ask many more questions to get more information than they can use in the story. *San Jose Mercury-News* reporter Eric Nalder (2004) said he asks sources for their entire life story as a way to get more information.

"Get the life story, even in cases where you don't intend to use it," he explained on the Project for Journalism Excellence's Journalism.org Web site. "Even when I interview a lawyer about a case, or a bureaucrat about a government policy, I get the life story if I have time. I get useful information and ask better questions as a result."

For stories in which the subjects must recount an experience, Nalder said he has them walk through the event again as if they were experiencing it in real time. "When people reach an important part of a story, slow them down and turn them into storytellers," he said. "Ask where they were standing, what they were doing, what they were wearing, what was the temperature and what were the noises around them? . . . This is how you get a story, not a bunch of facts." (Reprinted with permission from Eric Nalder, investigative reporter, *San Jose Mercury-News*.)

Reporters need to be able to recognize good quotes that become direct quotes in stories. When someone expresses a point in a unique way or has a distinct way of talking, that comment can tie a story together. Opinion, insight, colorful expressions, or an especially clear translation of complicated terms makes for good quotes. Reporters should paraphrase or use as an indirect quote routine or factual information. They should avoid using clichés and sparingly quote people quoting other people. The latter must be attributed clearly.

Telling the Story with Anecdotes

With more feature styles being used in news stories these days, good anecdotes as well as good quotes are important. Anecdotes illustrate points. They are the little stories that speakers tell about their childhood, their first job, or their favorite grandparent. A riveting anecdote might end up being the lead of the story, so good reporters are always on the prowl for them. John Brady, author of *The Craft of Interviewing*, a timeless book on interviewing, said reporters must insist that sources give them anecdotes (1976). He explained:

> If he says, "I owe my 40 years of marriage to absolute understanding and compatibility," ask him, "What do you mean by understanding and compatibility? Can you give me some examples?" Follow-up questions do more than secure specifics—they brace rapport. They indicate that you are genuinely curious about the subject's life and charred times. With sufficient rapport, the writer can even get away with a hard-bitten closed question.

Questions that begin with *when* seem to elicit a few more anecdotes, said Brady, but all the W's and H can work. *When* takes people back in time to recall a story or anecdote. When did you first decide you wanted to be governor of the state? When did you realize your invention was going to revolutionize cell phone technology? Reporters usually have to tighten up anecdotes, but the speaker's words can reveal humor, emotion, and empathy, so direct quotes should be part of the anecdote.

Reporters also should be on the lookout for what Brady called "The Definitive Anecdote" that can be used for the lead or might give an excellent summation at the end of a feature story. Brady quoted the late freelance journalist Richard Gehman, who wrote: "Quite often, in the course of interviews about a subject, the writer will stumble upon the single telling anecdote that either sums up the character or illumines one facet of it compellingly. If that anecdote 'feels' right, he ought to write it at once and put it aside for later use."

Getting Down the Quotes

Note taking often gives student journalists trouble. As a skill that is developed over years, practice does make perfect. The first rule of note taking: It is better to overdo it—to have more notes than you need. Reporters typically take notes on 50 percent to 75 percent more than they will use in their stories. In the writing process, the story might take an unexpected direction, so notes that seemed unimportant before might take on significance later.

Second rule: Reporters never stop taking notes during the interview. They even take notes during the final informal chatting at the end of the interview just in case the source pops out a good quote. They take notes even when using a working tape recorder. Any background noise might make the tape difficult to hear, the tape recorder might malfunction, or they won't have time to listen to the tape before writing the story.

If you plan to use a tape recorder, make sure it is working, and take plenty of batteries and tapes for the interview. Put the tape recorder in an inconspicuous place—not between you and the source where it can become a focal point. Above all, remember: Take notes. The audio might not be clear, and if you do not have notes, you do not have a story.

Third rule: Reporters take notes on more than words. They include description of the source's clothes, his or her mannerisms, and even what's on the office walls. They use their senses to describe the taste, smell, and feel of the environment in addition to what they see and hear.

Final rule: Good reporters write or type their interview notes as soon as possible. Memories fade quickly, and a hastily written scrawl will soon be illegible. Even if there is no time to type up notes formally, reporters should go through the interview notes, make illegible words legible, and flesh out sentences. Such diligence is needed so reporters don't lose track of needed information. See Figure 3.1 for Don Fry's tips on note taking from speedy interviewers.

Establishing Rapport

Usually reporters try to put their sources at ease by beginning with small talk, such as commenting on office décor or remarking on some aspect of the news. They interact with sources as much as possible, using eye contact and body language to keep the sources talking. Reporters respond with nods, a tilt of the head, a responsive "hmmm" to let sources know they are paying attention. Reporters have to be careful that such body language and comments do not make a source infer the reporter agrees or disagrees. The reporter's mannerisms should not be misconstrued.

Apart from their body language, reporters need to remain as neutral as possible in phrasing and asking their questions. Bias should not creep into the way questions are phrased. Reporters should assess their attitudes and potential biases toward the story topic and the story's sources. Cultural bias is discussed in Chapter 5. Reporters have to be aware constantly of their potential biases when approaching a source. For example, in 2000, when a team of reporters at the *New York Times* did a 15-part series called "How Race Is Lived in America," they had to be aware of their own beliefs about race. "We're all

FIGURE 3.1   Tips on Note Taking from Speedy Interviewers

- Always get the source's correctly spelled name, address, and phone number.
- Staple business cards into the notebook. Always ask if the card is correct.
- Don't crowd the notebook. Leave space for annotating notes.
- Leave the inside covers blank to write down questions to ask later.
- Take 20 times as many notes as you put into the story.
- Jot down the time every five minutes or so to remember the rhythm of interview.
- Draw diagrams of rooms, stages, scenes, flags, etcetera.
- Inventory the space around the source, and ask follow-up questions.
- Spell out sourcing agreements in the notebook.
- Close the notebook at the end of the interview, and use the Columbo Effect.
- Annotate the notes as soon as possible, preferably on site.
- If the notes get cold, make extracts.
- On longer projects, keep a journal or daily memos.
- Let lawyers set policy on how long to keep notes.

Source: Don Fry, writing coach, all rights reserved.

racial in some way," said Soma Golden Behr, assistant managing editor at the *Times,* in an interview on the Poynter Web site (2000). "We all have a race or some perception of a race. You have to audit your feelings out of anything you're working on."

The need to put feelings aside arises whenever a hot-button story develops. The 1980s tested journalists' ability to put their personal feelings and fears aside when conducting interviews on the AIDS crisis. Jacqui Banaszynski's series of stories in the *St. Paul* (MN) *Pioneer Press* (Steele, 1992) were the first on the topic to win the Pulitzer Prize, and she said that dealing with an emotional subject and complex family relationships were challenges in the interviewing process.

The subject of her stories was Dick Hanson, a 37-year-old gay man who farmed in Glenwood, Minnesota. Banaszynski met Hanson and his partner, Bert Henningson, and wrote three stories about Hanson's battle with AIDS, which resulted in his death a few months later. In addition to the depth with which she explained Hanson and Henningson's gay relationship, she spent much of the third story in the series discussing how Hanson's three brothers had rejected him. The charged situation led to one brother's verbal attack on her and to tough decisions about what interview material to use in her stories. Banaszynski's series illustrated that for emotionally charged interviews, insight and self-awareness seem to be a good guard against inaccurate or melodramatic stories.

Journalism ethicist Bob Steele (1992) said Banaszynski's series upheld the highest ethical standards of journalism with its truthful and in-depth storytelling. She was not manipulated by her sources or the emotional topic, yet she also acted responsibly by minimizing harm to her sources. For example, she said she decided against using a quote from Hanson's brother about how he would like to "put a bullet in [Dick's] head." Banaszynski said she felt she had already described adequately the family rift. The rapport Banaszynski built with all her sources served her stories well.

Louise Ritchie, a former journalist for the *Washington Post* and the *Detroit Free Press* who has a Ph.D. in clinical psychology, said journalists sometimes have to think like therapists when interviewing (1997). Psychology has a number of techniques that are helpful for journalistic interviewing, she said. When Ritchie was a journalist, she might not have pursued questions about a person's behavior that didn't make sense. But psychology training has taught her to ask about any unusual behavior. She said the behavior that seems odd might seem perfectly normal to the interview subjects, so they will talk about it.

First meetings hold much importance to psychologists, and they should for journalists as well, Ritchie said.

> Journalists who pay attention from their first contact with their interview subjects may learn important information about how the person handles surprises, stress, and life in general.

Being quiet during an interview also helps interview subjects talk more. All psychologists know to use silence to elicit more from patients; journalists can use the same techniques. If a subject becomes emotional when talking, the best technique is either to remain silent and see whether the person continues talking or ask a follow-up question to find out why the person became emotional. "Ask the question and then, like a good psychologist, close your mouth and wait for the revelation," Ritchie explained.

However, in another technique, unlike psychologists, some journalists reveal more about themselves in an effort to get a subject to talk. By revealing shared experiences, journalists make the interview subjects feel more comfortable about talking. They might share a similar interest in a sports team or the loss of a sibling at a young age. Watch out: Reporters have damaged their relationships with sources—and the subsequent relationships of other reporters—by becoming too chummy with sources who revealed information the sources believed "was just between friends."

Difficult Moments in Interviewing

Reporters face challenges when a source is reluctant to talk with them. Shirley Biagi in *Interviews That Work* (1992) said that reporters should first try sources who are most likely to say yes to an interview. If that doesn't work, she lists several things that might persuade the source. She said to try to appeal to the source's "sense of pride or purpose." Tell the person the story is going to be written whether he or she comments, and it will look better if the source makes a comment.

Or the reporter might appeal to the person's "instinct for justice," "the ability to represent a point of view," or "need for attention." The reporter can explain how the story serves the public interest and how the public is interested in the source's perspective. The story might give the source a "sense of professional or personal prestige," which might appeal to his or her ego. Finally, the reporter can appeal to the source's "desire for community welfare," indicating that the source is setting a good example by speaking to the media.

Reporters also might run into a problem if the source suddenly tries to go "off the record." Reporters do not quickly agree to off-the-record interviews because it means they cannot identify or quote the source, which lessens the credibility of the information. First, reporters should try to persuade the source to be interviewed on the record. Sometimes sources don't understand what off the record means. They might not realize that they would not be mentioned in the story if they were off the record, but the reporter could still use the information.

If the source still wanted to remain off the record, the reporter would have two choices: Find another source or negotiate what off the record means. Some reporters would allow an off-the-record interview if it meant they could still use the information as background, just not identify the source. Reporters make their decisions about off the record based on how important the information is. If going off the record is the only way to get information crucial to a story, reporters might have no other choice.

In some cases sources might ask to read a story before it is published. All journalists typically say no to this request. They understand human nature—most sources will want to rephrase their quotes or will question the focus of the story. However, in complex stories, many journalists will check back with sources to assure the accuracy of facts and specific quotes or check definitions of jargon. If a source asks to read a story, offering such follow-up fact checking often diffuses the request. The sources see that they and the journalists want the same thing: an accurate story. And they don't have to read the story to make that happen.

The end of the interview often is the most crucial moment because generally the source relaxes and might become more talkative. Savvy journalists always ask a few final questions of a source as they leave, such as "What is the most important thing the readers/viewers should know about this topic/you?" With such open-ended questions, reporters cover all the bases, capturing any information they might not have known to ask. The reporter should end any interview with a request to call the source with any additional questions that might arise while writing the story. The channels of communication between the source and reporter should remain open. In some circumstances, a reporter might send a thank-you note after the interview.

USING QUOTES EFFECTIVELY

In beginning newswriting classes, students are told to put direct quotes "high up" in the inverted pyramid story, meaning they should be in the first three or four paragraphs. This advice serves working reporters well because it makes sure an overzealous copy editor won't cut an important quote, and it introduces sources early on. However, no hard and fast rule exists about where to place quotes in news or features. In a long magazine piece, some reporters might sprinkle only a few lengthy quotes throughout the story.

For news reporters on deadline, strong quotes sometimes can be used like a nut graph to clarify the impact of a story. When an event that many felt was an outrageous disregard for human life happened in Fort Worth, Texas, in 2002, *Star-Telegram* reporter Deanna Boyd found the perfect quote to evoke that feeling. A 25-year-old nurse's aide who had hit a homeless man with her car drove home to her garage. There he remained alive and lodged in her windshield for several days, and then after he died, she enlisted friends to help her dump his body in a park. Here are the first seven paragraphs of Boyd's story:

> FORT WORTH—When Gregory Glenn Biggs' body was found in October in Cobb Park, evidence pointed to a hit-and-run.

But in the past two weeks, police have learned that Biggs lived for two or three days after he was hit, lying on a car hood in a southeast Fort Worth garage, his body trapped in the windshield.

Despite Biggs' pleas, police said, the driver refused to help and left him to die. Afterward, the body was dumped in the park.

"I'm going to have to come up with a new word. Indifferent isn't enough. Cruel isn't enough to say. Heartless? Inhumane? Maybe we've just redefined inhumanity here," said Richard Alpert, a Tarrant County assistant district attorney.

What happened to the 37-year-old Biggs, police said, was not a simple case of a driver's failure to stop to help an injured man. It was homicide, they said.

"If he had gotten medical attention, he probably would have survived," traffic investigation Sgt. John Fahrenthold said.

Wednesday, police arrested Chante Mallard, a 25-year-old nurse's aide, basing their case primarily on Mallard's confession about four months later of what happened on an October night as she drove near the East Loop 820 split with U.S. 287. (Reprinted with permission from the *Fort Worth Star-Telegram.*)

The assistant district attorney's quote sums up what most people probably thought when they heard about this crime—that inhumane acts had hit a new level. The second quote Boyd used from the traffic sergeant is not as flowery, yet effectively states the most important fact from the case: that Biggs might have lived if Mallard had helped him. In June 2003 Mallard was sentenced to 50 years in prison for the murder of Biggs.

Boyd's story became a finalist in the Best Newspaper Writing Awards. Because of the sensational nature of the story, she had to tread carefully in her reporting and interviewing. One aspect of her thorough reporting became a particularly difficult interview moment. Biggs was estranged from his family, but Boyd used a people-tracking Internet service called Autotrack to find Biggs's relatives. When she finally reached his mother, Boyd said it was clear that his mother did not know officially that he had died or how he had died. Boyd made the decision that it was more compassionate to tell Biggs's mother herself than let her read about it in the newspaper the next day.

"I was honest, and Meredith Biggs appeared to appreciate it," Boyd said. "She thanked me profusely for giving her the answers, albeit painful, that she had been seeking over the past few years." (Reprinted with permission from the Poynter Institute, St. Petersburg, Florida.)

Other reporters have had to break bad news to families. The best approach comes when reporters identify who they are and why they are calling and express their condolences. Some family members might reminisce to help them through their grief. Others might not want to talk, and reporters should respect their request not to answer questions.

TYPES OF INTERVIEWS

Interview types and styles depend on the kind of story being written. Your research should have determined the type of interview you need. Not every interview needs to be in person or can be, particularly if a reporter is working under deadline pressure or if a source is in another country, state, or city. Whenever possible, a reporter should go to the source and meet face to face. For several types of interviews, an in-person interview is crucial.

■ **New beat, new source interviews.** Beat reporting requires building relationships with sources the reporter will use over and over. Reporters need to know faces and personalities and determine whether the source will be someone who will take calls. Is this source articulate and well spoken, and will he or she provide good information? Will the source understand deadlines?

The first interviews with sources should be face to face because they launch the rapport important to both the source and the reporter. Beat sources are not "one-hit wonders," whom the reporter might never interview again and therefore not have to worry about how the source will respond to the story. Beat reporters have to go back to the same sources sometimes for years, so they must keep source–reporter relationships stable.

Throughout the relationship beyond that first interview, sources might not like every story, even though the stories are as accurate, complete, and fair as possible. That's where the relationship with the source becomes crucial. The reporter should answer openly and honestly any of the source's complaints about a story. Sometimes it will mean just reminding the source how journalism works—that all sides of a story must be told, not just the side the source likes. If the beat source trusts a reporter, he or she will continue to be available to the reporter.

Ken Metzler said about beat reporting in *Creative Interviewing* (1997): "While you are sizing them up, they are doing the same with you. The rapport and trust established on initial contact will affect future interviews, not only with one source, but also with many others. Word gets around."

Often reporters interview new sources who might provide information periodically but not on a routine basis, as a beat source does. Or a source might seek out a reporter to provide information. The reporter must also establish rapport but realize that one interview might be the extent of their contact. In that instance, the reporter also must assess why a specific source wants to be interviewed. Is it his or her job, such as a public information officer? Is it a desire to keep the source's issues in the media? Is it a method of retaliation against issues or people to whom the source is opposed? Whatever the reason, the reporter must be aware of hidden agendas so all sides of an issue can be discussed.

■ **Personality profile/feature interviews.** To capture someone's personality for a story, a reporter must spend time with the subject. Throughout the interview, the reporter tries to get a sense of who the person is. Depending on the focus of the story, the interview environment is important. Reporters need to get a full picture of the person, so interviews should take place at the source's office, home, and even at the site of his or her favorite hobby, such as on a tennis court or in a fishing boat. Observation of the individual, his or her home turf, and mannerisms will be part of the personality profile.

For these types of interviews, the reporter should do extensive research beforehand. The reporter should be familiar with news stories written about the person, the person's résumé, and interviews with friends, enemies, and associates. If a reporter appears uninformed during an interview, the source might lose respect for the reporter's abilities and try to cut the interview short. Also, the background research on the person will allow the reporter to move on to more in-depth interview questions. For example, because the reporter has already seen the source's résumé, he or she does not need to ask the subject's college major. Instead, the reporter can ask why a person who is now a Wall Street tycoon majored in theater in college. That type of question also confirms information the reporter might have discovered—and lets the source know that the reporter has done his or her homework. The reporter should confirm résumé information; sometimes people claim to have college degrees they never earned.

When Dana Kennedy profiled actor and former rapper Mark Wahlberg in the *New York Times* (2000), tough questions needed to be asked about Wahlberg's criminal past and time in prison for stabbing a man in the eye. Here's how Kennedy handled it:

> Mr. Wahlberg, who is soft-spoken and genial in person, is resigned to questions about his past. The only time he becomes uncomfortable during the interview is when he is asked if he has ever sought out Tranh Lam, the man who lost his eye in the attack, and apologized to him . . .
>
> Mr. Wahlberg says he apologized to Mr. Lam in court but has not had contact with him since. "It would be unfair to all the other people that I messed up if I only singled him out," he said. "I'm certainly sorry for what I did. I did this every day until I was sent to prison."

Research will give reporters enough background so that they can ask questions to get anecdotes and quotations that will complete the story. Detail and description about individuals and their lives makes personality and feature stories captivating for audiences.

■ **In-depth information interviews.** In these types of interviews, the reporter gathers extensive background material or information essential to the story. For example, the source might provide a chronological explanation of a manufacturing plant's demise and the effect on workers in the community. Or a scientist might "walk" a reporter through the discovery of a more environmentally friendly way to dry clean clothes and how the process works.

In a "fishing expedition"–type interview, the reporter has some information but needs much more for a story. These interviews might have two types of sources, depending on the source's willingness to talk. With a helpful source, the reporter can say directly what information he knows and what additional information he needs. If the source does not know, the reporter always asks for names of people who might have the information.

With an unwilling or hostile source, the reporter must be well prepared so he or she can allude to the needed information and ask the source to confirm it. Reporters should have carefully prepared questions for a hostile source, who will want to give as little time as possible to the interview. Hostile sources actually are easier to deal with in person than on the phone; the telephone makes it too easy to end the interview with a click. In person, most sources know to maintain their composure in front of a reporter.

Any in-depth interview should be arranged well in advance so the source knows the time commitment. Reporters should expect such interviews to last several hours and require copious notes.

■ **Telephone interviews.** These interviews remain the staple of daily reporting. In beat reporting, the telephone interview works well because reporters already have a rapport with numerous sources who can be called for a quick quote or confirmation of a fact if a reporter is working on deadline.

Other advantages for phone interviews are the time saved and the ability to type notes directly into the computer so they can be cut and pasted into the story. Now that so many people have cell phones, reporters can reach people easier—if they have sources' cell phone numbers.

The obvious downside of telephone interviews: People can hang up. Efforts to reconnect might be in vain. Telephone interviews do not allow reporters to see people's reactions to questions or to add detail. It is also easier for reporters to make mistakes in writing down words that they did not hear clearly. And cell phones might cut off when either party hits a nonservice area or runs into interference, such as high-tension electric lines.

■ **Electronic mail interviews.** Interviewing via email is still a new frontier in the journalistic process. Although email has been around for a number of years now, journalists have been slow to accept it as an interviewing method. In 2002 University of Miami researcher Bruce Garrison investigated how journalists used electronic mail. He found that the majority of the 201 journalists he studied still used the telephone and in-person methods, with only 6.5 percent reporting using email for interviews. However, a majority of the journalists viewed email interviews positively. The more prevalent use of email by journalists was for "contacting groups, organizations, and public officials about policy issues when reporting," Garrison reported. More than 80 percent of the journalists had used email for this purpose.

Garrison also found that generally journalists felt secure when using email for information gathering or interviews. They were more concerned about the impact of the technology in swamping them with junk email or wasting their time with useless correspondence than the quality of the email information. However, their bosses worried about information gathered through email. Garrison reported:

> Editors are much more concerned about the security and credibility of information in electronic mail than others in the newsroom. They appear to be much more concerned about problems that may occur in information obtained through electronic mail than are beat or general assignment reporters.

Journalists have to be cautious in email interviews that the responses came from the source and not from an assistant who has access to his or her boss's email.

■ **On-the-scene-interviews.** When covering any event, crime, or disaster, the reporter has to talk to participants, witnesses, and officials. From a feature on the state fair to a school shooting, sources who experienced the event should be interviewed. Such interviewing can be as simple as walking up to people at the event to get their comments or as time consuming as knocking on doors in a neighborhood where a major crime has occurred. These important interviews grab sources in the moment; they can tell the reporter right away what they saw and felt.

Reporters must remember that people who have witnessed a traumatic event, such as a child being killed by a car, might not be completely reliable sources. Reporters must be aware of people's psychological states when interviewing them. A reporter who interviews four witnesses to an accident might get four slightly different versions. People who witness or who have suffered trauma perceive those events in different ways. Reporters might have to reinterview a source later after he or she has had some time to recover from the shock of the event.

Judith Lewis Herman in her book, *Trauma and Recovery* (1992), notes that telling about an event can be part of the healing process. That could prompt people to talk about tragic events. But reporters must be fair and considerate in questioning trauma victims and double-check the accuracy of their information.

CONSIDERATIONS FOR BROADCAST INTERVIEWS

Several of the interview styles mentioned here translate well to broadcast media. Because of the need for on-camera interviews, the on-the-scene interview is the most useful type for broadcast reporters. Frederick Shook, in *Television Field Production and Reporting* (2000), said: "While visuals tell the story in television news, interviews provide the little moments of emphasis that punctuate the story. Without sound bites the television story is essentially barren." Interviews in TV stories add spark and spontaneity.

Shook said: "Interviews impart a sense of authority and spontaneity to television news stories and provide intimate detail that otherwise would be unobtainable. Interviews further help to reveal something of the person being interviewed."

But broadcast reporters, especially those working for TV stations, have to manage interviews carefully. It can be intimidating for people to have a video camera and lights pointed in their faces, especially for "regular people," rather than government officials or experts who are used to being on camera. Shook said it was crucial that reporters establish rapport with interview subjects before turning on the camera and lights. Interview subjects must have time to become comfortable with the equipment. They may have to use a wireless microphone, rather than a larger microphone held before their faces, which might distract them.

Setting can make the broadcast interview more visually interesting and put the subject at ease. If reporting in a workplace or other organization with ongoing activities, ask the subjects to show you what they do each day. A videographer for WDSU in New Orleans explained: "So many journalists interrupt reality. They stop the person and slap them in front of a wall for the interview, instead of talking with the interview subjects as they keep working." It's just human nature for people to feel more comfortable in a familiar setting, so that is where reporters should interview if at all possible.

Shook also recommended several rules for good broadcast interviews. The 5 W's and an H should be the basis for creating interview questions. The reporter should consider the questions the viewer or listener wants answered by the interview. Don't ask, "How do you feel?" Shook explained. It is better to make an observation about a situation and then ask the subjects what they think. Also, try to make the interview as conversational as possible because it will elicit more meaningful responses.

Former CNN reporter Victoria McCullough Carroll said in *Writing News for Television* (1997) that good broadcast reporters also write their own notes of everything interview subjects say both on and off camera. Good information for the story might be revealed when the camera stops rolling, so reporters should have their own notes to rely on, she said.

Silence can be a beneficial technique in any interview for any medium, as noted earlier in the chapter. Ask a question and then allow for several seconds of silence. The subjects will try to fill the silence or might expand on the topic the reporter did not ask. Veteran *60 Minutes* reporter Mike Wallace said (Carroll, 1997): "The single most interesting thing that you can do in television, I find, is to ask a good question and then let it hang there for two or three or four seconds as though you are expecting more. You know what? They get a little embarrassed and give you more." When used with a good question, silence may elicit a good sound bite from the subject. The sound bite is crucial because, unlike print reporters, broadcast reporters have only five to twenty seconds to devote to the interview.

Choosing the Sound Bite

A 15-minute interview for a print reporter might yield a 15-inch story that would include direct quotes and paraphrases, but a broadcaster has to find two or three sentences from that 15 minutes for a 10-second sound bite. (Depending on the newsroom, a sound bite might be referred to as a SOT, sound on tape.) Carroll said that reporters and editors require practice to find good sound bites, but eventually one jumps right out. In addition to allowing viewers to hear directly from people in a story, sound bites can add emotion and feeling to a story.

Sounds bites should be evaluated carefully, however. Some sound bites might have to be rejected because they use profanity or conflict with the facts of a story. Sound bites in which the interview subject uses poor grammar or extra words can be edited to a shorter length. But sound bites should be edited with care. The meaning of someone's words should not be changed through editing.

The format of attribution differs between a broadcast and a print quote because the audience needs to know who is talking before seeing or hearing the statement. In a print story, the attribution will typically come before or after the first sentence of a direct quote so as not to "bury the quote" and also to identify quickly the speaker if the story quotes more than one source. In TV and radio, the interview subject has to be introduced before the sound bite. A smooth transition is needed from the news anchor or reporter into the sound bite.

Carroll said most broadcast news writers choose the sound bite they will use in the story before they write the script. That way they can find the focus of the story because the focus will be built around the best sound bites available for the story. Selecting the sound bites first also makes writing the script easier, she said, because you already have the words of the interview subject. Then the writer can select sentences that flow into and from the sound bite without being repetitive of the actual sound bite.

The NewsLab (2002a) gave the following example of a good sound bite for a story about witnesses being called for a grand jury hearing. Officials suspected some county commissioners in Florida delayed action on a plan to help the county hospital as a way to pressure the hospital to buy from a medical equipment salesman and financial backer of some commissioners:

> SOT: Commission Chairman Tom Scott: I cannot be bought. No one owns me. I do what is right for this community.

This sound bite runs about five seconds, but it clearly conveys that the chairman is claiming his innocence.

THE CONTINUED IMPORTANCE OF INTERVIEWING

Even with the onslaught of information from the Web and the ease with which so many people can be interviewed, nothing will replace interviewing in reporting. News stories are not really about numbers or meetings or crime. They are about people. People need to speak in news stories whether they are quoted in print or lead sound bites. Ken Metzler in *Creative Interviewing* (1997) reports that interviewing remains one of the most important activities for print reporters, who estimate that they get 75 percent to 80 percent of their material through interviews. Interviews are just as important for broadcast journalists.

GLOSSARY

Attribution: The name and title of the source of a quote or paraphrase. Full attribution is given the first time the source is used in a print story; for example, Mark Smith, former city council member, said. On second reference, only the last name is used, for example, Smith said.

Nut graph: The graph that contains the news peg or point of the story.

Off the record: The source will give information to the reporter only if guaranteed that he or she will not be identified in the story.

SOT: Sound on tape, or an on-tape interview with a person for a TV news story; runs between five and twenty seconds in length.

Sound bite: An on-tape interview with a person for a TV news story between five and twenty seconds in length.

ACTIVITIES

1. Examine the front-page stories of your daily newspaper today. Identify how much information came from interviews. Can you trace all information to specific sources? Would you estimate 75 to 80 percent of the information came from interviews?

2. Clip a front-page story from your local newspaper and evaluate its direct quotes. What do they add to the story, and why were they placed where they were? Evaluate the quotes with the eye of a broadcaster. Which one quote would be effective enough to be used as a sound bite?

3. Watch one of the many TV interview or talk shows. Evaluate how the interviewer elicits information from the subjects. Are questions open ended or closed ended? How does the interviewer establish rapport? Is the interview focused or rambling? Can you identify specific techniques that would be useful to you as a reporter? What techniques did you see that you would not use? Why?

4. Practice creating questions and gathering quotes. Come up with 10 questions for your roommate or a friend. Avoid using yes–no questions. Ask the questions and try to get down five full-sentence and meaningful direct quotes.

5. Look at several public relations textbooks to investigate what public relations practitioners tell their clients to do when being interviewed. Make a list of these recommendations. Write your reaction to how powerful sources try to "handle" reporters. Develop some strategies to get around what PR people advise.

6. Role play with another student in your class. Pick an issue on your campus. One student will be the reporter and the other will be the unwilling source who will try to use the public relations recommendations to avoid answering directly.

7. Based on the research you did in Chapter 2 to gather information about a campus leader, draft a list of questions and schedule an appointment with him or her. Do the interview, then write a three- to four-page story, focusing on the

individual or on a topic the individual is knowledgeable about. Write the story for the campus newspaper.

RESOURCES AND WEB SITES

Information on how-to's of interviewing: www.notrain-nogain.org and Journalism.org

REFERENCES

Biagi, S. (1992). *Interviews that work.* Belmont, CA: Wadsworth.
Boyd, D. (2003). Lessons learned. Best newspaper writing 2003. St. Petersburg, FL: Poynter Institute, p. 314.
Boyd, D. (2002, March 17). Bizarre details of man's death revealed. *Fort Worth Star-Telegram.* www.dfw.com/mld/startelegram/2809134.htm.
Brady, J. (1976). *The craft of interviewing.* Cincinnati, OH: Writer's Digest.
Carroll, V. M. (1997). *Writing news for television.* Ames, IA: Iowa State University Press.
Garrison, B. (2002, August). *The use of electronic mail as a newsgathering resource.* Paper presented at annual meeting of the Association for Education in Journalism and Mass Communication, Miami Beach, FL.
Herman, J. L. (1992). *Trauma and recovery.* New York: Basic Books.
Kennedy, D. (2000, October 15). With echoes from a dark past. *New York Times,* section 2, p. 13.
Metzler, K. (1997). *Creative interviewing.* Boston: Allyn & Bacon.
Nalder, E. (2004). Loosening lips. www.journalism.org/resources/tools/reporting/interviewing/loosening.asp.
NewsLab. (2002a). Clarity. Simplify complex relationships. www.newslab.org/video/BA/baclarity.htm.
NewsLab. (2002b). Steps to a strong interview. www.newslab.org/interview.htm.
Ritchie, L. R. (1997). Getting the measure of a soul on deadline. Interviewing tips from a psychologist. www.freep.com/jbspage/academy/psych.htm.
Self-awareness. (2000, October 27). Poynter Institute. www.poynter.org/centerpiece/RemJ/att3.htm.
Shook, F. (2000). *Television field production and reporting.* New York: Longman.
Steele, B. (1992, December). Doing ethics. *Quill,* pp. 28–30.

■ ■ ■ ■ ■

CHAPTER 4

GATHERING INFORMATION ETHICALLY AND LEGALLY

A reporter covering city hall is shopping at a local mall when she happens to see an assistant city finance officer who has been a source on several stories. The city official asks the reporter to join him for a cup of coffee. While they chat, he tells the reporter that someone in the city budget office has been embezzling city funds. He offers to let the reporter into his office after hours to use his computer to access records. The finance officer names the budget director as the embezzler and says the embezzling had gone undetected for at least six months. He has not said anything for fear of retribution and asked the reporter to protect him as a source.

What does the reporter do? Going into the city's computer after hours might be deemed computer hacking, trespassing, even stealing, although a city employee allowed access via his password. Going to higher-level city officials and asking about the embezzling charges might get the assistant city finance officer fired, or it might tip off the embezzler to cover his or her tracks.

In such cases, easy solutions might not exist. That's why reporters need a firm grasp of the legal and ethical guidelines that govern journalism. In this scenario the reporter should ask the assistant city finance officer to provide proof of the embezzlement through documents. In any scenario, the reporter should tell her editor about the situation to make sure that she follows proper newspaper procedures in protecting sources and in gathering information. The newspaper's attorney also might be consulted. If the reporter agrees to protect the source, she must keep her word and not reveal the source's name. In some cases, reporters have gone to jail to protect their sources. In this case, however, with documents proving the embezzlement, the reporter can pursue the story and avoid naming the source.

When they go after information, reporters do not have free rein to do anything they want to get a story. Personally, they are bound by the ethical norms of their profession and their own moral code. That includes not stealing information or illegally accessing records. Legally, they must follow the law so that they do not wrongly hurt someone's reputation, invade privacy, or violate laws on what information is open to them.

In this chapter, you will:

- Learn what codes of ethics say about journalists' behaviors,
- Consider how ethical behavior enhances journalistic excellence,
- Learn what constitutes copyright,
- Get a definition of libel and protections for journalists,
- Learn how to avoid invading someone's privacy,
- Find out when a public meeting is legally open or legally closed,
- Learn how to protect your notes and sources, and
- Be reminded how journalists are not protected if they break the law.

GUIDING JOURNALISTS' BEHAVIOR

Many in the general public perceive the idea of journalism ethics to be a contradiction of terms. Every few years an incident happens to reinforce that perception, such as when *New York Times* reporter Jayson Blair acknowledged faking or plagiarizing at least 36 stories in 2003. He resigned in disgrace, but as one positive outcome, the incident ignited a national discussion about journalism ethics. "The incident is serving as a wake-up call for journalism, prompting many papers—the *Globe* among them—to redouble efforts at accuracy and accountability, and inspiring readers to new levels of vigilance as error watchdogs," said the ombudsman for the *Boston Globe,* where Blair had worked as an intern. The number of readers reporting errors increased sharply after the Blair incident, and the *Globe* began running many more corrections. The *Globe* and other newspapers nationwide began tightening their checks and balances on reporters, rethinking use of anonymous sources, and reminding reporters that they must always attribute information they obtain from other news sources.

Alex Jones, director of the Joan Shorenstein Center on the Press, Politics and Public Policy at Harvard University, explained in an interview on WNET-TV (WNET, 2003) that because of the heavy deadline pressure in daily journalism, editors and news directors have to trust their reporters to behave ethically.

> The position of being a reporter on a major newspaper is a position of great trust because reporters not only do their reporting and writing, they also do their own fact-checking. There really is no independent way to do that and meet deadlines. So a newspaper has to depend on the integrity and honesty of the people . . . that represent it, and whose bylines appear. So when you have that position of trust, historically it's been a worthy thing to do. But, in the case of Jayson Blair, he was not deserving of that trust.

Jones recommended newsrooms make two major changes following the Blair incident. First, news organizations have to make it clear to their staffs and the public that they truly want to know about any mistakes they make, he said. Obviously, the goal is to strive for no errors, but when they do happen, the news organization should acknowledge them and correct them openly. Second, Jones said news organizations should begin a policy of randomly fact checking all reporters' stories occasionally.

Jayson Blair is an exception among reporters. Most journalists take ethical considerations seriously. No laws force them to behave ethically because such a law would violate the First Amendment that frees the press from restrictions. The fact that most do behave ethically is a testament to their personal integrity and respect for the expectations of their profession.

Codes of Ethics

No laws dictate journalistic ethics, and no standard code of ethics covers all mass communication professions. Ethics codes of professional organizations, such as the Society of Professional Journalists (SPJ), the Radio-Television News Directors Association, or the American Society of Newspaper Editors, guide journalists. Other mass communicators, such as public relations professionals, also have ethics codes through their professional groups, such as the Public Relations Society of America (PRSA). Ethics codes vary from a few paragraphs to pages of guidelines. Newspapers and other media have developed their own codes that might be more stringent than what their professional organizations have adopted, such as the Gannett newspaper chain's code of ethics. The news organization substantially rewrote its code after the company paid a reported $15 million to the Cincinnati, Ohio–based Chiquita company to avoid a lawsuit after a reporter accessed executives' emails. The reporter was working on a series about the company, including its operations within the United States and in Latin America. The *Cincinnati Enquirer* fired the reporter, who was also convicted of trespassing. The editor subsequently lost his job with Gannett.

The American Society of Newspaper Editors developed a code of ethics in 1926. SPJ used it until the 1970s, when it developed an ethics code to cover journalists in all media. The recent version of the SPJ code of ethics has four main components: "Seek Truth and Report It; Minimize Harm; Act Independently; and Be Accountable." The tenets easily apply to all mass communicators.

In seeking the truth, journalists should do the most accurate reporting possible. They should identify all sources and only in rare cases use anonymous sources. If they do, they should keep their promises of confidentiality no matter what the costs. For example, in the ultimate ethical sacrifice, Houston-based writer Vanessa Leggett sat in prison for almost five months rather than turn over to a federal grand jury in Texas the interviews she had gathered for her nonfiction book on the death of a Houston socialite. Leggett said she was covered by reporter's privilege, which protected her from being forced to disclose confidential sources. She stood by her principles because she felt she needed to uphold her integrity and objectivity as a journalist.

Journalists also have to present facts as given to them. They should not alter any information in a story, digitally change photos, or stage news events.

Journalists should try to keep bias out of their reporting by examining their own beliefs and making sure they are not letting them slip into their stories. More about cultural bias is covered in Chapter 5. They should try to cover all perspectives in a story, even those they don't like or agree with personally. Their stories must be fair and balanced as well as complete.

To minimize harm, journalists need to understand how their reporting will affect both sources and readers and make sure all topics and people are treated with sensitivity and respect. By ensuring that they use qualified sources and present verified facts, journalists can minimize harm. Harm can be defined as emotional pain, social ostracism, or financial loss. Journalists should not sensationalize a story to make it seem more newsworthy or gripping to audiences. They must be aware of libel laws and issues regarding invasion of privacy, both discussed later in this chapter.

Journalists should act independently, meaning they should not have any obligation except to inform the public. They shouldn't join partisan organizations, accept gifts or special treatment, or work for anyone other than their media employer. They should not allow special-interest groups or advertisers to influence the news.

Journalists should be accountable to everyone in their audience and to their colleagues. They should avoid even the appearance of a conflict of interest. If a mistake is made, it should be admitted and then corrected promptly. The media should provide a forum where the public can voice complaints, even those against the media. Journalists need to be willing to listen to media criticism and examine their motives to determine whether the criticism is justified.

Keeping Journalists Credible

Reporters who want to be excellent at their jobs and noted for the quality of their work have to be ethical. A reporter's reputation can be ruined by sloppy, incomplete, and inaccurate information. Reporters who violate source confidentiality or who obtain information illegally or in less than honest circumstances will be branded as unethical. Once that happens, the credibility of the reporter and the medium he works for is tarnished. No story is worth sacrificing your reputation. Reporters under pressure to produce front-page, visible stories might think they could fabricate sources or quotes. When they get away with such lying once, the pattern might continue. But eventually, their lying will be their downfall, as seen with Jayson Blair and other reporters who stole colleagues' work and did not credit them. University students know that if they plagiarize inadvertently or deliberately on work for any class or media, they can be failed, put on probation, or expelled. The same rules apply when they become professionals.

Bob Steele, an ethics expert at the Poynter Institute on Media Studies, said ethics in journalism and excellence in journalism go hand in hand. "You make tough choices that have an impact on people, on the subjects in your stories, on your sources, and on the people in the community who rely on your news gathering skills. Ethics and excellence are inseparable," he said in *Covering the Community: A Diversity Handbook for Media* (Aldrich, 1999). He explained that journalists have to make tough decisions that combine accuracy with fairness. Steele gave an example from the sports coverage of tennis star Jennifer Capriati. Ten years after her tennis successes, journalists continued to include paragraphs of run-ins with police and drugs during her troubled teen years. Steele pointed out that her teen problems were long past and were minor offenses anyway. Steele (2001) noted:

> The Capriati story demonstrates the challenges journalists face when it comes to honoring the values of accuracy, context, and fairness. Certainly reporters have an obligation to get the facts right in a story, but they also have an obligation to get the right facts into the story. Journalists must make important journalistic and ethical choices about which facts to write about and how they are used. . . . Journalists must ask themselves tough questions every time they consider tying her tennis success story to her teen troubles. Yes, reporters must be truthful in their reporting, but we often leave facts out of stories because they are not relevant or important. (Reprinted with permission from the Poynter Institute, St. Petersburg, Florida.)

Steele did not advocate ignoring important historical information about a person, but he argued that the ethical journalist would not continue to stigmatize and label someone with information that was no longer relevant. Good reporters have to wrestle with such ethical decisions daily. Often ethical decisions require a group opinion, that is, the reporter consults with editors—or even lawyers.

Although ethical judgment is the first step that keeps a reporter honest, another is the threat of lawsuits. Ethics codes do not bind reporters legally. But reporters must abide by specific laws and case laws that dictate behavior. These laws pertain to libel, privacy, access to documents, and interpretation of the First Amendment. Losing a libel or an invasion of privacy lawsuit can cost media organizations millions of dollars, and if the court finds the reporter at fault, he or she is usually fired. Such a firing can follow a reporter and prevent him or her from getting another job.

Copyright Issues

Plagiarizing someone else's work will get you fired, and depending on the circumstances, it also might be copyright infringement and get you sued. Citing facts is fine and not considered copyright infringement. Copyright law applies to unique or creative works of any kind, from writings to photos, choreography to artwork, films to music. For example, if a reporter lifts a significant amount of someone's Web commentary and puts it into his story without attribution, he has just committed copyright infringement. Anyone's individually published creative expression is "property" under copyright laws, and someone who wants to cite the material has to get the author's permission first, unless it falls under a fair use aspect of copyright law.

Fair use allows people such as journalists, book authors, critics, or scholars to quote small amounts of a copyrighted work as they report or critique the information in the public interest. Basically, as long as someone is quoting the copyrighted material for news or educational purposes and not to make money, the use is considered fair. Four considerations fall under fair use: how the copyrighted material will be used, what the characteristics of the copyrighted material are, what the quality and quantity of the use will be, and what the financial effect of the use will have on the copyrighted material.

If the copyrighted material has never been published before, courts tend to favor the rights of the author to have the right of first publication. A famous writer might never have published her collected letters, but she still owns the copyright and the right of first publication. If a journalist is quoting only a small portion of the copyrighted material, such as a few paragraphs out of a 500-page book, that is considered fair use. If a newspaper reprints a poet's complete poem as a sidebar to a profile of the poet, however, the newspaper should get copyright permission because it is publishing an author's copyrighted work in its entirety. If publishing the copyrighted material will cause its owner to lose money, publication is not fair use.

Reporters must be aware that just because a work does not display the copyright symbol, ©, does not mean the work is not copyrighted. Under international copyright agreements, the second an author fixes the work in some kind of tangible form, meaning when it is out of the author's brain and onto paper, videotape, or a computer disk, the work is protected. In the United States, people must formally register their works with the U.S. Copyright Office to protect themselves from copyright infringement.

Reporters who work as full-time employees for newspapers, magazines, Web sites, newsletters, or broadcast stations also should understand how copyright applies to their own writings. As employees of a media organization, they do not own the copyright of anything they write or produce for that organization. Typically, the media organization is the legal owner of the copyright of any material it publishes or broadcasts.

Freelance journalists have to negotiate copyright ownership issues when they work for media organizations. The bottom line: They want ownership of their material so that it can be resold in another format and they can continue to earn income from their work. Such earnings have become a major issue in recent years because people have made unauthorized copies of songs rather than buying compact discs, videos, or DVDs. Artists make money, or royalties, from the sale of their music or movies. Further complicating the conflict has been who owns the copyright: the artist or the distributor?

While the copyright issue in the music industry has been a leading story, most journalists just need to be aware of plagiarism and copyright issues. Bottom line: Journalists should carefully cite material they use, and if they are not sure whether a usage might violate copyright, they should check with an attorney. In most cases, artists or other writers will grant permission. In some cases, a fee will be charged. In preparing this textbook, the authors had to secure permissions to use much of the material reprinted from newspapers, Web sites, and other locations. In most cases, media did not charge for the use but requested that credit be given.

WHAT IS LIBEL?

Even if news reports prove accurate and truthful, media are not immune from libel lawsuits. News stories contain dozens of facts and quotes, and each bit of information, if incomplete or the result of a misinformed source, could lead to a lawsuit against a media organization. People sue media organizations for libel or defamatory statements and also for methods used in gathering information. Many plaintiffs have little chance of winning against the media, but their suits still make it through the court system.

No matter what the outcome, such litigation hurts the media. First, the average cost to defend against a libel charge through trial usually tops $100,000. Second, libel suits can take lots of time. A local district attorney sued the *Philadelphia Inquirer,* and the case went through the courts for 23 years until the *Inquirer* finally lost. Third, if a libel lawsuit goes before a jury, the media organization will typically lose because many jurors, who are members of the general public, have negative views of the news media and what they perceive as overwhelmingly biased reporting. Almost all the libel cases lost before juries are won by the media organization on appeal, but the damage—financial and reputation—has been done. Finally, numerous high-profile libel lawsuits add to the public's mistrust of the news media, further damaging their credibility.

Libel Defined

Libel is a defamatory statement written or printed. Basically it is a false statement, and if a plaintiff can prove falsity, he or she could win a lawsuit. Libel applies to newspapers, magazines, newsletters, the Internet, news releases, advertisements, and television and radio broadcasts. Libel law covers TV and radio reporting because segments are transcribed or taped. Defamatory statements can hurt a person's standing in the community. The statements attack the individual's character or professional abilities, and the result might be tangible such as the person losing his or her job, family, or reputation in the community. Media that lose libel suits can be ordered to pay damages.

Even reporters who do their jobs well can be sued for libel. Accurate reporting can draw a libel lawsuit. If reporters correctly quote someone who makes a defamatory statement, the reporters and their employers can be sued for libel. Reporters should also remember that the word *allegedly* does not protect them from libel lawsuits. Media organizations are responsible for every word and image that appears, even if those words are from a reliable source who happens to libel someone.

In a libel lawsuit, anyone associated with the publication or distribution of the information or anyone who has the opportunity to prevent publication or correct the information before it appeared can be sued. Editors who question facts and quotes must send the stories back to reporters or hold the stories until information can be double-checked. In a perfect reporting world, all information would be correct, and such back checking would not be needed.

Elements of Libel

The elements of libel law, which arose from the 1964 precedent-setting *New York Times v. Sullivan* case, are identification, publication, defamation, falsity, harm, and fault (see Figure 4.1). Individuals who bring a libel suit must show all elements—not just one—exist or they will not win the case. The libelous material must *identify* a person in some way, such as by name, in a photo, or through some identifying detail such as a home address. Individuals who are members of large groups cannot sue for libel because courts have ruled there is no identification. For example, a local attorney cannot sue because of a story that makes derogatory comments about lawyers. But he could sue if a newspaper ran a photograph of an unusual and readily identifiable house in town—his house—and reported that the house's owner sold drugs to teenagers.

FIGURE 4.1   **Elements of Libel**

To win a libel suit, a plaintiff must prove six elements of libel—all six.

Identification: The person must show he or she was clearly identified by name, in a photo, or through description.

Publication: The information must have been published, aired, circulated via memo, or just read by a third party other than the writer and the person who was defamed.

Defamation: The person has to show that the information printed, aired, or circulated exposed him or her to public ridicule or contempt.

Falsity: The person must show that the information was not true. To win a case, the media could have the burden of proof to show that the information was true.

Harm: Also known as injury, harm damages a person socially, emotionally, or financially. If media lose a suit, they will have to pay more if the person can show actual monetary loss as a result of the libelous material.

Fault: The individual must prove that the medium was at fault in publishing, airing, or circulating the libelous information.

The supposedly libelous materials also must be disseminated or *published,* meaning that at least three people have seen it. That means a secretary who types a news release with a defamatory statement can be one of the three parties: the writer, the person libeled, and the secretary.

Any story can make *defamatory* statements such as suggesting that:

- Someone has broken the law.
- Someone or some business is incompetent, unethical, or corrupt, or participates in illegal activities.
- Someone is dishonest or cruel.
- Someone is mentally ill.
- Someone has a particularly loathsome disease.
- Someone is a terrorist or aligned with a threatening political group.

In the fourth element of libel, the plaintiff must show in court that the information in the media report is *false.* A common problem that can lead to a libel suit is misidentifying someone with the same name as a person charged with a crime. In one case, a young reporter had the name of someone charged with a crime. Instead of double-checking with police on the person's address, the reporter looked in the phone book, found the name, and reported the name and address in the newspaper. The person in the phone book just happened to have the same name as the person charged with the crime and was listed as the charged party. When the wrongly named individual complained, the newspaper settled out of court because editors knew they could not win the case. The person was given a check and asked to sign a document that said he would not sue the newspaper. The reporter was fired.

A plaintiff in a libel suit must also show *harm,* that is, that the statements or story damaged him socially, emotionally, or financially. If the plaintiff can show actual monetary loss, he can ask for compensation. For example, if the lawyer noted earlier could show that he lost clients and income because people suspected he sold drugs to teenagers, he could try to recoup the lost income. That could increase any monetary amount the newspaper would have to pay if it lost the suit.

Finally, *fault* is determined based on the status of the person who has been libeled. If the plaintiff in the libel case is an average citizen and has proved the other elements of libel, he or she has to show only that the reporter was negligent. From the earlier example, the reporter knew to check the correct address with police and didn't. He was negligent.

Reporting on public officials or celebrities is less risky in regard to libel law because they have a higher burden of proof for fault. If they feel the media have defamed them, they must show the media acted with actual malice. Actual malice means the journalist knew or suspected incorrect or false information in a news story and published it anyway.

The Supreme Court explained in *New York Times v. Sullivan* why it has created a different libel standard for public officials. First, these individuals made a decision to enter the public arena, through either running for public office or pursuing high-visibility careers. Through their public activities, they invite attention and comment. Second, because of their public status, they have access to the media to try to counteract any false statements about themselves. If they call a news conference, the media will attend, unlike an unknown person who tries to gain media attention.

Protections for Journalists

Journalists libel people all the time. But journalists have legal protections, otherwise nothing would ever be printed or aired. If reporters consider these protections while writing the story, libel becomes moot. An individual could sue, but he or she would not win.

Journalists should look for three primary points when evaluating whether defamatory content in a news story is potentially libelous. First, is the information true? If the information is true and the reporter can prove it, he or she is typically protected from a libel charge. *Truth* is the primary libel defense.

Second, is the information part of a fair and accurate report from a court trial, legislative debate, or government action or report? Absolute privilege protects from libel the spoken and written words of public officials acting in their official capacity. The notion is that elected officials in debate and judicial proceedings need to be free to say what needs to be said without fear of a libel charge. Examples include comments said on the floors of the Senate, House of Representatives, state legislatures, and public meetings of city councils and county commissions.

That protection translates into what is called *qualified privilege* for journalists when they report on official government meetings or judicial forums, such as courtrooms, grand jury rooms, hearings, and trials. Anything that reporters quote in those venues would be protected. Someone might also report the substance of an official government report or statement and remain immune from libel. Journalists should make sure the government meeting is covered by qualified privilege, and their reporting must be a fair and accurate or a truthful summary of what was said. Quoting someone outside a meeting or trial might not be privileged, so journalists should be careful.

Third, journalists writing columns or opinion pieces are protected by common law practice called *fair comment and criticism*. The opinion piece should be about a person who invited public attention. The courts see statements of opinion as expressions of belief or judgment rather than assertions of truth. Opinion is protected against libel lawsuits if it cannot be proven false or if it uses exaggerated rhetoric that no one would understand to be a statement of fact. An editorial, opinion column, or movie, music, theater, or book review obviously contains opinions. For example, a review would be protected by fair comment as long as the critique does not stray into the performer's private life. The courts look at the journalistic context of the statements, which means defamatory opinion quotes in a news story would not be protected.

Other Defenses or Protections

Journalists have other protections in libel suits. In some states if media use a story from a wire service and the story contains false information, the media outlet is not liable. That comes under the *wire defense* rule. Media subscribe to wire services because they can't send reporters to every event and rely on wire services to provide accurate information. Case law holds that media who reprint errors contained in wire stories are not liable.

Also, *statutes of limitations* dictate when individuals can sue for libel. Depending on state laws, people cannot sue after a specific time, such as one or more years. Reporters should know what the statute of limitations is for libel in their respective states.

Also reporters cannot be sued for libel by the government. Writers can criticize the ineffectiveness of local government to respond to a natural disaster and not worry that they could be sued successfully. However, they could not write that the director of relief programs bungled aid distribution without the facts to back it up.

Apart from these points, attorneys for media organizations have some recommendations for preventing libel suits. Some people sue for libel because they are irritated at the way they were treated when they complained about an error. Anyone answering the newsroom phone should handle complaints without rudeness. People who are more upset after speaking to someone at the media organization might make the next call to their lawyer. Media organizations should run a quick and clear correction of any incorrect information without restating the erroneous information. Responding quickly can mitigate damages in a libel suit. In more serious cases, media could print a retraction that might be part of a written settlement to keep someone from suing for libel.

INVASION OF PRIVACY

Unlike libel, which deals with a person's reputation, privacy law deals with emotion. People sue media organizations because journalists have invaded their "right to be left alone." To get access, reporters might step beyond what is legally allowed—or at least what is considered ethical in the pursuit of information. Reporters attract negative attention when accused of invading someone's privacy, particularly if the person is not a public official or celebrity. Privacy law is typically state law, and four states still do not recognize the right of privacy: Minnesota, North Dakota, Vermont, and Wyoming.

Privacy laws have been determined by precedents from court cases, and although the newsworthiness of a story is always a good defense against an invasion of privacy lawsuit, fighting cases can cause the same kind of negative publicity for media organizations that libel suits can. Journalists should take care that certain stories and facts are relevant and that they understand privacy law.

Where Privacy Begins and Ends

Privacy law falls under four areas: intrusion, private facts, false light, and appropriation.

Intrusion occurs when journalists use physical, electronic, or mechanical devices to invade another's privacy. It is based on the idea that people have a reasonable expectation of privacy in certain places such as their homes. Intrusion focuses on how information is gathered. For example, if a reporter secretly records conversations, uses overly aggressive surveillance of someone, or hacks into someone's email or computer files, such actions might be considered intrusion.

Many states have laws that prohibit secretly recording a phone conversation or secretly taking a photo or video. Those laws also cover publishing the content of those calls. Journalists should be familiar with the laws in the state where they are working. Surveillance is considered lawful, however, when people are in public or quasi-public places. People must assume they might be photographed or recorded when they are in a public place, especially if they are public officials carrying out public duties. As long as they don't harass, trespass, or otherwise intrude, journalists can photograph, film, and record what they easily see or hear in public places. Reporters must also be clear on what is a public place. For example, shopping malls are not; they are privately owned.

If a reporter calls a source on the phone, 12 states require that the reporter tell the source before he or she records the phone conversation. Other states have what is called a one-party notification whereby only one party, in this case, the reporter, has to be aware that the conversation is being taped.

Also considered intrusion, as well as a criminal offense, is trespassing. Journalists should be careful to avoid trespassing on someone's property when pursuing a story. The property need not be damaged; just going onto property without proper permission is trespassing. Proper permission means consent from the owner or person in possession of the property. Law enforcement officials, for example, cannot give permission for journalists to go onto private property.

Journalists also might be considered as trespassers if they refuse to leave when asked, misrepresent the purpose of the interview, or fail to identify themselves as reporters. Using undercover reporting and hidden cameras might put a reporter at risk for trespassing charges. In the well-known *Food Lion v. Capital Cities/ABC* case, in 1992 the TV reporters used hidden cameras and went undercover to reveal unsanitary food practices at one store of the grocery story chain. Because the reporters lied to get hired and misrepresented themselves to get access to food preparation, the court considered their behavior to be trespassing and fined ABC $5.5 million. Although ABC ultimately was fined only $1 on appeal, the case confirmed that the courts might consider going undercover as trespassing (Barringer, 1999).

When public property is involved in a news story, public officials have the ultimate control over access. When a public area becomes a place of disorder or disaster, public officials have the right to deny access. Public officials can often exclude journalists from the scene, and courts have said that exclusion is justified because the officials are trying to protect lives or property. If someone refuses to move from the scene of a calamity, he or she might be charged with criminal trespass, obstruction, or disorderly conduct. Only California, with its high incidence of earthquakes, has adopted legislation permitting journalists access to the scenes of disasters.

Private facts, also known as "embarrassing facts," is the publication of private information that would be considered highly offensive to a reasonable person and is not considered of legitimate concern to the public. Private fact plaintiffs sue for shame, humiliation, and mental anguish. Plaintiffs sue over the publication of information that, although true, is so intimate and personal the general public has no need to know it. The information has to be distributed to a large audience and must be very personal to be considered highly offensive.

Most media organizations can win these cases if they can show the information has newsworthiness. In fact, 11 states don't recognize this type of privacy case because they don't believe the media should be punished for publishing true information that they obtain legally. When a Vietnam veteran foiled an assassination attempt on President Ford, the *San Francisco Chronicle* reported that the veteran was gay. He sued under private facts, claiming his sexual orientation was private and not relevant to the story. The *San Francisco Chronicle* won by explaining that his sexual orientation was newsworthy because President Ford seemed to be slow to thank the veteran when he found out. Also, the veteran was already known as a gay man in San Francisco, and the gay community was touting him as a hero for saving the president's life. The veteran did not prove his case.

False light is a type of privacy law similar to libel. In it, the plaintiff claims to be a victim of falsehood and might have to prove actual malice against the media organization. The plaintiff must show that the media knew their report was false and distributed it anyway. These plaintiffs, however, sue for mental anguish, not for loss of reputation. Today, these cases crop up primarily in TV docudramas. TV producers can avoid these lawsuits by getting proper consent from anyone depicted, dropping any reference to the actual people involved, or changing the show to fiction so that it does not reflect actual people's lives.

Appropriation deals with commercial use of someone's name, likeness, or identity and rarely involves print journalists. In these cases, advertising or public relations people might be sued if they use a photo of someone in an ad or promotion for a product without consent. The courts have said that unless they have signed away their rights, people should be given the monetary rewards that result from the use of their names, likenesses, or identities to sell products or services.

Consent forms protect against lawsuits in these cases. Typically, news photographers do not need to request that subjects in public places sign consent forms because placing someone's image in a newspaper to illustrate a news or feature story is not considered commercial use. However, if news photographers take a picture in a private or restricted area or if the subject is under 18, they would be wise to have a signed consent from the subject or, in the case of a child, the subject's parent or guardian. Freelance photographers have to be more careful about gaining consent from subjects because they are selling their photos as a product to newspapers and magazines, which could make them subject to appropriation lawsuits. "There have been cases in which the selling of a photograph without the permission of those in the image had been held to be an appropriation of the person's likeness," said Michael Sherer in *News Photographer* (1987).

CHALLENGES OF NEWS GATHERING

Reporters' legal access to information and people cannot be found in one document or court case. The First Amendment does not guarantee that the general public or even a reporter can go to a city council meeting, obtain government documents, or visit government property. The First Amendment has been interpreted as a way for people to confront their government, not to report on its activities. For example, reporters tried to claim a First Amendment right to conduct face-to-face interviews with some California prisoners. The reporters argued they needed the access as part of their activities as a free press. The courts said the Constitution does not require the government to give the press access to information not available to the average citizen.

Over decades of cases, the Supreme Court guaranteed public access first only to criminal trials (*Richmond Newspapers, Inc. v. Virginia*, 1980) but has extended the principles to cover other judicial proceedings. To force reporters to turn over notes or to testify in cases, judges have used the Fifth Amendment right to due process and the Sixth Amendment rights to a speedy trial and to confront witnesses.

Although the courts have not been supportive of the rights of news gathering, federal and state governments have further guaranteed these rights through Freedom of Information Act (FOIA) laws, discussed in Chapter 2, and open meetings laws, discussed in Chapter 6.

Protecting Your Sources and Notes

At times in pursuing a story, a reporter might have to promise confidentiality to a source. Reporters should know first the rules at their publication or news station; some editors and news directors do not allow unnamed sources in stories. Others might allow confidential sources for background information only. Confidential sources should be a last resort: when criminal activities are involved, when sources are afraid they will get fired, or when sources want to stay out of the limelight for justifiable reasons. No laws protect confidential relationships between journalists and sources as they do for relationships between lawyers and clients, doctors and patients, or priests and penitents.

But case law might. A 1991 case established a precedent that indicates journalists should keep their promises of confidentiality or face financial consequences. In *Cohen v. Cowles Media Co.,* editors at the St. Paul and Minneapolis newspapers decided to name a source to whom a reporter promised confidentiality. They felt that readers needed to know that the story came from an opposing political party's campaign office. When the source lost his job because of the story, he sued the newspaper company and won. The court said the source and the reporter's relationship was based on a promise, which, when broken, caused an injustice for the source. The source won $200,000.

Remember the example earlier in the chapter when Houston-based writer Vanessa Leggett went to jail to avoid revealing sources and interviews? Reporters and their employers must decide where to draw the line when journalists have information critical to a criminal case or judicial proceeding. That's when the judicial system and the rights of journalists come into conflict. If a journalist has information about a criminal case, judges, lawyers, and law enforcement officials want journalists to testify in court just like everyone else. Journalists counter that if they don't keep their promises of confidentiality to news sources, sources will no longer trust them, and they can't report effectively. Also, based on their ethical standards, journalists say they are supposed to remain neutral, and any involvement with either side of a legal conflict compromises that ability.

Judges invoke the Sixth Amendment as the reason journalists must comply with their orders to testify or turn over notes and other materials. The Sixth Amendment protects the right of criminal defendants to obtain evidence in their favor and to confront witnesses against them. When a subpoena is issued for them to testify, journalists argue that the First Amendment protects them from being forced to disclose confidential information. If they revealed confidential information, they say, people would be reluctant to speak to reporters and the First Amendment interest in the free flow of information would suffer. The Supreme Court has partially endorsed this idea, and subsequently many states have passed shield laws that give journalists leeway in protecting sources. Thirty states have shield laws, and reporters should know if they are protected in their respective states.

The courts have said the government must establish three criteria before a journalist can be forced to testify: The government should have a probable cause to believe that a reporter has information "clearly relevant" to a specific violation of law; the government should show evidence that the information sought cannot be obtained by alternative means less destructive of First Amendment values; and the government should establish a compelling and overriding interest in the information. States that have shield laws have similar requirements. In addition, shield laws establish who is defined as a journalist, what kinds of information the privilege protects, and when the privilege is waived.

While no federal shield law exists, U.S. Department of Justice rules govern federal courts and regulations. Under these guidelines, Justice Department employees must seek alternative sources other than reporters when possible. They also must negotiate with the media when possible. They can seek subpoenas only if they have reasonable grounds to believe information is relevant and essential to a case. The scope of the Justice Department's subpoena should be as narrow as possible. Also, under Section 403 of the Federal Rules of Evidence, judges might quash a subpoena if the information from reporters would duplicate information already available. A federal judge might consider, therefore, whether alternative sources for the information are available.

Staying on the Right Side of the Law

Courts have never said reporters can violate the law when pursuing a story. They will be fined or imprisoned just like any other person who breaks the law. In 1998, for example, a Maryland freelancer argued he was doing research for stories on how police enforce child pornography laws when he received and downloaded child porn, which violated Maryland law. The court didn't buy the argument and said the First Amendment does not protect reporters who violate the law. The reporter was sentenced to 18 months in prison.

As noted earlier in this chapter, reporters must develop their personal moral and ethical standards, and they should know their news organization's code of ethics. Whenever they have questions or concerns about the ethics or legality of a situation, journalists should consult their supervisors or news organizations' attorneys.

Reporters who do their jobs conscientiously and carefully do have protections if they are sued for libel or invasion of privacy. Case law over the years has favored journalists when they legally obtain truthful information through their reporting. Shield laws also have added protection to keep reporters from having to reveal sources, and freedom of information and sunshine laws allow them to gain access to public records and meetings. However, reporters should remember that in most other areas, such as trespass or criminal activities, they will be prosecuted just like any other citizen if they break the law.

GLOSSARY

Actual malice: Occurs when a journalist knew or suspected there was incorrect or false information in a news story and published it anyway.

Code of ethics: A document that outlines for individual members of an organization specific rules of conduct and consequences for not following those rules.

Copyright: Protects any unique or creative expression once it is fixed in a tangible form. In the United States to sue for copyright infringement, people must formally register their works with the U.S. Copyright Office.

Defamation: Expression that tends to damage a person's standing in the community through words that attack an individual's character and professional abilities. Defamation might cause people to avoid contact with the person attacked.

Fair comment and criticism: A defense in libel that allows reviewers and columnists to comment on the performance of an individual who invited public attention.

Fair use: Allows people such as journalists, book authors, critics, or scholars to quote small amounts of a copyrighted work because they are reporting or critiquing the information in the public interest. The four considerations under fair use are how the copyrighted material will be used, what the characteristics of the copyrighted material are, what the quality and quantity of the use will be, and what the financial impact of the use will be on the copyrighted material.

False light: A type of privacy law that is similar to libel. A plaintiff must claim to be a victim of falsehood and show that the media knew their report was false and distributed it anyway.

Falsity: One of the six elements of libel; the information was not true.

Fault: One of the six elements of libel that shows a journalist was negligent. For public officials or public figures, fault is the higher standard of *actual malice*.

First Amendment: States that Congress shall make no law abridging freedom of the press or freedom of speech.

Intrusion: When journalists use physical, electronic, or mechanical devices to invade another's privacy, such as his or her home.

Invasion of privacy: An area under which individuals can sue journalists. The four primary areas are intrusion, private facts, false light, and appropriation.

Libel: Publication or broadcast of a statement that injures someone's reputation or that lowers that person's esteem in the community.

Negligence: What private people must prove in libel cases. It is defined as the media failing to properly take care in their reporting or failure to follow the established practices of journalism such as double checking facts or failing to call an obviously knowledgeable source.

Private facts: The publication of private information that would be considered highly offensive to a reasonable person and is not considered of legitimate concern to the public.

Qualified privilege: Protects journalists when they report on what is said in official government meetings or judicial forums, such as courtrooms, grand jury rooms, hearings, and trials. Someone might also report the substance of an official government report or statement and remain immune from libel. Sometimes called absolute privilege.

Shield law: Allows reporters to protect sources without fear of going to jail to do so.

Sixth Amendment: Protects the right of criminal defendants to obtain evidence in their favor and to confront witnesses against them.

Sunshine law: Also known as open records laws, based on the notion that government work should be out in the sunshine or in the open.

Wire service defense: Protects any media that reprint a libelous statement sent out by a wire service.

ACTIVITIES

1. Get into groups and discuss each of the four main headings in the Society of Professional Journalists' Code of Ethics. What do these concepts mean to the group members? How are your interpretations different? Discuss examples of how you can avoid violating the code of ethics.

2. Find police or crime stories in your local or regional newspaper. Look for word usage and writing style that helps the newspaper avoid a libel case. For example, did the article make sure to cite a police report or police officials? Did the article avoid naming suspects and wait until someone was charged with a crime to name them? Did reporters hide behind or overuse the word *allegedly?*

3. Discuss the concept of consent from news sources. Give examples of how you know you have a source's consent to publish the comments. Discuss unique scenarios in which you might need to get special consent, for example, in a hospital or school, and how you would handle it.

4. Research the open meetings law in your state. Then get the meeting notice for a local government meeting and see whether it complies with the law.

5. Read *American Journalism Review's* "The Vanessa Leggett Saga" (Garcia, 2002), and discuss the case. How and why was the judge in Texas able to imprison her for so long?

RESOURCES AND WEB SITES

American Press Institute: americanpressinstitute.org
American Society of Newspaper Editors: www.asne.org
ASME guidelines: http://asme.magazine.org/guidelines/index.html
Copyright Web site: www.benedict.com
Freedom of Information Center: www.missouri.edu/~foiwww
Gannett guidelines on ethical news gathering methods: www.gannett.com/go/press/pr061499.htm
Public Relations Society of America: www.prsa.org
Radio-Television News Directors Association: www.rtnda.org. Also known as the Association of Electronic Journalists.
Reporters Committee for Freedom of the Press: www.rcfp.org
Society of Professional Journalists: www.spj.org
Student Press Law Center: www.splc.org
U.S. Constitution: www.house.gov/Constitution/Constitution.html
U.S. Copyright Office: www.loc.gov/copyright
Your state press association

REFERENCES

Aldrich, L. S. (1999). *Covering the community: A diversity handbook for media.* Thousand Oaks, CA: Pine Forge Press.

The attorney general's guidelines on subpoenaing the news media. (1988). Reporters Committee for Freedom of the Press. *Confidential Sources & Information.* www.rcfp.org/csi/ag_guide.html.

Barringer, F. (1999, October 21). Appeals court rejects damages against ABC in Food Lion case. *New York Times,* p. A1.

Chinlund, C. (2003, June 23). New era on errors. *Boston Globe.* www.boston.com/dailyglobe2/174/oped/New_era_on_errors+.shtml.

Cohen v. Cowles Media Co. (90-634). 501 U.S. 663 (1991).

Garcia, G. X. (2002, March). The Vanessa Leggett saga. *American Journalism Review,* pp. 20–27.

Guide to taping conversations in all 50 states. (2003). Reporters Committee for Freedom of the Press. www.rcfp.org/taping/index.html.

Lester, P. M. (1991). *Photojournalism: An ethical approach.* Hillsdale, NJ: Lawrence Erlbaum.

Libel Defense Resource Center. (2002). *Report on trials and damages.* New York: Libel Defense Resource Center.

Pell v. Procunier, 417 U.S. 817, 822, 94 S.Ct. 2800, 2804, 41 L.Ed.2d 495 (1974).

PEN American Center. (2002). PEN/Newman's own First Amendment award recipient, Vanessa Leggett. www.pen.org/freedom/pressrel/case.htm.

Richmond Newspapers, Inc. v. Virginia. 448 U.S. 555 (1980).

Sherer, M. (1987, January). Short course: Invasion of privacy. *News Photographer,* pp. 18, 22.

Sipple v. Chronicle Publishing Co. 154 Cal. App. 3d 1040, 201 CaL.Rptr. 665, 10 Media L. Rptr. 1690 (1984).

Society of Professional Journalists. (1996). *Code of ethics.* www.spj.org/ethics_code.asp.

Steele, B. (2001, June 27). The Capriati story—Does she always wear the scarlet letters "TT"? Poynter Institute. www.poynter.org/talkaboutethics/062701.htm.

U.S. v. Matthews. 11 F. Supp. 2d 656 (1998).

Student Press Law Center. (1995). Using the tools of the trade, a Freedom of Information Law primer. www.splc.org/legalresearch.asp?id=14.

New York Times v. Sullivan. 376 U.S. 254 (1964).

WNET. (2003). Journalism ethics. *Religion & Ethics Newsweekly.* [News transcript]. www.pbs.org/wnet/religionandethics/week637/perspectives.html.

CHAPTER 5

COVERING DIVERSE COMMUNITIES

One day a student from a newswriting course approached her journalism professor to ask about a story idea. She said she knew a student on campus who was black and Jewish. The student was active in both the Black Student Union and the campus Jewish group at a time when the two groups were locked in conflict over some racist and anti-Semitic insensitivity that had occurred between them. The journalism student wanted to know whether the student might be the subject of a good profile story. The professor answered with an emphatic "Yes."

The journalism student's completed feature made the front page of the campus newspaper, and the campus community received significant information about how one person on campus successfully negotiated her racial and religious identities.

This example illustrates that sometimes the story of community diversity can be embodied in one person. Too often the media miss these stories of diversity, not because of an unwillingness to cover the topic but just out of ignorance about the many groups that make up their communities. Some communities, however, might not be diverse. Reporters should know what unique groups make up their communities and make sure each has a voice.

In this chapter, you will:

- Learn why diversity coverage is important,
- Consider steps to include diversity,
- Find ways to cover census information and blended ethnic categories,
- Learn how disability and aging groups are diversity issues,
- See how to overcome bias,
- Examine why terminology is important to diverse groups, and
- See where socioeconomic class fits in diversity coverage.

ENSURING DIVERSITY IN COVERAGE

Covering diverse groups in a community is a sign of excellence and accuracy in reporting because it means the news media are presenting a truthful and balanced picture of their communities. Most media outlets know the importance of covering diversity in modern times. David Yarnold, executive editor of the *San Jose* (CA) *Mercury-News,* said (2002): "It comes down to a question of credibility: If readers don't see themselves and hear their voices in your pages, they will no longer view you as a credible source of information."

He added that covering diversity is as important as making sure sources' names are spelled correctly. "It's a fundamental component of accuracy," he said. Covering diversity also makes good economic sense because readers won't subscribe to a newspaper or watch a TV news program that does not cover topics of concern to their community. As Dorothy Gilliam, a *Washington Post* columnist and a former president of the National Association of Black Journalists (NABJ), said (Aldrich, 1999): "A media that does not reflect its community eventually will not survive."

Understanding and Broadening the Definition

So how is covering diversity defined? Leigh Stephens Aldrich, in *Covering the Community: A Diversity Handbook for Media* (1999), said: "Diversity describes an environment, such as a community, that includes representation of multiple groups. Diversity places an emphasis on accepting and respecting differences by recognizing that no one group is intrinsically superior to another."

Journalists incorporating diversity follow three guidelines in coverage: using proper language, using accurate information rather than stereotypes, and remembering to write about all the people in their communities, omitting no group. Later in this chapter terminology and language, as well as stereotypes, are addressed. Aldrich said not omitting groups is the most important guide for media to remember. Enlightened journalists know to avoid racism, sexism, or homophobia in their stories, but omission of groups from coverage can also misrepresent them. If they are left out of news coverage, society forgets they exist.

For example, few media organizations report on Native people and American Indian tribal issues, even though they "are one of the most politically vulnerable racial groups in America," said American Indian journalist Jodi Rave (2002). Typically, the media ignore Native people except when a Redskins sports mascot or an Indian-run casino draws controversy, Rave noted. By failing to cover American Indians, journalists for a long time missed a major news story: that for decades the U.S. Bureau of Indian Affairs mismanaged a $10 billion trust fund earmarked for 300,000 Native people, Rave said.

Omissions often occur because many journalists tend to return to the same expert sources and might miss diverse sources and other perspectives on a topic. The Society of Professional Journalists (SPJ) has tried to remedy this problem by creating the Diversity Toolbox, which has a searchable sourcebook ranging from aging issues to youth and family issues. Sally Lehrman, national diversity chair for SPJ, said the goal is for journalists to have the resources they need to include voices that have been underrepresented in the news (2002). "If you're not checking with a breadth of sources, chances are, your story has holes," she said.

This type of coverage is not only writing the occasional story on an ethnic festival or a feature on Black History Month but also making sure that diverse groups within a community are covered equally to other groups. KRON-TV in San Francisco takes a multifaceted approach to covering its community, which is about 50 percent nonwhite. The station instituted weekly diversity group meetings to talk about how to widen its coverage of the many racial and ethnic groups in the city. Craig Franklin, producer of news special projects at KRON (Arviso, 2002), said the results have been stories such as "a feature on Filipino veterans who had been denied government benefits. An award-winning, two-part series on racial profiling of Arab Americans."

Expanding the Source List

To avoid omitting diverse sources, journalists have to avoid what are called "Rolodex interviews"—calling the same expert sources from their files over and over for stories. Stephen Magagnini, who covered ethnic affairs and race relations for the *Sacramento Bee*, said (Aldrich, 1999) he has developed a huge list of ethnic and racial sources, just from people he has met over the years.

The *Diversity Handbook for Media* (Aldrich, 1999) recommends that "not only should you include the usual experts, such as doctors, engineers, and educators, but you should include key community contacts such as a barber, a religious community member, a grocery store clerk, and a city street worker." Stories will be more complete and will include an array of perspectives when reporters call on diverse sources.

How can reporters develop a large number of trustworthy sources from the divergent groups in a community? They have to become familiar with those groups and their cultures. Reporters might begin by visiting community centers or festivals or checking out ethnic media, group specialty publications, or Web sites. All provide a wealth of story ideas and sources.

Magagnini said (Aldrich, 1999) reporters should have extensive sources in each cultural group. One trustworthy source in the group can recommend other group members who both agree and disagree with the source. Reporters need to be aware of cultural differences in reporting on ethnic groups, he added. For example, Magagnini had difficulty interviewing American Indians on the phone. He discovered that the Indian way is to talk in person. He also learned to smooth the interview by starting with the name of the person who recommended that particular source. Also, if a language barrier exists, he recommended finding competent translation.

The American Society of Newspaper Editors (ASNE) launched a continuing initiative in 1999 on diversity and accuracy, and a number of media rose to the challenge to retool their coverage. It noted:

Several papers restructured beats to reflect a less-institutional bent. Examples from California: The Fresno Bee has an immigration beat; The (*Stockton, Calif.*) Record has an urban affairs beat and a reporter covering generations X and Y; and The Orange County (*Calif.*) Register has created beats to cover Asians, cultural connections, Latin affairs, small businesses and aging. The Modesto Bee has a reporter who covers relationships, including the family, gay and lesbian issues. (Reprinted with permission from the American Society of Newspaper Editors.)

Other techniques to improve access to diverse sources include having community groups critique news coverage and make suggestions. The Lansdale (PA) *Reporter* created an 18-member community diversity committee for just that purpose. The paper has instituted a computer database of minority group sources, and the deputy news editor maintains and keeps it current. Other newspapers have created focused columns on specific diverse groups in their midst such as the Rock Hill, South Carolina, *Herald's* initiation of a column on the Catawba Indian Nation near there. And the Jackson, Michigan, *Patriot's* editor reported: "We are having brainstorming sessions to find ways to be more inclusive, to rely less on official sources."

RACE, ETHNICITY, AND THE CENSUS

Although race and ethnicity are not the only aspect of diversity reporting, they are the kind most often considered by media organizations. Famed Watergate journalist Carl Bernstein said (Aldrich, 1999): "Race is the most important story in America, straining the fabric of our national existence, touching on all our problems. We're terrified of it, unsure how to begin covering it, and afraid of being incendiary, so we ignore it and the obvious questions."

Although some media organizations have tackled the story of race relations and racial issues, many continue to ignore it. A University of Missouri *Guide to Research on Race and News* (Kelley, 2000) reported, "News content still reflects the concerns of white male news managers writing for a presumably all-white audience." Although women and minorities are slowly gaining managerial slots, the news content at most media does not reflect substantively the ethnic and racial makeup of the communities.

Paying Attention to Coverage

Problems in diversity coverage arise because many media organizations might not understand how they report incorrectly on race or they might not perceive an imbalance in coverage. For example, TV news tends to report on people of color in the context of crime or ethnic festivals primarily, according to *White News: Why Local News Programs Don't Cover People of Color* (Heider, 2000). A TV assignment editor in Albuquerque said the station did not link people of color and crime too often, but a Latino activist there disagreed, saying most of the coverage on the Hispanic community centers on crime.

Media need to have ethnic communities assess their coverage to determine whether an imbalance exists—or is perceived. Reporters on the front line also can ask sources to suggest stories that are not being covered. Media should welcome suggestions and input to ensure coverage represents their community's ethnic and racial makeup.

A major aspect of modern diversity coverage is a new definition of ethnicity in which people embrace several racial categories. The U.S. Census in 2000 began to reflect this change. Steve Doig, an expert in census reporting at Arizona State University, said the census is the important tool in understanding trends in racial issues. Doig (2000) noted:

> No problem in American society has been more chronic and vexing than that of race relations. Add to that the strains of demographic change caused by immigration to the United States of millions leaving their countries of birth to seek a better life here. The resulting frictions and adjustments are the source of many important stories for journalists, and Census data is one of the best ways of measuring those changes. (Copyright 2000 by Stephen K. Doig. Used with permission.)

The 2000 Census itself illustrates how the United States allows racial categories to be fluid. In 1997 the U.S. Office of Management and Budget (OMB) ruled that the census allow people to select as many racial categories as they felt fit their background. It allowed respondents to acknowledge all parts of their heritage. Tests of the census survey forms before they were administered in 2000 found that in some areas 5 percent to 11 percent of the population responded as multiracial.

In doing comparison stories on the census, the new categories do make reporting difficult, Doig said, because the 1980 and 1990 censuses allowed respondents to pick only one of five racial categories. For example, in the 1990 Census, Spanish/Hispanic was not a racial category; only Hispanic was. The 2000 Census allowed for 126 configurations of racial categories. In his *Reporting Census 2000, A Guide for Journalists* Web site, Doig has created a method that allows reporters to compare the 1990 and 2000 censuses and explains the Index changes. In addition, Phil Meyer of the University of North Carolina at Chapel Hill and Shawn McIntosh of *USA TODAY* updated their 1991 *USA TODAY* Diversity Index to accommodate the 2000 Census multiracial categories.

Finding Story Ideas

The census can provide dozens of story ideas, from political redistricting to changes in family structure, Doig said. Two years after the short-form census data are released, the Census Bureau releases the long-form census data, which every six households completes. "This data covers *all* the census questions, allowing you to pursue a wide range of topics including income, education, immigration, workplace, commuting, and a variety of housing questions," Doig (2000) explained.

For example, *St. Louis Post Dispatch* reporter Jim Getz's story (2002) from Census 2000 data illustrated that the number of black homeowners tripled over the decade in the Metro East area of St. Louis. But census stories don't just report numbers; they tell the stories of the people behind the numbers. Getz's story allowed several families to share their joy about home ownership. " 'We'd been renting apartments since we were 19, and we figured it was time to get a home,' said Lawanda Moore, 30, who with her husband, Lawrence, bought a house in French Village in November 1998. 'It's like only $5 more a month, but it's mine.' "

Reporters who surf onto the Census Bureau Web site, www.census.gov, can quickly find profiles of their communities, which will show the diversity changes that might be taking place. For instance, another *St. Louis Post Dispatch* story on the census revealed that Asians were the fastest-growing ethnic group in that area over the past 10 years (O'Connor, 2001). Further investigation into that statistic showed that many Asians were from India and had information technology jobs.

Another category of census data cuts across all ethnic groups: information about people with some form of disability. Census 2000 included two questions that had six subparts to identify people with disabilities. The 1990 Census included four questions used to identify people with disabilities. Based on census data, approximately one-fifth of Americans have some form of disability, which makes them a large demographic group and one whose issues the media only rarely focus on.

In addition to relying on census data, reporters need to observe their communities by driving around neighborhoods, checking out business areas, and going to restaurants. They should notice where ethnic or racial groups tend to congregate and whether groups appear to be integrated. When reporting stories that include various ethnic or racial groups, journalists need to be careful how each is represented so that readers do not form misperceptions about any group.

For example, in one North Carolina town, a corner near a convenience store had become increasingly popular as a pickup spot for day laborers. As the number steadily grew, police had more problems with minor fights, drinking, and drug use among workers who were not hired and who stayed at the corner throughout the day. At the same time, the town had become increasingly Hispanic as were many of the workers at the pickup location. The reporter covering the story—which appeared several times as complaints came in and police and town officials worked on a solution—took special care to avoid any references that the Hispanic workers were the prime troublemakers.

DISABILITY AND AGING AS DIVERSITY

When most reporters think of diversity, they think of ethnic groups, racial groups, or even sexual orientation groups. However, people with physical and mental disabilities are the largest group of people in a diversity category, accounting for about 20 percent of the U.S. population, according to the U.S. Census Bureau (1997). Like other societal groups, they have been advocating to stop discrimination against them and to achieve greater civil rights since the 1960s.

The social change that disability rights groups have brought about has implications for the rapidly aging U.S. population, many of whom will likely develop a disabling condition as they age. A researcher for the Newspaper Association of America said: "The adult population (is) more age-diverse. In 1960, very few people were over the age of 65; today, still fewer than one in six adults is over 65. By 2030, individuals older than 65 will make up more than 30 percent of the adults in this country—and half of these senior citizens will be older than 75" (Sullivan, 2002).

Legislation Reporters Should Know

Several society-altering pieces of legislation have resulted from the advocacy of groups focused on disability issues. Journalists covering disability, health care, education, or government issues should become familiar with this legislation: the Rehabilitation Act of 1973, the Individuals with Disabilities Education Act of 1975 (IDEA), and the Americans with Disabilities Act of 1990 (ADA). Each has implications for reporters' beats from local government to education to health.

The Rehabilitation Act began to be enforced in the 1980s and "prohibits discrimination based on disability in Federal employment and federally funded programs and services, by Federal contractors, and in the availability and use of Federal agencies' electronic and information technology," according to the U.S. Architectural and Transportation Barriers Compliance Board. That independent federal agency works to improve people's access to all parts of society—from physical to educational.

Soon after the Rehabilitation Act, IDEA was passed and, when enforced, guarantees free and public education to U.S. children and young people with disabilities. The ADA is the broadest civil rights legislation for people with disabilities and applies to society as a whole, not just the federal government as the Rehabilitation Act does.

The U.S. Department of Justice, which enforces parts of the ADA, summarizes it this way: "The ADA prohibits discrimination and ensures equal opportunity for persons with disabilities in employment, state and local government services, public accommodations, commercial facilities, and transportation. It also mandates the establishment of Telecommunications Devices for the Deaf (TDD)/telephone relay services" (2002).

Basically, except for some businesses and organizations with exemptions, the ADA applies to much of U.S. society. In addition to being a disability rights story, the ADA is a business story. A number of U.S. businesses fought against complying with the ADA's accessibility and employment requirements because they contended it would be expensive. The power of the business lobby caused some lopsided coverage of the ADA by journalists who had many sources in the business community but who didn't know where to find the disability angle.

The Society of Professional Journalists' Rainbow Sourcebook and the government-grant-funded Center for an Accessible Society, whose mission is to provide journalists with information about disability issues, have tried to fill the void for journalists with their online resources. See the resources list at the end of the chapter.

Accessibility as a Diversity Issue

Almost any story has a disability angle. When the local school district builds a new elementary school or when the local hotel renovates, the ADA requires that both be accessible to people with disabilities. Journalists should be aware to ask about the impact. Disability and aging groups advocate for a concept called universal design. As the American Association of Retired Persons (AARP) explains (2003), universal design "fits everyone—young and old, tall or short, large or small, able-bodied, or challenged by disabilities." It is not only wheelchair ramps but also items such as flashing smoke detectors for people with hearing impairments or door handles that are easier to grasp. Some local governments have been notorious for continuing to be inaccessible to people with any kind of impairment, even after the ADA. And government noncompliance with laws always makes for a good story.

In the aftermath of September 11, 2001, the U.S. news media hardly covered the failure of building evacuation plans to assist to safety people who used walkers or wheelchairs or who have mobility impairments. Reporters also missed earlier stories from the 1994 California earthquake: Disaster relief centers used inaccessible shelters and turned away deaf people when they couldn't communicate with them. From voting booth access to disability unemployment statistics to aging baby boomers, disability topics are everywhere.

OVERCOMING BIAS

Journalists need to develop self-awareness about potential biases they might have so that they can report stories fully, fairly, accurately, and honestly. Journalists who don't understand a culture, disability, religion, or whatever can misinterpret the story or fall into the trap of using stereotypes. For instance, when interviewing a person with a disability, able-bodied journalists might have to confront their own fears about the ease with which anyone can become disabled. These underlying fears can lead a reporter to produce either a story that presents the disabled person as a tragic, pitiable figure or one that presents the disabled person as an inspirational "Supercrip," who supposedly deserves kudos for getting on with daily living. Either presentation is inaccurate.

Stories That Don't Look Like You

Journalists' bias can creep into any story. Biases crop up when journalists are confronted with issues and people outside their experiences. Journalists have to consider their own backgrounds, upbringing, religion, sexual preference, gender, education, race, ethnicity, and on and on, when approaching a story. Being aware of potential biases enables reporters to write stories that are fair, balanced, and accurate.

For example, after the events of September 11, 2001, U.S. journalists, who come from primarily Judeo-Christian backgrounds, scrambled to try to understand Islam. Confronted with both their own ignorance about the religious traditions of Islam and their own internal biases, journalists unconsciously or purposefully might have blamed Islam for the terrorist attacks. Journalists struggled to understand that Islam has many forms, just as Christianity or Judaism comes in many forms.

Pulitzer Prize–winning reporter Caryle Murphy, a *Washington Post* religion reporter and formerly the *Post's* Cairo bureau chief, wrote about the diversity within Islam in her book, *Passion for Islam, Shaping the Modern Middle East: The Egyptian Experience.* She explained in a live chat posted on washingtonpost.com (2002): "There is a broad spectrum of Islamists—from radical, violent ones to moderate, non-violent ones. . . . I'd say that the radical, violent Islamists—who are a minority—don't consider the damage they cause with their violence. They are blinded by a distorted religious dogma."

Misunderstandings and bias also might cause journalists to misinterpret or incorrectly report events, such as the lives of Muslim women. Murphy (2002) explained:

> There's a lot of misperceptions about women in the Middle East. Just because a woman wears a head scarf or veil doesn't mean she's repressed.

In a similar fashion, when journalists focus on how someone with a disability deviates from the norm or on what they sense as tragedy to add drama to a story, they might send a message of pity to readers. HolLynn D'Lil, a wheelchair user, explained in the disability lifestyle magazine *Mainstream* (1997):

> Being told that you're inspirational when you're doing something ordinary is an assault on your self-concept. Suddenly you're reminded once again of the traditional attitudes about disabilities, that no matter who you are, what you do, how you feel, to some people you'll always be a tragic figure.

She reminded journalists that "a life with a disability is still a life after all, to be enjoyed and lived to the fullest."

WRITING ABOUT SEXUAL ORIENTATION

In addition to ethnic or disability issues, bias might creep into reporters' stories when they write about gay and lesbian issues or are interviewing sources with a sexual orientation different from their own. An even larger problem might be omitting coverage of gay and lesbian issues.

The National Lesbian and Gay Journalists Association reports that issues such as same-sex marriage, gay families, parenting and adoption, gays in the military, sex education in the schools, civil liberties, gay-related ballot initiatives, gay bashing, and anti-gay violence deserve significant media attention. The University of Southern California (USC) Sexual Orientation in the News (SOIN) project reports that the media cover sensational stories about gay issues such as the murder of Utah student Mathew Shepard, comedian Ellen Degeneres's coming out, or celebrity Rosie O'Donnell's same-sex marriage to Kelli Carpenter. They do not focus, however, on stories from local gay and lesbian communities. "Broadcast stations and newspapers favor high-visibility, dramatic stories over the hard digging associated with ongoing local stories involving gay and lesbian issues," said USC communication researcher Sheila Murphy (Stewart, 2000).

One media development that illustrated increased attention to gay and lesbian issues happened in August 2002 when the *New York Times* began printing stories about same-sex commitment ceremonies, in the same way it printed marriage announcements. Poynter ethicist Bob Steele applauded the *Times'* decision:

> Covering same-sex unions is a matter of factual accuracy. A newspaper is obligated to truthfully reflect the reality of what is happening in the communities and society it covers. . . . Reporting gay couples' ceremonies is also a matter of fairness. This is a human rights issue, and individuals should not be discriminated against—deprived of news coverage—based on their sexual orientation. USC research reported that 144 U.S. newspapers had run same-sex union announcements by fall 2002. (Reprinted with permission from the Poynter Institute, St. Petersburg, Florida.)

KEEPING LANGUAGE CLEAR AND SPECIFIC

Words have power to define groups, so many diverse groups are concerned about the terminology the media use when writing about them. Reporters might be misled by their own beliefs; they may not even think to check *The AP Stylebook* because the offending word is one they always use. Or they are misled by sources who are still using terms that have fallen out of favor. Whatever the reason, using incorrect terms to refer to people or groups becomes an accuracy issue.

The Associated Press Stylebook (2002) is clear on these terms, and various societal groups typically approve its entries. Reporters are expected to follow *The AP Stylebook* or other style guides used by their media organizations, and each guide indicates the preferred terms. Using the wrong terms can cause ill will between the media and community groups, which in turn can affect a group's trust of the media and make diversity coverage more difficult.

For example, wheelchair users rightly explain that they are not "bound" or "confined" in their chairs; in fact, wheelchairs allow people mobility and independence, not confinement. Although *The AP Stylebook* clearly states not to use terms such as *handicapped, wheelchair-bound,* or *confined to a wheelchair,* journalists continue to use those terms. For disability terms that *The AP Stylebook* doesn't cover, journalists can go to the online style guide created by the National Center on Disability and Journalism (2002) in San Francisco, at www.ncdj.org.

In regard to ethnic references, Tom Arviso Jr., who is publisher and editor of the *Navajo Times,* the largest American Indian–owned weekly newspaper, said the term *redskin* is the equivalent of the *n-word* for African Americans. He adds that reporters can use American Indian or Native American in their stories, although American Indian is considered more modern. When identifying American Indians in a story, it is best to be as specific as possible and identify them by their tribal affiliation, such as Navajo or Cree. Arviso explains (2002):

> If you (do) not, then your story or broadcast is basically untrue and inaccurate, and you are adding to the longstanding ignorance of non-Native media as well as perpetuating stereotypes of Native Americans. Most importantly, though, you will lose the respect of the Native person you are writing about as well as those who are aware of your ignorance. It is important to always be aware and respectful of a person's culture and heritage when you are writing about them.

The same holds true for any ethnic group. Each wants to be represented accurately in all aspects of the story, including the use of correct terms when referring to it. Checking terms prevents reporters from using labels that stereotype or misrepresent groups. Because language changes, reporters should consult their stylebooks, even when they think they are using the correct terms.

SOCIOECONOMIC CLASS AND POVERTY

Finally, journalists need to be conscious of one societal group that cuts across all racial, ability, and gender lines: the poor. The news media have been criticized for giving little attention to poverty in the United States. Critics state that media audiences are predominantly middle and upper middle class, so media cater to those socioeconomic groups. Also, poverty coverage typically is not breaking news but takes in-depth reporting on issues such as public housing, public health, and the welfare system.

Poverty affects every community in the United States. The government definition of poverty is a family of four with an annual household income under $14,128. About 33 million Americans were classified as poor in 2002, according to TomPaine.com, a public-interest journal. A number of poor people fall into the category of "working poor," meaning they were in the labor force at least 27 weeks in a year. And the number of poor Americans is growing significantly: Two million more people lived below the poverty line in 2002 when compared with 2000, according to the U.S. Department of Labor (2002).

Hunger and homelessness are visual aspects of poverty. Many media focus on them primarily during the Christmas holidays, but each is a significant story year round in most urban areas. A study by the U.S. Council of Mayors (2003) found that requests for emergency food assistance in 2000 grew by an average of 17 percent, with 83 percent of cities showing an increase in 2003. The mayors' survey found that 62 percent of people asking for emergency food assistance were members of families, that is, children and parents.

School systems have more and more programs to provide poor children with adequate breakfasts and lunches. In 2000, the average demand for emergency shelter grew by the highest one-year increase in 10 years (15 percent). Seventy-two percent of cities saw an increase in requests for shelter from homeless families.

In addition to hunger and homelessness, poor people lack health insurance and adequate medical care. Many states have adopted programs to provide health insurance to millions of children who are not covered by Medicaid, the government's health program for low-income people. Lack of adequate medical treatment can have long-term effects on the poor, particularly children, who might not live healthy lives as youngsters or succeed in school.

The weak U.S. economy since 2001 contributed to an increase in the number of poor residents and also affected the ability of many nonprofit organizations, such as shelters and poverty assistance programs, to help. Poverty also drains a community's resources, including government finances. Even though people living in poverty might not be media consumers, they still are part of the fabric of U.S. society. Stories about them should be written because journalists need to report on topics concerning all echelons of society. And in many cases, when stories of less fortunate residents appear, helping agencies and the needy get a boost.

Some stories might reveal an underlying prejudice against lower-income residents, not even those who are at or below the poverty level. One southern community required developers to include affordable housing within any new neighborhoods. That meant that in a neighborhood where the average housing price was $350,000, some homes had to be priced closer to the mid-$150,000 range. When one developer learned that a family with five children planned to move into one of the affordable houses in her development, she rewrote the neighborhood covenant. The changes prohibited any toys left in the yard and required homeowners to keep hedges trimmed and yards mowed. The implication was clear: Lower-income homeowners do not take the same level of pride in their yards and need written requirements. The story made some readers uncomfortable and angry, but the reporter did her job in covering the story completely.

POSTSCRIPT

Any journalist is best served by doing an "attitude check" before beginning a story on an unknown or controversial topic. Self-awareness and information are the keys to avoiding bias in reporting. The more a reporter tries to understand a topic and the people involved, the more likely he or she will write a fair and balanced story.

GLOSSARY

American Indian: A race of people living in North America when Europeans arrived. The preferred term, not Native American, according to *The Associated Press Stylebook.* If possible, reporters should list a person's tribe affiliation.

Disability: "A person who has a physical or mental impairment that substantially limits one or more major life activities; has a record of such an impairment; or is regarded as having such an impairment," according to the government definition from the Americans with Disabilities Act.

Diversity: "Describes an environment, such as a community, that includes representation of multiple groups. Diversity places an emphasis on accepting and respecting differences by recognizing that no one group is intrinsically superior to another," said Leigh Stephens Aldrich in *Covering the Community: A Diversity Handbook for Media.*

Ethnicity: Subgroups of racial categories based on geographic origins, language, cultural traditions, religion, diet, and so on. In writing about a person's ethnicity, the reporter should ask sources to self-identify their ethnicity.

Long-form census data: Every sixth household completes this form; gathers information about housing, income, education, immigration, workplace, and commuting.

Medicaid: A government program from the state and federal levels that provides medical care for those who cannot afford it because of poverty; provided regardless of age.

Poverty: A family of four with an annual household income under $14,128, according to the federal government definition.

Race: A group of people who share the same ancestry and physical characteristics. The U.S. Census Bureau now allows people to self-select one or more race categories.

Rolodex interviews: Calling the same expert sources from reporter files over and over for stories.

Universal design: "The design of products and environments to be usable by all people, to the greatest extent possible, without the need for adaptation or specialized design," according to the Center for Universal Design.

Working poor: People whose income is poverty level, but they were in the labor force at least 27 weeks in a year.

ACTIVITIES

1. Do an audit of the diversity in your class. Have each student do an abbreviated family tree showing ethnic or racial diversity of parents and grandparents. How many groups or cultures are represented by you and your classmates?

2. Contact your local independent living center that serves people with disabilities. Invite a specialist from the center to take the class on an "audit" of your school's compliance with the Americans with Disabilities Act. For example, are there accessible entrances to all buildings? Are there centrally located telecommunications devices for the deaf on campus? Write a story about your school's compliance.

3. Visit the U.S. Citizenship and Immigration Services and U.S. Census Bureau Web sites and research what immigrant groups have increased in your community. Do a story about why the group settled in your community. Make sure you have diverse sources.

4. Do a story about cross-racial adoption. Some of your college classmates might have parents who are of a different racial group than they are. See whether the students would be willing to be sources to discuss how they define their ethnic identity. If you can't find classmates who are adoptees, contact an organization that assists parents who adopt from outside the United States, such as Ichild for India Adoption Resources, www.serve.com/ichild.

5. Find out the poverty statistics for your community from the U.S. Department of Labor. Find sources at the local public housing complex or through poverty assistance programs for a story about "the face of poverty" in your community.

6. Localize a story about same-sex marriage. Find people from all walks of life in your community and get their opinions on the topic. Find out the stance of members from the local gay community. Write a story about residents' beliefs on the subject.

RESOURCES AND WEB SITES

American Society of Newspaper Editors: www.asne.org
Asian American Journalists Association: www.aaja.org
Census statistics and story ideas: www.census.gov

Center for an Accessible Society: www.accessiblesociety.org
National Association of Black Journalists: www.nabj.org
National Association of Hispanic Journalists: www.nahj.org
National Center on Disability and Journalism: www.ncdj.org
National Gay and Lesbian Task Force: www.ngltf.org
Native American Journalists Association: www.naja.com
Poynter Institute of Media Studies: www.poynter.org
Society of Professional Journalists: www.spj.org
Student Press Law Center: www.splc.org
U.S. Citizenship and Immigration Services: http://uscis.gov

REFERENCES

AARP. (2003). Finding universal design solutions that meet your needs. www.aarp.org/universalhome/solutions.html.

Access Board. (2003). The Rehabilitation Act of 1973: www.access-board.gov/about/Rehab%20Act.htm.

Aldrich, L. S. (1999). *Covering the community: A diversity handbook for media.* Thousand Oaks, CA: Pine Forge Press.

American Society of Newspaper Editors (ASNE). (1999). Time out for diversity and accuracy. Best practices: Coverage (ideas at a glance). www.asne.org/kiosk/diversity/1999timeout/coverage.htm.

Arviso, T. (2002). Watch your language: Words have power. *SPJ-Diversity Toolbox.* www.spj.org/diversity_toolbox_words.asp.

The Associated Press. (2002). *The Associated Press stylebook.* Cambridge, MA: Perseus Publishing.

Azocar, C. (2000). Does race still matter? *Newswatch.* www.newswatch.sfsu.edu/academics.

Blow, R. (2002, September 26). A poverty reporter wins a genius award. TomPaine.com. www.tompaine.com/feature.cfm/ID/6457.

Center for an Accessible Society. (2001). Disaster experiences of people with disabilities. www.accessiblesociety.org/topics/independentliving/disasterprep-1.htm.

Center for Universal Design. (1997). What is universal design. www.design.ncsu.edu/cud/univ_design/ud.htm.

D'Lil, H. (1997, November). Being an "inspiration." *Mainstream,* pp. 14–17.

Doig, S. (2000). *Reporting Census 2000: A guide for journalists.* http://cronkite.pp.asu.edu/census.

Getz, J. (2002, June 19). Home ownership by blacks jumped in Metro East in '90s. *St. Louis Post Dispatch.* www.stltoday.com.

Haller, B. (2001, April 29). Confusing disability and tragedy. *Baltimore Sun,* p. 1C.

Heider, D. (2000). *White news: Why local news programs don't cover people of color.* Mahwah, NJ: Lawrence Erlbaum.

Kelley, R. (2000). *Guide to research on race and news.* Columbia, MO: University of Missouri.

Lehrman, S. (2002). Diversity is accuracy. *SPJ-Diversity Toolbox.* www.spj.org/diversity_toolbox.asp.

Murphy, C. (2002, November 25). Passion for Islam: Shaping the Modern Middle East: The Egyptian Experience with Caryle Murphy, author and *Post* staff writer. [Online chat transcript]. http://discuss.washingtonpost.com/wp-srv/zforum/02/sp_books_murphy112502. htm.

National Center on Disability and Journalism. (2002). Style guide. www.ncdj.org/styleguide.html.

O'Connor, P. (2001, July 4). Asians are among fastest growing racial groups in the St. Louis area. *St. Louis Post Dispatch.* www.stltoday.com.

Rave, J. (2002). Why media should report on Native issues. *NewsWatch, Covering Indian Country.* http://newswatch.sfsu.edu/journal.

Steele, B. (2002, August 22). Reporting same-sex union. *Poynter Online.* www.poynter.org.

Stewart, S. (2000, September 7). Lesbians and gays in the newsroom—10 years later. [Press release]. www.usc.edu/schools/annenberg/asc/projects/soin/research/pressRelease.html.

Sullivan, D. (2002). A tidal wave of change in our nation's communities. Newspaper Association of America Growth Opportunities Leveraging Diversity Network. www.naa.org/diversity/gold/press/wave_of_change.html.

U.S. Census Bureau. (1997). Disabilities affect one-fifth of all Americans. *Census brief,* CENBR/97-5.

U.S. Council of Mayors. (2003, December 14). Mayors' Sixteenth Annual Survey on "Hunger and Homelessness in America's Cities" finds increased levels of hunger, increased capacity to meet demand. [Press release]. www.usmayors.org/uscm/news/press_releases/documents/hunger_release.htm.

U.S. Department of Justice. (2002). ADA home page. www.usdoj.gov/crt/ada/adahom1.htm.

U.S. Department of Labor. (2002, March). *Profile of the working poor, 2000.* [Report 957]. www.bls.gov/cps/cpswp2000.htm.

Yarnold, D. (2002). Why diversity? *SPJ-Diversity Toolbox.* www.spj.org/diversity_toolbox.asp.

CHAPTER 6

COVERING THE BASICS OF LOCAL GOVERNMENT

The editor of a community newspaper has decided to hire another reporter to cover county government issues. In the last five years, new housing developments have sprung up throughout the county, attracting hundreds of new residents. The school system is feeling the crunch of additional students, and school officials are putting pressure on county commissioners for more funding. One reporter has been covering schools and another county government. The editor wants a third reporter who can take on county growth issues as well as swing between county government and schools as needed.

In covering local government, beats often overlap. An education reporter needs to know how county government financing works if the school system depends on allocations from the county commissioners. The county government reporter covers a range of stories from growth and resulting infrastructure issues to the actions of intragovernmental authorities such as water and sewer boards. Reporters assigned to cover cities within the county must know city government issues and also how the city interacts with county government. City reporters might also work on stories with education reporters if any of the school systems are city based. The specific responsibilities of education reporters are covered in Chapter 8.

Reporters who work in larger newsrooms, whether for newspapers or television stations, might be assigned to cover a specific city or a county and all that happens there. In smaller media organizations, such as community newspapers or radio stations, one reporter might cover all local government agencies. How local government is structured will affect how beats are divided. In some states, cities are so large that they are the principal government rather than a city and county government. In other states, townships have the same responsibility for services that counties do. Other states clearly delineate municipal and county governments and their respective responsibilities.

Local government reporters must also understand the relationships between local government and the state and between local government and the federal bureaucracy. Most local governments get their powers from their respective state constitutions or local charters. State statutes might also dictate the responsibilities and powers of local governments. For example, a city might not be able to pass an antipanhandling ordinance without permission from state lawmakers. One county might have legislative authority to assess a certain fee that is not permitted in the adjoining county. Reporters must know the limits on authority for the local governmental entities they cover.

In this chapter, you will:

- Get an overview of city and county government,
- Learn how governmental agencies interact,
- See how local government beats overlap,
- Be introduced to the major players in local government,
- Learn the issues facing local government leaders,
- Learn how to cover a meeting, and
- See how state and federal governments affect local governments.

THE BREADTH OF LOCAL GOVERNMENT

According to the Census of Governments, more than 87,000 governmental units operated in the United States in 2002. More than one-third, or 35,000, comprised special district governments, such as airport authorities. Municipal or city governments totaled slightly more than 19,000, town or townships about 16,500, and county governments about 3,000. State and federal laws affect how these local governments operate as do city and county ordinances and regulations.

Each state differs in how its local governments are set up. Denver, Colorado, has a strong mayor and city council form of government that oversees the city and county of Denver with no separate county government. Polk County, Florida, encompasses 17 municipalities and towns, each with its own governing body. The largest, Lakeland, has a city commission form of government; Polk County government operates separately.

Some states have many local governmental units, such as city councils or commissions, county commissions, transit authorities, airport authorities—any agency or organization that spends tax money. The national average is 27 governmental units per county. The New York metropolitan area has 1,400 units; San Francisco has 900.

A city or county manager or administrator generally oversees the day-to-day operations. The elected council, commission, or board hires and fires the administrator, who in turns hires and fires department heads. Reporters must know the unique roles of elected officials and professional administrators and their relationships. How much power is given to the manager versus elected officials? Where do they get their power? State law? City or county charter? What are the specific responsibilities of each as required by law or voter expectations?

Cities and counties often offer the same services, such as libraries, emergency medical services, and parks and recreation departments. In some instances, cities and counties share responsibilities, such as a jointly operated water and sewer system, and they can enter into joint financing agreements to provide parks, rescue squads, or animal shelters, among services.

Generally cities have been assigned or have assumed responsibilities for services needed in urban areas: fire protection, law enforcement, refuse collection, water and sewer services, and street maintenance and improvement. County responsibility has evolved into services people have needed areawide, such as health, education, and welfare. Responsibilities used to be more delineated. Georgia in the 1970s, for example, expanded the services allowed only to cities to counties as well. The Georgia Municipal Association in *A Reporter's Guide to Covering City Hall* noted that "unlike most other states, cities and counties in Georgia are empowered to perform many of the same functions" (Bean, 2003). Reporters need to find out the specific services permitted to local governmental units on their beat.

One way is through organizations such as the Georgia Municipal Association. Each state has a similar association or league that assists city governments and usually one for county governments. Those sources should be first stops for any reporter trying to learn a local government beat. For example, Capitolimpact.com is a gateway to comprehensive information on towns, law enforcement agencies, courts, school systems, and even zip code lists. Reporters can click on a state and find information that relates to the governmental unit they cover.

Reporters need to know the breadth of local government agencies in their media's coverage area and what services each government entity provides. Reporters should not waste time trying to find someone in city hall to answer social services questions or someone at the county to deal with streets when those tasks are handled elsewhere. Some reporters can get a headstart in learning their local government beat. The Georgia Municipal Association has prepared specifically for reporters a 40-page document, available online, that outlines the structure of city government. It can be found at www.gmanet. com/data/pdf/reporter.pdf. The material came from the *Handbook for Georgia Mayors and Council Members*, published by the Carl Vinson Institute of Government at the University of Georgia.

While getting background on the forms of government, reporters should also check to determine laws relating to the ethical performance of government officials. Public officials are required to disclose any situation in which they might benefit. For example, if rezoning property could enhance a city council member's business, he would have to reveal that before a vote and abstain during voting. Reporters could check state press associations to find out the ethical guidelines governing public officials in their respective states.

A LOOK AT CITY GOVERNMENT

As noted earlier in this chapter, almost 36,000 municipal, town, or township governments operate in the United States. More than 174 million U.S. residents lived in municipalities (or cities, towns, boroughs, or villages, depending on where you live and what you call them) at the beginning of this century, and 76 million of them lived in cities of 100,000 people or more. About half of the nation's municipalities are small and have populations of fewer than 1,000 residents (2002 Census of Governments Report).

Reporters can examine statistics from the Census of Governments to find out how many municipalities operate within their state. The National League of Cities also has information about demographic changes in cities over the last decade. For example, small cities grew faster than large and medium-sized cities (Woodell, 2003). Cities in the South and West had faster growth than cities in the Northeast and Midwest, and the general demographics are changing in many small cities and towns.

The 2002 Census of Governments notes: "The number of municipal governments per state varies widely. Illinois, Pennsylvania, and Texas each has more than 1,000, while at the other extreme, there are 8 states with fewer than 50 municipal governments each: Connecticut, Hawaii, Maine, Massachusetts, Nevada, New Hampshire, Rhode Island, and Vermont."

Forms of City Government

Cities follow one of four forms of city government: mayor–council, which often is considered in two forms: strong mayor–council and weak mayor– council; a council–manager form; a commission form; and sometimes a town meeting form. The strong mayor–council and council–manager forms are considered to have the most effective administration, according to the National Civic League.

Sometimes cities start one administrative structure and then change, such as in Providence, Rhode Island, where city officials decided to return the mayor to a part time position, as noted in this article in the Providence *Herald-Journal* (Randall, 2003):

> . . . City officials hired (Vern) Keeslar in June to run the day-to-day operations of the city and oversee planning. Keeslar worked as a transportation planner for the city of Provo for the past eight years. . . .
>
> Officials in January decided to advertise for a city manager with planning experience and return the mayor to part time. Mayor Alma Leonhardt had been serving as both mayor and city administrator.

David Lawrence and Jake Wicker discuss four forms of government in their book, *Municipal Government in North Carolina* (1995):

■ The mayor–council form with a strong mayor or weak mayor. The mayor–council form has an elected city council. The mayor is elected separately and has administrative authority based on the weak or strong form. The council sets policy and appoints department heads. Many small cities and towns have this form of government. The mayor or council might hire an administrator or city manager, who does not have the authority or power found in a council–manager form of government.

The strong mayor form is often found in large cities and less frequently in small and medium-sized cities. Some towns that do not have a manager will have a mayor who carries out many of the responsibilities and duties a professional administrator would handle. In the Denver, Colorado, model, the mayor is a true executive, and the city council has executive powers. In the weak mayor form, the mayor has little authority and has no veto power.

■ The council–manager form has a manager, who is hired by the city council. The council sets policy, and the manager sees that those policies are carried out. Generally a professional, the person oversees the daily operation of the city, hires and fires department heads, and drafts the budget. The mayor presides over the council; the mayor and the council are elected. This form is predominant in U.S. cities.

■ The commission form of government is found less often and not in some states. Less than 3 percent of cities with populations greater than 2,500 use it. Voters elect three to seven people to the commission. Each commissioner might be assigned certain responsibilities to supervise, such as streets.

■ The town meeting form of city government developed in New England and is still used there. Towns hire a town manager, and elected officials oversee some duties. Citizens meet to enact ordinances, elect officials, and levy taxes.

No matter the form, reporters must be aware of who really holds the power. A manager who serves at the pleasure of a city council might not be quite so open with reporters if he fears for job security. A mayor facing re-election might seek media attention. Reporters must consider officials' personal agendas.

Getting to Know the Players in City Government

Once a reporter knows the form of government, he or she can start getting to know who holds the power. A city Web site is a good starting point to find out names and titles of government officials as well as names, addresses, possibly occupations, and telephone numbers of elected or appointed officials.

Part of learning the sources on the beat is figuring out who wields the power and whether a government depends on a public information officer or officers to release information. Often town employees are told to follow guidelines in answering media questions and might refer an inquisitive reporter to a higher-ranking official or designated representative. How officials are elected—whether the mayor is popularly elected or appointed by fellow council members—is essential in knowing how responsive officials will be to citizen needs and interests. Knowing the dynamics will help reporters approach sources and avoid getting pulled into personality quagmires.

■ **The mayor.** Mayors might have few powers in some communities but exert great influence. Mayors preside at meetings, break tie votes, and sign proclamations. The office of mayor is often the most visible to voters, and in most cities, the mayor is elected. In the nation's larger cities, mayors might be professional administrators and charged with running city government. In smaller communities, the mayor might also be an administrator. In most municipalities, the mayor will serve a ceremonial role.

■ **Aldermen, council members, or commission members.** Who serves on the council, town board, or city commission is essential to the reporter. The city or town charter will tell how the board is made up, including size, how members are elected, and term of office. Members might have staggered terms, either four years or two years, so that each board has some experience and continuity. Some cities elect officials at-large or by districts, whereas others elect solely from districts. Some communities mix it up. Most municipal elections are nonpartisan, though most people make public their party affiliation. State laws will lay out the council's or board's responsibilities.

In addition to a board member's name, occupation, address, and phone number, the reporter needs to know how long the person has served; what has been his or her voting record, for example, is she prodevelopment or antigrowth; does she form a voting bloc with other members and if so, who are they; is the member outspoken or reticent?

■ **City or town manager.** Managers generally serve at the pleasure of the city council, commission, or board of aldermen. The manager's responsibilities, however, might be laid out in state law. Managers might hire and fire department heads and, thereby, exercise a great deal of control over town administration. In some cities, council members might hire certain positions, such as the police chief. Managers might analyze issues, such as a rezoning, and make a recommendation to the council, board, or commission. Most managers are responsible for developing and administering the municipal budget.

The manager's job is often difficult. Managers might also walk a tightrope between what elected officials want and what they see as the best course for the town. Elected officials might want to provide certain services that they know will make them popular among their constituents, but the manager might have to show that those services are too costly. Reporters can find out more about city managers through the International City/County Management Association at www.icma.org.

■ **Department heads.** Each administrator at this level is the best source for how services are delivered. Each department, such as transit, public works, police or fire, finance, or utilities, has a top administrator. Some might have worked up through the ranks, while others might be newer to town administration. Such people are good sources for background or casual conversation when a reporter is not pursuing a hot story. Building solid relationships with these sources can pay dividends later.

■ **Employees.** At the bottom of the administration ladder are employees. They keep the town going day-to-day and can be the best sources for a reporter new to the beat. Reporters must be sensitive to any employee's fear of talking too much about the job or department head. Such sources should be protected when necessary. A complaining employee can provide a clue to a city's internal work climate, as can a former employee. But a reporter needs to be cautious not to become embroiled in a personal controversy that has broad implications for the town or town government. In some states employees might be members of unions, and union leaders should be added to the source list.

A new reporter to the beat can learn a great deal about the players from the former beat reporter, if he or she is still around. The next place to go is the newspaper library morgue to become familiar with previous stories about the council, commission, or committee and its members. Earlier coverage will answer many questions and provide background on issues. Minutes of meetings, agenda packages that contain reports, and other documents can provide context for continuing issues.

Once the reporter has a handle on who makes up the board, it is wise to schedule some time to meet with each member, the town manager, and major department heads. The initial meeting can be an informational one to get to know the individual and to learn more about the beat and its issues. Don't expect to get a story from each of these meetings. Keep it more informal and unstructured. If an idea surfaces, set up a time later to do the interviews for the story. More about new beat interviews can be found in Chapter 3 on interviewing.

Use the informational sessions to get an assessment of the town, its operations, and others who are involved in its operation. Often sources will offer comments on other council members' performance. Tuck that information away for later use. For example, when officials are elected, even though in nonpartisan races, such details can lead to questions and indepth coverage.

Services That Cities Provide

Reporters should check state statutes and statewide governmental organizations such as their state League of Municipalities or the Association of County Governments to learn what services each local government unit oversees. For example, the National League of Cities represents 49 state municipal leagues, which in turn include more than 18,000 cities. A list of states and their municipal leagues can be found at www.nlc.org/nlc_org/site/membership/state_municipal_leagues/list_of_state_municipal_leagues.cfm.

Traditionally, cities have provided services such as streets, water and sewer, law enforcement, fire protection, public transportation, and parks and recreation. As noted earlier, some municipalities operate school systems as well as special authorities that oversee airports, utilities such as electricity and gas, or other fee-based services. Others "support cemeteries, art galleries and museums, and auditoriums, coliseums, and convention centers," note Lawrence and Wicker in their book *Municipal Government in North Carolina* (1995).

What Are the Issues?

Most reporters who cover local government can identify issues that affect their communities on a daily, weekly, or annual basis. Some stories are written regularly, such as about budget, elections, back to school, or Founder's Day events, and others surface periodically such as annexations, construction, employee hiring or firing, or long-range planning. Reporters can uncover these issues by reading past news stories, checking in with local officials and local government watchers, monitoring local government Web sites, and keeping an advance or futures file to remind them about upcoming events.

In thinking broadly about issues, reporters might find useful the pressroom at the National League of Cities' Web site. The pressroom link can also give lots of ideas for stories. For example, one news release based on a survey of 330 cities and towns showed that municipalities were raising fees and taxes while cutting staff members and infrastructure spending to deal with tight budgets. The Web site also has links to each state's comparable organization for story ideas and issues closer to home.

In addition, the National League of Cities launched a project to determine what issues officials faced through its Municipalities in Transition Project (Woodell, 2003). By identifying the issues, the League hoped to help identify policies and solutions. Through interviews with 70 officials in 27 communities across the United States, League researchers identified six recurring themes:

■ **The "new" economy.** This trend represents more service than manufacturing jobs. "Globalization has meant that an American city might now trade more with Hong Kong than that city's direct neighbor," the report said. Some communities are stagnating while others are booming. Officials said that the economy was "at the root of other important issues and trends facing their cities."

■ **Limited revenue capacity.** This problem has occurred from a variety of causes, among them federal and state mandates and changes in funding levels; the economy; and suburbanization and sprawl, the report noted. Cities are also limited on how they can raise revenues.

■ **Movement of people and businesses.** As people move into a community, they need time to adjust, whether to schools, neighborhoods, or the economy. When people move out, that can change the demographics economically, as well as the need for services and programs.

■ **Suburbanization and sprawl.** The League report stated that officials felt both were unavoidable. Suburbanization is the growth of the suburbs for residences and businesses, while sprawl is "an uncontrollable pattern of development that is fostered by suburban growth," the report noted. While they are unavoidable, cities have to pay the consequences of both, and officials say they have little control over either.

■ **Education.** Education is a "key indicator of a community's desirability" for both residents and businesses, the League report stated. Schools contribute to an educated workforce, while at the same time they "cope with and try to solve a variety of deep-seated social problems."

■ **Changing city government roles and relationships.** Officials interviewed cited a number of changing roles. Some mentioned more and others less citizen participation; most reported a decline in trust by citizens in government officials; many said cities have a "more business-like approach" because cities find services that can be supported directly with fees; and citizens want cities to "provide core services in a more efficient manner."

Diversity is an issue on any local government beat. The National League of Cities (2003b) noted in its "Demographic Change in Small Cities, 1990–2000" that Hispanics, Asians, and African Americans showed gains in all regions, but Hispanic growth particularly in the South at least doubled in small cities everywhere. The report cited that demographic changes, including overall growth and increased diversity, "are important because they present challenges to local leadership and policy making . . . infrastructure, service provision, and fiscal capacity." Reporters need to monitor those changes locally, explain the impact, and include a diversity of voices in any story. Diversity is covered in greater detail in Chapter 5.

COVERING COUNTY GOVERNMENT

Forty-eight of the 50 states have operational county governments, according to the National Association of Counties (NACo). Connecticut and Rhode Island have counties but no functioning county governments. Neither does the District of Columbia. Counties vary in geographic area from 67 square kilometers in Arlington County, Virginia, to 227,559 square kilometers in North Slope Borough, Alaska (Alaska calls its counties "boroughs"). In regard to population, Loving County, Texas, is home to 140 residents compared to Los Angeles County, California, and its 9.2 million people, NACo notes.

The NACo Web site has much data about counties and notes the organization's membership totals more than 2,000 counties, representing more than 80 percent of the nation's population. In NACo's "About Counties" section, a reporter can click on a state and find out how many counties it has and also access each county's Web site. For example, if a reporter is preparing to move to Montana, she can find out from NACo's Web site that Montana has 56 counties, the name and population of each county, the county seats, and when each county was incorporated. The reporter can also find a Census Bureau profile of Montana.

According to the 2002 Census of Governments, the number of county governments per state varies. Texas has 254 compared to some states with fewer than 20. In some states, cities and counties have merged into one governmental unit that is counted as a municipal government, such as the Denver example. Between 1997 and 2002, seven county governments were abolished, and two merged with city governments. The Census report notes that more than 10 percent of the U.S. population is not served by a county government, and the majority of county governments each serve fewer than 50,000 residents.

Forms of County Government

Like cities, county government can be organized in several ways. Most counties operate under a county-manager form of government and a board of commissioners that sets policy, hires the manager, and approves the budget, among other tasks. Boards vary in size, method of election, term of office, and administrative structure. Board members can range from three to eleven, and terms of office range from two to four years, although more counties have moved to four-year staggered terms. Unlike municipal elections, county elections are partisan, that is, candidates state their political party affiliation. More about elections is in Chapter 13.

The county as a geographic unit has been a logical choice for certain services and programs. Among the responsibilities within counties have been operating schools, conducting elections, overseeing and maintaining property tax records, and managing agricultural, environmental, social services, and public health programs, including mental health and rabies control. In some states, court systems are housed within the county but are actually state administered. Counties also provide some of the same services as cities: law enforcement, public libraries, fire protection, water and sewer systems, parks and recreation, and hospitals. They also manage convention centers and museums.

A board of commissioners might delegate some responsibilities to other boards, such as agriculture or social services. School districts will have school board members to establish policy, but they will rely on the counties to collect revenue and appropriate school operating and capital improvement funds. More information about budgets is in Chapter 7 on financing local government, and a specific discussion on school governance is included in Chapter 8 on covering the education beat.

People on the Beat

Becoming familiar with the county beat parallels learning the structure of the city beat.

■ **County commissioners or a governing body.** The size, members' terms of office, administrative structure, how the chair is chosen, and type of government will vary county by county. In addition to a commissioner's name, occupation, address, and phone number, the reporter needs to know how long the person has served; what has been his or her voting record; whether he or she forms a voting bloc with other members and if so, on what issues; and whether the commissioner represents a specific constituency such as farmers.

■ **Commission chair.** The chair of the governing body might be selected from among the elected members by those members. In some instances, voters elect a chair. Like a mayor, the chair might have some administrative authority, but in most counties, that person acquires and exercises influence because of the office. The chair could call special meetings if necessary and would also serve as the ceremonial leader to represent the county at special events.

■ **County manager.** Like the city manager, the county manager is a professional hired by the county commissioners or governing board. He or she is responsible for the day-to-day operations, drafts and oversees the county budget, and keeps the commissioners informed and up-to-date. The manager basically executes the policies and directives of the county commissioners.

■ **Department heads.** Just like with city or any other government, counties are organized into departments with administrators. Reporters should know who leads each department and develop relationships with those sources. In many cases, department heads have been with the county for many years and can offer background and perspective on operations other than their own. The county attorney and the county clerk can be excellent sources, although neither usually oversees a department.

■ **Employees.** Among a reporter's sources should be county employees. Departmental secretaries and administrative assistants keep calendars and know what is happening day to day. Other employees, especially long-term employees, know trends and the history. They usually live in the community and give reporters leads on what other residents are saying about county government. County government reporters should follow the same advice for reporters in the city government section of the text and be sensitive to employees' willingness to be sources. Some might fear retribution if they talk too much, and if so, that could be the beginning of a story about personnel problems.

In learning who's who on the beat, reporters must also be sensitive to and aware of the relationships of commissioners and managers, managers and department heads, department heads and employees, commissioners and the voters, and on and on. Commissioners will feel they must be responsive to the voters, while managers feel responsible to the board that hired them but at the same time feel a duty to the general public. Personalities often come into play in stories, and reporters must decide when those personalities should be and are actually part of the story.

Using minutes of previous meetings, just like in covering the municipal beat, can be valuable to any county government reporter. Minutes will include the routine as well as the revealing, as from this partial account from a meeting of the Dorchester County, Maryland, commissioners in Figure 6.1. All caps indicate the action, and the explanation follows.

Reporters have used minutes to research commissioners' attendance at meetings as well as to track issues as they have been brought up for discussion.

FIGURE 6.1   The County Commissioners of Dorchester County, Regular Meeting Minutes, September 3, 2002

The County Commissioners of Dorchester County met in regular session on September 3, 2002, with the following members present: Thomas A. Flowers, President; Effie M. Elzey; Jay L. Newcomb, Glen A. Payne, Sr., and Jane Baynard, County Administrator. E. Thomas Merryweather, County Attorney, and Molly Foreman, Administrative Specialist, were also present. Commissioner Newcomb joined the meeting late. William Nichols, Vice President, was absent.

REGULAR SESSION

The Commissioners convened in a Regular Session with Commissioner Flowers presiding.

INVOCATION AND PLEDGE OF ALLEGIANCE

Commissioner Flowers asked for a moment of silence and Commissioner Payne led the Pledge of Allegiance.

COMMENDATION: CORNELIUS "SNAP" JOHNSON, AIRPORT

The Commissioners issued a commendation to Cornelius "Snap" Johnson, an employee of the Airport, recognizing him for his heroism in extinguishing an aircraft that was on fire at the Airport on August 26, 2002. Commissioner Newcomb joined the meeting at this point.

REVIEW AND APPROVAL OF MINUTES

The Commissioners approved minutes from August 27, 2002 as amended.

REVIEW AND APPROVAL OF VOUCHERS

The Commissioners reviewed and approved the County vouchers. . . .

Issues to Be Covered

A county government reporter never lacks in story material. Issues facing county governments are broad and plentiful. As noted earlier, counties can encompass huge geographic areas, so reporters might have a lot of territory to cover physically. Within a county might be a cosmopolitan city, a university town, and acres of farmland—all housing people of varying interests and lifestyles. Counties provide services for all those residents.

In recent years, counties have faced increasing financial pressure, as discussed more specifically in Chapter 7. Lack of funds has forced governing officials to make tough choices about which services to expand and which to cut. State and even federal governments have reduced funding levels, and many counties are moving more and more to fee-based services and programs to raise money.

Because counties run health departments, federal legislation has increased county responsibilities. The federal Health Insurance Portability and Accountability Act of 1996, known as HIPAA, required all medical offices, whether private or government funded, to tighten policies regarding release of patient records. Patients must sign forms that they are aware of what information can be released and what cannot; the signed forms become part of their files at their doctors' offices. County-operated health departments and clinics must comply, adding more paperwork and staff time to each patient visit.

County governments have also borne the expense for complying with the federal Homeland Security Act. Public safety personnel who are known as "first responders" have had to be additionally trained since 9/11. Airports have tighter security and have had to hire and train more personnel. Because the federal government has provided little funding for the additional safety requirements, county governments have had to absorb those costs. More about public safety in regard to terrorism is discussed in Chapter 10.

Under the federal Clean Skies and Clean Air acts, county governments as well as state governments have had to adopt measures to lower pollution levels that can contribute to higher ozone levels in the summer and higher particulate matter, such as car exhaust and emissions from power plants. Many people are familiar with the different color codes for ozone levels, from the safest, lowest green to the dangerous purple. Weather forecasters air the levels daily, while county governments must implement measures to comply with more stringent standards. Governments that fail to comply by federal deadlines will face penalties, such as cuts in their federal transportation dollars.

In some communities, county officials are dealing with increased growth and the resulting impact on services, schools, the environment, highways and other roads, and even landfills. All these growth issues are continuing stories: They occur over and over, and new angles appear constantly. Reporters should consider how these issues affect all income groups, age groups, and racial and ethnic groups. Each will have a different take. For example, if a county has to cut back on bus service that links several towns within the county, lower-income residents will be more severely affected than individuals who own cars or who can drive.

In reporting these issue stories, reporters should remember the money trail. Financing is critical, and reporters should know who is paying, how, and how much. County managers look at places other than county taxes and fees to finance projects. A resource for county officials as well as for reporters is the NACo Web site that includes deadlines for grant applications, such as $100,000 grants for community-based, collaborative environmental and health projects that would use EPA tools to improve local air quality or address public health concerns. The site also has links to federal legislation affecting county governments, copies of testimony before Congress, and fact sheets. One item even tells local government officials "How to Influence Congress without Leaving Home." Such items are food for reporters' stories.

PLANNING AND ZONING

Growth, up or down, significantly affects all aspects of local government. Areas of the country that are growing fast often cannot keep up with the demand for infrastructure as houses go up, more malls are built, and schools are needed. Highways become overcrowded. Pollution levels rise. Although more people generate more income, often the demand comes well before governments have in hand money from increases in property taxes to add needed services or to build roads or sewer lines.

For example, if a company locates in the county, the county will not collect any tax revenue until the plant is operating, which could take two years from the groundbreaking to the grand opening. As part of the economic development package to attract the plant, the county might have agreed to lay water and sewer lines to the site and resurface and widen the rural road that eventually will be the primary access. Let's suppose that the plant will bring in 500 employees who will add 425 children to the school system in grades kindergarten through twelfth. The school system might need more teachers— or possibly another elementary school if the system has had growth apart from the plant's arrival. Those activities cost money, and the plant has yet to pay any property taxes.

Much of the growth in recent years has been in nonmetropolitan areas, which means out in the countryside and outside of cities. Development of farmland and forests has put pressure on local governments to plan the type of growth they want and to avoid environmental damage. In some areas, however, lack of planning has resulted in miles of haphazard mini shopping malls, business areas, and commercial development encroaching on neighborhoods. In other locales, boards have been more proactive and developed long-range plans that govern what can be built where. Cities often have extended their planning jurisdiction out into counties, and in more progressive areas, cities and counties have worked together to develop master plans to control growth. State laws might require cities and counties to approve comprehensive growth plans.

Local growth affects state governments, too. When more schools and teachers are needed, state budgets feel the strain because states fund a large portion of local schools' budgets. Increased traffic increases pollution, which could put states in violation of federal Environmental Protection Agency guidelines. Reporters should investigate growth's impact beyond local borders.

Zoning Classifications

For decades city and county planning departments have used zoning classifications to define the types of development within a geographic area. Maps on the walls of zoning offices might have brightly colored geometric shapes that show where businesses, manufacturing plants, and residences are allowed or have been built. Zoning regulations even control size and location of signs. For example, many towns have restricted recognizable logos of fast food chains so that they conform to local regulations.

Zoning codes set designations for each type of development, such as R for residential development or O-I for office and institutional. Following an R might be a number designation that relates to the number of housing units allowed per acre. The higher the number, the denser the development per acre. For example, a designation of R-1 would mean one dwelling per acre, while R-40 would be an apartment complex. Zoning regulations can also dictate the types of structures, the number of parking places per apartment unit, the amount of park or green space per acre, where construction is allowed, curbs and gutters, and other requirements.

Zoning regulations also apply to commercial and building developments. Some communities might exclude certain kinds of commercial operations such as factories of any type. Others might restrict commercial and business operations to specific areas of town to protect residential neighborhoods from noise and traffic. Zoning requirements might limit in-home businesses that would generate more traffic in a residential area. Some parts of a community might be designated as no build areas, such as in flood plains or watershed areas that supply a community's water.

Changing a parcel's zoning classification can bring out residents by the score, as can a city's plan to annex property. Residents become defensive, argumentative, and confrontational when they believe their property values or way of life might be compromised by less restrictive zoning that would allow apartments, homes of lesser value, or business growth nearby. In an annexation, county residents might not want the burden of additional city taxes, even if it means water and sewer line service instead of septic tanks or more regular police patrols.

Reporters must recognize that issues associated with planning and zoning often prove to be emotional ones for residents, who will be vocal at public hearings and even threaten officials and their chances for reelection. Antigrowth groups might suddenly appear and demand coverage. Planning commission members might take firm stances. Reporters must ensure that stories are balanced and reflect the emotion and impact on all sides.

For example, residents in Clark County, Nevada, objected after the Clark County Commission approved projects throughout the Las Vegas Valley that were "contrary to existing land-use guides" and "threw long-range master planning into disarray," according to the *Las Vegas Sun*. Neighborhood residents became angry and upset over changes they felt could affect property values and neighborhood quality of life, the *Sun* reported.

Planning and zoning can be a huge and important beat for any newspaper or other media organization. Growth and development stories overlap other local government beats, and they affect every resident. The American Planning Association's (APA) Web site at www.planning.org advertises that its public affairs coordinator can put reporters in touch with planning experts to explain or comment on planning topics. The APA has an annual public service award for newspapers that publish stories to benefit city and regional planning.

Stories on the Beat

When a developer wants property to be rezoned, he has to follow a procedure that starts in the planning office. Reporters can find out the process from planning staff, but at the least, adjoining residents must be notified and signs posted on the affected property about the rezoning. A public hearing date before the governing board will be set, and the planning staff will make a recommendation for or against the rezoning. In theory, governing boards are not to consider the specific use of the property, such as a rezoning request that would turn farmland into the site of a superstore. It should consider whether changing farmland to a business or manufacturing zone fits with long-range development plans.

The planning approval process can take months and even years. Local officials might demand changes to an initial plan or concessions, such as the developer paying for street improvements before they give final approval. William Spence's story (2003) in the *Daily Inter Lake* about a mall development in Kalispell, Montana, hints at the process and just how long it might take:

> Hoping for a favorable decision on an impending master plan amendment, a Tennessee firm also submitted a zone-change request on Monday regarding a proposed regional mall.
>
> Wolford Development wants to build the largest shopping center in Montana on 481 acres located near the intersection of U.S. 93 and West Reserve Drive.

For the project to proceed, the company needs both the amendment to the Flathead County Master Plan and the zoning change and then must subdivide the property. It could also face other regulatory hurdles related to sewage disposal and stormwater runoff.

Developer Bucky Wolford submitted a master plan amendment request in July. The Flathead County Planning Board will hold a public hearing on that issue on Sept. 10; it then goes to the county commissioners for a final decision.

If the amendment is denied, the zone change would be moot. (Reprinted with permission of the *Daily Inter Lake*.)

A reporter will follow the story, sometimes even before the actual rezoning request is filed. A company such as Wal-Mart might announce plans to build a new store in a community on a specific site. Part of the property might not be zoned for commercial development, and so the rezoning process begins. The reporter will write stories about the request, any objections or support, public hearing, and final vote and throughout all stories explain the jargon that goes with the beat. The outcome affects more than just the planning reporter, as shown in this story by Kirsten Orsini-Meinhard (2003) in the Fort Collins, Colorado, *Coloradoan*:

When developers dropped their plans for a lifestyle center in Windsor, the town lost more than just upscale stores.

It also lost the potential to generate sales tax revenue and, most importantly, say Windsor officials, the ability to upgrade its highway interchange that is in bad need of repair.

The decision affected town officials and residents because the center would have been at an intersection of Interstate 25 that needed upgrading. The development could have pushed state officials to make improvements sooner, although the intersection was way down the priority list of road projects.

Planning stories often go beyond just a local focus and pull in state and national agencies and resources. A county or several counties might be affected by federal policies or votes. When President Bush and the Department of Energy announced in 2002 that Nevada's Yucca Mountain would be the site of a high-level nuclear waste dump, state and local officials went into action. Governor Kenny Guinn vetoed the presidential decision, which was called a historic action on the part of a governor, according to a story in the *Las Vegas Sun* (2002). Congress overruled Guinn and upheld Yucca Mountain as the site that eventually would have 77,000 tons of high-level nuclear waste.

Yucca Mountain is about 90 miles northwest of Las Vegas. The decision affected states other than Nevada. A resolution opposing Yucca Mountain as the site showed up on the agenda of the Salt Lake City, Utah, City Council, although Salt Lake City is 350 miles north of Yucca Mountain. Inyo County, California, which is 180 miles west, noted on its planning department Web site (2003) that it was one of ten "Affected Units of Local Government" from the Yucca Mountain site. "The County maintains an oversight and impact assessment office to monitor ongoing activities at the proposed high-level radioactive waste repository at Yucca Mountain, Nevada," noted the site, which includes departmental responsibilities, the county's growth plan, and its zoning ordinances.

SPECIAL GOVERNMENTS AND DISTRICTS

The Census of Governments (2002), which is conducted every five years, defines special district governments as:

> independent, special-purpose governmental units (other than school district governments) that exist as separate entities with substantial administrative and fiscal independence from general-purpose local governments. [They] provide specific services that are not being supplied by existing general-purpose governments. Most perform a single function, but in some instances their enabling legislation allows them to provide several, usually related, types of services . . . from such basic social needs as hospitals and fire protection to the less conspicuous tasks of mosquito abatement and upkeep of cemeteries.

The number of special districts has almost tripled since 1952 but grew only slightly between the 1997 and 2002 census counts. The growth, however, reflects the public's demand for services not offered or performed by existing governments, the Census of Governments points out. The number varies by state; eleven states—California, Colorado, Illinois, Indiana, Kansas, Missouri, Nebraska, New York, Pennsylvania, Texas, and Washington—have at least 1,000 special district governments, according to the Census of Governments. Alaska, the District of Columbia, Hawaii, and Louisiana have fewer than 50 special district governments.

Nine out of 10 special district governments perform only one function. More than one-third are responsible for functions "related to natural resources such as drainage and flood control, irrigation, and soil and water conservation. The next most frequent function . . . is fire protection followed by housing and community development, and sewerage," the Census of Governments reported. About 15 percent provide water supplies.

Special district boards often face criticism and tough challenges, as in this story from the *Sacramento Bee* (Lee, 2003):

> The struggling Port of Sacramento needs to embrace public uses such as recreation and tourism, and restructure its governing board, according to a draft report from a port advisory committee.
>
> With those changes, the port might get enough political support to obtain federal money for much needed improvements to its maritime business.
>
> Faced with losses of more than $900,000 each of the last two years and increasing pressure from West Sacramento residents, port leaders are seeking a new vision that will allow them to get along with their neighbors and make a profit.

"If we do nothing, it doesn't get any better," said Robbie Waters, Sacramento city councilman and port commissioner. (The *Sacramento Bee*, 2003. Reprinted with permission.)

In some areas, existing local governments, such as municipalities and counties, fund the special district governments. In other states, these governments can levy taxes or assess fees to raise operating revenues. If a special district requires infrastructure, such as a new pumping station at a water treatment plant, the cost might be paid through other resources, such as bonds issued by the governing agency and approved by the voters. Bonds are discussed in more detail in Chapter 7 on financing local government.

Just as with other aspects of the local government beat, a reporter must know which special district governments are included in the beat. Special district governments mean another set of sources, documents, meetings, agendas, and stories. Unless the special district government has a large budget or extensive authority or influence, little or no coverage might appear. A reporter might cover special district governments sporadically, only when an issue comes up, such as an increase in fees or a report that shows a problem with services.

Reporters should not let special district governments go unnoticed or unreported. In some cases, individuals have established their own "kingdoms" in which they have wielded great power and influence because of their positions within these governments or their advisory boards. Other governmental units might make their budgets look good by assigning money-losing services to special authorities or districts.

One Example: Utilities

Municipalities, counties, or cooperatives might operate and manage utility systems, which in turn are regulated by state utility commissions that must approve any rate increases. Utilities cover a range of services: natural gas, petroleum, electricity, nuclear power, wind power. Some local governments might have cooperatives to provide utilities, such as water and sewer service. Local governments might also oversee telephone systems. For the most part, companies or independents rather than local governments operate cable systems. At least one channel might be designated as a local government access channel on which public hearings, meetings, or other government business can be aired.

These utilities generally are managed by separate boards or districts, and their revenues must support the utility's operating expenses. Most media do not have a reporter assigned specifically to the utilities beat. Utilities might be covered as part of a business beat or a state or a local government beat. In addition to the utility board members and local government officials, reporters have other resources to consult in learning and covering a utility beat. Dow Jones Newsletters in July 2003 started a new service, Dow Jones Energy Legal Beat, "tailored to legal, investment and regulatory professionals who need insight into complex legal issues affecting individual energy companies and the sector as a whole," according to the news release distributed on BusinessWire.

"When something happens in the energy industry, you can bet there are attorneys, regulators and lobbyists involved. And there's plenty happening now—the Bush Administration's new energy plan, investigations of energy trading companies, new regulations and executive orders changing current regulations, as well as lawsuits affecting energy companies and the way they operate," said Michael Rieke, editor of Dow Jones Energy Legal Beat, in its news release. "Dow Jones Energy Legal Beat brings its readers news on all these fronts in one place, organized so that readers can quickly find the information they need."

The Investigative Reporters and Editors (IRE) Web site has tip sheets on how to cover aspects of the utilities industry, developed after blackouts in 2003. They can be ordered for a minimal fee. In addition, the site has links to federal reports that utility companies must file as well as to "State Electricity Profiles," which give the electrical generation capacity of each state. A reporter can find out the largest generating plants in a state; the type of generation, such as water, coal, or nuclear; and the generating capacity in megawatts. Such information is valuable when a reporter wants to compare his or her state with other states' types of power generation, for example.

Companies that provide energy must submit annual reports to regulatory agencies such as the Federal Energy Commission and to the Securities and Exchange Commission if they are publicly traded. Those documents provide insight into the cost of power, expansion, and even forecasts of energy capacity. In the wake of the August 2003 blackout in the Northeast, many utility reporters, in search of the cause, consulted such documents as the fingerpointing began and continued.

Beyond the Usual Story

Many utility stories focus on rates and lack of service. When bills are going up because the power company has secured a rate increase, readers and consumers want to know how much their pocketbooks will be hit. When power is out and when it will come back on also make for attention-getting news. Rising gas prices, particularly near holidays such as the Fourth of July when more people travel, lead the news. Reporters must include what is forcing prices up, such as the war in Iraq or the traditional increases at high-traffic times.

Not all utility news is negative. Often utility companies show their corporate hearts, as in this story from the *Great Falls* (Montana) *Tribune* (Dennison, 2003):

> HELENA—NorthWestern Energy Wednesday offered up an extra $1.7 million of ratepayer funds to help poor customers pay heating bills this winter, saying the money is the unspent balance in related accounts.

NorthWestern made the offer to Gov. Judy Martz's new energy task force, which later agreed the money should be transferred to the account that funds programs helping NorthWestern's low-income customers.

The funds will increase by more than 50 percent the money NorthWestern plans to spend on these programs this year.

Wednesday's action came at the first meeting of Martz's Consumer Energy Protection Task Force, which will make recommendations on how to tackle urgent energy problems facing the state. (Reprinted with permission of the *Great Falls Tribune*.)

In addition to showing the benefit in NorthWestern's service area, the story ties the gift to the governor's energy task force and sets a broader context for the story.

Alternative energy makes for big news, as in this story from the *Arizona Business Gazette* (Scott, 2003):

What is thought to be the nation's first subdivision powered by solar energy and propane, a community of 487 houses that won't be connected to the electrical power grid, is taking shape 30 miles east of Kingman.

GreenWood Ranch Estates will offer modular homes on forested 5-acre lots. Each will be equipped to generate electricity by harnessing the 320 days of sunlight the area receives annually.

OVERLAPPING BEATS

Often what happens on one local government beat affects another beat. For example, if the county commissioners must approve the budget and resulting appropriation for the local school system, the education reporter must be familiar with the county government staff. The county government reporter must clue in the education reporter when budget discussions begin, or just cover that section of the meeting and give the notes to the education reporter.

Some news organizations assign separate reporters to county government and to education. In smaller operations, one reporter might cover schools, county government, and municipal government—a huge beat in terms of geography, people, and issues.

The health reporter and the county government reporter might work on stories because the county administers the health department. The county government reporter, in looking at the National Association of Counties' Web site, might notice a report that was done by NACo in conjunction with the National Association of Community Health Centers. Information from the survey could be the basis for a solid joint reporting project between the health reporter and the county government reporter on issues facing county administrators in regard to health issues. Reporters who want to see the report can find it on the NACo Web site.

A police reporter might team up with the county government reporter to write a series on the impact of the federal Homeland Security Act on local governments and first responders, as public safety people are called in the legislation. NACo has a fact sheet on its Web site about the Homeland Security Department and the need for congressional funding so that local departments can comply with the legislation.

The lead from the following story by Sanjay Bhatt (2003) of the *Seattle Times* shows local governments' interaction:

> Anyone hoping to become the next superintendent of Seattle Public Schools will have to get an "A" from the seven School Board members and perhaps an unofficial eighth: Mayor Greg Nickels.
>
> The School Board has asked Nickels to meet privately with each finalist. According to the Mayor's Office, Nickels also will meet with the board's search consultant, Nancy Noeske. When the board last selected finalists for the superintendent's job in 1995, it didn't discuss the idea of involving then-Mayor Norm Rice.
>
> Board President Nancy Waldman said the board decided to involve Nickels because it's important for the superintendent and mayor to work well together. But would a thumbs-down from Nickels doom a finalist? Waldman said the board hasn't had a chance to discuss that.
>
> Increasingly, mayors of large cities are playing a more prominent role in shaping the future of their schools. Since the mid-1990s, mayors in Chicago, Boston and Cleveland have brought their school systems under their administrations with state lawmakers' backing.
>
> Mayors have exercised less direct control in Philadelphia, Detroit, Los Angeles and New York by hand-picking school-board members and flexing their muscles in other school matters, according to "Powerful Reforms with Shallow Roots: Improving America's Urban Schools." (Copyright 2003 Seattle Times Company. Used with permission.)

THE CHALLENGE OF COVERING MEETINGS

The most visible part of any government beat is the meeting, and government officials meet often and at great length. During meetings, local government officials transact business, out in the open, in the public eye. Covering meetings can be one of the most challenging assignments for a reporter because of the number of players, the issues, deadlines—and the number of meetings.

Laws That Open Meetings

Congress passed the Federal Sunshine Act legislation in 1976 that required about 50 federal agencies, commissions, boards, and councils to meet in public. The act states that the public should be allowed to observe the decision-making processes of the federal government whenever practical. The same agencies covered by the Freedom of Information Act—discussed in Chapter 2—are covered by the Sunshine Act, and most of the FOIA exemptions also apply. The additional exemption in the Sunshine Act is No. 10, which allows a meeting to be closed for discussion about the issuance of a subpoena or the government body's participation in a court or administrative proceeding.

All states have their own open meetings laws as well. Reporters can check online for their state press association's guidelines to meeting coverage, actual language of the open meetings law, and updates. States vary in the type of exemptions and in the procedures reporters must follow to object to official closure of meetings.

Legally, a public open meeting has two aspects to it. First, it requires public notification of the meeting, which can be as simple as a flyer tacked on a bulletin board in a government building. State laws outline the provisions for notification, including time, such as 48 hours in advance.

Second, a public meeting generally is said to occur when a quorum of the members discusses or acts on any item that is the business of the group (but check your state's open meetings laws). That's where local government bodies get into trouble. They might be in violation if city council members get together for dinner before the council meeting and discuss city business. Under the open meeting definition, the council was in session, not just having a meal. A reporter might need to find out where the council eats and attend the dinner. Some states might have more restrictive laws that define an open meeting.

State laws generally do provide exemptions when government bodies can go into private or executive sessions. Those exceptions are specifically noted in the law. What should a reporter do if kicked out of a meeting that should be open? Media organizations offer a number of suggestions. First, before the public and media are excluded, a reporter should ask the legal reason for closing the meeting and find out which open meetings exemption applies. Reporters should notify their editors, who, in turn, should contact the media organization's legal counsel or the attorney for the state press association. Also, reporters should find out which official asked that the meeting be closed and why he or she did so.

For college journalists, the Student Press Law Center advises: "If officials still tell you the meeting is closed, ask that your objection and their response be read into the minutes and then leave. Upon leaving, be sure to record the names and titles of everyone you talked to and carefully note what was said."

News organizations have filed suit when meetings have been improperly closed. If the media bring a lawsuit against the board and win, any action taken behind closed doors is null and void. If the meeting was illegally closed, most editors will ask that the journalist write a story about the closure and any subsequent stories about legal action against the illegal meeting. Bad publicity might make elected officials rethink violating the open meetings statute.

Why Local Boards Meet

Local governments have several types of meetings, as outlined in the Georgia Municipal Association's *A Reporter's Guide to Covering City Hall* (Bean, 2003):

■ **Regular council or commission meetings.** Here the governing body conducts business, such as approving expenditures and passing regulations and ordinances. Such meetings fall under state laws requiring public notification. Reporters have access to agendas in advance to know what to expect at each meeting.

■ **Executive sessions.** A local government can go into executive or closed session to discuss away from public scrutiny specific matters, such as real estate transactions, personnel issues, lawsuits, or special awards to employees. Usually the board has to vote in public to go into closed session, and the public is entitled to written confirmation of the topic discussed.

■ **Work sessions.** Such meetings are set for board members to discuss topics in more detail than allowed at a regular meeting. The public can attend but might not be allowed to speak. Boards will schedule work sessions, for example, during budget deliberations.

■ **Special meetings.** Such meetings can be called to discuss a specific issue or a few issues. Although such meetings are not often set, the board is still compelled to notify the public and the media.

■ **Public hearings.** Such sessions allow residents a chance to give their views about specific issues. For example, boards hold public hearings on rezoning changes. A public hearing could be called to get residents' input on where to locate a school or a public park or budget proposals for the coming fiscal year. Hearings require the same notification as other meetings.

Up-Front Work

When a reporter takes on a local government beat, he or she must find out which meetings are routinely covered and then the details, such as when and where the governing board meets, notification procedures, when and where to get agendas, the procedure for adopting an ordinance, and where the minutes are kept. For example, the county commissioners might meet once a month at the county administrative offices and also once a month at another location that might be more accessible to residents in the southern part of the county.

Beyond the twice monthly or weekly town council meetings might also be scheduled meetings for the appearance commission, planning and zoning board, transportation advisory board, and any number of other committees and commissions. Some newsrooms do not cover all the subcommittees or commissions and wait until those bodies' reports come to the governing board. If a major issue, such as a rezoning case, is at the forefront, a reporter might attend a planning board meeting, although those meetings are not part of routine coverage.

To get ready for that first meeting, a reporter should get a copy of the agenda. In some cases, the agenda might be one page, listing what issues will be discussed and by whom. In most cases, however, the agenda for one meeting might be a several-inch-thick package that includes an outline for the meeting, with times assigned for each issue and supplemental material for each issue. For example, if the council will consider a developer's request to build a commercial office building, the agenda package could include impact reports from the planning and zoning board, the transportation advisory committee, and the appearance commission.

For a continuing issue, minutes from earlier meetings would reveal what has been discussed, council members' views on prior projects, names of proponents and opponents, and other relevant data. To clarify agenda items, a reporter might have to call the town manager, a council member, a department head, or someone else to find out what action, if any, might be taken.

Once a reporter has done the up-front work prior to a meeting, an editor might want an advance story. The advance story basically outlines the agenda and lets residents know what will be discussed at the meeting. A reporter might need to provide some background for readers. If the town council has held a public hearing on a rezoning application, it might vote on the rezoning at the upcoming meeting.

The advance story would include when and where the meeting will be held and would note if residents could watch the proceedings on public access television, available in many communities. Any controversial aspects would be highlighted. This advance story from the *Bristol* (CT) *Press* (Collins, 2003) outlines the upcoming meeting and what will happen after that vote:

> BRISTOL—Concerned about the preservation of historic buildings, city councilors will decide Tuesday whether to move ahead with a plan to buy time before some old buildings are knocked down.
>
> Officials are also looking into other measures that could lead to more protection for threatened buildings and to update the city's 25-year-old list of structures worth saving.
>
> As a first step, city Councilor Ellen Zoppo said that extending the city's automatic delay from 60 to 90 days would give officials a chance to search for alternatives that might allow threatened historic buildings to survive.
>
> "It gives us a little more time," said Jonathan Rosenthal, the city's economic development director.
>
> Councilors plan to introduce the proposed change to the city's statutes Tuesday. A public hearing would be held in early October and final approval would likely come at the Oct. 14 council meeting. (Reprinted with permission of the *Bristol Press*.)

Before attending the meeting, a reporter should discuss with an editor which aspects of the agenda might be most noteworthy. Some local governmental meetings last three to four hours. Everything that is discussed, approved, postponed, or noted might not make it into the paper. A reporter should have an idea of where to focus attention, but still be ready to cover the unexpected reaction or the agenda item that exploded in importance.

Newspaper reporters working for a morning paper might have a deadline before the meeting ends. Reporters have to be prepared to file or send a story in before the important action happens. Print reporters could send electronically or call in a story complete with background. Then right at deadline, they could write the lead of the story with the latest action or information. Broadcast journalists face the same kind of pressure in getting the action on air. Stations will go "live" so reporters can give up-to-the-minute accounts of what has happened.

Figure 6.2 has a meetings checklist that gives tips on what to do at the meeting.

Writing It Up

The lead of the story needs to set up the action that occurred. For example, the town council might vote unanimously to rezone 50 acres south of Middlebury

FIGURE 6.2   Meetings Coverage Checklist

- Get there early.

- Sit close to the elected officials.

- See where everyone is sitting and get names.

- If you are covering a public hearing, check names of people who have signed in to speak, if that is the procedure. Note their backgrounds or affiliation.

- Use a tape recorder to back up notes.

- If necessary, briefly leave the meeting to interview people who are leaving because you might not be able to find them later. Obviously, do not leave during a crucial discussion or vote.

- Be prepared to interview as many people as possible after the meeting but before they leave the site.

- Get follow-up information from council or committee members when the meeting ends. If the meeting is at night (and most meetings are), you might not be able to get up with them the next day before you have to write a story.

- Describe people who spoke, such as the way they talked or what they wore.

- Note other aspects about the meeting, such as standing room only, people hanging around outside, picket lines, or flyers that a group is handing out.

- Figure out crowd estimates.

despite a public hearing at which dozens of residents opposed the rezoning. Your lead might read:

> The Middlebury Town Council voted unanimously Monday night to rezone 50 acres adjacent to Southern Estates, despite outspoken opposition to the rezoning proposal at the council meeting last week.

Avoid using language such as:

> The Middlebury Town Council agreed to vote unanimously . . .

Or

> The Middlebury Town Council met Monday night and voted unanimously . . .

Or

> The Middlebury Town Council decided Monday night to vote unanimously. . . .

If they voted, the members voted and that's the final action. You don't need to say they agreed to vote or decided to vote. The action had to come at a meeting, so noting that aspect is unnecessary. When you write the story, you need to focus on the substance. The main focus might be the vote on an issue, such as the rezoning. The most compelling aspect of the meeting might be conflict or differing opinions during a public hearing or a discussion at a meeting. For example:

> City council member Maryann Jones yelled at fellow council member Anjanette Hartley at Monday night's meeting for her continuing votes against affordable housing, calling Hartley "the greatest un-friend struggling lower-income residents have ever seen in Middlebury.
> "We have had six proposals come before the council to build affordable housing that would be within reach of numerous lower-income citizens," Jones pointed out. "And Council member Hartley has voted against each one. What's the matter with you?"

Personnel issues might lead a story, particularly if the council sets raises for town employees or an employee resigns.

> The Sussex Town Council voted to give town employees a 3 percent raise during the next fiscal year while the town manager and department heads will see 4 to 6 percent increases in their salaries.

Or:

> If, as Caswell Beach commissioner Frank Bausch said, a vote of confidence on his performance as beach commissioner represented a "battle of wills" between him and Mayor Harry Simmons, Bausch was the victor, but not by much.

Of five commissioners, two voted their confidence in Bausch. Three others, including Bausch himself, did not vote. By rules of procedure, those non-votes were recorded as affirmative votes.

Often a reporter has several issues that must be reported in a story. Some editors will want separate stories on each issue. Others will want one longer wrap-up story to cover all the issues. The lead will set up the organization for the story, as in:

The Sussex Town Council voted to give town employees a 3 percent raise during the next fiscal year and also received the resignation of town manager Vincent Rose.
In other action, the council appointed three new members to the planning board and set Friday as the deadline for applications for director of public works.

The reporter sets up the four issues that will be discussed in the story: raises, a resignation, planning board appointments, and an application deadline. The order of the items indicates the order of importance. The reader knows what to expect and can read the entire story or scan to find those items that he wants to know more about. The reporter has set the agenda for the story, listing those issues that she thinks are the most important for the reader. The town manager might have submitted his resignation just before the end of the meeting, but the reporter cannot write the story chronologically. Important information would then be at the end of the story. Town residents will want to know quickly that a favorite town official is leaving.

Often a lead will need to give context rather than only list an action, as in:

A proposed ordinance that would attempt to keep community development in check with local schools' capacities encountered brief opposition Monday at a Washington County commissioners' meeting.
Three years of work has spawned the ordinance, which would require developers to submit a permit to the Washington School Board inquiring whether school facilities have enough classroom space for the potential development's incoming children.
Following input from community residents, the council approved unanimously the ordinance that will go into effect immediately.

Reporters should also include local officials' and local residents' reactions. Quotes can add description, opinion, color, and context to meetings coverage, as shown in council member Maryann Jones's quote earlier. The town manager would be quoted to explain his reasons for resigning.

Many publications, online sites, and television stations include reporters' email addresses so that readers or viewers can respond to stories. They also list government officials and how residents can contact them about issues and concerns.

OTHER CONSIDERATIONS OF LOCAL GOVERNMENT BEATS

No text can cover every aspect that a beginning reporter will face on a beat. But often what goes on at the local level begins somewhere else, such as with the actions of the state or federal government or an event elsewhere.

How State and Federal Actions Affect Local Government

All levels of government—city, county, state, and federal—have a relationship. As noted earlier in the chapter, state legislatures still retain some control over local governmental functions. At the turn of the twentieth century, most local governments raised their own revenues. That has changed. Counties are the primary revenue-producing entities at the local level; that is, they raise taxes that are shared by the cities and the county. But the state and federal governments do provide part of local government budgets, including school budgets.

Federal funding for homeland security shows the interrelationship of federal, state, and local governments. Homeland Security Director Tom Ridge met with mayors in summer 2003 to assure them that states would be required to pass along federal dollars earmarked for local governments' costs for meeting federal requirements for homeland security.

According to the U.S. Conference of Mayors' Web site, Ridge noted that he favored local governments deciding which equipment and security measures, such as metal detectors in governmental buildings, would be best. The federal government funneled funds through the states, which in turn allocated money to local governments. Mayors had complained that their states had not acted with speed.

Ridge said: "If there is a problem with that process, we need to change it. If money's not reaching the cities, that's not the way it's supposed to work," adding that state delays in getting money to local governments could result in states losing their 20 percent share of federal funding. States facing huge budget deficits in 2002–2004 could not afford to lose any dollars. Local reporters needed to keep an eye on that story.

Reporting Local Angles on National Stories

Most news organizations get international and national news from wire services, such as the Associated Press, Reuters, or Gannett News Service. Editors and reporters read trade publications and national news magazines to find out trends and issues in other areas as well as reactions to national news events.

In many cases, reporters will investigate and develop stories they first see on the wires or in other publications to determine whether they can find a local angle. The example of when Homeland Security Director Tom Ridge met with mayors shows how local angles come out of national stories. Each municipality and county government has to comply with the federal homeland security regulations—hence a local angle to that story.

When the blackout of August 2003 shut down power in seven states and parts of Canada, local reporters followed soon after with stories about whether a similar blackout could occur in their cities or counties. Lead after lead in stories from the Associated Press in California to the *Minneapolis Star-Tribune* told readers the likelihood of whether such a blackout could happen in their backyards. For example, this AP lead out of Los Angeles noted:

> There was no risk of the blackout that hit the Northeast Thursday affecting California, officials said.
>
> "Everything is operating normally here," said Tom Boyd, a Southern California Edison spokesman. "We are isolated from this problem."

The lead in a story from the *St. Petersburg Times* (Adair & Hau, 2003) stated:

> Florida is wired into the same power grid as the region crippled by Thursday's massive blackout, but energy experts say the state is less likely to suffer a similar catastrophe.
>
> They say it is less reliant on imported energy than many states, and its robust internal grid withstands frequent lightning and the occasional hurricane without statewide shutdowns.

Enterprising reporters must realize that sometimes what seems to be no story might actually be a story. Local reporters should always be thinking about national and state stories that could affect their communities. Even some international stories could tie into local coverage. Local residents might collect nonperishable food and clothing to aid flood victims in Mexico, a city might adopt a sister city in Russia, or a Hmong community might increase the town's diversity.

GLOSSARY

Advance story: Article that previews activities, discussion, or action expected at an upcoming meeting or event.

Charter: A document similar to a state or the federal Constitution that creates a municipality or county and specifies its powers.

Federal Sunshine Act: Legislation that required about 50 federal agencies, commissions, boards, and councils to meet in public; passed in 1976.

HIPAA: The federal Health Insurance Portability and Accountability Act of 1996; required of all medical offices, whether private or government funded, to tighten policies regarding release of patient records; patients must sign forms that they are aware of what information can be released and what cannot; the signed forms become part of their files at their doctors' offices.

Homeland Security Act: Passed by Congress in the wake of 9/11; establishes guidelines from the federal to state to local law enforcement and emergency personnel about precautions and guidelines to protect the country in the event of another terrorist attack; provides some funding to states and local governments; also established a color-coded alert system that dictates level of security measures.

Special district or authority: Oversees airports, toll roads, ports, utilities such as electricity and gas, or other fee-based services; its budget is generally separate from the local governmental unit, and it is expected to be self-supporting.

ACTIVITIES

1. Look at today's edition of your local newspaper. See how many stories you can identify that are related to local government or local government action. Categorize the stories, for example, city council action, watchdog group opposition, advance story on meetings or public hearings, follow-up story to city council action, and so forth.

2. Go to your city or town's official Web site. Look at the list of committees and boards that have an advisory or policy-making role to the city council. How many did you count? If you attended all the meetings of these boards and committees, how many meetings would you cover each week? Each month? How can you get information from those meetings without having to attend them?

3. Invite a local reporter who covers city or county government to class. Have the reporter outline how he or she learned the beat. Who are his or her best sources? How did he or she cultivate sources? What are the top three issues? What are other tips for covering the beat? For covering other town boards, commissions, or committee meetings?

4. Get an agenda for an upcoming city or town council or county commissioners meeting. Check the local government's Web site for minutes of previous meetings that might relate to items on the agenda. Make sure you have a list of the elected officials who will be at the meeting. Arrange for the city or county manager or one of the elected officials to come to class and review what will be up for vote or discussion at the meeting. Have the manager outline the meeting structure and provide any other background to prepare you for the meeting.

5. After the preparation in Activity 4, attend the meeting. Arrange in advance for either the council or county commission member or the manager who came to class to be available for questions afterward. In class and before writing, discuss possible stories from the meeting. Should topics be divided into several stories, or can the entire meeting be covered in one story? Write at least one story.

6. Based on actions in the meeting you covered, develop an angle for a follow-up story. Make a list of sources. Write the story using the meeting actions as background.

7. Assign each student in the class to a local government beat: city, county, social services board, health department, special authority such as airport or water and

sewer board, and so on. Have the student develop a beat report that would include the following:

- An overall description of the beat (e.g., I am covering social services that provides assistance to low-income residents. Assistance ranges from food stamps to teen pregnancy prevention programs to health care).
- Who the major players are and the roles they play.
- Where the money comes from (e.g., social services gets funds from the county, state, and federal governments).
- When and where the policy-making boards meet. When and where agendas for the meetings are available.
- What the important/interesting issues on the beat have been in the past few months. Use as a source stories that have been written; start a clip file for the beat.
- How to keep track of what's happening on the beat.
- List written sources (at least five) in addition to media.
- Other than the policy-making group, the other organizations that relate to the beat (e.g., a local group that monitors the town's tax rate).
- List at least two ideas for beat stories.

RESOURCES AND WEB SITES

Investigative Reporters and Editors: www.ire.org. Resources, training, stories showing how to do investigative projects.

International City/County Management Association: www.icma.org. Has huge "links" section to local government sites.

National Association of Counties: www.naco.org. Provides information on counties nationally, helpful "model county" database.

National Association of State Budget Officers: www.nasbo.org. Has information and training on state and local budgets.

National League of Cities: www.nlc.org. A lobbying agency with links ranging from policy to homeland security issues.

State and local government on the Internet: www.statelocalgov.net. Links to all state Web sites, also with links to state offices, county Web sites, and many city Web sites.

U.S. Conference of Mayors: www.usmayors.org. Business-oriented site is helpful when researching the role of local leadership.

REFERENCES

Adair, B., & Hau, L. (2003, August 15). Northeast blackout: Officials say Florida system more resilient. *St. Petersburg Times.* http://209.157.64.200/focus/f-news/964972/posts.

Bean, B. (2003, August 15). *A reporter's guide to covering city hall.* Atlanta: Georgia Municipal Association.

Bell, A. F. , II, & Wicker, W. J. (1998). *County government in North Carolina* (4th ed.). Chapel Hill, NC: Institute of Government, University of North Carolina at Chapel Hill.

Bhatt, S. (2003, August 23). Nickels to meet school finalists. *Seattle Times.* http://seattletimes.nwsource.com/html/localnews/2001597439_mayors23m.html.

Carroll, T. (2003, September 4). Formal approval? That's not my way of doing things, Harry. *State Port* (NC) *Pilot.* www.stateportpilot.com/stories/caswell.html.

Collins, S. (2003, September 5). Council eyes plan to delay demolition of historic buildings. *Bristol Press.* www.bristolpress.com/site/news.cfm?newsid=10116948&BRD=1643& PAG=461&dept_id=10486&rfi=6.

Dennison, M. (2003, August 28). NorthWestern offers utility aid for needy. *Great Falls Tribune.* www.greatfallstribune.com/news/stories/20030828/localnews/144988.html.

Dow Jones newsletter launches weekly newsletter covering energy law and industry oversight. (2003, June 24). BusinessWire. www.businesswire.com/webbox/bw.062403/231755498.htm.

Government Organization. (2002, December). 2002 Census of Governments, Vol. 1, No. 1. Retrieved July 24, 2003, from www.census.gov/prod/2003pubs/gc021x1.pdf.

Harris, J., Leiter, K., & Johnston, S. (1992). *The complete reporter: Fundamentals of news gathering, writing and editing* (6th ed.). New York: Macmillan.

Investigative Reporters and Editors. (2003, August 26). How to cover the blackout. www.ire.org/inthenews_archive/blackout.html.

Inyo County Planning Department. (2003, August 26). www.sdsc.edu/Inyo/planning.html.

Lawrence, D. M., & Wicker, W. J. (1995). *Municipal government in North Carolina.* Chapel Hill, NC: Institute of Government. University of North Carolina at Chapel Hill.

Lee, M. (2003, August 27). Port told to change its focus. *Sacramento Bee.* www.sacbee.com/content/business/story/7303594p-8248142c.html.

National League of Cities. (2003a, May 27). Cities raise fees and taxes, cut projects and staff to deal with increasing fiscal squeeze. [News Release]. www.nlc.org/nlc_org/site/newsroom/nations_cities_weekly/display.cfm?id=9E4EC88F-1639-453C-951CE56E55776B13.

National League of Cities (2003b, June). Demographic change in small cities, 1990–2000. [Research brief on America's cities.] www.nlc.org.

Orsini-Meinhard, K. (2003, August 27). Developers pullout big blow to Windsor. *Coloradoan.* www.coloradoan.com/news/stories/20030827/news/138148.html.

Randall, M. (2003, August 28). Providence manager fitting right in. *Herald-Journal.* http://hjnews.townnews.com.

Scott, L. (2003, August 28). Solar subdivision is a 1st. *Arizona Business Gazette.* www.azcentral.com/abgnews/articles/0828solar28.html.

Spence, W. (2003, August 28). Mall zoning request submitted. *Daily Inter Lake.* www.dailyinterlake.com/NewsEngine/SelectStory_AD.tpl?command=search&db=news.db&eqskudata=49-816522-66.

State Electricity Profile. (2003). Investigative Reporters and Editors. www.eia.doe.gov/cneaf/electricity/st_profiles/toc.html.

2002 Census of Governments Report. (2003, July). www.census.gov/govs/cog/2002COGprelim_report.pdf.

Veiga, A. (2003, August 14). California electrical grid not affected by Northeast blackout. *Sacramento Bee.* www.sacbee.com/content/news/story/7221772p-8167108c.html.

Woodell, J. (2003, June). Major factors affecting America's cities. National League of Cities' Municipalities in Transition Project. www.nlc.org/nlc_org/site/files/reports/major.pdf.

Yucca Mountain year's top story. (2002, December 27). *Las Vegas Sun.* www.lasvegassun.com/sunbin/stories/text/2002/dec/27/514440668.html.

CHAPTER 7

FINANCING LOCAL GOVERNMENT

A reporter for a campus newspaper learns that the university is considering a sizable contribution to the town to support free bus service for all riders, including university employees and students. The reporter is curious how the town's bus service is funded and whether the university's seemingly large contribution is justified. But she has never looked at a city government budget and has no idea where to find figures on transportation revenues and costs.

A reporter assigned to cover a local government agency—or most any organization—will have to write about money at some point. Most reporters do not like to cover budgets and write budget stories because they do not want to deal with the numbers. All budgets contain columns of dollar figures that show income and expenditures. Budgets have their own language and terminology, which can be daunting. Reporters fear that they won't be able to make sense out of the columns of numbers or understand financial jargon such as revenues, fund balance, disbursements, debt service, and the like.

The reporter's greatest challenge is understanding what all the numbers mean. That understanding is essential if reporters are to explain the numbers and their impact. Reporters must interview officials and experts who can translate the figures in simple and tangible terms. Reporters also must seek people outside of government to add a balanced voice to any story.

The advantage of covering government finances over a private company's finances is access to information. Government agencies must make their budgets public under state public record statutes, as discussed in Chapter 2, and generally the budget process is conducted out in the open at public meetings as well.

In covering any financial story, reporters must recognize that money is power. Elected officials might try to use or manipulate that power to get services or programs for their respective constituents or to promote their political careers. Reporters must be attuned to official language and hidden agendas when interviewing officials or reading their assessment of government spending.

The power game also can lead to conflict. Conflict can arise from the very nature of the budget: Someone, such as taxpayers, or some agency has to

127

put money in, and someone is making a decision about how that money is spent. The money provider, let's say a taxpayer, might not agree with the money spender, a town council, for example. Many town council meetings over budget matters have become antagonistic—and have resulted in lively coverage for reporters.

In this chapter you will:

- Find definitions for budget terminology,
- Learn how local governments finance day-to-day operations and construction projects,
- Follow the budget-making process,
- Get leads on where to find budget stories,
- Learn what goes into budget stories, and
- Become more comfortable with using budgets as sources of information.

COVERING THE BUDGET

When it comes to government financing, the annual budget is the single most important document. A budget is more than just an accounting of where funds come from and how they are spent. Within that one document is the outline or blueprint of how a city, town, county, or governmental unit, such as a school district, operates. How officials choose to spend money is a reflection of philosophy, policies, and priorities. Reporters can also find the salaries of top officials who make the budget decisions.

Every agency or organization has a process for developing its annual operating budget. In addition to the operating budget that covers daily expenses, a government unit usually has a capital budget to pay for equipment, buildings, or other items that are one-time expenses or nonrecurring. State laws might outline the process, including the mandate that a local government's budget be balanced. A budget is not balanced if estimated revenues do not match estimated expenses. Anyone who follows national news, however, often hears that the federal government's budget is not balanced. Joseph S. Ferrell, professor at the School of Government at the University of North Carolina at Chapel Hill, notes (2003):

> The real difference between federal budgets and state or local budgets is that it is very easy for the federal government to borrow money to balance its budget. It is very difficult for state and local governments to borrow (*money*) because most state constitutions require voter approval for debt incurrence.

Not every budget will have the same revenues or expenditures. Most city or county budgets will include revenues or income from certain taxes or fees and expenditures such as personnel, construction, or debt payments.

Some services might be covered by one government agency but not by others. For example, counties generally administer social services programs, whereas cities can operate utility companies. To cover the budget process thoroughly, reporters must know what programs a particular governmental body oversees. Those responsibilities are discussed in Chapter 6 and might be set out in a state constitution. Reporters must know and understand how money is collected and spent. And they must know the terminology that budget officers and managers use to describe what's in the budget document.

The Budget Process

Each governmental unit spends money, but not all can levy taxes or set user fees to raise money. Some governmental bodies are dependent on others to raise their income. In Texas individual school boards can levy taxes. In North Carolina, about two-thirds of school district funds come from the state and federal governments and another portion from county property tax and sales tax revenues. No matter where their funding comes from, however, governments have to set budgets.

Government agencies have specific timetables for developing their budgets. Reporters must know when each agency's fiscal year begins and ends and the time line for the budget process. The fiscal year is the 12-month period in which revenues are raised and expended. Budgeting is a year-round process, but the public view of the budgeting process usually begins four to six months before officials actually approve the budget. For agencies that operate on a July 1 to June 30 fiscal year, the budget process is well under way in January. Some local governments, such as Colorado Springs, Colorado, operate on a fiscal year that parallels the calendar year, January 1 to December 31. The public phase of its budgeting process will begin during the preceding summer. Most governments will post on their Web sites the timetable for the budget process.

In the first step in the budget process, individual departments assess their financial needs for the coming fiscal year. Most governments have long-range goals that come into play during budget times. For example, the police chief might decide that she needs four additional police officers at a cost of $160,000. The town has a long-range goal of strengthening public safety. The parks and recreation department needs $75,000 to renovate and upgrade town soccer fields, a move that fits with the town council's promise of improving recreational sites. Or the school board might allocate $425,000 for adding broadband cable to the high schools as part of its commitment to convert the schools to high-tech campuses.

Once department heads have their budgets completed, they send their requests to the city, county, or school financial or budget officer for review. The lead governmental administrator, such as the city or county manager or school superintendent, might also get a copy at this time. The finance or budget officer—or in a smaller operating system, the top administrator—then has the daunting task of assessing each request. Most governmental units cannot take all wish lists, add up the total, and then increase budget revenues each year to do all that's needed or wanted. At this stage, cutting, wheedling, and dickering take place. The city manager will meet with each department head to determine just what is essential to maintain town services and possibly improve them. Or the schools' budget officer will determine a priority list for funding requests.

After the departmental meetings, the administrator draws up a proposed budget that includes anticipated income and expenses and shares it with elected officials. More tweaking might occur in work sessions before a draft is ready for public comment. Then the city council will set public hearings at which residents can support, oppose, or offer changes. In this high-tech age, some local governments have solicited public comment via Web sites or email. Residents can also watch budget deliberations on local access cable channels. School boards, too, will follow a similar process of work sessions and public hearings to get residents' ideas and opinions.

After the public hearings, the governmental body will vote on the budget, including any tax or fee increases or decreases for the coming year. In some cases, a budget is not approved before the fiscal year starts. The governmental legislative body can adopt a continuing resolution to allow money to be spent while budget negotiations roll on. In regard to local governments missing the budget deadline, Ferrell (2003) from the UNC-CH School of Government said: "No harm is done unless a pay day rolls around before adoption. Other bills just go unpaid."

Reporters must follow all steps of the budget process, and year to year they might notice a pattern in how a particular governing board proceeds, for example, whether it continuously misses budget deadlines. As departments are determining their needs, reporters are writing stories about how those departments are faring in the current fiscal year, for example:

> Additional state budget cuts have forced University administrators to take another 1 percent reduction in operating revenues throughout the campus, and several deans noted Tuesday any more cuts will mean laying off employees.
> The cuts came as the University prepared its budget proposal for the coming fiscal year, and University administrators feared that some programs might face the budget ax if mid-year cuts become a common practice.

When initial budget projections are released, reporters write about cuts, increases, impact on services, and other issues. For example:

> The Board of Education has proposed a record $34.2 million budget that board members say is essential for the school system to meet federal mandates in the No Child Left Behind Act.

This year six out of eight schools did not meet the guidelines set out in the act, and administrators have requested additional funds to hire teachers and reduce classroom size so they can meet the criteria laid out in the Bush administration's effort to improve education.

When the public comments, reporters are there to hear and record.

More than 100 Leesville residents crammed into the small county commissioners' meeting room Monday night to protest the proposed budget that includes additional revenue from the expected annexation of the community south of Harrisburg.

"We live in the county and not in the city because we don't want to pay higher taxes," said Wilbur Norton, who lives in the house where his parents were born. "It's not fair to plan to annex our community just so the city can get more money from property taxes and other fees."

And when the final budget is approved and tax rates are set, reporters tell the community.

The Town Council approved late Thursday night a budget for the coming fiscal year that holds taxes at the same rate but still has money for a modest pay increase for town employees and for town park improvements.

"The completion of the South Hills Mall added enough commercial space to our tax base that we have enough revenue to increase the budget for some special needs but not raise taxes," said City Manager Linda Howell.

Where in the Budget to Find Stories

When the proposed budget is released, the reporter's first stop should be the administrator's letter or statement at the beginning of the budget. That section is a gold mine to see in what areas the budget will grow or shrink, what revenues will change, and whether a tax increase will be needed to fund growth. The letter might even note that because revenues increased in some areas, a tax decrease is recommended for the next year. The administrator's letter will summarize what happened with the budget in the current fiscal year, the agency's fiscal health, and where the budget is headed in the next fiscal year. The administrator might even comment on the well-being of the state and national economies and their effect on the community and its finances. Some of those comments might be stories in themselves.

John Link, county manager in Orange County, North Carolina, responded critically in his 2003 budget message after the state withheld sales tax reimbursements to counties so the state could ease its budget woes. The state collects sales tax, or the amount per dollar charged on consumer purchases, and returns a portion to the counties each quarter. North Carolina, like many other states in recent years, has faced huge budget shortfalls. North Carolina's deficit in fiscal year 2003 was close to $1 billion. Governor Mike Easley decided not to return sales tax revenues to counties to give the state more income. County Manager Link in his budget message noted:

> As outrageous as this seizure of county funds may be, we have realistically and conservatively assumed loss of these funds in our calculations of available fund balance for next year. . . . My proposed budget includes funding of about $3.1 million from State reimbursements owed to us. While doubtlessly unrealistic, that assumption is intended to send a clear message to Raleigh [*where the Legislature meets*]—that it is wrong and unacceptable for the State to seize funds that rightfully should come to the citizens of Orange County.

Such strong language is definitely the basis for a news story about how local government administrators feel about the state's budget constraints and the impact on local government. Reporters should also probe how local governments will replace withheld revenues or whether they will reduce services to keep their budgets balanced.

National events can also affect local government finances. In 2003 here's what Colorado Springs City Manager Lorne C. Kramer wrote:

> Although the terrorist attacks of September 11, 2001, had a definite impact on the economy, most economic indicators showed a slowing prior to that event. The national, State and local economies continue to feel the effects of a lingering recession that began early in 2001. This unfavorable economic climate has had an adverse impact on City revenues, which we anticipate will continue through 2003.

Kramer noted sales tax and use tax collections had dropped, and during the 2002–2003 fiscal year, Colorado Springs started a selective hiring freeze, froze all overtime pay except for emergency reasons, and suspended all capital improvement projects. Anticipating another shortfall, Kramer warned that the next fiscal year budget would include sacrifices, such as trimming less essential services and postponing new equipment purchases. The changes were necessary to avoid laying off significant numbers of city employees.

Such statements are helpful to reporters in determining trends, new ventures, the status of the town's fiscal health, and other topics. The city manager's summary might note a modest pay increase for town employees, a transfer of funds or the use of the fund balance (equivalent to a savings account) to cover essential services, or a delay in renovating city hall. The summary puts into words the columns of numbers that the budget contains and helps reporters determine what stories need to be written.

Also within the budget document will be summaries before each department's budget figures. Department heads will note what services will be added or deleted, which goals from the previous year were reached and which were not, and other specific points related to the department and its budget. Again, such discussions put numbers into words and language that reporters can understand and use as a starting point to develop stories. Reporters should also consider departmental budgets vis-à-vis the local government's philosophy and priorities. Are designated areas of importance getting the dollars needed to do the job? Why or why not? In Maryland, for example, state job cuts one year laid off the person in charge of keeping the Maryland terrapin (the real turtle not the university's mascot) from going extinct. The *Baltimore Sun* did a story just about that employee.

In Every Budget Story

Every budget story is different as officials go through the process of getting a budget balanced and approved. But in writing any budget story, reporters must be sure that basic information is covered. Every budget story should note the current year's budget in dollars and the projected year's budget amount. Based on the current fiscal year's figures, reporters should note the proposed increase or decrease in dollars and percent of the existing budget. They could even put the numbers in an Excel spreadsheet and make sure the government budget adds up correctly.

All stories need to include the effect on residents. That impact needs to be translated into tangible terms. It doesn't work to tell citizens that the budget is 7 percent higher than last year or that town employees will get a 2.5 percent pay increase. Readers or viewers need to know how that translates in dollars and cents: Seven percent might be $1.75 million higher while a 2.5 percent raise translates to $600 for the average employee earning $24,000 a year.

Sometimes budget changes can be simply translated into how a tax rate increase will affect the owner of a house valued at $100,000, the sample most reporters seem to choose. In some communities, the average house might cost twice that amount, and reporters should note the effect based on the average housing cost in their communities. If town officials vote to charge for certain permits for the first time or raise fines for parking tickets, residents need to know the exact amounts.

The first story that announces the proposed budget is the most important because it is the first look that taxpayers have at what they can expect for the coming year. That story shows the government's fiscal health. The reporter obviously will include the information mentioned here as well as the percentage increase or decrease in the budget overall, departmental changes and which departments have the greatest increases or decreases, and specific changes in taxes or user fees.

Residents want to know how the budget will affect their pocketbooks and their quality of life, and they will want to hear those explanations from town officials. Budget stories should include the time line for approving the budget and when citizens can voice their reactions.

Reporters should determine what parts of the budget are important to their audiences and write the stories in human terms. If the school board adopts a budget that is not sufficient to hire custodial help, parents need to know.

> Although the students in Barbara Evans' first-grade class are pretty good about cleaning up, she admits that she still spends about 20 minutes every day straightening and ordering the room for the next day.
>
> Next school year, though, she'll be doing even more. The Middlebury Board of Education adopted Monday night the next fiscal year budget that reduces the custodial help at each of the system's eight schools. That means teachers like Evans will be emptying trash, sweeping floors, and doing light housekeeping chores three days a week.
>
> "Every year it seems that teachers have to pick up something that is not related to academics," Evans said. "Having a tidy classroom is important to learning."

Resources beyond the Budget Itself

Reporter Dave Herzog developed twenty tips to covering a municipal budget for staff at the *Providence* (RI) *Journal-Bulletin* (1998b). His tips can work with any budget. See them in Figure 7.1.

Herzog also suggested documents that can help reporters who write about budgets. Among them are the following:

■ **Annual reports.** Herzog notes that towns (or counties or school boards) might publish annual reports, what he called the "feel-good document," describing the positive aspects. Local governments use annual reports as a summary of the year's accomplishments. In some communities the reports are published in local media as a supplement.

■ **Audited financial statements.** State laws might require local governments to be audited, and the auditors' reports will describe deficits, litigation, and any other problems. A management letter will tell how and why a problem occurred and any proposed remedies. Reporters should monitor a board's progress in making those changes.

■ **Bond official statements.** These statements are prepared when a town, school district, or county plans to issue bonds to borrow money. The statement includes town demographics and "helps investors in deciding whether to invest in the bonds," Herzog noted.

■ **Credit reports.** Issued by firms such as Moody's and Standard & Poor's, the reports analyze the financial condition of the local government.

Some reporters use spreadsheets to look at specific budget items. They can put in budget data and analyze departmental increases and decreases. Or they will get experts to look at parts of the budget to detect changes or problems.

FIGURE 7.1   Dan Herzog: One Reporter's Tips for Covering Budgets

1. Break out of the mindset that a budget is a dry collection of numbers that you report on a couple of times during the financial season. Remember that it is a document that charts your town's plan for the coming year and reflects the political values of the people who put it together.

2. Approach the budget and town financial reporting as a cycle that unfolds during the year. As you do the event-driven stories, keep an eye open for possible enterprise stories.

3. Look at the bottom lines. If spending is greater than income, your town will run a deficit.

4. Look for stories you can do before the budget is released. For example, you can analyze the budgets from the past five or ten years and discover trends that are important to readers.

5. Always adjust for inflation when looking at budgets over time. This will save you from making the embarrassing mistake of writing that spending has doubled in your town. The best way to adjust for inflation is by using the Consumer Price Index (CPI). The formula for adjusting 1988 spending to 1998 dollars would be: (1988 amount × 1998 CPI) / 1988 CPI. In the example below, you can see that what looks like a 50 percent rise over the past decade really is a 5.7 percent rise. (The CPI is available on the U.S. Bureau of Labor Statistics Web site.)

1988	$1,000,000
1988 adjusted	$1,418,624
1998	$1,500,000
CPI 1988	119.2
CPI 1998	169.1
Real difference	$81,375.8
Real change	5.7%

6. Put your budget-day stories into context by telling readers whether taxes will go up and by how much. Illustrate by showing what would happen to the tax bill of a "typical" property.

7. Make budget day stories meaningful for readers by telling them what services they're going to be getting or losing. Find out who are the winners and losers.

8. Reduce clutter in your stories by taking some of your numbers out and putting them into graphics.

9. Get wish lists from department heads and check to see whether their priorities got into the budget. If not, what are the implications?

10. Pick one interesting or unusual part of the budget and write about it sometime during the budget cycle. Tell readers something they didn't know before.

11. Look at independent audits. These documents cast a cold eye on a town's spending and show what really happened in a fiscal year. Look for deficits in all the funds—not just the general fund.

12. Check whether the budgeters are moving functions into enterprise funds. These funds are supposed to pay for themselves and cover government functions that you can measure. An example: providing water service.

(continued)

FIGURE 7.1   Continued

---

13. Read the management letters in the audits. There's where you will find criticism of the town's policies and practices.

14. Read credit reports and bond official statements. The bond official statements will report, in gory detail, the financial condition of the town and possible risks to investors. The credit reports, available from ratings agencies (Moody's and Standard & Poor's), do a nice job of outlining a town's finances in clear terms.

15. Learn how to use a spreadsheet and use it to analyze your budgets.

16. Get reports from the Rhode Island Public Expenditure Council and read them. They contain useful information about town finances and taxation. (While this suggestion is specific to Rhode Island, you can find in your state similar agencies that monitor local government finance.)

17. If your town has big year-end surpluses, ask why. They might say it's from conservative fiscal practices. It might be because they are intentionally asking for money in the budget and not spending it.

18. Look to see if the town is setting aside money for legal fees and settlements. If that's happening, the town may be planning to close a lawsuit by settling with a plaintiff.

19. Find out whether municipal contracts are set to expire. If the town is negotiating contracts, what effect will these contracts have on the budget (and vice versa)?

20. Remember that the budget is a living document that has application year-round. Keep it on your desk and refer to it often.

Ferrell from the UNC-CH School of Government said close analysis can help reporters determine whether a local governmental body might run a deficit. A deficit budget can be concealed by inflating revenue estimates. He advised comparing revenue estimates for the projected year's budget with current revenues and question any that seem unrealistic or out of line.

Reporters should also find out the basis of accounting in their communities, Ferrell said. Is the method cash, accrual, or a combination of the two? Ferrell (2003) explained:

> A cash-basis budget forecasts only actual receipts and expenditures. An accrual budget forecasts income that the town is entitled to receive (whether it actually materializes or not) and expenses that it owes (whether actually paid or not).

A local government might base too much of its revenue projections on funds it expects to receive. If funds do not come in as expected, a deficit can occur. The same scenario would occur if an unemployed college student bought a car and expected her parents to pay the car loan. If the parents renege, the student has no income to pay the loan.

Who's Who in the Budget Process

The primary players in local government budgets are the top administrators such as the county or city manager or the school superintendent, as discussed in local government structure in Chapter 6. Your best source will be whoever has the responsibility of developing the draft budget, working with elected officials, and overseeing spending. That person could be a city manager, a finance officer, or both. Other key players follow.

■ **Individual department heads or directors.** They know firsthand their departments' needs. During the fiscal year, reporters should check with department directors to see whether funding levels are adequate to carry out services or if concerns arise. Employees can also be sources, especially in years of service cuts or few or no pay raises. Reporters have to be sensitive to employees' willingness to talk, however, if they fear consequences from their boss. Employee union representatives also might be willing to talk.

■ **Directors of special authorities or boards.** Some communities have airport authorities, bridge or highway boards, or other agencies that oversee special uses. Each might have some role in raising and spending money. Reporters need to know how those agencies relate to one another and which ones are dependent on others for revenue. For example, the airport authority might get funds from the county as well as from the two largest cities in the county. Reporters should look carefully at these authorities, their financial health, and their relationships to the primary government. A city budget might look healthy if money-losing functions are shifted into special authorities, noted Ferrell of the UNC-CH School of Government.

■ **Elected officials.** They must maintain and often expand services at the same time they hold the line on taxes and fees. They must be responsive to citizens, who in turn will decide whether the officials are reelected. Public hearings on budget proposals can be battlegrounds between residents who want improvements, such as bicycle paths, and city council members who are trying to offset lower revenues and to avoid raising property taxes. Reporters should develop a list of full-time government officials who have a financial role.

■ **Watchdog organizations.** Reporters should also be aware of local watchdog organizations that keep an eye on tax rates and services. Every community has one, and some statewide organizations monitor trends that affect local communities. Such sources can provide a different, though often prejudicial, look at how money is collected and spent. Elected officials might be sensitive to their viewpoints, depending on how many votes each organization controls in the next election.

■ **Auditors.** When they review budgets, they can explain why a municipality or school board is having problems. Reporters should find out if state laws require a review of local government finances. Audits might be investigative, that is, requested because of suspected problems, or performance audits conducted on a routine basis.

■ **Governmental groupies.** Every community has people who are extremely interested in local politics and actions. They attend all city council, school board, or county commission meetings. They follow board actions and can provide a context and valuable information to new reporters. Of course, reporters must recognize any bias, such as an antigrowth sentiment, on the part of these governmental hangers-on. Reporters must guard against using these people as sources too frequently because they are easy to find. Reporters also need to look for people who are affected but who are not so vocal. Visiting community centers or senior centers might be one way to find "average citizens."

■ **State officials.** Reporters should also put state officials on their source lists in covering local government finance. Certain state agencies assist cities and counties when they want to finance construction. A few states such as Maryland and North Carolina have institutes or organizations that advise local government officials. Individual state associations of county commissioners, education officials, and city officials plus their national equivalents can assist reporters who have questions about how a specific local government's budget compares to another similar unit. Thousands of local government sites can be accessed through www.statelocalgov.net.

REVENUE, OR WHERE THE MONEY COMES FROM

Local governments collect money from many sources. For cities and counties, the largest chunk of funding generally comes from property taxes and sales tax. They also get money from user fees paid when residents use recreation facilities or pay fines for overdue library books; special taxes such as a tax on hotel and motel rooms; state and federal governments; special assessments, such as for water and sewer or for education; utility fees; availability fees charged when new construction taps into a service, such as water or sewer; and even interest on what's in their bank accounts.

Each state differs in the types and amount of taxes and fees its local governments collect. In some states, local governments often depend on state resources and legislators' largesse for part of their income. They have to get permission from their state legislatures to charge special taxes or fees, such as an entertainment tax on event tickets sold at a sports arena. Some states started instituting control over local governments' budgets after the Depression in the late 1930s to ensure that local units would not be in default. Reporters must be familiar with the income sources for the particular governmental unit they cover and understand the relationship between local governments and state government. Let's look at some of the taxes that provide revenue for local governments.

Property Tax As a Primary Revenue Source

Property tax is based on value of real property, that is, buildings and land, in a community. Some states also tax personal property, such as cars and boats. All the taxable real property is called the tax base, that is, the sum total or value of the taxable property in a county or geographical unit. As the property appreciates, or increases in value—as real estate generally does—the tax base of the county increases or becomes richer. The more rural and less developed a county, the less it will collect from property tax and the more dependent it might be on outside sources, such as federal aid, to fund services. School systems that depend on property tax for revenue might suffer if they operate in poor districts. The primary beneficiaries of property taxes will be the county, municipalities, and school districts.

Counties assess property values on a regular basis. Assessors use complex techniques to determine the assessed valuation or tax value of each residence and business within the county. New valuations—often higher—are sent to property owners, who can contest a valuation that they consider incorrect. In North Carolina, counties must reassess property values at least every eight years. Many states reassess more often than that. That process is called reevaluation.

Some states set property taxes at a cent amount per $100 valuation. If the tax rate is 65 cents per $100 valuation, a person who has a house valued at $220,000 will pay $1,430 a year (do the math: 220,000/100 = 2200 × .65 = 1,430). Other governments use a mill or one-thousandth of a dollar and expressed as $1 per $1,000. In a story about Michigan's special education tax that is set in mills and collected by the state, *Kalamazoo Gazette* writer Craig McCool (2003) explained the tax this way:

> "People will see an increase of 5 mills on their tax bill for the state education tax," said Kalamazoo City Treasurer Wade Carlson. "They will also then notice a 5-mill decrease on their winter tax bill."
>
> One mill is $1 of tax for every $1,000 of taxable value. A house with a market value of $100,000 and a taxable value of $50,000 would pay $250 on a five-mill levy.

In addition to residential property, local governments also tax commercial property, such as office buildings, malls, individual businesses, or retail stores. A substantial commercial tax base can reduce a local government's dependency on residential owners for property tax income. Often county or city officials will set up economic development offices and heavily recruit business development to increase the commercial tax base. For example, Boise, Idaho, city government has been heavily marketing an industrial park along Interstate 84 to attract businesses and jobs. When businesses locate there, Boise's commercial tax base will increase. The city possibly could reduce its tax rate and still generate the same level of income. Or it could keep the same rate and have more income to spend on city services. See how that works in Figure 7.2.

FIGURE 7.2   How Tax Base Affects Tax Rate

- At a tax rate of 65 cents per $100, a city's commercial tax base of $100 million produces $650,000 (100,000,000/100 = 1,000,000 × .65 = $650,000).
- If the commercial tax base increases to $102 million, the city needs a tax rate of 63.7 cents to generate about the same income (102,000,000/100 = 1,020,000 × .637 = $649,740).
- If the city kept the tax rate the same while the tax base increased, the city would bring in $663,000 with the higher commercial tax base.

As part of learning intergovernmental relationships and covering budgets, reporters need to know who collects local property taxes. Counties might collect property tax for themselves, special districts, and small municipalities. Larger cities might collect their own taxes.

In theory, everyone pays property tax in one way or another. College students might own a condominium and, thereby, pay property tax as owners. But if they rent that condominium and the town raises property taxes, the owner will need more money to cover the higher taxes. As a result, the condominium renters might see their monthly rent go up to cover the owner's higher property tax bill. University students who shop on Main Street might pay slightly higher prices for pizza or T-shirts if the store owners are paying higher commercial property tax bills.

Sales Tax Depends on Consumer Spending

Sales tax also brings in money for counties as well as for cities and municipalities. Sales tax is set at cents per dollar spending, such as four cents for every dollar spent added in as sales tax. Not every state has a sales tax. In some states, such as Mississippi and Rhode Island, the state sales tax can be twice as high as the rate in other states such as Colorado and Virginia. Some states collect sales tax on food, while others do not because officials believe such taxes are regressive or they do not tax items that are necessary for survival. The tax unfairly penalizes lower-income people, they say.

Local governments get authority from state legislatures to charge a sales tax in addition to what the state rate might be. For example in Colorado, local governmental units can add up to 5 cents above the 2.9-cent state rate. In Nevada the state sales tax is 6.5 cents, but local governments can tack on 7.5 cents more. The additional tax rate can vary county to county. One county might charge 2.5 cents additional sales tax, while the neighboring county might set its rate at 2 cents per dollar.

States collect the sales tax and then return a portion to the counties or other governmental units. As noted earlier in this chapter, in 2003 the state of North Carolina withheld sales tax payments to counties to help balance its state budget. That created deficits for local governments across the state. Such action by the state shows local governments' dependency on outside sources for revenue. When that revenue stream is pulled, cities and counties are hurt, which in turn affects services to local residents.

The more dependent a local government is on sales tax, the more it is affected during a recession. Reporters should pay attention to sales tax and the effect an economic downturn can have on local governmental budgets. When consumers buy fewer items, sales tax collections decline, and government at all levels suffers.

In Georgia, school boards and local governments can ask voters to approve a Special Purpose Local Option Sales Tax, affectionately known as SPLOST. If approved, the tax stays in effect for a set number of years or until the amount is raised. For example, Clayton County, Georgia, put before the voters in fall 2003 a SPLOST of $240 million for five years to raise funds for road improvements, including sidewalks, overhead pedestrian walkways, and recreational facilities. The SPLOST would remain for five years or until $240 million had been raised, whichever came first. The SPLOST was critical to all Clayton County departments because without the sales tax funds for road repairs, the commissioners would have to take money from each department's budget to cover the costs. That would mean fewer books for the library, for example, or the inability to renovate some buildings to make them handicapped accessible. Voters approved the SPLOST, thereby agreeing to higher taxes to keep and improve services.

User Fees Pay Their Way

Local governments can set user fees that are charged to residents and even nonresidents for using services. For example, a community swimming pool might charge $2 each time a city resident wants to swim but $3 for a noncity resident. A city might require hotels and motels to collect a room tax each night a room is occupied. The county charges when residents dump trash at the landfill, apply for a marriage license, or sell property. The county might also require residents to get licenses annually for each cat or dog they own or charge them if they use the county's emergency medical transport service. City and county planning departments charge for building inspections. City or county libraries charge fines for overdue books, videos, or other loaned materials. City or county-managed airports charge airlines landing fees to use runways and taxi up to terminals.

Although these fees do not bring in huge amounts of money in some communities, they do support the cost of providing the services. In Boise, Idaho, user fees are expected to bring in 38 percent of the city's revenue in fiscal year 2005 compared to 34 percent from property tax.

Proponents of user fees support the notion that whoever uses the service pays. For example, a city recreation department would charge fees for summer camp programs that would cover the cost of hiring personnel and buying supplies. The fees stay within the department or unit that assesses and collects them rather than going into a general fund, or the pot of money that pays day-to-day operating expenses.

Local governments aren't the only ones that rely on income from user fees. One that motorists often find is a toll on roads and bridges, an effort monitored by statewide road or bridge authorities. For years, the state of Virginia charged tolls on Interstate 95. At that time, for example, a Georgia resident who drove to Washington, DC, passed through several tollbooths and deposited change from Colonial Heights through Richmond. Legislators set the tolls on certain highways and bridges to recoup or pay for the cost of highway construction. Once the state has paid the debt, the toll booths might come down. Or the state might use the tolls to have a continuous revenue stream.

Debate has surfaced more and more over user fees as state and federal contributions to local governments have decreased. Critics claim that fees are actually taxes disguised as user fees. An example is impact fees that local governments collect to offset the cost of expanded services needed because of growth. Impact fees are often associated with school systems, which need more classrooms and buildings to handle additional students as neighborhoods are built or expanded. The impact fee is a one-time payment that goes through the developer to the school system and is usually paid at the time the house is sold. Some people, however, contend these fees are actually taxes rather than user fees because all residents pay them, regardless of whether they have school-aged children.

Critics of user fees also contend that they can be regressive; that is, they affect people who do not have the ability to pay and might prevent equal access. Low-income residents who could not afford to join a health club also could not be expected to pay the $300 fee for a week at a school system–sponsored summer camp. A city hall reporter should explore how local programs will be financially accessible to all residents, regardless of their income. A reporter also must know the range of user fees and how much they directly support program costs.

State and Federal Dollars Add In

Prior to 1980, many local governments received federal aid and grants directly. The Reagan administration adopted policies that channeled those funds through the states, however, and at the same time cut the amount of federal money to the states. In some cases $2 out of $3 sent directly to local governments disappeared.

Today local governments still get federal funds directly for transportation, from specific federal agencies, or as community development grants. Transportation dollars support highway construction and bus services, for example, and development grants help build low-income housing. A county might get funds from the Federal Emergency Management Agency to build a firefighter training center. Other federal aid, such as Medicaid that covers the cost of health care for low-income residents, goes to the states and is reallocated to county governments. More and more local governments and even the states have had to pick up Medicaid payments because of a drop in federal money.

Consider this story from the *Daily Camera* in Boulder, Colorado. The story has implications for every state. See how writer Ryan Morgan (2003) ties the story to several departments and needs within Boulder city government.

Colorado residents are smart.

So says new census data that shows Colorado is the second-most educated state in the union, behind Massachusetts, with 32 percent of residents holding at least a bachelor's degree.

But when it comes to lobbying the feds for money, local governments don't look good.

Colorado is near the bottom of the list—48th place—in the amount of money local governments are able to sweet-talk from the federal government. Local governments pocketed $797 in federal money per resident in 2000—chump change compared to the $3,843 per resident first-place Arizona's local governments took home from Washington, D.C. Virginia and Nevada took home less money than Colorado.

Mike Beasley, the state's director of local affairs, disputed the U.S. Census Bureau figures. Colorado may have lagged badly in 2000, he said, but "I would be stunned if we're 48th today. I would say that taking a one-year snapshot is not particularly accurate."

Census officials tallied the money that flows to local governments, and they didn't count federal funding for programs at the University of Colorado or federal offices.

Officials in Boulder said the census figures pretty accurately reflect reality, and they want a piece of the federal action, which could help pay for roads and other pricey infrastructure.

"This is the first year we're making a more concentrated effort," said Amy Mueller, the city's intergovernmental liaison. "We need the money, and we didn't want to be left behind."

Mueller returned Monday from Washington, D.C., where she spent a week meeting with members of Colorado's congressional delegation, along with members of the Beltway lobbying firm Smith, Dawson and Andrews. Boulder is paying the firm $60,000 to help win money for road and water construction.

The city wants to receive federal dollars to pay for a hoped-for "transit village," a multimodal transportation center at 30th and Pearl streets, as well as money to help pay for construction along the 28th Street corridor.

City water engineers are also hoping for federal assistance to study the possibility of installing a pipeline to replace the feeder canal that carries water from Carter Lake, near Loveland, to the Boulder Reservoir. Water quality experts in Boulder worry the water coming through the canal is being tainted by heavy construction activity, and they say they think a pipeline could be the key to keeping the water clean. But first, they need to pay for expensive studies.

Federal money "would allow the process to move forward a lot sooner and probably more completely," said Chris Rudkin, the city's water quality coordinator.

Getting approval to shell out $60,000 in a year when the budget was already tight wasn't easy, Mueller said.

"It's hard in a difficult budget year to say, 'Hey, let's spend some money,'" she said.

But if the city wins funding for even one of the many projects it hopes to get, it will be more than worth the money, Mueller said.

"We've realized that other cities are able to generate much more federal support for their projects," she said. "There are a lot of projects we wouldn't be able to do without federal help." (Reprinted with permission of Boulder Publishing.)

Morgan catches the reader with a short lead then quickly gets to the nut graph or point of the story in paragraph four. The story has some numbers to add the context, but Morgan relies on specific project examples to let the reader know the impact federal dollars can have on transportation and water and sewer service. He uses quotes from the experts—and even one bureaucrat who doubts Colorado's nearly last finish in securing federal funding.

Any reporter at another newspaper could do a similar story showing its local government's share of federal dollars and what officials have done and are doing to supplant any decreases. Local officials need to explain whether their share is less and what they are doing to retain and get available monies.

Enterprise Funds

In some budgets, reporters might see a category for enterprise or service funds. Those expenditures support government services that are enterprises or bring in revenue. For example, the cost of operating a municipal electric company might be included under enterprise expenses. The sheriff's department's expenses might be paid out of the general fund because it does not bring in any revenue, but emergency medical services expenses might come out of enterprise funds because it charges users for the service.

Enterprise fund expenses would be the same as for any other department: salaries, supplies, utilities, equipment, services such as computer support, and travel.

Savings for a Rainy Day

Local governments, whether city, county, or schools, have fund balances, which are equal to a savings account. The fund balance is the amount of money in the general fund that can be carried over to the next fiscal year. When governments plan their budgets, they do not normally rely on the fund balance as a revenue source. Governments maintain fund balances as reserves for emergencies, unexpected expenses, or cash flow problems. These funds sometimes are called rainy day accounts.

Budget officers usually recommend that local governments maintain a fund balance that is at least 8 percent of annual expenditures, excluding capital or building projects. Some governmental units might retain less. Fund balances are invested, and cities and counties collect interest, just like an individual's money market checking account earns a little interest.

Towns can also assess property owners for improvements that the town is making to enhance the value of their property, such as streets, water lines, and sewer lines. For example, home owners could be charged for a sidewalk at a rate based on the length of the property along the street. Or owners of lots who live around a city lake could be assessed for dredging and lakeside improvements.

More and more communities are counting on availability fees. They can be charged for new construction to tap into water or sewer services or to get garbage or trash collection. They can also be one-time charges to raise money to improve or repair infrastructure such as a water system. One reporter in Winchester, Virginia (Van Meter, 2003), noted:

> BERRYVILLE—The Clarke County Sanitary Authority is counting on availability fees from 15 new connections to its water utility to halve the $41,000 deficit in its water service budget.
>
> The authority charged $4,000 for each connection. The budget had estimated six connections. An additional nine connections would generate another $36,000.

State Taxes and the Effect on Local Governments

States assess and collect some taxes that local governments do not. Most states assess an income tax, much like the federal income tax, on individuals and corporations. Some states, such as Alaska, Florida, and Nevada, do not have a state income tax. But they will get income another way, such as higher fees for driver licenses, vehicle inspections and tags, or motor fuels tax.

The motor fuels tax is assessed on gasoline, diesel, and alternative fuels. Those funds support highway construction and are not assessed locally. For example, in 2003 Nevada did not have a state income tax, but it had one of the highest motor fuels taxes, assessing an additional 24 cents per gallon on gasoline and 27 cents per gallon on diesel as well as a statewide sales tax of 6 cents. In a state that has high tourism, Nevada feeds its financial tank each time a visitor fills up, eats out, or buys souvenirs.

States might charge what's called an excise tax on cigarette packs. In some states, cities and counties can also tax a pack of cigarettes. Among states that allow local governments to tax cigarettes are Alabama, Illinois, Missouri, New York, Tennessee, and Virginia, according to the Federal Tax Administrators Web site (2003). The taxes range from a high $2.05 per pack to 3 cents. States also levy taxes on tobacco products such as chewing tobacco, snuff, and cigars.

States also charge liquor taxes on distilled spirits, and in 18 states government controls the sale of liquor. The excise tax on liquor goes into state coffers, but sales tax charged on liquor could find its way back to local governments. Most states do not control the sale of wine; a few, such as New Hampshire, Pennsylvania, and Utah, do. Some states levy excise taxes on sales of wine and beer. Rates on all taxes change, and updated comparisons can be found on the Federation of Tax Administrators Web site at www.taxadmin.org.

States periodically initiate amnesty programs whereby individuals or corporations can pay back income tax or other owed taxes with no penalties. Such programs often result in huge collection windfalls for states. For example, Louisiana set up an amnesty program in September and October 2001; the state collected $173.1 million in owed taxes, according to the Federation of Tax Administrators Web site. Such programs obviously make good stories.

LIABILITIES, OR WHERE THE MONEY GOES

Just as individuals spend money on rent or mortgage payments, food, clothing, or entertainment, governments spend money on buildings, utilities, salaries, services, and debts. Any budget document will specify where income is spent. Some budgets will include charts or graphs that show quickly where funds go.

In recent years, local governments have had increasing problems raising enough revenues to cover expected expenditures. A 2003 survey by the National League of Cities showed that of the cities that responded to the survey, a high percentage were increasing taxes and user fees and using reserves to meet expenses. The survey noted that municipalities were facing the worst financial conditions since the league started the survey in 1985.

According to the survey, four out of five cities (79 percent) reported they were less able to meet financial needs than they had been during the previous year. In a survey only a year earlier, 55 percent of cities responding said they were less able to meet financial needs. Some found a 4 percent gap between revenues and spending. On average they had a 1 percent drop in revenues and a 2.9 percent increase in expenses.

While the lagging economy has affected local governments' ability to meet expenses recently, so has federal government action. Local governments have faced pressure to comply with Homeland Security initiatives and to meet education requirements under the federal No Child Left Behind Act. Neither federal mandate has provided sufficient funds to cover expenses, but local governments have still been expected to comply.

Local governments, including city, county, and school districts, differ in how they categorize expenses, but most have some sort of general fund that covers day-to-day departmental costs, capital costs for one-time construction or expansion projects, and debt service to repay funds borrowed. In learning about the budget, reporters must get a specific breakdown of how the governmental unit groups departments, services, projects, equipment, and other items.

General Fund Expenses

All governments have a general fund that pays day-to-day operating expenses, such as salaries, utilities, supplies, cars, travel expenses for officials, office equipment—whatever it takes to keep government operating. The fund might represent the major share of expenses because it includes most departments. In some cases, the general fund covers departments that do not generate revenues, such as the administrative offices, human resources, public safety, or technology. For example, a town might spend 45 percent of its general fund revenues to pay fire and police expenses including salaries, vehicles, uniforms, office supplies, or other materials.

Expenditures in a city's general fund and a county's general fund might be similar as well as different. Both pay for public safety or police, fire, and emergency medical services. Each might also pay for libraries, parks and recreation, environmental protection, education, and general government administration. The county generally covers social services and health services. A city might be responsible for maintaining its streets, while county roads might come under the state's jurisdiction.

Capital Improvements Cost Extra

Infrastructure such as water and sewer lines, buildings such as a city vehicle maintenance garage, and equipment such as generators needed in a utility plant are called capital expenses. Capital budget items are listed separately in budget documents. If the project is small enough, officials might cover the cost through revenues or what is saved in the fund balance. But generally local governments do not have enough money to pay such large expenses at one time, so they will finance such construction by borrowing funds.

Local governments can finance construction or equipment by selling bonds, or written notes that promise that the borrower—such as the city—will repay the amount along with a fixed rate of interest. Selling bonds is often called "floating" a bond package. Payments are stretched out over 20 or 30 years.

The principal—or amount borrowed—plus the interest that must be repaid each year is called the debt service. A reporter can think of debt service as being similar to what a student would owe each year to repay a college loan. The initial amount borrowed plus interest and any service fees would be included in the payment. If a local government has issued bonds for several projects, reporters will find a debt service item for all the bond repayments owed that fiscal year. In looking at budget expenditures, reporters might see an amount for capital expenditures, including debt service, or a separate amount for debt service.

Local and state governments can issue general obligation bonds to support broad projects, such as airport improvements. Nearly all states have constitutional provisions that require voter approval for general obligation debt, said Ferrell (2003) of the UNC-CH School of Government. "General obligation means that the government promises the lenders that it will use its taxing power to whatever extent is needed to pay off the loans," he added.

Governments can sell revenue bonds that are to be repaid through the revenues generated by the purpose or facility, such as a concert hall that will sell event tickets. Taxpayer approval is not required for government officials to sell revenue bonds.

To sell any bonds and to get an interest rate that is not too high, local governments must have a good bond rating. Investment firms such as Moody's and Standard & Poor's rate governmental units. The highest rating, an AAA rating, is given when a local government has a healthy tax base, does not have a lot of debt, and is considered by financial analysts to be a good risk for investors. Rating firms also evaluate states, essential if they are floating or issuing bonds to cover state government projects. States might seek voter approval for multibillion-dollar bond packages that will finance projects across public universities and community colleges, for example, or cover extensive highway improvements.

Most states have requirements that govern local governments' sale of securities, such as bonds, or any other obligation that requires a specific source to repay the debt. In Michigan, for example, any municipality that sells a security or bond must report the sale and other pertinent information to the state Department of the Treasury within 15 days of issuing the security.

Reporters should be aware of how much debt a local government is carrying. The debt might be for improvements to the police station or library, water and sewer lines, or airport expansion. Just as home owners can refinance their houses for a lower interest rate, local governments can do the same. The city council of Boise, Idaho, refinanced part of its general fund debt service to reduce its payments by $2.5 million. The council allocated the savings to other projects.

Paying the Unexpected Expense

As noted earlier in the discussion on fund balance, local governments must set aside funds for emergencies or surprises. The city of Reno, Nevada, amassed unexpected legal expenses in a multiyear project to upgrade its rail system. Here's how reporter Anjeanette Damon (2003) clearly outlined the newest and earlier unanticipated costs in a story in the *Reno Gazette-Journal:*

> The Reno City Council has approved a $200,000 contract for outside lawyers to handle construction litigation for the train trench project, an expense that was not anticipated in the original budget.

The city has hired Los Angeles–based Gibbs, Giden, Locher & Turner to manage construction claims arising from the project and change orders to the $170.7 million design–build contract. The project's $26.4 million contingency fund will be tapped for the expense, which is not to exceed $200,000.

Chief Deputy City Attorney Randall Edwards said the cost was not included in the original budget because the city did not know how complicated the legal matters would become.

"We didn't anticipate there would be such complicated issues that we would need outside counsel," Edwards said. "Now, as we get more into the project, we felt it would be smart on our part to get people experienced with these issues." There are no lawsuits pending for which the lawyers would be needed, he said.

"We're hoping to avoid any litigation altogether," he said. The law firm handled similar issues for the Alameda Corridor, a 20-mile train trench project in Southern California.

Reno's $282 million project is designed to separate trains from vehicle and pedestrian traffic along a 2.1-mile corridor through downtown. Construction, which is under way, is scheduled to be complete in early 2006.

The contract for outside lawyers comes one month after the council tapped the contingency fund for a surprise contract overrun of $158,392 for a Los Angeles law firm. O'Melveny & Myers had a $690,000 contract to help arrange for a federal loan and negotiate an agreement with Union Pacific Railroad for the trench project. That firm did not handle construction litigation issues.

In the year since the trench construction contract was awarded, the city has accumulated $4.2 million in surprise costs, which will be covered by the project's contingency fund. Other costs include a $3.6 million lawsuit settlement over relocation of the Kinder Morgan pipeline and an estimated $600,000 in modifications to the Rusty Spike power substation along the Truckee River. (Reprinted with permission of the *Reno Gazette-Journal*.)

Damon explained the most recent unexpected expense and includes a reference to the $4.2 million already spent to settle a lawsuit and modify a power substation. She tells readers that such expenses are paid out of a $26 million contingency fund. Readers are also told what the overall project entails and when it will be finished.

WRITING FOR CLARITY

As noted earlier in the chapter, some reporters shy away from budgets and financing because they aren't familiar with the language or jargon. In any story, reporters must explain terminology and not quote sources' words that they don't understand thoroughly. Chip Scanlan in a piece for the Poynter Institute (2003) noted that reporters use the term *shortfall*, or how a budget or quantity falls short, to mean "shortage, decline, unpaid bill, difference, unmet budget, request, debt, remainder, and deficit." He cautions to avoid jargon. "Bureaucrats may use terms such as 'revenue' and 'expenditure,'" he said, but "keep it simple with 'income' and 'spending.'"

In Damon's story about the Reno City Council, a few phrases might cause readers to pause and wonder, "What is a change order?" "What is a design–build contract?" "Litigation" can also be translated into "lawsuit."

In writing about budgets—or any numbers for that matter—reporters must guard against piling numbers into sentences and paragraphs. Most writing coaches recommend that no two numbers touch in writing. For example, you would not write: "Out of the $45,768, $13,032 is earmarked for new recreation programs." Readers have to work hard to sort out the two figures. Better writing: "Out of the $45,768, commissioners set aside $13,032 for new recreation programs."

Whenever Professor Phil Meyer at UNC–Chapel Hill talks about numbers, he recommends that important numbers should be highlighted and summarized early in a report. He also notes that one or two statistics that stand out should be used. If reporters have lots of numbers, it is best to meet with the graphics department to have the figures organized into a readable and clear chart.

To make budget stories clear to readers, a reporter might want to create a list of budget definitions. Such a list could run as a box next to a story. Taxpayers hold officials accountable for spending funds to benefit their communities and make them the best places possible to live in. To do so, residents must understand fully what the reporter has found and is showing them. Reporters have a challenging role to ensure that often-complicated budgets are reported clearly, completely, accurately, and fairly.

GLOSSARY

Assessed valuation: The value put on a piece of property and used to determine how much taxes are to be paid. The assessed value is generally a little less than the market value or how much someone would pay for the property on the open market.

Budget: A local government's financial blueprint for how it will raise revenues and spend funds; shows the government's philosophy and priorities.

Capital expenditure or outlay: Funds that are appropriated to cover the costs of capital improvements, such as buildings; a budget separate from recurring annual expenses because construction costs are one-time expenses.

Capital improvements: Physical structures, such as buildings or additions; can also be infrastructure such as water and sewer lines.

Contingency: Money set aside for emergencies or unanticipated needs.

Debt service: The annual installment of principal and interest owed by a government on outstanding bonds. For example, a school district could carry a debt service for classroom buildings.

Fiscal year: The 12-month period on which a budget is based and during which funds are acquired and spent; most local governments operate on a July 1 through June 30 fiscal year. The fiscal year 2003–2004 is referred to as FY '04.

Fund balance: Akin to a savings account; the amount of money a local government has at the end of a fiscal year after all expenses have been paid; that amount can be carried over to the next year.

General obligation bonds: Bonds that pledge the issuing authority's taxing power as security for repayment; normally issued to finance large projects, such as airport improvements; require the approval of voters because they mandate taxes over many years.

Mill: Unit of measure equal to one-thousandth of a dollar or one-tenth of a cent; some governments set property taxes in mills and others in cents on assessed property value.

Operating budget: That part of the budget that covers general activities of the local government, such as human resources, public safety, transportation; such activities are permanent, recurring expenses as opposed to capital budgets that would cover one-time construction or infrastructure costs.

Personal property: Items, such as boats, cars, and other vehicles, and business machinery and equipment, that are taxed by local government.

Property tax: Paid by residents on land, buildings, cars, boats, and mobile homes.

Real property: Real estate, that is, land and buildings; counties establish values for land on a rotating basis, generally every eight years.

Reevaluation: The process in which a county reassesses the value of real property.

Revenue: Money collected or received by a local government; funds include user fees, sales tax, federal payments, and so on; revenues are used to support services.

Revenue bonds: Bonds sold that are to be repaid through the revenues generated by the purpose or facility, such as a concert hall that will generate enough revenues to support itself and repay the bonds; taxpayer approval is not required for government officials to sell the bonds.

Sales tax: Tax paid on items purchased; a rate per dollar, such as 5 cents per dollar, is set by the state. States allow counties to levy a specific sales tax that is collected by the state and remitted to counties. Counties receive the funds based on a formula set by the state; state payments are sent to local governments quarterly.

Tax base: The total assessed value of real property within a city or a county.

Tax rate: The rate at which real property is taxed, either cents per $100 valuation or set in mills, equal to one-thousandth of a dollar of the assessed property's value.

User fees: Fees paid by residents or users for specific services, such as library fines, use of a community center pool, participation in a recreation league, and so on.

ACTIVITIES

1. Read five days' worth of your local newspaper. Identify stories that relate to local government budgets, whether the story is about city or school financing.

Count the numbers (or dollar amounts) used. As a reader, are you clear on what the numbers mean? Is the story overburdened with numbers? Does the reporter translate the numbers into tangible terms, that is, specifically how residents will be affected? Does the story have sufficient background so you have context for the numbers? Is the language clear? What terminology did you not understand? How could the reporter explain the terminology more clearly?

2. Use your responses as a reader of these stories to develop your own guidelines in writing about local government finance.

3. Go online and find a copy of your city's budget. Find the manager's summary. Look for and identify:
   - Current tax rate.
   - Proposed tax rate.
   - Goals that were not met in the current fiscal year that need to be addressed in the next fiscal year.
   - Comments about the city's fiscal health.
   - Programs to be funded in the next fiscal year.
   - The three largest income producers.
   - The three areas of greatest expenditures.

   Based on what you found in the manager's summary, identify six stories you could write.

4. In looking at the city budget, how dependent is the city and/or county on property taxes? What makes up the tax base in your community? Interview the appropriate city or county manager to find out how the tax base has changed in the last 10 years. Develop a story that can explain the change and the impact on residents.

5. How dependent is the city and/or county on user fees? What are the largest user fees? Check your state constitution or department of revenue or treasury to determine what controls state government exerts on local governments in regard to types of fees they can charge. Interview the appropriate city or county manager to find out how user fees have changed in the last five years. Develop a story that can explain the change and the impact on residents. Be sure to include opponents and proponents of user fees.

6. Look at your local school district's budget. If the superintendent or other administrators are getting raises, can you determine whether they deserve the increases? Did they meet objectives set out in the current year's budget? What were the school system's goals? Were they reached?

7. Go through the budget, either the schools' or the city or county government's, by department. Find the goals and expected accomplishments. What happened last year? Were goals met? What can you find out about the department from reading the budget, such as number of employees, priorities, goals?

8. Select a local governmental budget. Look for debt service. What is the government paying for? How much is the annual debt service? How many more years before the debt is repaid? Also find the unit's bond rating. What is it? What does that mean?

RESOURCES AND WEB SITES

Government Financial Officers Association: www.gfoa.org. Includes a comprehensive "digital finance library" with helpful links.

The Rockefeller Institute of Government: www.rockinst.org. Has a large government finance section.

Timothy Kelsey's "Financing Local Government": www.farmfoundation.org/2001NPPEC/kelsey.pdf. Basic run-through of what is included in local budgets.

U.S. Census Bureau government finances: www.census.gov/govs/www/index.html. Links to financial data from every level of government.

Individual county and city finance departments, which include budgets, managers' messages, accomplishments from previous years

State Offices of State Budget and Management generally provide links to state budgets and some helpful analysis

REFERENCES

City of Boise, Idaho. (2003, July 20). www.cityofboise.org/financial_management/debt_strategy.pdf.

City of Colorado Springs, Colorado. (2003, July 20). www.springsgov.com.

Damon, A. (2003, July 17). Reno Council approves contract for outside lawyers. *Reno Gazette-Journal*. www.rgj.com/news/stories/html/2003/07/17/47235.php?sp1=rgj&sp2=News&sp3=Local+News.

Federation of Tax Administrators. (2003, July 18). www.taxadmin.org/fta/rate/sl_sales.html.

Ferrell, J. (2003 July). Interview. School of Government. University of North Carolina at Chapel Hill.

Hart, J. (1998). Reporting on budgets. www.facsnet.org/tools/nbgs/p_thru_%20z/r/reprtngbu.php3.

Herzog, D. (1998a). Part 2: Writing better budget stories. *Providence Journal* Company. www.projo.com.

Herzog, D. (1998b). Twenty tips for covering and writing about budgets. *Providence Journal* Company. www.projo.com.

Link, J. (2003). 2002–03 Budget Message. www.co.orange.nc.us/budget/0203/budgetmsg.pdf.

McCool, C. (2003, June 28). Summer tax collection begins for school funding. *Kalamazoo Gazette*. www.mlive.com/news/kzgazette/index.ssf?/xml/story.ssf/html_standard.xsl?/base/news-5/105679592356800.xml.

Morgan, R. (2003, July 1). Colo. No. 48 in federal money: State officials dispute census statistics. *Daily Camera*. www.dailycamera.com/bdc/state_news/article/0,1713,BDC_2419_2079907,00.html.

National League of Cities. (2003, May 27). Cities raise fees and taxes, cut projects and staff to deal with increasing fiscal squeeze. [News Release]. www.nlc.org/nlc_org/site/newsroom/nations_cities_weekly/display.cfm?id=9E4EC88F-1639-453C-951CE56E55776B13.

Pollos, J. A. (2003, September 5). Training for the taking: Northern Lakes fire received FEMA grant for facility at airport. *Cda Press*. [Couer d'Alene, Idaho.] www.cdapress.com.

Scanlan, C. (2003, March 5). Avoiding numeric novocain: Writing well with numbers. Poynter Institute. www.poynter.org/content/content_print.asp?id+23390&custom=.

Van Meter, V. (2003, May 28). Authority depending on availability fees. *Winchester* (VA) *Star*. www.winchesterstar.com/TheWinchesterStar/030528/Area_fees.asp.

Yopp, J. J., & McAdams, K. (2003). *Reaching audiences: A guide to media writing*. Boston: Allyn & Bacon.

CHAPTER 8

■ ■ ■ ■ ■

COVERING THE ESSENTIALS
OF EDUCATION

Many student journalists get experience covering their own university or college. Some years they write about routine issues such as tuition increases or sports teams; other years the campus explodes with controversies and the stories are endless.

One such year occurred at a state university in Maryland. In 2002 for the first time in 22 years, Towson University hired a new president, Mark Perkins. Controversy began even before Perkins arrived when news stories surfaced that problems had existed at his previous job as chancellor of the University of Wisconsin–Green Bay. Towson officials put any concerns aside, however, and planned for an inauguration. The University of Maryland system approved the purchase of a presidential home for the new hire, and renovation of the house began.

But renovations to the presidential house cost much more than expected, and the $850,000 price tag almost doubled. Members of the University System Board of Regents, upset by the cost overruns, felt the new president should have kept them better informed and kept the costs in check more effectively. Eight months after he began, the new president agreed to leave.

The university newspaper, *The Towerlight,* and the *Baltimore Sun* gave the story—the biggest to hit the university campus in its 135-year history—ongoing coverage. In writing numerous front-page stories, journalists at the student newspaper received a crash course in how to cover complex higher education stories, including budgets and personalities.

Many journalists, especially young or college-age reporters, believe they know the intricacies of education reporting because they have just been in, or still are in, an educational system. Being a student does not make you knowledgeable, however, or give you access to the behind the scenes goings-on of a school district or university. In addition, educational entities vary widely, from private to public schools, from preschool to graduate school. All have a myriad of special programs at every level. State laws can also affect how a school system is organized, governed, and funded.

Education reporting also blends with other topics such as government or business. *Baltimore Sun* education reporter Jon Rockoff (2003) said beginning education reporters have to "understand that it (the education beat) covers a lot of ground: politics, policy, crime, etc., in addition to education. Other than that, the general rules of reporting apply."

In this chapter you will:

- Learn the skills needed to cover education,
- Examine financial issues involved in K–12 education,
- See models for student achievement,
- Consider unique aspects of the K–12 beat and child/youth issues,
- Look at higher education and its issues, such as sports, and
- Think about getting good visuals for education stories.

PREPARING FOR THE EDUCATION BEAT

The Education Writers Association (EWA), a group of more than 500 journalists who cover U.S. education, calls education the most enjoyable beat because of its huge diversity of stories. The Association said in its 2001 book, *Covering the Education Beat:*

> No other assignment sweeps across people's lives from infancy to old age. In most communities, education is a major industry. In most states, it consumes the largest share of tax dollars. A journalist writing about education will cover everything from budgets to blustery encounters over values, from clever innovations by students in the computer lab to ground-breaking inventions discovered in the research lab, from threats of local lawsuits to U.S. Supreme Court rulings, from teacher education to charter schools. (Reprinted with permission from the Education Writers Association.)

Higher education as a subset of the education beat has some unique aspects. Scott Jaschik, who has covered higher education at the *Chronicle of Higher Education* for almost 20 years, said (Stepp, 2003): "Higher education is a mix. You have the latest student silliness, and you have the world of great ideas. That's what makes it interesting."

However, EWA says much media coverage of education still tends toward dull school board coverage instead of digging into the "issues and trends that touch the lives of readers." News audiences deserve detailed reporting on education because it affects the readiness of the next generation to function as knowledgeable citizens, and taxpayers fund education. Political leaders stress the importance of education in U.S. society by spending much time discussing it when they give speeches.

Basic Skills Needed

Because education is a complex beat, journalists should be prepared for all types of stories. EWA (2001) lists seven crucial skills education reporters should be able to do: "Size up a school; use computer spreadsheet and database programs, such as Excel and Access; cultivate extensive sources; read a budget; interview students; analyze statistics, especially test scores; and understand school politics."

Sizing up the school means reporters should be able to judge the quality of a school with a visit. Rockoff (2003) said: "Get to know the basics about the school system, such as number of students, schools, and employees. Figure out the major issues, and identify future issues." However, reporters need to be careful about their judgments and weigh their impressions against objective evidence such as test scores or teacher turnover. "News reports on school quality can profoundly affect the reputation of schools, so it is of course crucial that reporters get it right. The stakes are high," EWA said. Rockoff added, "There are also topics particular to a school system, for example, minority achievement in districts with sizeable minority populations."

Much data from states, school districts, and higher education are available these days, and education reporters need to know how to read spreadsheets and use database programs. "News organizations now routinely use spreadsheet and database programs to sort, summarize, analyze, and publish test scores, dropout rates, and other information on the morning after the (report's) release date," EWA reports. For example, the New Orleans *Times Picayune* analyzed six years of standardized text scores from 80 elementary schools with a spreadsheet program to see how the students progressed through the schools. The newspaper found large discrepancies in the test scores and began digging to find the reasons why. Reporters discovered that one principal told teachers to read the test to students with reading problems instead of letting them attempt it. Another principal barred some low-scoring students from taking the test.

Education reporters should also know how to read a budget because every level of education has one. They should know statistics because they might report trends in test scores, dropout rates, or racial demographics. Education reporters should be able to calculate percentages and understand the difference among mean, median, and mode. Reporters need to understand per-pupil funding in which money is allocated based on the number of students in a school. The newest twist to this funding is governments tying allocations to adequate academic performance by the students.

To cover this diverse beat, education reporters must develop a stable of sources from parents and teachers to administrators to teacher union leaders to local businesspeople to education experts. All types of stories arise on the education beat, from condom distribution in high schools to college tuition increases to new prekindergarten programs. Reporters must be comfortable interviewing children and teenagers. Because they might be less at ease with a reporter's questions, more finesse might be needed to interview them, as compared to adults.

Finally, education writers must understand that schools and universities have distinct internal politics. EWA (2002) explains:

> Schools are political organizations as well as learning institutions. School board members, teacher unions, and administrators all engage in political tugs and pulls for control and power. So reporters need to be skillful in detecting when school initiatives are launched more for political rather than educational ends.

Reporters also have to be prepared to learn and decipher educational jargon. Educators talk in abbreviations, acronyms, and outcomes. The *Sun's* Jon Rockoff called this "education-ese, the abstract jargon employed by educators and education policy makers." Reporters should make certain to translate clearly and state what the terminology means. Often reporters assume a level of knowledge by readers and lapse into using terms such as *DAP* (developmentally appropriate practices) that confuse readers.

FINDING SOURCES AND BASIC INFORMATION

When getting started on the education beat, reporters should make appointments with key people throughout the district to get a sense of local issues. Among those sources are superintendents and assistant superintendents, principals, school board members, teachers, administrative staff, school attorneys, and parents. These informational interviews can be invaluable in gaining sources and finding the hot topics in that school district. Larger school systems will have public information officers who can make introductions; smaller systems probably will have secretaries who serve as intermediaries for key administrative personnel.

Looking Outside the Schools

In addition to the usual sources, reporters should also make contact with various advisory board and union leaders, said Marjorie Hampson, Baltimore County Public School System public information officer (PIO). "These stakeholders are very influential in most schools systems," she said (2003). "Baltimore County has several advisory boards, including the PTA council, educational, special education, minority, gifted and talented, and technical. Volunteers, who do not actually make policy, but influence the system greatly, form these boards." She added that reporters should contact presidents of any unions for employees in the school district. These groups range from teacher to clerical to administrators' unions.

Among Hampson's other tips, she noted: "Attendance at board meetings is a must. Visitations to schools are a plus. Get a school calendar! Study the system's Web site. Call the communications office early and often for help and information."

Media studies show that most people receive news about education and local schools from print media more than from electronic media. Hampson said that means education reporters have a significant responsibility to keep local citizens informed. "Education reporters have the task of reporting what readers *should know,* and have the *right to know,* and getting the information from knowledgeable and reputable sources," she said. "A new reporter needs to do his homework and discover how the system works—with all of its intricacies—as well as who controls it."

Interviewing Your Sources

In addition to understanding funding issues, reporters on the education beat face a unique challenge because so many potential sources are under age 18. Interviewing young people has legal as well as privacy implications. Reporter Elizabeth Stone offered insight into interviewing young people in a 1999 *Columbia Journalism Review* article that can be accessed at www.cjr.org.

The Education Writers Association said reporting on youth creates ethical considerations because young people, and sometimes their parents, might not understand the consequences of media stories on their lives. "Reporters wield great power in the impact they can have on the lives of children and schools; that power demands responsibility," EWA (2002) said. "It is important to consider the possible unintended consequences of the stories we cover about the most vulnerable in our society."

For example, the *Oregonian*, as part of a series on the class of 2000, interviewed a 16-year-old and her mother about their struggles. The two revealed much intimate information ranging from the teen's learning disabilities to the fact that she had been raped. Although the story didn't mention the rape, it did discuss the teen's problems with truancy and her decision to drop out of high school. The *Oregonian* reporter explained to them what would be included in the story. However, "both were devastated when it appeared on the front page. Neither was prepared for the calls and comments from shocked friends and relatives," according to EWA.

EWA (2002) recommends the following guidelines when dealing with children in stories:

- Understand that youth, and even their parents, might be naïve about the impact of a media story on them. Find out if children will be harassed or teased if certain details appear in the media. Even if a parent consents to embarrassing details about a child for the story, the reporter should consider the potential harm to the child. Both parent and child should know what specifics will be in the story so they can voice any concerns. The *Sun*'s Jon Rockoff (2003) said: "Different newspapers have different rules. I prefer to speak with students with an adult's permission; schools like to check with parents."

- Reporters should treat young people with respect.
- Children should always have the option to stop an interview if they are uncomfortable. EWA recommends interviewing young people in small groups, which proved effective when reporters covered a 1998 school shooting in Oregon.
- Parents of children under 16 should be informed if their children and their comments will be in a story on a sensitive or controversial subject. However, when the story is a light feature or on a noncontroversial subject, prior notification is not necessary. For example, when *Maryland Family* magazine published a feature on David Dalrymple, who at age 11 was a junior in college, the story was noncontroversial. All the details revealed positive aspects of his life, such as he could do triple-digit math with negative numbers at age 2 (Burrell, 2003).
- Baltimore County schools PIO Hampson (2003) said students receive a student handbook when the school year starts. "In the book is a tear-out that must be signed and returned to the principal stating that the parent(s) do *not* wish to have their student interviewed, videotaped, photographed, etc. by the media," she said. "If the media are doing a story in a school, all other students may participate." Even for noncontroversial stories, school personnel refer all requests for stories or interviews to the Office of Communications for approval first. However, "in controversial cases, requests for information may have to be submitted in writing to the system's law office," Hampson said. "The waiting period may be up to 30 days, according to the (state) Public Information Act." Enterprising reporters with good contacts can easily find their way around this restriction by going to parent groups and others outside the district who are willing to speak to them.
- If negative or unflattering intimate details of a youth's life, such as sexual abuse or learning problems, will be revealed in a story, the reporter should consider concealing the child's identity. As EWA said, "It is difficult to imagine, for example, how we could identify a teenager and write about his or her sexual activity without causing harm."

LynNell Hancock, a former education and youth reporter and now Columbia University journalism professor, teaches a course in "covering the youth beat." She agreed with these ethical tenets, but added that when interviewing children, reporters have to modify their style. Children should be interviewed in a location that is safe and familiar and has few distractions.

Interviews should also be age-appropriate lengths. Children under age 9 can be interviewed for a maximum of 30 minutes; for ages 10 to 14 about 45 minutes is appropriate, and for teens, one hour, she said. The reporter should sit eye-to-eye with the young person and literally not look down on the youth. For the best results, questions should move from the general to the specific; they should be open ended rather than yes–no or either–or. "Not, 'do you live with your mother?' But, 'who lives with you at home?' Yes–no questions may frustrate the child, or result in false agreement," Hancock (2003, June) explained.

In addition, she advised: "Don't use false praise or make statements that reward a child for talking to you. Children learn to give answers that please the teacher in classroom. You don't want answers meant simply to please the interviewer. So, instead of saying 'good answer, yes, you're right,' say, 'you've been very helpful, you've helped me understand,' and so on."

RESOURCES ON CHILDREN AND YOUTH ISSUES

Hancock criticized the stereotypical and sometimes superficial ways that youth and their issues are covered. "Kids are either victims or perpetrators, angels or devils," she said. "Teens are inscrutable, alien mutants, or honor students. Children are either completely innocent or miniature adults with a remorseless streak." A 2002 study of youth coverage confirmed that crime and violence dominate the media stories on children. Many stories were one-dimensional and lacked context, according to the Casey Journalism Center on Children and Families. Another study of TV news coverage of children found similar misrepresentation. "Local television news broadcasts under-represent the presence of children in society, distort the level of crime committed by and against children, and rarely focus on public policy issues that affect American families," according to Children Now (2001), a research and action group that advocates on behalf of children.

Stories about youth issues should have depth and context. Hancock explained: "The realistic voices of kids and the adults around them should be central to the purpose of every story. Flesh out multi-dimensional humans. Not angels or devils, but complex people with distinctive voices, nuanced responses, and messy lives." Reporters can learn about youth perspectives generally through *Youth Outlook*, an online youth magazine that features young people's views. Education reporters should also be on the mailing list for school newspapers in the districts they cover. These can be a wealth of information about an issue at a specific school.

In addition to using young people as sources, reporters should find qualified experts in child development, education, social services, juvenile justice, law enforcement, religion, the military, and recreation. In reporting on education issues specifically, child advocates might have a different take on a story than do education officials. Organizations such as Keep Schools Safe, a general organization that works on reducing school violence, or InsideSchools.org, an independent group that helps New York City parents find schools and speak out about the city school system, advocate about educational issues important to parents. Also, Child Trends provides nonpartisan children's research on a variety of topics. Its publication, *Child Indicator*, gives a state-by-state study of the impact of the federal No Child Left Behind legislation. The publication also reports on topics such as youth risk behavior and school readiness.

FINANCING K–12 EDUCATION

Financial issues drive many aspects of the education beat and surface at most school board meetings. Education reporters have to be aware of the unique stories about funding within the beat.

Free public education is a foundation of the United States, but education is not free for the local, state, and federal governments. Costs have been sky-rocketing since the 1950s, and most school districts function as independent government entities, levying taxes to pay for their services.

How Schools Are Funded

The 2002 Census of Governments reported that of the 15,000 public schools systems in the United States in 2002, most were independent and could raise taxes. About 1,500 depend on other governments. Thirty-one states provide public schools solely through independent school districts, an arrangement more common in western states. Fifteen states have mixed systems, while the District of Columbia and four states—Alaska, Hawaii, Maryland, and North Carolina—have dependent school districts, administered by systems that are agencies of county, municipal, or state government. In North Carolina, all school systems are dependents of county government. Municipal govern-ments operate school systems in 13 states and the District of Columbia.

In the 2001–2002 school year, the United States spent $411 billion on K–12 education, which was more than the country's defense spending that year. Even with that high price tag, many children still received a mediocre to poor education. Funding disparities have plagued school districts for decades because some districts use property taxes to gain revenue for their schools. That means that neighborhoods with wealth and higher property taxes have more money for their schools than do poorer areas. Governments at all levels have been trying to alleviate these disparities.

EWA's *Money Matters: A Reporter's Guide to School Finance* (2003) states that reporters should understand the following facts to cover school finances:

- Funding for public schools comes from taxes.
- Mostly, local school boards develop district budgets and levy taxes to fund those budgets. Occasionally, city or county governments direct dis-trict budgets.

- State governments, however, contribute the most funding to K–12 education, accounting for about 50 percent of revenue. Local governments contribute another 43 percent, and the federal government funds about 5 percent to 8 percent of K–12 education.
- States spend 35 percent out of their total state budget expenditures for K–12 education—the most of any one purpose. They spend another 13 percent on higher education.
- Districts get their funding through property taxes, which are assessed based on the value of commercial and residential property in a community. Property taxes are discussed in Chapter 7.
- Because some districts are in poorer areas or have students who require more services to educate them, states have created a formula that calculates the cost per student enrolled in the schools, or what is called per-pupil funding.
- Most of a school district's operating budget goes for salaries and benefits—about 85 percent—with the rest for transportation, food, teacher training, maintenance, and materials.
- The average salary for a U.S. public school teacher in 2000–2001 was $42,898.
- New school buildings or renovations are funded outside the operating budget. Many times bonds, which allow the school district to borrow money at a lower rate of interest than banks provide, fund these projects. Voters within the school district must approve the bonds because they might have to be repaid through higher taxes.
- In recent years, school finance has been linked to student achievement. *Money Matters* states that the current question for districts is: "How much money does it take to graduate young people who are able to actively participate on a jury in a complex legal case, for instance? A new paradigm has developed, educational adequacy, which emphasizes how much money is needed to reach certain outcomes, and is beginning to overshadow the concern for equitable distribution of money."

The economy in recent years has affected states' ability to fund school districts. When states face budget shortfalls and bad economic times, school systems receive less funding. As mentioned earlier, states account for the largest part of school district funding, so when states are in an economic crisis, school districts suffer. In tight times, though, "education usually comes off better than any other system, short of criminal justice," said James Gutherie (EWA, 2003), an education finance expert at the Peabody Center for Education Policy at Vanderbilt University. "The long-run trajectory for American education is to get more and more—it's an article of faith."

Models for Student Achievement

Most school districts are trying to figure out a funding model that yields the best-educated students for the money under what is called the adequacy movement. The venture ties funding to how much money is needed to provide teachers and resources so students can score well on tests or other measures.

For public schools, "adequacy" is defined as "sufficient funds for schools to teach all but the most severely disabled to meet state and district standards or some other clearly defined educational outcome," according to *Money Matters* (2003). Two events led to the adequacy movement. In 1983, a national commission warned that U.S. schools were mediocre, which led to states adopting strict educational standards and then testing students on those standards. In 2002, Congress passed President Bush's No Child Left Behind initiatives, which require schools to show that their students are improving on standardized tests or face penalties—basically less money.

States have devised a number of models to meet the level of adequacy required by their states. Education reporters should know which models or hybrids their school districts use. Some states, such as Ohio, Mississippi, and Illinois, use the *successful schools model.* They look at past per-pupil funding in districts in which students were achieving state academic standards. The per-student funding from those successful school districts is averaged and then applied statewide. In the *professional judgment model,* states such as Maine and Oregon gather experts—teachers, administrators, and school finance consultants—to decide what resources are needed to create schools in which students will achieve state standards.

In the *evidence-based model,* school districts research proven successful practices that improve student achievement and then establish a funding level to attain those outcomes in all school districts. New Jersey's court-ordered school reform is an example. By 2001 that state had created a funding system that was equal for both poor and rich school districts.

Another model bases its structure on statistical data. "The *cost–function model* gathers a high volume of data including test scores, teachers' salaries, and student demographics, applies a statistical formula to it, and then determines how much an average student needs in the way of resources to succeed," according to *Money Matters.* Other states use hybrid models, which combine elements of several models.

COVERING HIGHER EDUCATION

Sometimes the media give higher education short shrift unless they cover a college town. In its 2003 analysis of higher education coverage, *American Journalism Review* (*AJR*) found that many newsrooms let that beat remain vacant or combine it with the K–12 beat (Stepp, 2003). In addition, only 8 percent of EWA members list themselves as covering the higher education beat. Those media that do make the effort to cover the beat find many compelling stories to interest news audiences. "There's a greater recognition among the general public that a college education in some form is really needed. So there is a lot of interest in higher education," Sharon Jayson, the higher education reporter for the *Austin American-Statesman,* stated in the *AJR* article.

Story Ideas on the Higher Ed Beat

Higher education reporters dig into finances, admissions, course offerings, enrollment fluctuations, crime and safety, substance abuse, student lifestyles, and grade inflation, among other topics on college campuses. They also look at who really controls higher education. In November 2003 the *Atlanta Journal-Constitution* did an in-depth look at who sat on the University of Georgia Board of Trustees and the state's Board of Regents after members of both boards criticized UGA President Michael Adams. The story plus the thumbnail sketches of both boards' members was a who's who in Georgia.

What's being taught in colleges, who's teaching, and the rigor of those courses attract journalists' interest. Patrick Healy of the *Boston Globe* noticed (Stepp, 2003) while covering a routine spring commencement that a huge number of Harvard graduates received honors. His research at Harvard's historical archives revealed a growing trend—that Harvard's honors rate was 91 percent, compared to 51 percent at Yale. The lead of his Pulitzer-nominated story (2001, October) read:

> Since the Vietnam era, rampant grade inflation has made [Harvard's] top prize for students—graduating with honors—virtually meaningless. . . .
>
> While the world regards these students as the best of the best of America's 13 million undergraduates, Harvard honors has actually become the laughing-stock of the Ivy League.
>
> The other Ivies see Harvard as the Lake Wobegon of higher education, where all the students, being above average, can take honors for granted. It takes just a B-minus average in the major subject to earn cum laude—no sweat at a school where 51 percent of the grades last year were A's and A-minuses.

Other higher education stories explore the life of today's college students. Reporters also search for new trends in college life. The Associated Press's John Affleck said reporters covered 9/11's impact on college study abroad programs and on colleges' growing interest in Islamic studies.

However, some higher education reporters say coverage of university life has been too superficial, sensational, or underreported. For sensational stories, reporters too often focus on crime, drugs, or student drinking. "I have always been dismayed at the extent to which so much attention is going to issues surrounding tuition, admissions, and ratings," Gene I. Maeroff, formerly a *New York Times* education reporter and director of the Hechinger Institute on Education and the Media at Columbia University, noted in the *AJR* piece (Stepp, 2003). "These three areas tend to get undue coverage. It would be really helpful to see higher-education reporters think more in terms of teaching and learning."

AJR reported that education reporters said among the list of undercovered stories were "even more on what student life is really like; what goes on inside classrooms and research labs; and what happens at non-elite, non–East

Coast institutions, especially community colleges." Other topics that need covering are distance education and commuter-student issues.

Journalists need to think about "the big picture" when covering higher education stories, said Holly Stepp, who contributed to EWA's *Covering the Education Beat: A Current Guide for Editors, Writers and the Public* (2001). They need to "demystify the work of higher education and explain its impact on readers."

Jaschik, who has covered higher education at the *Chronicle of Higher Education* for almost two decades, said higher education reporters need to do three main things: "Pay attention to all institutions, not just the biggest; pay attention to context; and go to campuses and talk to students and faculty members" (Stepp, 2003).

Financial Issues on the Higher Ed Beat

Because taxpayers, in large part, fund the hundreds of state colleges and universities, financial stories attract audiences. The 2002 Census of Governments reported that every state has one or more state-operated institution of higher education. Local public higher education systems operate more than 600 colleges and universities, of which three-fourths are operated by independent school districts and one-fourth by county or municipal governments. Most operate at the junior college level. More than 900 private colleges and universities exist in the United States as well, according to the National Association of Independent Colleges and Universities. Without a public funding stream, their finances are more difficult to access.

Reporter Jayson explained in *AJR* (2003): "Higher education is big bucks. There's a lot of money invested. That has made people more aware of what's at stake." The *Hartford Courant*'s education reporter Robert Frahm, also quoted in the *AJR* story, agreed: "Two stories in particular—admissions and cost—are of huge interest to many, many readers. Every time I do a story about the cost of college, my phone rings the next day and people want to know more."

More and more universities have launched huge fund-raising campaigns to add to their endowments. The University of North Carolina at Chapel Hill embarked in 2000 on the largest capital campaign ever: $1.8 billion. By mid-2003, the campaign had crested $1 billion. Funds will be used for building construction and renovation, financial aid and scholarships, endowed professorships, and other uses. Many campuses look to their endowments to provide educational support in addition to what they might receive from state governments, if they are public institutions, or federal grant money. In some cases, the latter can amount for as much as one-third of a university's annual income, and grants will support faculty as well as graduate students.

In looking at university finances, the *Houston Chronicle* exposed questionable practices in the University of Texas's investments. "As financial markets slide, the people charged with managing a trust fund that benefits Texas' largest state universities are hiding the performance of some of the fund's highest-risk investments," the paper reported. In California, the *Riverside Press-Enterprise* saw a good story in the financial difficulties of UC-Riverside's business school, which had accrued a $2.5 million deficit out of its state money. That newspaper commits eight full-time reporters to the education beat and five more who cover school districts and colleges as part of their geographic beat, noted the *AJR* article on higher education.

When college tuition rises, both college and community journalists latch onto this anger-inducing story. The College Board (2002) reported that in 2002–2003 college tuition and fees rose an average of about 6 percent at four-year private institutions, almost 10 percent at four-year public institutions, and about 8 percent at two-year public institutions. Students, parents, and taxpayers pay attention to the rising cost of higher education.

Developing and Cultivating Sources

Good higher education stories, like on any beat, come from good sources. College journalists might have an advantage over community journalists because they literally live in the middle of higher education stories, sitting next to sources in classes or taking classes from them. Often college journalists break or report university stories first. Overburdened reporters at the local metropolitan newspaper rely on tips, news releases, and student newspaper stories to tell them what is going on. Astute college journalists have a well-developed roster of sources among administrators, faculty, staff, and students. They should know about campus news even before the university news release comes out.

Mike Morris, who was senior editor with *The Towerlight* and wrote most of the Towson University president stories mentioned at the beginning of this chapter, had to work a wide range of sources to keep up with the ongoing controversy. After that experience, he (2003) suggested: "Use sources that you are very confident with, and know that they have somewhat of an authority to speak on the matter. Don't be shy. Persistently call high-ranking administrators and people who are relevant or critical to your story." Even sources' behavior can give you good information about the stance of a source. It's also important to get to key sources early in the reporting before they begin to clam up. Morris said:

> More likely than not, you'll be surprised by how revealing anything they do or say is. The fact that someone hangs up the phone on you or doesn't return your calls says an awful lot. I personally would spend a large amount of time building a relationship with my sources and having them feel comfortable enough to divulge key information, only to be silenced by their bosses when they read their quotes in the next newspaper. I had to find alternative means of getting information for my articles, which usually meant convincing the person to talk—but off the record. I took a gamble with one of my best sources and used her extremely colorful quotes to support my articles.

The source did get into trouble with her bosses so Morris used her only for background information in subsequent stories. Morris also had to make an ethical decision not to name a source he needed to reveal Towson's top finalist to replace President Perkins. "I opted to say as much as I could without giving the person away, which still accomplished the same goal of informing the campus on the matter at hand," he explained.

In addition to protecting sources, higher education reporters face other interviewing challenges. High-ranking higher education officials can be difficult-to-reach sources. They have secretaries or public information officers who block access. Board members such as trustees or regents are often political appointees and might be wary of talking so they don't lose their appointments. They also have other lives outside their political appointments. For example, Morris had to track down members of the University of Maryland System Board of Regents at their workplaces when the regents were not meeting. Morris (2003) added:

> Be suspicious about what anyone tells you because most people involved with higher education have hidden agendas. Be curious and question what your sources tell you. For example, a Towson University administrator was quoted in August 2001 as saying what "excellent condition" the Guilford (presidential) house was in. Yet about six months later, (President) Perkins said hundreds of thousands of dollars were spent on asbestos and lead paint removal.

Using Public Documents

Freedom of information conflicts also arose in Morris's pursuit of the Towson University president story. When the Board of Regents dismissed Perkins from the university, it would not release any information about the severance package he received. Rumors flew around the state about how the package gave Perkins hundreds of thousands of dollars over the next few years. Morris explained that the story needed to be pinned down, but the Board of Regents said Maryland's Freedom of Information Act did not cover personnel information. Journalists in the state disagreed because the salaries of all state university administrators had always been considered an open record.The Board of Regents never officially released the information, but Morris got the information from one of his regular sources. No one corrected his reporting on the information, and the *Baltimore Sun* even credited Morris's story as the definitive information on the severance package.

SPORTS ON THE EDUCATION BEAT

Information found through freedom of information searches can also be an important entrée into a major higher education beat—sports. Although the large majority of higher education stories involving sports are event coverage, occasionally important stories surface within the education side of sports. Many times documents, such as those from athletic department budgets, bring these stories to the fore.

In covering sports, any reporter functions just like all other journalists digging for a story. According to the *Associated Press Sports Writing Handbook* (Wilstein, 2002):

> They do their detective work armed with powerful other resources: the federal Freedom of Information Act, state and county records, utility company files, reverse telephone directories, computer databases, and other elements of computer-aided research. With tools like that, reporters can get information on such things as: college athletic budgets; incomes of coaches; compliance with Title IX requirements for equality of male and female programs; phone records for coaches and recruiters; unauthorized use of state funds in recruiting; distribution of tickets to coaches, players, businesses, and alumni; and the addresses of athletes.

The balance between athletics and academics surfaces constantly. How universities allocate funds between the academic and athletic sides, particularly in hard financial times, sparks controversy. Endowments or special booster organizations might subsidize athletics or provide scholarships. When a high-profile coach is hired at a spectacular salary, many people question a school's priorities.

In addition, faculty members lament when students—whether high school or college—have to miss classes so they can participate in sports contests. While acknowledging the benefit of sports to a student's education, teachers do not want students to miss important instruction. They also fear students will focus too much on athletics and not enough on knowledge that will help them later. Not every athlete signs a lucrative contract with the National Football League.

The National Collegiate Athletic Association (NCAA) has been in discussions in recent years about the academics–athletics balance, particularly student-athlete graduation rates. Those rates have fallen for many schools. As part of its academic reform, the NCAA implemented new rules in 2004. Schools whose athletes perform poorly in the classroom will lose lucrative postseason contests. Under a system of graduated penalties, they will be ineligible for postseason championships and bowl bids. The Coalition on Intercollegiate Athletics made up of NCAA representatives and educators endorsed the NCAA reforms and will monitor their success in improving athletes' academic performance.

At middle schools and high schools, much attention in recent years has focused on sportsmanship. Some schools have implemented programs that penalize schools whose teams do not behave properly even off the field. Players could be suspended for drinking, missing classes, or any other number of infractions. The education reporter who covers the beat adequately has to delve into the sports arena and pay attention to those issues where athletics and academics clash. The sports reporter generally pays attention to the play-by-play on the field, but on some occasions the two may team up to write stories that span both beats.

A Case Study of a College Sports Investigation

In one of the major investigative journalism projects involving college sports, the *St. Paul Pioneer Press* uncovered extensive academic fraud among players at the University of Minnesota. Sports editor Emilio Garcia-Ruiz (2000) detailed the exhaustive investigation in the *IRE Journal*, explaining the newspaper's reporting team was guided by one overriding tenet: "Only evidence that school and NCAA investigators could not refute would appear in print."

The other major aspect of the investigation was patience. *Pioneer Press* reporter George Dohrmann spent three months tracking down proof of cheating among about two dozen players. The first lead: a letter sent to the NCAA by an academic counseling office manager who was a tutor for athletes. At first, she refused to acknowledge any wrongdoing. But Dohrmann kept in touch with her over two months, and finally she admitted that she had done course work for more than two dozen players. Dohrmann needed proof, however, not just her statement.

The tutor had saved all the work on her computer and allowed Dohrmann to download the course work. He and other *Pioneer Press* reporters tracked down several former players who admitted that the tutor did their course work for them, thus confirming the tutor's story. The newspaper ran the story before an NCAA basketball tournament and faced a firestorm of criticism and 600 subscription cancellations. Many Minnesota residents saw the newspaper as attacking their home team.

Once every other Minnesota media outlet got on the story, Garcia-Ruiz said the newspaper put together a team to continue the investigation. The newspaper decided to focus strictly on one topic: academic fraud. Other media looked into what the basketball coach knew and when he knew it. In the course of its reporting, the *Pioneer Press* did document that the coach knew what was going on; the university dismissed him with a $1.5 million contract buyout.

The investigative team created a spreadsheet to analyze all the course work player by player. The team dug into players' academic records, which were used as background but did not appear in the newspaper because of possible legal complications. Reporters submitted numerous Freedom of Information Act requests to the university for all its NCAA filings and other information. The reporters discovered that the University of Minnesota team had one of the worst graduation rates in the Big Ten.

Three months after the first story by the newspaper, the university president admitted the basketball team's wrongdoing, saying, "The Gopher basketball team was guilty of 'numerous instances' of academic cheating." About 18 players over the course of five years cheated or committed other NCAA violations. The final result: the suspension of four players from the NCAA tournament, the coach's ouster, a self-imposed ban on postseason play, and contracts not renewed for five high-level athletic department officials. (From the *IRE Journal*, March/April 2000. Excerpted with permission of Investigative Reporters and Editors, Inc. and the author.)

VISUALIZING THE EDUCATION BEAT

Features on the education beat can be easily illustrated in photographs or on videotape. Stories such as carnival fund-raisers or student design competitions vibrantly depict excited young people. However, the tough stories to depict can be the most important ones to cover, such as testing issues or budget crises. Often education reporters resort to head shots of officials, students bending over desks as they take exams, or teachers lecturing to classes. In many cases, students cannot be identified without prior consent, particularly if a story deals with a sensitive topic, such as cheating.

TV journalists especially struggle to report on the "hard news" of the education beat. Yvonne Simons, a reporter for WRAL-TV in Raleigh, North Carolina, said: "Testing on a good day is basically a dull story." She noted in an account on the EWA Web site (2003) that she faced a struggle when reporting on the state's accountability system, an important story to the entire state. Many parents did not understand that students and their schools would be held accountable if they did poorly on standardized tests. With a fellowship from EWA, she produced an eight-part series, which in addition to being broadcast had an added online component on the station's Web site. To illustrate the story, she got footage of students resolutely trying to do well on the test at a school about to face penalties.

Getting permission to get images from inside classrooms can be a challenge but well worth it to illuminate a significant topic. As noted earlier in the chapter, reporters will have to get permission. The *Sun*'s Jon Rockoff (2003) said: "What goes on in the classroom is the biggest story topic, especially when classroom instruction is being altered. And the impact of the accountability movement is a major topic of interest now, for example, how has high-stakes testing affected instruction and administration."

GLOSSARY

Adequacy: "Sufficient funds for schools to teach all but the most severely disabled to meet state and district standards or some other clearly defined educational outcome," according to the EWA.

Cost–function model: "Gathers a high volume of data including test scores, teachers' salaries, and student demographics, applies a statistical formula to it, and then determines how much an average student needs in the way of resources to succeed," according to the EWA.

Educationese: The abstract jargon employed by educators and education policy makers.

Evidence-based model: School districts research proven successful practices that improve student achievement and then establish a funding level to attain those outcomes.

Professional judgment model: Gathers experts—teachers, administrators, and school finance consultants—to decide what resources are needed to create schools in which students will achieve state standards.

Successful schools model: It looks at past per-pupil funding in districts in which students were achieving state academic standards. The per-student funding from those successful school districts is averaged and then applied statewide.

ACTIVITIES

1. Research the county or city school system where you live. How is it funded? Who sits on the Board of Education? Are members appointed or elected? How many students does the system have? What is the system doing to assess students?

2. Have the school superintendent or another top administrator come to class. Interview him or her about three issues facing the school system. How much does each issue rely on funding to be resolved? Write a story about one of the issues, using the interview as a basis. Include comments from three other education sources, such as teachers, parents, volunteers, or students.

3. Pick a current educational issue, such as "no pass, no play" for student athletes, and find out what the local district's policy is.

4. Investigate special education in the local school system. What type of model is being used, mainstreaming, or inclusion, or separate classes? Research the federal Individuals with Disabilities Education Act (IDEA) and how it is applied in the school system.

5. Go to the National Center for Education Statistics Web site, http://nces.ed.gov, and compare your local high school to that of another school on the list. On the Common Core of Data page, you can search for data on specific schools. What do the differences tell you about important issues at either school?

RESOURCES AND WEB SITES

Sites from the Education Writers Association:
Education Index: www.educationindex.com. An index site; links to sites on thousands of topics.

K–12
American Federation of Teachers, AFL-CIO: www.aft.org. The teachers' union.
American School Board Journal: www.asbj.com
Child Indicator: www.childtrends.org/store/search.cfm?#URLToken#
Child Trends: www.childtrends.org
The Children's Beat: A Journal of Media Coverage: www.casey.umd.edu. Free quarterly magazine written by and for journalists.

Education Daily: www.educationdaily.com
Education News: www.educationnews.org
Education Next: www.educationnext.org
Education Week: www.edweek.org
Education World: www.education-world.com
Educational Leadership: www.ascd.org
Harvard Education Letter: www.edletter.org
InsideSchools.org: www.insideschools.org
Keep Schools Safe: www.keepschoolssafe.org
National Education Association: www.nea.org. Links to legislative activity.
National School Boards Association: www.nsba.org. Lots of downloadable reports for free; good site for information on hot topics and on school governance.
Phi Delta Kappan: www.pdkintl.org/kappan
Rethinking Schools: www.rethinkingschools.org
The School Administrator: www.aasa.org/publications/sa
Stateline: www.stateline.org/education
Teachers College at Columbia University links: www.TCRecord.org
Youth Outlook: www.youthoutlook.org.news. Looks at the world through young people's eyes; a Pacific News Service online project.

Higher Education
Black Issues in Higher Education: www.blackissues.com
Change Magazine: www.aahe.org/change
Chronicle of Higher Education: www.chronicle.com
Community College Week: www.ccweek.com
National CrossTalk: www.highereducation.org/crosstalk
Peterson's Education Portal: www.petersons.com. Good site for basic research on colleges and universities.
Postsecondary Education Opportunities: www.postsecondary.org
www.uwire.com. Connects college media.
University Business: www.universitybusiness.com

Data Sources
College Board: www.collegeboard.com
Education Commission of the States: www.ecs.org
Educational Research Service: www.ers.org
ERIC: www.askeric.org
ERIC Clearinghouse on Higher Education: www.eriche.org
The Grapevine Survey, the Center for the Study of Education Policy: www.coe.ilstu.edu/grapevine
National Assessment of Educational Progress: http://nces.ed.gov/nationsreportcard
National Center for Education Statistics: http://nces.ed.gov
National Center for Public Policy and Higher Education: www.highereducation.org
National Center on Education, Disability and Juvenile Justice: www.edjj.org
National Library of Education: www.ed.gov/NLE
TIMSS, Third International Math and Science Study: http://nces.ed.gov/timss
U.S. Department of Education, Office of Educational Research and Improvement: www.ed.gov/offices/OERI

Children and Youth Resources from LynNell Hancock
Child Welfare
Administration for Children and Families: www.dhhs.gov. U.S. Department of Health and Human Services. Compiles data on welfare, child support, domestic violence, adoption, foster care, family support, child abuse, and neglect.

American Bar Association Center on Children and the Law: http://www.abanet.org/child. A public policy and law organization that focuses on child protective services, foster care, and termination of parental rights.

American Public Welfare Association: www.awpa.org. Compiles state data on children in out-of-home care.

Annie E. Casey Foundation: www.aecf.org. Advocacy and research group that promotes neighborhood-based foster care.

Child Welfare League of America: www.cwla.org. A national advocacy group that looks at states' statistics on child abuse and neglect.

National Clearinghouse on Child Abuse and Neglect Information: www.calib.com. A federal clearinghouse that offers a wealth of information on child abuse statistics and more.

National Coalition for Child Protection Reform: www.nccpr.org. A committee founded out of a Harvard Law School conference in 1991 dedicated to reforming child welfare systems.

National Committee to Prevent Child Abuse: www.childabuse.org. Publishes an annual survey of child abuse data from voluntary state reporting.

National Council of Juvenile and Family Court Judges: www.ncjfcj.unr.org. Represents judges with jurisdiction over delinquency, abuse and neglect, divorce, custody, and domestic violence cases and acts as clearinghouse for statistics and identification of model court projects.

The Pew Commission on Children in Foster Care: www.pewfostercare.org. Develops research and recommendations to improve policies for children in foster care.

School Shootings

Department of Justice report, "Kids and Guns," (2000, March 7): www.ncjrs.org/html/ojjdp/jjbul2000_03_2/contents.html

The Harvard Civil Rights Project and the Advancement Project released a June 2000 report on "Opportunities Suspended: The Devastating Consequences of Zero Tolerance and School Discipline Policies." www.civilrightsproject.harvard.edu/convenings/zerotolerance/synopsis.php

Justice Policy Institute's "School House Hype" report, realities of school violence: www.cjcj.org. JPI is a project of the Center on Juvenile and Criminal Justice.

National Conference of State Legislatures: www.ncsl.org. "School Violence: Lessons Learned" and its "Colorado After Columbine: The Gun Debate."

National School Safety Center: www.nssc1.org. Details violent school deaths in the United States since 1992.

National Youth Gang Center: www.iir.com/nygc. (links to sources of youth-violence information)

Poynter Institute's "Another School Shooting": www.poynter.org

The Secret Service National Threat Assessment Center report (2000) on 37 school shootings over the past 25 years: www.treas.gov/usss/index.shtml

U.S. Department of Education: www.ed.gov. "Guide to Safe Schools." It followed up in 2000 with "Safeguarding Our Childen: An Action Guide."

Health

National Head Start Association: www.nhsa.org

National Institute of Mental Health: Child and Adolescent Mental Health: www.nimh.nih.gov/publicat/childmenu.cfm

Policy and Research Groups

Annie E. Casey Foundation's Kids Count Data Book Online: www.aecf.org/kidscount/databook. Census data on the age, sex, race, and living arrangements of U.S. children.

The Child and Family Web Guide: www.cfw.tufts.edu. From Tufts University, research in education, mental health, child care, and adoption.

Child Trends reports: www.childtrends.org. An annual collection of data measuring all aspects of children's well-being in America.

The International Clearinghouse on Child, Youth and Family Policy: www.childpolicyintl.org.
    Cross-national, comparative information about policies, programs, benefits, and ser-
    vices in the industrialized nations.
Kids Count Network: www.kidscountnetwork.net. Reports, issue briefs, and data books by
    state, topic, or type of document.
National Center for Children in Poverty, Columbia University School of Public Health: www.
    researchforum.org. Research on poverty, welfare, education, and children's health.
The Urban Institute: www.urban.org. Nationwide clearinghouse for family and child policy
    research.

Training for Education Reporters
The Education Writers Association offers the National Fellowships in Education Reporting
    and regional and national seminars on timely education topics, led by researchers and
    education reporters. Topics: the First Amendment and public schools, school leader-
    ship, college costs, and school reform in California (see www.ewa/offers/seminars or
    www.ewa/offers/fellowships).

REFERENCES

Burrell, J. (2003, July). College by 9, David Dalrymple stands out at UMBC. *Maryland Family*,
    pp. 16–17.
Casey Journalism Center on Children and Families. (2002, February 19). Crime and suffering
    dominate news coverage of children, context rarely reported. [News release]. http://casey.
    umd.edu/home.nsf.
Child Trends. (2002). The impact of President Bush's *No Child Left Behind Act* on state educa-
    tion indicators. *The Child Indicator*. www.childtrends.org/w_welcome.asp.
Children Now. (2001, October 23). Local TV news distorts real picture of children, study finds.
    [News release]. www.childrennow.org/newsroom/news-01/pr-10-23-01.cfm.
The College Board. (2002, October 24). $90 billion available in student financial aid, with schol-
    arship growth outpacing loan growth. [News release]. www.collegeboard.com/press/
    article/0,3183,18420,00.html.
Education Writers Association. (2003). *Money matters: A reporter's guide to school finance*. Wash-
    ington, DC: EWA.
Education Writers Association. (2002). *Standards for education reporters*. Washington, DC: EWA.
Education Writers Association. (2001). *Covering the education beat: A current guide for editors,
    writers and the public*. Washington, DC: EWA.
Garcia-Ruiz, E. (2000, March/April). Proving NCAA violations in Minnesota basketball. *IRE
    Journal*, p. 18.
Government Organization, 2002 Census of Governments. Vol. 1 No. 1. (2002 December).
    http://www.census.gov/prod/2003pubs/gc021x1.pdf accessed 7/24/2003.
Hampson, M. (2003, August). Email interview with Baltimore County Public School System's
    public information officer.
Hancock, L. (2003, June) Covering the youth beat. www.jrn.columbia.edu/studentwork/chil-
    dren.
Healy, P. (2001, October 7). Harvard figures show most of its grades are A's or B's. *Boston Globe*,
    p. A1
Morris, M. (2003, March 15). Email interview with the senior editor of Towson University's
    The Towerlight.
Rockoff, J. (2003, August). Email interview with the *Sun*'s Baltimore County education reporter.
Stepp, C. S. (2003, January/February). Higher examination. *American Journalism Review*.
Stone, Elizabeth. (1999, September/October). Using children as sources. *Columbia Journalism
    Review*. http://archives.cjr.org/year/99/5/children.asp.
Wilstein, S. (2002). *Associated Press sports writing handbook*. New York: McGraw-Hill.

CHAPTER 9

THE BROAD BEAT OF BUSINESS

When the United States invaded Iraq in spring 2003, the *Dallas Morning News* staff went into gear. As reporters busily chased news from the Pentagon, the White House, Army headquarters in Saudi Arabia, and battalions on the move in Iraq, business reporters examined the impact falling bombs would have on the U.S. economy.

The night the war started, the *Morning News* tore up its business front and devoted it entirely to the war's possible impact on the national economy and local mainstays. The main story explored different scenarios and had economists speculate on how each scenario could affect the economy. What effect would a quick decisive victory have versus a drawn-out, Vietnam-style war? What if Saddam Hussein unleashed his "weapons of mass destruction"?

Sidebar or companion stories looked specifically at industries that could be affected by the war, for example, the impact on airline traffic and Fort Worth–based American Airlines, which at the time was fighting to avoid filing for bankruptcy. Another story looked at the flow of crude oil and how the war could influence oil prices and, ultimately, the price of gas at the pump. Besides a consumer angle, this story also had a strong Dallas angle because of petroleum giant ExxonMobil being based there.

A third story explored the issue of advertising during wartime: How would companies change advertising strategies during the war? How would major publications and TV networks handle advertising during prime-time war coverage? Would advertisers want to be associated with the war coverage or would they shy away? A final story checked out the war's possible impact on tourism, conventions, hotel reservations, and visitor spending.

Just about every story has a money angle or business connection. Schools, churches, sports teams, the media—all take in and spend money, some for profit and some nonprofit. That means business interests affect every beat, and often business reporters will team with reporters on other beats to produce stories.

Business reporters and business sections play a large role in putting daily news events into context and showing their impact on people's wallets.

The story might not be as dramatic as a war. Natural disasters, such as hurricanes and tornadoes, carry huge price tags. Parishioners tithe at their churches, providing budgets to hire staff and pay for missions. The widespread power outage in the Northeast on August 14, 2003, cost New York businesses more than $750 million. The price tags for new stadiums or players negotiating contracts highlight the business side of sports. Every government action requires an expenditure of personnel and the paper the document is printed on, at the very least.

While business publications such as the *Wall Street Journal* are still widely read, more and more media have added business sections over the last decade. In the early 1990s, many newspapers moved from one page of business news to entire sections, often marketing those sections one day a week. Now large dailies in particular have a business section every day. Online sites have links to business stories or cover solely business news.

Business news used to focus on promotions, new companies, mergers, and stock listings. Today, business news ranges from the opening of a local ice cream shop to the collapse of business giants such as Enron. Business reporting staffs might have two reporters to cover local stories or dozens of reporters assigned to specific business beats such as financial institutions, retail, computer or technology, consumer spending, textiles, dot.com companies, and on and on.

In this chapter you will:

■ Be introduced to business beats,
■ Learn major documents that business reporters use to get information,
■ Meet the major players on the business beat,
■ Learn how to read an earnings report,
■ See some major business stories and how they got reported, and
■ Get an overview of nonprofit organizations.

BREAKING COVERAGE INTO BEATS

Media that have the resources to hire enough staff will divide business beats based on the size of the paper and the types of businesses or industry prevalent in a given area. Here are some key beats that media consider, said Pete Johnson (2003), assistant business editor for the *Dallas Morning News*, which has a business desk staff of more than 50 reporters and editors.

■ The economy beat makes sense of the many, often conflicting, reports issued by state and federal governments assessing the status of unemployment, consumer confidence, consumer spending, gross domestic product, and sales of durable goods, to name a few. Reporters on this beat must not be afraid of numbers.

■ The markets beat analyzes movements in the major stock markets, looking for trends that give clues about the future direction of the economy. Again, comfort with math benefits a reporter on this beat.

■ The technology beat is a must-have beat today. In fact, most major metropolitan newspapers have subdivided this beat into specific specialties. (The *Dallas Morning News* has five to six tech writers, including one whose job is to test the latest computer and video games and write reviews.) The beat runs the gamut of reporting company-specific news, such as earnings and new products, to spotting and exploring new trends among technology companies or technology users. A reporter on this beat must have a love for gadgets.

■ The auto beat is not only for gear-heads any more. Auto coverage includes trends in auto sales; rebates and incentives; automakers' earnings; environmental issues and government regulation; consumer safety; corporate intrigue; and new products. Johnson added: "It may help to know something about cars, but it's not essential to know the displacement of a 450cc engine."

■ The health care beat from a business perspective does not cover the disease of the week. This reporter explores issues related to the rising costs of health care and their impact on consumers, companies, and health providers. An overlooked beat for some time, more media see it as critically important.

■ The real estate beat is perfect for people who love to know what their neighbor's house sold for and whether their house is increasing or decreasing in value. The real estate reporter does not cover every transaction but can tell readers which neighborhoods are hot and which are not. This reporter explores trends in housing sales, office vacancies, mortgage rates, among others, and breaks news on major real estate sales or development plans.

■ The transportation beat, depending on the region, could involve covering airlines, railroads, shipping, and ports. For example, the *Morning News* has an airlines reporter covering locally based American and Southwest Airlines; a business travel reporter who covers online travel agencies and hotels and writes consumer-oriented pieces; and an aviation reporter who covers air defense contractors based in Dallas–Fort Worth as well as the railroad based there. Story topics include airline flights and traffic, company performance (earnings, on-time results, etc.), corporate leadership, union contracts, and consumer pieces on prices, security, and even airline food.

■ The sports beat has become more and more a business story. Player transactions are still the province of a newspaper's sports department. But more and more papers cover the buying and selling of professional teams in the business department. Professional sports franchises and their financial dealings with cities and states, vendors, sponsors, and lenders are all part of this beat. So, too, are the players and their corporate endorsements. Some athletes, such as Tiger Woods or Michael Jordan, are corporate enterprises in their own right, though they don't file quarterly earnings reports. On this beat knowledge of sports is helpful.

- The retail beat covers a mix of industry trend stories, company-specific news, and consumer-driven stories. News about retail sales often is viewed as a good indicator of the state of the economy. Individual retailers are important employers in a community, and their sales, earnings, and overall health become a major concern. As consumers, readers want to know retail trends, store openings or closings, or changes in the sales tax.

- The energy beat ranges from the companies that produce the power to the environmental groups that monitor them. Johnson noted: "We love to hate utility companies, but we can't live without them. The same is true with the oil and gas companies. These companies make news that affects readers where it hurts: A proposed rate hike by the electric company hits just before the hot summer months; OPEC cuts the supply of oil and prices at the pump soar; and Enron manipulates its revenues to give an inflated picture of its profits." Environmental issues, such as the development of alternative sources of fuel, might overlap on this beat. The environment as a science beat is covered in Chapter 12.

- The legal affairs beat looks at the legal community, "which is an important, yet under-reported, power broker in every city," Johnson noted. Enron, Worldcom, Imclone, HealthSouth, Martha Stewart—the list of companies or corporate officers involved in some type of legal morass grows longer each day. A legal affairs reporter helps make sense of the allegations and government efforts to rein in the abuses.

- The media beat covers issues related to newspaper, television, and radio ownership, advertising, and influence. The media beat has been hot recently with media mergers as well as proposals by the Federal Communications Commission to loosen limits on media ownership. "Not for the timid since you may find yourself writing about the company that supplies your paycheck," Johnson pointed out.

- The personal finance beat, a very consumer-oriented beat, helps people spend, save, or invest their money wisely. The beat has seen a growing emphasis at newspapers.

- The labor beat depends on the region of the country for the amount of attention and size of staff. While not a big priority at southern papers, such as the *Dallas Morning News,* in cities not heavily dependent on factories and manufacturing, labor becomes important in the industrial Northeast and Midwest. Reporters write stories related to organized labor, including pay, benefits, and working conditions.

Although not every newspaper can afford huge business staffs, the beats just defined can serve as a guide to any business reporter as to the range of topics covered on the beat. The solo business reporter at the small daily might find he or she covers all these beats at some time each year. Or editors might establish local business news or the impact of national news on local businesses as the parameters for the business beat. Media in Iowa, Wisconsin, or other agriculture-dependent states would assign a reporter to an agribusiness beat. That beat reporter could cover industries ranging from dairy in Wisconsin to walnut growers in California to corn in Iowa to cattle in Texas. Trends in cost of cultivation as well as family farm life would make stories on an agribusiness beat.

KEY DOCUMENTS ON THE BUSINESS BEAT

Documents jump start many business stories. Simply, documents can give you details, sometimes quite revealing, about a company's health and wealth. They can prepare you to interview the company's chief executive officer or attend an annual meeting. Business reporters must know which reports companies file, what the deadlines are for filing, and when they can get access to them.

Publicly traded companies are required by law to file a series of reports in a timely fashion to help investors understand what's happening with them. These documents go to the Securities and Exchange Commission and can be accessed via the Web site. Johnson at the *Dallas Morning News* and his colleague, staff writer Eric Torbenson (2003), said the following are basic reports that reporters, analysts, and investors pay the most attention to.

- **10-Q:** These quarterly filings appear when a company reports its quarterly earnings. They are not audited numbers, but they give a pretty good indication of what's happening with the company. They include something called "management's discussion and analysis of financial condition and results of operations," just basically a long title for "what's going on at our company." Torbenson said the statements are "generally good stuff where we get a sense of how business is going and see trends in revenue and costs." The 10-Q also features balance sheet information, which is crucial for a company such as American Airlines's parent company, AMR. The *Morning News* wants to know that information so reporters can calculate when the company is going to run out of cash.
- **10-K:** Like a 10-Q, the 10-K is the annual report for the company. Unlike the 10-Q, it is audited by an accredited accounting firm so the numbers are reliable. It too includes a management discussion of how the year went, though more thorough because it is the big report for the year. It also details litigation facing the company and gives a broad overview of the company's industry. Reporters can think of it as a more beefy 10-Q, Johnson added.
- **8-K:** When something newsworthy happens to a company—something that investors would really, really want to know about as soon as possible— companies are required to file an 8-K. The document generally deals with events that would have a material effect on a company's outlook.

It's a pretty broad category and open to interpretation. Sometimes it can be a profit warning, or executives leaving the company, or even good news like a major contract being awarded. But they're worth watching out for. They almost always guarantee news.

- **DEF-14A,** also known as a proxy statement: Each year public companies have annual meetings where they discuss business, elect directors, and handle big issues in front of their shareholders. A guide to that meeting, the proxy lists names of people up for election to the board of directors, entertains shareholder proposals, and outlines other business. The proxy includes key information on who holds the shares of the company, what the officers are paid on an annual basis, and the stock incentive plans that most companies have. From a reporter's point of view, the proxy statement might be the most important document a company produces.

- **Form 4:** These forms must be filed when officers of the company or directors on the board sell stock. Sometimes they will sell it, other times they will buy stock. But no matter, they have to disclose what they did. Generally there's a substantial time lag between when the stock action happens and when they report it. If the president is dumping all his stock in a company, it usually means bad things are happening. Likewise, officers buying lots of stock are betting the company will do well.

- **11-K:** Like an annual report (a 10-K), the 11-K deals with a stock ownership plan and how that is going.

- **S-type forms:** S-forms often are prospectuses on either a brand-new stock offering for a public company or a new securities offering for a company that's already being traded publicly. These often include key information on the state of the company and why it is going to the market for money.

Reading an Earnings Report

Each quarter, a publicly owned company must submit a "consolidated statement of income"—otherwise known as an earnings report—to the federal Securities and Exchange Commission. This document gives a picture of how the company is performing and is closely scrutinized by Wall Street. A good or bad report by any of the select companies that comprise the Dow Jones industrial average, or other major corporations, can dramatically move the stock market on a given day. Television business shows might preview a particular company's earnings report to come out that day while shareholders and investors anxiously await.

The reports have page after page of numbers. Reporters—and investors—watch essentially three sets of numbers: total revenues for the quarter (often expressed by retailers as total sales); net income or loss; and diluted earnings per share (essentially the amount that each share would earn if the profit were divided among all outstanding shares of common stock plus all stock warrants, stock options, preferred stock, etc.). In each case, the numbers for the just-completed quarter are compared with the same quarter from a year ago to give a sense of the company's direction.

The basic information, therefore, would be Company XYZ reported a second-quarter profit of $25.2 million, or $1.01 per share, compared with $19.8 million, or 85 cents per share, for the same quarter a year ago. Revenues were $750 million compared with $675 million a year ago. That means the company increased its sales, its profit, and the value of its common stock. All that is good news for stockholders, who could receive higher dividends and might see the price of their stock rise. Companies also use this report to forecast their performance for the following quarter and the full year, though an increasing number of major corporations, such as Coca-Cola, have chosen to stop providing guidance.

Interpreting an earnings report is not as simple as looking at profits and losses. For example, a company such as Time Warner Inc. might post a loss. If it is a smaller loss than a year ago, or if the loss is less than analysts predicted, it is good news. Similarly, a company might post a profit, but if the earnings per share are less than analysts expected, or if they are less than the company forecast, then even an increase is considered bad news.

A myriad number of complications can alter the picture. A company might show strong gains in revenue but post a net loss because of a charge against earnings for such things as a corporate restructuring, a legal judgment, or the divestiture of an underperforming unit. Companies usually explain these changes in the text that accompanies the financial statement.

Based on the earnings report in Figure 9.1 from Max & Erma's Restaurants, business in the third quarter of 2003 was a disappointment compared with the same quarter in 2002. The company's revenues grew by almost $3.9 million, but its expenses grew by $4.5 million. Max & Erma's still managed to make a profit, though it was less than the profit made in the third quarter of 2002.

In the earnings statement for Max & Erma's Restaurants, reporters can see where money is spent and what is left (net income) after all expenses are paid, including taxes. They can also see what the profit would be worth to shareholders if it were evenly divided among all those owning shares of common stock, stock options, or stock warrants.

In the case of Max & Erma's, the August 2002 profit was $881,386 with nearly 2.6 million shares outstanding, resulting in net income per share of 34 cents. In August 2003, the company realized $619,840 in profit and the number of outstanding shares had risen above 2.6 million. The combination of less income and more shares lowered the earnings per share to 24 cents. Net income per share measures what the profit would be worth to shareholders if it were evenly divided. The board of directors decides whether shareholders

FIGURE 9.1 Earnings Statement Filed with the SEC for Max & Erma's
Restaurants, Inc., Condensed Consolidated Statements of Income (unaudited)

	TWELVE WEEKS ENDED		FORTY WEEKS ENDED	
	August 3, 2003	*August 4, 2002*	*August 3, 2003*	*August 4, 2002*
REVENUES:	$39,589,993	$35,712,493	$127,599,012	$115,992,136
COSTS AND EXPENSES:				
Costs of Goods Sold	9,833,941	8,672,221	31,413,934	28,576,383
Payroll and Benefits	12,994,300	11,395,408	41,758,349	37,274,130
Other Operating Expenses	12,240,073	10,796,877	39,727,347	35,087,016
Pre-Opening Expenses	275,496	217,055	642,994	472,983
Loss on Disposition of Assets	158,239		158,239	
Administrative Expenses	3,009,247	2,926,622	9,871,428	9,341,889
Total Operating Expenses	38,511,296	34,008,183	123,572,291	110,752,401
Operating Income	1,078,697	1,704,310	4,026,721	5,239,735
Interest Expense	373,606	474,924	1,259,704	1,644,782
Minority Interest in Income of Affiliated Partnerships	19,251	—	38,502	38,503
INCOME BEFORE INCOME TAXES:	685,840	1,229,386	2,728,515	3,556,450
INCOME TAXES:	66,000	348,000	551,000	993,000
NET INCOME:	$ 619,840	$ 881,386	$ 2,177,515	$ 2,563,450
NET INCOME PER SHARE:				
Basic	$0.25	$0.38	$0.89	$1.10
Diluted	$0.24	$0.34	$0.82	$0.99
SHARES OUTSTANDING:				
Basic	2,474,839	2,319,028	2,437,502	2,336,895
Diluted	2,628,741	2,582,193	2,652,408	2,597,210

actually get a dividend. The board could decide to put the profits into growing the company instead of paying a dividend. For example, Microsoft chose not to pay a dividend for years but opted to pay one in 2003, as noted in the following Associated Press story:

SEATTLE—It's payday for Microsoft investors.

Microsoft Corp. is issuing its first dividend Friday, shelling out more than $850 million to shareholders, from the smallest investor right up to co-founder Bill Gates.

At 8 cents a share, the annual payout won't be huge to the average investor, analysts said. But it still marks a significant change for the Redmond, Wash., software company that went public in 1986 and has long hoarded its cash—now $43.4 billion—for research, acquisitions and legal claims.

Of course, there are the not-so-average investors.

Mr. Gates, who directly owns more than 1.2 billion shares of stock in the company he helped found in 1975, will receive a dividend of about $96.5 million. Microsoft chief executive Steve Ballmer will receive about $37.7 million.

Microsoft announced the dividend in January and issued a two-for-one stock split in February. The company has about 10.7 billion shares outstanding.

When announcing the dividend, chief financial officer John Connors noted that Microsoft was the only company of the 30 in the Dow Jones industrial average not to issue a dividend.

The payment is a monumental change for Microsoft, said Howard Silverblatt, an analyst for Standard & Poor's.

"It's kind of a changing of mentalities and thought and process," he said. "Going zero to anything is the biggest change you can have." (Reprinted with permission of the Associated Press.)

KEY PLAYERS FOR THE BUSINESS BEAT

Just as assistant business editor Johnson listed beats essential to business coverage, any business reporter should cultivate essential sources:

■ **Board of directors.** A group of individuals elected by a corporation's shareholders to oversee the company and, among other tasks, appoint senior management, issue stock, and declare dividends. A company's top executives usually sit on the board as inside directors. Outside directors from other businesses or from the community also serve on the board to advise on policy matters. The individuals are paid a set fee for each meeting they attend.

■ **Chairman of the board.** The highest ranking corporate officer. Often, but not always, also the company's top executive.

■ **President.** The second-highest ranking officer after the chairman of the board. Appointed by the board, the president reports to the board. In smaller companies, the president is usually the chief executive officer (CEO) and is responsible for day-to-day management and policy decisions. In larger corporations, the CEO title is usually held by the chairman, leaving the president as a chief operating officer (COO).

■ **Chief executive officer (CEO).** The executive chiefly responsible for the activities of a company. Usually an additional title held by a senior officer such as the chairman of the board or the president.

■ **Chief operating officer (COO):** The executive chiefly responsible for the day-to-day management.

■ **Chief financial officer (CFO):** The executive responsible for handling funds, financial records, and financial planning.

■ **Board of directors members.** A generally broad-based group appointed to set policy and to advise company executives. Members also vote on issues such as whether to issue stock and might have the authority to hire and fire the CEO. Members can come from the corporate, civic, government, and education sectors.

Beyond the officials who run the company, reporters will cultivate other sources.

■ **Media relations people.** Many companies have media relations people who handle reporters' inquiries. They can often provide background in addition to scores of fact sheets, news releases, copies of executives' speeches, and other materials to help a new reporter learn the company.

■ **Employees.** Department heads such as the vice president of retail services for a financial institution should also be cultivated. These people might be hard to reach, depending on the size of the company, without going through a public relations person first. Reporters should look for employees who might be willing to talk. Often reporters hear from disgruntled employees who want to complain about treatment or benefits. Reporters should listen, then investigate before writing a story. Former employees might also be good sources, but again reporters should determine their credibility.

■ **Consumers.** People eat in restaurants, shop in malls, find bargains at outlet centers, shop online—or wherever. Their comments add the personal touch to business stories. Reporters must remember that to interview people in private locations, such as malls or eateries, they must get permission—or wait in the street on city-owned property. They do not want to get charged with trespassing in the effort to get a story.

■ **Forensic accountants.** Some enterprising reporters have consulted what are known as forensic accountants. These people work much like forensics experts who aid police. They can look at financial reports and determine a company's health, if the company is reporting income and expenses correctly, or if any numbers just do not add up. Such forensics experts became critical in uncovering the Enron scandal—and some were just business reporters doing their job.

■ **Analysts and economists.** Other key sources include the analysts and economists at banks and brokerage houses who study a particular company or market sector, such as technology stocks, large retailers, or oil and gas companies. It might be difficult to locate an analyst for every small company, but reporters generally can find an analyst who covers that company's larger competitors and can speak on business trends or conditions in that sector. Most economists and analysts are happy to talk with reporters—the publicity helps their business, after all—and their comments provide balance and theoretically an independent viewpoint.

■ **Federal agency staff members.** Also useful as sources are the staffs at federal agencies that oversee businesses, such as the Securities and Exchange Commission, the Federal Communications Commission, the Federal Trade Commission, or the Federal Aviation Administration, to name just a few. Most states also have their own set of regulatory agencies overseeing aspects such as utility service and rates.

■ **Experts.** Reporters should also cultivate outside experts, such as university professors, independent consultants, or private investment advisers, who can provide perspective for a news story. For example, an economics professor at the nearest college could comment on the state of the local economy.

■ **Union leaders.** Many sectors have employee unions. Leaders can provide another perspective in addition to the expected topics of contract negotiations, benefits, and employee working conditions.

■ **Financial services.** Reporters whose employers can afford it can subscribe to financial services such as Bloomberg or Dow Jones newswires. Through these services, which might cost as much as $1,500 a year, reporters can retrieve a wealth of information on publicly traded companies, commodities such as gold or oil, bond markets, foreign currency exchange rates, and a whole lot more.

Reporters probably use Bloomberg most for information on stock prices, Johnson said. Reporters can find the current price of a particular company's stock and what it sold for the day before, the month before, or 10 years before. You could find, if you wanted, the price of General Electric stock every day since it first went public. Or you could find what GE sold for in five-minute intervals on any given day.

Reporters can find the same type of information on commodities and the stock indexes, such as the Dow Jones Industrials. For example, you could chart the price of oil since the first Gulf War, you could track the path of the Dow since the stock market crash of 1929, or you could find how Japan's Nikkei 225 index has fared this century.

Beyond stock prices, Bloomberg is a tremendous resource for a host of financial information on companies. Annual and quarterly reports—as well as most of the other documents discussed earlier—are available through Bloomberg. A company's balance sheet, credit profile, and dividend summary also can be found there.

The identities of a company's top executives, the members of its board of directors, and their positions in other companies can be learned on Bloomberg.

Reporters can also find the analysts who cover a particular company, as well as their latest recommendations. Need a source to help explain why a company's stock is off by 10 percent? Bloomberg is the place to look.

■ **Specialty reporters.** Reporters at community newspapers who have to put the local angle on a story might want to consult a reporter at a larger media outlet who has covered the story for a while. Most reporters are quite willing to share information and to coach reporters fairly new to the beat—without giving away any of their favorite sources.

A SAMPLING OF STORY IDEAS

The business beat, as evidenced by the beats listed earlier in the chapter, covers thousands of stories a week. No textbook can outline for a beginning reporter all the stories that might pop up. Any wise business reporter scours other business sections to find story ideas and to get a context for what makes business headlines in other parts of the country. People behind the headlines make good news. A time-consuming but well-read story always is an in-depth look at who sits on company boards of directors.

Bankruptcy Filings

Companies going out of business, dotcom sites shutting down after a few months online, and individuals and business owners filing for bankruptcy dominate the negative side of the business beat. Enron-type stories can overshadow the news of local merchants who are forced to close after decades of operation. Business reporters need to follow bankruptcy proceedings, which can relieve people of debt or protect them from creditors while they come up with a plan to repay debts. Individuals or businesses can restructure or even eliminate debt if they file for bankruptcy as allowed under federal laws. People can file on their own, but the laws are complicated. A bankruptcy filing can affect an individual's credit for up to a decade or longer.

Different types of bankruptcy are Chapter 7, Chapter 11, and Chapter 13. Under Chapter 7, individuals can have their debts eliminated, but they will have to sell or liquidate their assets or property, except for what may be exempted, to pay as much of their debt as possible. Federal law requires disclosure of what is owned and has been owned for two years prior to the filing. Anyone who files for bankruptcy under Chapter 7 cannot file for bankruptcy again for six years.

Chapter 11 is for individuals who have a lot of debt and for businesses, which is when most audiences hear the term used. Under Chapter 11, individuals or businesses come up with a plan to reorganize their debt. Also a reorganization plan, Chapter 13 allows individuals to set up a plan to repay their creditors, usually on a monthly plan. Payments are made to a bankruptcy trustee who in turn pays the creditors. People can file a Chapter 13 bankruptcy to stop creditors from pursuing them or foreclosure on their home or property. The filing gives people time to come up with a plan to repay debts.

Reporters cover company bankruptcies more frequently than individual filings. The latter could be a trend story, however, and could indicate the economic health of a community.

Cyclical News

Some business stories, however, are cyclical. Earnings reports come out every quarter. Companies have annual meetings and, among other items, announce promotions that find their way into business roundups. Holiday sales become predictable stories as do back-to-school specials. Seasons influence business coverage: summer vacations to the beach, winter ski trips to the mountains, spring weddings and honeymoon hideaways, fall tours of the leaves.

Other stories give consumers basic information to guide their choices of when to buy a home, when to get life insurance, where to invest, which electronics are the best for the price, and on and on. The following story in the Honolulu *Star-Bulletin* notes housing prices on the island of Oahu. Housing costs interest a range of readers. Note the sources Russ Lynch and Lyn Danninger (2003) used:

> Despite home prices that have passed the peak of the 1990s bubble, Oahu's housing market is not heading for a fall any time soon, local economists say.
>
> Home resales on Oahu continued to soar in both volume and price last month, with the median price among single-family houses hitting $394,500, the highest since the Honolulu Board of Realtors began keeping records in 1987.
>
> "I'd say it's still a green light on Oahu," said Paul Brewbaker, chief economist at the Bank of Hawaii.
>
> The previous high of $392,000 was reached in 1990 at the peak of the . Japanese-investment bubble.
>
> But neither Brewbaker nor Leroy Laney, professor of economics and finance at Hawaii Pacific University, believes Oahu homes are overvalued today.
>
> "It's hard to make an argument that homes are overvalued in the broad sweep of time during which you would expect real estate to appreciate," Brewbaker said.
>
> Laney agrees.
>
> "As far as affordability, it's relative to everything else. At some point you'd expect it to exceed that high. Everything else, like personal income, has gone up so in (inflation-adjusted) terms; it's not yet as high," he said.
>
> During the Japanese bubble, which ended in 1990, the rapid price acceleration made the period a boom.
>
> The pace of price increases this time around has been relatively steady, Brewbaker said.

"It's not nearly as rapid a rate of increase," he said.

The August median, the point at which half the units sold for more and half for less, was an increase of 9.6 percent from $360,000 in the same month last year.

While condominium prices were not as high as they were during the boom, the median sales price of $179,400 was up 19.6 percent from the August 2002 median of $150,000.

Mortgage rates have begun to creep back up, but the sales momentum continues, with 425 single-family homes changing hands in August, up 24.3 percent from 342 in the previous August.

Brewbaker predicts the pace of sales could slow somewhat as a result of rising rates.

"There probably would be some slowdown," he said.

Last month, 646 condominium units were resold, up 16 percent from 557 a year earlier.

Fixed mortgage rates bottomed out in June and have since risen a point and a half, said Harvey Shapiro, research economist for the Board of Realtors. It is too soon to know if the higher rates will inhibit sales, he said.

The monthly figures report only sales that have closed, which can be a couple of months after sales agreements are reached, Shapiro said.

In other words, the August report covers many agreements made before mortgage rates began to rise.

Total dollar sales volume for the first eight months of 2003 rose to $2.2 billion, up more than 35 percent from $1.6 billion in the first eight months of last year, said Anne Keamo, chairwoman of the 4,000-member Board of Realtors.

The association reports only sales of previously owned homes, recorded in its computerized Multiple Listing Service.

Sales of newly built homes also have been strong, but developers have said new-home sales now are being inhibited by a dwindling inventory. (Reprinted with permission from the *Honolulu Star-Bulletin*.)

Look at the range of sources in the housing price story—a university professor, a bank economist, and a researcher with the Board of Realtors—who put the numbers in context. They even add a historical context, comparing the current housing prices to figures in 1990. Lynch and Danninger carefully attribute quotes so readers know who is talking throughout the story.

Another business topic that always interests readers is jobs. Angela Shah, a writer for the *Dallas Morning News,* did more than just report the numbers, as the lead to her story (2003) shows:

The labor market defied expectations again Friday as companies slashed 93,000 jobs in August.

Despite positive trends recently in corporate profits, consumer spending and the stock market, job creation—an essential ingredient for a healthy economy—is just not happening.

"A couple of indicators move in the right direction for more than a month, and then you get something like this," said Lyssa Jenkens, chief economist at the Greater Dallas Chamber. "I thought we had traction, but maybe not."

While the jobless rate for August dipped slightly from 6.2 percent to 6.1 percent, that only reflects a group of discouraged job seekers who have quit looking and have been taken out of the workforce. Also, the number of self-employed has risen, and they are not included in the statistics.

The report left economists—many of whom had expected a more positive report—searching for explanations. (Reprinted with permission of the *Dallas Morning News.*)

Shah sets up the contradictions: Despite some positive trends, the number of new jobs has not increased. And people who follow the labor market are puzzled. Readers have the basic information in the first four paragraphs and can find additional explanation further into the story.

REPORTING ON NONPROFITS AND CHARITIES

Often many business leaders sit on the boards of nonprofit organizations. Their contacts within the business community benefit nonprofits or charities when it comes time to raise money. Some businesses, particularly those that are family owned, have charitable foundations on the side. For example, the Knight Foundation, which received its endowment from stock in the Knight Newspapers chain (now Knight-Ridder), makes grants to journalism education, such as endowed professorships and copy-editing workshops for working journalists.

A few newspapers have what is called a philanthropy beat that covers organizations that give away money or offer services for little or no charge. Among nonprofits are churches, private foundations, and organizations such as the American Cancer Society or the broad United Way, which is an umbrella for hundreds of smaller nonprofits. In some cases, these organizations have taken over the responsibilities that were once provided by government. At the turn of this century, nonprofits found themselves hard pressed to raise money, particularly after a poor economy and 9/11 when so many people gave to charities that sprang up to help victims and their families.

Journalists trying to put together a philanthropy beat can find help at the Foundation Center, established in 1956, as a resource for nonprofits and others. Its Web site has helpful links, news releases, and other information. In the mid-1990s appeared the Independent Sector, a coalition of nonprofit organizations, foundations, and corporate giving programs, "promoting philanthropy, volunteering, and citizen action," according to its Web site.

Nonprofit or philanthropic organizations have fewer reporting requirements than do businesses or publicly traded companies, but they still have records that a reporter on a philanthropy beat can use for information. Types of tax-exempt organizations include those that are charitable, social welfare, labor, and agricultural oriented, and business leagues, social clubs, fraternal societies, veterans' organizations, employee associations, and political parties.

Any tax-exempt organization must submit a Form 990 to the Internal Revenue Service each year. Information from Form 990 must be provided to anyone who asks for it. But getting these organizations to comply can sometimes be difficult. Although the IRS does require disclosure, many organizations feel little threat of penalty if they do not comply. If a charity resists, reporters can eventually get the data from the IRS by asking in person or making a written request that must be filled within 30 days.

Keith Storey, an education professor at Chapman University in California, tried to show his students how to find out financial information about disability-related charities (1998). He chose five organizations—Easter Seals, the Muscular Dystrophy Association (MDA), the Arthritis Foundation, Special Olympics, and United Cerebral Palsy Association. He specifically wanted to investigate where the money donated to them goes. The first stumbling block was getting organizations to respond to his numerous requests for information, he noted in an article published about the project. It took him almost a year of phone calls and visits to regional offices of the organizations to get their Form 990 information.

Storey said he found good information about the five charities from the American Institute of Philanthropy. The Institute revealed how much each of the charities spent in salaries for its directors and top staff and what percentage of its money it spent on "charitable purposes." For example, Storey found out that MDA paid its executive director $300,000 for one year and that five staff members made more than $100,000 a year.

His investigation also looked at how much some charities paid commercial fund-raisers. In California, for example, Easter Seals and the Arthritis Foundation both hired the fund-raising firm of My Favorite Charities. By looking at the California Attorney General's Report on Charitable Solicitation by Commercial Fundraisers, Storey said he found much fund-raising money poorly spent: Easter Seals paid My Favorite Charities $3,399 although it raised only $101, and the Arthritis Foundation paid $3,350 for only $150 raised.

Because the organizations wasted money on fund-raisers and paid high salaries, they had much less money for direct disability services, Storey reported. Anyone investigating charities should use a multipronged approach, he said. First, see whether the charity lists its financial information on its Web site. Even if it does, it might not be complete. Call the charity and ask for its latest financial report and IRS 990 forms. If a phone call doesn't work, send a registered letter with the request, and someone there will have to sign for the package. If the charity still does not respond, you can request the Form 990 directly from the IRS.

In addition to the IRS information, reporters should see how the charity ranks with oversight organizations such as the American Institute of Philanthropy. Other organizations such as the Better Business Bureau and Guidestar also provide information about tax-exempt organizations. Finally, Storey said, don't forget to investigate the commercial fund-raisers that nonprofit organizations might hire. The state attorney general's office should have information on charitable solicitation by commercial fundraisers. You might find information for fund-raisers in your state as Storey did in California.

Journalists on the philanthropy beat should not be swayed by the good works that nonprofit organizations do. The organizations that solicit funds from the general public should be held accountable for how the money is spent. Officials should be willing to share information. Most do a good job with limited funds and staff, but once in a while, a story breaks that shows embezzlement or poor judgment in administration. Reporters have to be ready to cover those stories as well as the softer stories about the people who benefit from nonprofits' help and support.

GLOSSARY

DEF-14A, also known as a proxy statement: A guide to the annual meeting, the proxy lists people up for election to the board of directors, entertains shareholder proposals, and outlines other business. The proxy statement might be the most important document a company produces.

Earnings per share: What the company could pay per share based on net income if it were to pay a dividend to shareholders.

Earnings report: Usually a 10-Q filed by a business with the Securities Exchange Commission listing income and expenditures for a specific time period.

8-K: Required when something newsworthy happens to a company, such as a profit warning, executives leaving the company, or a major contract being awarded.

11-K: Like an annual report (a 10-K), the 11-K deals with a stock ownership plan and how that is going.

Forensic accountant: An individual who has the knowledge to look at a company's financial statement and uncover inconsistencies.

Form 4:   Filed when officers of the company or directors on the board sell stock.

Form 990:   The IRS form that tax-exempt organizations must submit and also a public record.

Independent Sector: A coalition of nonprofit organizations, foundations, and corporate giving programs.

Net income: What is left after all the bills, including taxes, are paid.

Philanthropy: Helping people or organizations generally through foundations that give away funds in endowments; the federal government requires foundations to give at least 5 percent each year, usually the interest earned on their investments.

Prospectus: A statement issued when a company plans to offer new securities or when a new company is going public. The prospectus gives financial information to attract investors.

S-type forms: Prospectuses on either a brand-new stock offering for a public company or a new securities offering for a company that's already being traded publicly.

10-Q: Quarterly filings when a company reports its quarterly earnings; features balance sheet information.

10-K: Like a 10-Q, the 10-K is the annual report for the company; audited and includes a management discussion of how the year went.

ACTIVITIES

1. Have a local business reporter come to class and share how he or she got started on the beat. Did he or she have an undergraduate degree in business or economics? What documents or reports are the most helpful? The most difficult to get? What's the most accessible way to get reports?

2. Look at the Oahu housing story in the chapter. How many records can you identify that the reporters used to write the story? Name them.

3. Choose a Fortune 500 company that has an office in your community or state. Use at least five documents to write a background piece about the company and an idea for a story that would be of interest to local readers.

4. Look at the annual report of the Fortune 500 company you selected in Activity 3. Find the president's or CEO's letter to stockholders. Can you identify at least three stories you could develop from that letter? What financial data would you need to back up the story?

5. From the Fortune 500 company you used in Activity 3, download the latest balance sheet from its annual report. Have a business professor come to class and show you how to read the financial statement.

6. Write a story about a local business in your community. You could divide businesses among students in your class so that some students write about businesses that have located within the last year and others write about businesses that have been in town longer. Get input from the local chamber of commerce, merchants association, downtown revitalization group, or other agency tied to business development or growth.

7. What is the economic health of your community? What factors would you use to report that story? Write a story comparing its economic health today and 10 years ago.

8. Find a local nonprofit organization or charity based in your community, such as a food bank or battered women's shelter, and request its financial records. Look at how much of its money goes toward direct services and how much goes toward overhead costs. Write a profile of the organization.

RESOURCES AND WEB SITES

American Institute of Philanthropy: www.charitywatch.org
Associations on the Net: www.ipl.org/ref/AON. Research for associations from a variety of categories with the Internet Public Library.

BBB Wise Giving Alliance: www.give.org/reports/index.asp. Reports on charities and other organizations that solicit money.

Business Reporting. (2003, September 7). International Women's Media Foundation. www.iwmf.org/training/business.php

Common Wealth: www.epn.org/commonwealth. A collection of articles on nonprofits from *The American Prospect* magazine.

Council on Foundations: www.cof.org. A professional organization of more than 2,000 foundations.

Downes, J., & Goodman, J. E. (2002). *Dictionary of finance and investment terms* (6th ed.). Hauppauge, NY: Barron's Educational Series.

FirstGov Information for Nonprofits: www.nonprofit.gov. Government-agency-specific information for nonprofits.

The Foundation Center: http://fdncenter.org. Information for and about foundations.

The Foundation Directory: http://fconline.fdncenter.org. From the Foundation Center, a directory of grantmakers. Subscription needed to access it.

GAO report on tax-exempt organizations: In PDF format, GAO report from April 2002 that gives a detailed introduction to the IRS Form 990 and regulation of nonprofit organizations. www.muridae.com/nporegulation/lobbying.html

GuideStar: www.guidestar.org. National database of nonprofit organizations.

Hamilton, J. (2003). *CCH journalists' guide to writing about securities* (2nd ed.). www.cch.com

Independent Sector: www.independentsector.org. Information about nonprofits and foundations.

IRS FAQ about charities and nonprofits: www.irs.gov/charities/article/0,,id=96430,00.html. Charities and nonprofits file Form 990 as tax-exempt organizations.

National Center for Charitable Statistics: http://nccs.urban.org. Data on the nonprofit sector from the Urban Institute.

Nonprofit Coordinating Committee of New York: www.npccny.org/Form_990/990.htm. How to read the IRS Form 990.

Oatis, J. (2003, September 7). Web sites for journalists. www.oatis.com/bageht.htm

Taparia, J. (2003). *Understanding financial statements: A journalist's guide.* Oak Park, IL: Marion Street Press.

REFERENCES

Associated Press. (2003, March 7). Microsoft paying out first dividend. *Dallas Morning News,* p. 12D.

Debt and Bankruptcy. NOLO Law for All. (2003). Retrieved November 30, 2003, from www.nolo.com/lawcenter/ency/index.cfm/catID/734BECB6-ADDE-4041-AEC595AF30EA15CE.

Johnson, P., & Torbenson, E. (2003, September). Business beat reporting at the *Dallas Morning News.* Responses to questions via email interview.

Lynch, R., & Danninger, L. (2003, September 4). Simple housing sales prices still climbing: August's $394,500 media price beats the peak set during the Japanese boom. *Star-Bulletin.* http://starbulletin.com/2003/09/04/news/index2.html.

Shah, A. (2003, September 6). Layoffs offer dose of recovery reality. While economy grew, firms shed 93,000 jobs in August. *Dallas Morning News,* p. 1A.

Storey, K. (1998, March/April). Telethons and the Special Olympics: Where does that money really go? *The Ragged Edge.* www.ragged-edge-mag.com/mar98/telethn.htm.

CHAPTER 10

COVERING PUBLIC SAFETY AND DISASTER

A newspaper reporter in Texas took a few hours on a Sunday, her usual day off, to interview local hospital nurses being trained to obtain evidence in rape cases when victims came to the emergency room. The interviews produced a feature story about the new program. The nurse manager of the emergency room, pleased with the article, became a willing and reliable source for the reporter.

A few weeks later when a gunman shot nine people at a public event, the reporter benefited from that trusting relationship. The late-night shooting sent the reporter to the hospital on deadline to get the shooting victims' conditions and their names. The nurse manager told the reporter that the hospital typically did not release victims' names while they were being treated. But she found an alternative way to get the names to the reporter: She left the list of names in plain sight at the nurses' station and told the reporter where to find them. (Based on Texas open records laws, the nurse manager knew that victims' names would be released in a day or two anyway.) The reporter added the names to her story in time for the paper's first edition.

The above scenario illustrates the crucial role that reporter–source relationships play on the public safety beat, which typically covers police and fire departments. Those units are also the first called during disasters, such as derailed trains, overturned trucks loaded with toxic chemicals, or communities flattened by tornadoes. Because the public safety beat deals with crisis and death, reporters have to be careful, skilled, and sensitive in covering their beat.

In this chapter, you will:

- See how to build good relationships with public safety sources,
- Review law enforcement procedures and how they vary from jurisdiction to jurisdiction,
- Get insight on interagency relationships,
- Find out how to report although access has become more restrictive post 9/11,
- Consider how to deal with the trauma for victims and journalists when covering this high-pressure beat,

- Get an overview on campus crime,
- Learn how to report on disasters, both human-made and natural,
- Recognize the need for differences between broadcast and print media in covering public safety, and
- Find stories beyond daily public safety events.

LEARNING THE CULTURE

Good relationships with reliable sources are the lifeblood of the public safety beat reporter. Jamie Stockwell, a police reporter for the *Washington Post,* said even when she was covering the high-profile sniper shootings in September and October 2002, her core relationship with her police sources did not change. "The size, the magnitude, and the interest was greater than any other story I've been involved in, but it is still a good old-fashioned cop story," she said in an *American Journalism Review* article (Lisheron, 2002).

Stockwell explained how she doggedly had to build relationships with her sources when she began covering police in Prince George's County, Maryland, outside of Washington, DC. She had reported on crime in a small Texas community before moving east and had an open rapport with law officers there. In Prince George's County, police protected a population of 815,000, and police problems ranged from brutality complaints to 100 homicides a year.

To get to know Prince George's system, she made herself known to police as often as possible. "I'd go to every single homicide scene, the ones nobody seemed to care about, the ones cops call the run-of-the-mills. I'd be the only one there from the press. I'd talk to officers and the detectives working the homicide. Pretty soon they knew who I was," she said in *AJR* (2002). She knew she had made a breakthrough when the head of the police union invited her for a beer. She admitted that not all the police like her, or ever will, but "there are enough of them I trust and respect that if I want information, I can get it."

Reporters need to remember that they and the police are pursuing the same thing—details of the crime and the guilty party—just for different reasons. Mark Lisheron (2002) of the *Milwaukee Journal Sentinel* explained in the *AJR* article:

> The issue is information. Cops and reporters chase the same information trying to answer the who and the why of the crime. They go to the same crime scenes, talk to the same witnesses, work with the best evidence they have. Each develops a barter system for information based on trust. The reporter and the cop size each other up and determine their ability to exchange and share information.

Identifying the Sources

Reporters new to the public safety beat must identify the key players in the police and fire departments. The city's public safety structure will determine the levels of authority and responsibility. Some cities have separate fire chiefs and police chiefs. Some have a public safety director who oversees both functions. The top administrator of each would be responsible to the city manager or mayor.

In a county system, the sheriff would be the top law enforcement officer, and a fire marshal would investigate fire-related incidents. A public safety reporter would also have to consider as part of the beat the emergency management service that provides ambulance service as well as disaster assistance.

"You have to get to know the people," said Bill Toohey (2002), a former radio journalist who became the public information director for Baltimore County police in Maryland. Every police chief, sheriff, fire chief, fire marshal, or precinct commander has a different way of running a department, and reporters need to understand each officer's specific views on public safety topics. They also need to learn how each department works and the types of cases each investigates.

Reporters need to understand more than just what is going on in the department. For example, to find out what is on the minds of officers—their concerns about benefits, salaries, and safety, for example—they can check out the police union's Web site. Stockwell and Toohey suggested that new public safety reporters go to events that might not make stories but will make contacts, such as promotion ceremonies and recruit class graduations. "You get to meet people and make connections," Toohey said.

In addition, "the culture of each agency is different," Toohey (2002) explained. For example, in the city of Baltimore, homicide detectives are much more willing to talk to reporters than are detectives in Baltimore County. The city has about 300 homicides a year. The few public information officers cannot handle the hundreds of media requests, so detectives pitch in. The county has about 30 homicides annually, and homicide detectives rarely talk to reporters, leaving that job to Toohey.

To understand public safety broadly, Toohey suggested reporters talk to community group members about crime, not just to police officials. Most larger jurisdictions have some type of police–community relations councils, and the public can attend the meetings. In Baltimore County, the department runs a 10-week Citizens Academy in which community leaders learn about the police department. Toohey always includes several journalists. "It's a chance for reporters to meet with community people," he said.

Reporters should remember that police departments often work in conjunction with state law enforcement and the Federal Bureau of Investigation to solve crimes. A police reporter should have contacts there as well. A local fire department might also consult with a state law enforcement agency if arson could be a cause. If a fire results in a death, both fire and police departments would be called in.

"Good police reporting is good reporting. It's developing sources, finding information, learning how things are done," Toohey said. "Building relationships, that is so important—in the community, in the police department."

The Burden of Accuracy

Reporting public safety stories places an extra burden on reporters to be accurate. Getting information right is crucial in any story, but especially so in stories where people are hurt, die, are taken hostage, or are charged with crimes. Victims and perpetrators need to be identified accurately. Information on incidence reports and from public safety officials might not always be correct. For example, some reports have misspelled names, and officers might have difficult-to-read handwriting.

If reporters have doubts about an individual's identity or how a crime took place, they should seek clarification through additional sources or records. Many people have the same name, and reporters need to be careful not to misidentify people. The phone book and Internet are not good ways to check names. Reporters should use additional sources: police records, police officials, fire officials, and the people involved in the crime. Qualified privilege will protect a reporter from libel, as discussed in Chapter 4, but no reporter wants to make numerous errors because police or fire reports were wrong.

Law Enforcement Procedures

Law enforcement procedures might seem straightforward: Criminals break the law, they are arrested, they are charged, and the process toward trial or plea bargain begins. However, this process varies depending on the state, county, or city. "The police reporter needs to learn the pipeline from arrest to prison," Toohey said. Public safety reporters must learn the criminal laws of their states and the court procedures in the jurisdiction they cover so they know where police take criminals after an arrest. Chapter 11 on covering the courts gives a general overview of the process from criminal charges to verdict.

Although many local police departments follow the FBI's Uniform Crime Reporting System for reporting statistics, many states are inconsistent in their definitions of crimes. Figure 10.1 shows a list of the FBI's definitions.

For example, Toohey (2002) said first-degree murder in New York State is different from first-degree murder in Maryland.

> The whole homicide/murder distinction is not at all simple. Homicide and murder are different. Homicide is, most basically, the killing of one human being by another, but it is not always a crime. For example, one of our officers shot and killed a knife wielding man the other day. That is homicide, but the State's Attorney will probably decide it was not the crime of murder.

Reporters also need to understand any departmental rules that govern a law officer's interaction with the media. Some departments simply want reporters to speak to the public information officers before approaching detectives. Although a department might not have a formal rule, breaking even the unwritten rules could have consequences for the reporter's continuing relationship with the department. Toohey said: "You may not like the rules; the

FIGURE 10.1   Crime Definitions from the FBI Uniform Crime Reporting Handbook (2002)

(These definitions are used only for the FBI statistical reporting. Various states have different definitions of crimes.)

Aggravated assault: An unlawful attack by one person upon another for the purpose of inflicting severe or aggravated bodily injury. This type of assault usually is accompanied by the use of a weapon or by means likely to produce death or great bodily harm. In reporting assault, attempts are included because serious personal injury could result if the crime were successfully completed.

Arson: Any willful or malicious burning or attempt to burn, with or without intent to defraud, a dwelling, house, public building, motor vehicle or aircraft, personal property of another, etc.

Burglary: The unlawful entry of a structure to commit a felony or theft. The use of force to gain entry is not required to classify an offense as a burglary.

Forcible rape: The carnal knowledge of a person, forcibly and/or against that person's will. In reporting rape, assaults or attempts to commit rape by force or threat of force are also included.

Hate crime: Also known as a bias crime, it is a criminal offense committed against a person, property, or society, which is motivated, in whole or in part, by the offender's bias against a race, religion, disability, sexual orientation, or ethnicity/national origin.

Larceny or theft: The unlawful taking, carrying, leading, or riding away of property from the possession or constructive possession of another. It includes crimes such as shoplifting, pocket-picking, purse-snatching, thefts from motor vehicles, thefts of motor vehicle parts or accessories, bicycle thefts, etc., in which no use of force, violence, or fraud occurs.

Motor vehicle theft: The theft or attempted theft of a motor vehicle, including stealing of automobiles, buses, trucks, motorcycles, motorscooters, snowmobiles, etc.

Murder and nonnegligent manslaughter: The willful (nonnegligent) killing of one human being by another.

Robbery: The taking or attempting to take anything of value from the care, custody, or control of a person or persons by force or threat of force or violence and/or by putting the victim in fear.

rules may not have the force of law. You don't have to obey the rules but understand you may be sacrificing cooperation if you violate the rules."

As an example, Toohey noted one reporter who constantly violated the Baltimore County police policy about where reporters could go in the county police building. Her behavior so angered a police lieutenant that he and other police would no longer speak with her. That shut down most of her police reporting efforts. Police reporting requires give and take because journalists have to return to the same police officials day after day for information. "You don't have to be co-opted by the department, but you do have to show some respect for it—and understanding," Toohey explained.

The behavior extends to crime scenes, which is discussed later in the chapter. Police or firefighters will not want reporters any place where they could interfere with an investigation or with their efforts to put out a fire. Reporters who have a good relationship with public safety officials have a better chance of gaining access, and certainly gathering information, particularly on deadline.

Access to Information in Covering Public Safety

The reporter's ability to access police officials, fire officials, public safety officials, and their records varies from state to state, depending on the specific state Freedom of Information Act (FOIA) or open records laws. Some state laws exempt any part of an investigation record that could identify a victim or witness, particularly if police determine that releasing the information puts the person at risk. Information pertinent to an investigation might not be released. Juveniles' names are also protected under state FOIA laws. Some departments make accessibility to records easy, while others will refuse to put out reports on weekends, making reporters' jobs more difficult.

For example, a journalist can walk into a police station in Texas and look through a stack of the day's police incidence reports that are available in a pressroom. In Pennsylvania many law enforcement agencies will not give out any incidence reports and will allow reporters to view only the police blotter, which records only each police call. In fact, a 1997 case ruled that police incidence reports in Pennsylvania are to be disclosed; however, a reporter for the *Mirror* in Altoona investigated and found that a number of state police barracks did not provide incidence reports on request. Toohey (2002) reminded reporters to be careful when clarifying information on incidence reports. A supervisor, rather than the desk officer who might be seeing the incidence report for the first time, might be the most reliable source.

In covering a county or large geographic area, a reporter might have to contact several public safety departments, including a county sheriff's office, local fire departments, and an emergency management system. Because of the sheer geographic size, a reporter might not be able to visit each department every day. He or she might have to rely on telephone calls and the desk officer's idea of what is news for stories. A reporter's telephone skills might be crucial in determining how much information he or she can pull from a police officer. Again, the better the relationship, the more likely the reporter will get information. A reporter might also have to make daily calls, particularly on weekends, to the state patrol to check for accidents and deaths or injuries. In any instance in which a reporter gets information via the phone, he or she should be sure to get the name and rank of the officer quoted.

Public records laws note procedures, including costs, for obtaining records. Police departments have been known to charge fees for photocopying police reports that have been well above what is considered "reasonable." Such fees deter anyone—residents or reporters—from obtaining copies. Reporters and their state press associations should challenge any fee that seems out of line. These guidelines are spelled out in state open records laws.

Access to public safety information requires a balancing act for both sides. Officials' ultimate goal is to solve the crime, a goal that might be helped by releasing information via the media so the public can come forward with tips. That proved to be the break for law enforcement in the 2002 sniper shootings in Maryland. Police might withhold information so officers do not tip criminals that they are about to be caught. For reporters, the goal is to provide as much information as possible to the public. Ethical journalists, however, will withhold information to prevent injury or death.

Barbara Cochran, the president of Radio-Television News Directors Association (RTNDA), wrote in an *American Journalism Review* article (2002) that police and media butted heads in the Washington, DC, sniper case in fall 2002 because "law enforcement teetered between stonewalling and using the media to reassure the public and send messages to the killer." In the end, it wasn't police-released information that led to the two prime suspects' capture. "It was the widespread but unauthorized dissemination of information about their Chevy Caprice with New Jersey tags that led to the arrests of John Allen Muhammad and John Lee Malvo," said Cochran. A former FBI agent admitted that the media were "absolutely an integral part of the resolution of this case."

Even though news media can aid in solving crimes, it is unlikely that journalists will have more access to information in the future. States with the most open access to officials and records began tightening that access in the post-9/11 media environment. Many states have added antiterrorist security plans to the list of materials exempt from the public and the media. Since 9/11 some states have pulled from their Web sites locations of power plants and nuclear reactors, architectural drawings of government buildings, and state water resource locations, according to the Reporters Committee for Freedom of the Press (2003).

Cochran (2002) said that she believes that since 9/11, "the public has been much more willing to sacrifice its right to information out of a greater concern for security." The federal government has been tightening access and withholding more and more records in the name of security concerns. A "trend toward secrecy pervades the federal government," Cochran said. For example, government databases have been vanishing from the Internet. In the end, such secrecy will affect all aspects of journalism, especially public safety reporting.

Since 9/11, local public safety departments have reorganized to coordinate better their antiterrorism efforts and emergency preparedness, Public Information Officer Toohey explained. Local departments work more closely with state and federal law enforcement as part of Homeland Security efforts. Reporters need to be aware of these liaisons so they can approach the correct agency for information. With these new relationships, a local crime with suspected terrorism connections might end up with the FBI, not local law enforcement.

GETTING TO THE SCENE

Reporters must have access to the scene of a crime, fire, or disastrous event to cover public safety completely. Many police and fire reporters can get to the scene fairly fast because most news organizations have someone monitoring public safety scanners, either in the newsroom or from an outside source. For example, CNN in New York, several New York City TV stations, and the major New York City daily newspapers have signed on with Breaking News Network, which has about 400 people monitoring scanners from Virginia to Connecticut. The news organizations get leads on major breaking crime stories in their area and pay a fee for the information. However, Toohey reminded reporters that scanner information is not an official report. "It is only what people tell the police, not what really happened," he explained.

Some reporters, and especially photographers, have scanners in their cars and can arrive at the scene minutes after the public safety officials do. For example, *New York Daily News* photographer David Handschuh (2002) said he heard on the scanner in his car a call for all Manhattan fire companies to respond to a major fire at the World Trade Center on September 11, 2001. He arrived at the scene at the same time as several fire trucks.

As online technology grows, however, audio scanners might become obsolete. In northwest Louisiana, emergency service calls go directly on to a Web site for all to see. Reporters can view detailed information about each 911 dispatch. The police reporter at the *Times* in Shreveport said the system is superior to the audio scanner because he can more easily find the location of the emergency. "The Web site saves a lot of time because we can look up the address and find out which agency has been sent out to respond to an event," Seth Parsons of the *Times* in Shreveport, Louisiana, told *Editor & Publisher* (Sullivan, 2003).

How close a reporter or photographer can get to the scene depends on the police, fire, or emergency management's media guidelines. The Reporters Committee for Freedom of the Press (2002) said the police develop such policies with three things in mind: that the release of information "does not jeopardize an individual's rights, impair prosecution, or impede the law enforcement process." Most local law enforcement agencies have developed their own guidelines; only three states—California, Ohio, and Oregon—have state laws that address news media access to emergency scenes.

As noted in Chapter 4 about privacy, reporters may face trespassing charges if they venture onto private property without permission. Reporters can also be arrested if they hinder police in their investigations or arrests.

DEALING WITH THE TRAUMA

In violent crimes, fires, and disasters, people experience the worst time in their lives, and reporters must learn to balance their sensitivity to people in crisis with getting the story covered. TV anchors, reporters, and photographers as well as print news photographers have to be careful in how they present what they see to their news audiences. *The Rundown,* a publication for TV news personnel, recommends that when covering an airplane crash, for example (TV News, 1997):

> Anchors and reporters must be sensitive to the loss of lives, while still pushing to find out what viewers need to know about how this happened and what the consequences are. The tone should be calm. . . . The whole news team must work assertively to shield viewers from shocking images and content. In preventing gruesome material from being aired, it isn't just video that may be objectionable. Viewers may be uncomfortable with phrases such as "body parts." (Reprinted with permission from *The Rundown.*)

In disasters such as plane crashes, *The Rundown* said to edit all video carefully, especially live coverage. The photographer should be careful not to include graphic footage if the station will run the video live.

How to Talk to Victims and Witnesses

In addition to sensitivity in reporting the visual aspect of a crime or disaster, reporters have to exercise care when talking to survivors, witnesses, or grieving relatives. Reporters might be the one to tell a family member, inadvertently, that an accident has happened. Approaching sources takes sensitivity.

When talking to survivors or grieving relatives, reporters have to be sensitive to whether people want to talk. If they say "No," reporters must respect that decision. For example, when a TWA flight exploded near Long Island in 1996, the WNBC-TV news director set a policy that her news teams could not approach victims' families. Only if the families approached the reporters and indicated they wanted to talk could they be interviewed. Some relatives and survivors might want to talk so they can share stories about their loved ones or so they can tell the story of what happened.

The Dart Center for Journalism and Trauma offers much advice to reporters about how to report these tough stories without causing more trauma. Sometimes journalists let the victims initiate contact, as WNBC-TV did. When the *Boston Globe* covered the priest sexual abuse scandal in the Catholic Church, it decided to set up a "tip box" that allowed someone who wanted to report past clergy sex abuse to talk to a reporter, leave a confidential message, or send an email. The tip box resulted in a deluge of calls—several thousand over two years. Many victims felt betrayed by their church and willing and openly discussed the abuse, according to *Globe* reporters. *Globe* reporters told the Dart Center:

> The experience of having been shunned made many victims and their families even more willing to speak with us because they were so angry and disappointed and disillusioned as a result of their poor treatment by the church. Then, after our stories began to run, many victims grew even angrier, because they realized that the betrayal they had experienced was not an isolated event. If you had wondered whether the ostracism some victims and their families experienced made them reluctant to speak to us, I would say that was not the case; in fact, it made them more eager to share the indignities they had suffered. (Cox, 2003)

When the *Daily Oklahoman* covered the bombing of the Murrah Federal Building in 1995 and a high death toll from tornadoes in 1999, staff followed policies meant to provide dignity and respect to victims. Specific actions helped victims and their families feel better, such as callbacks to verify facts and quotes. The newspaper covered only public, not private, funerals of disaster victims. Also, the *Daily Oklahoman* emphasized "profiles of life" stories by writing about disaster victims' lives, rather than focusing on their deaths. "In most cases, victims' relatives wanted to talk when they realized that the reporter was writing a 'Profile of Life.' Some of these led to bigger stories, too," according to the newspaper (Hight, 2000).

Journalists Can Be Victims, Too

In addition to victims and viewers, journalists also have to be aware of the impact that covering gruesome or traumatic events has on their own mental health. "Recent studies by psychologists suggest that reporters and photographers experience the sometimes debilitating symptoms of post-traumatic stress disorder at rates comparable to firefighters, police officers, and soldiers," according to the Poynter Institute (Shapiro, 2002). As *Daily Oklahoman* managing editor Joe Hight (2000) explained:

> Journalists usually first encounter the wall of grief at the beginning of their careers. With little or no training, they are assigned the police beat. They learn and gain experience by covering one tragedy. Then another. Then another. Victim's coverage becomes a repetitive part of journalists' careers that builds into more than just memories.

But instead of dealing with the stress and trauma of covering these stories, many journalists deny or bluster through with false bravado. Hight (2000) called the impact on journalists of covering disasters the "Wall Effect."

> Like a tennis ball thrown against a wall, the victim's emotion, all that grief, can bounce back and absorb the person facing the victims—the journalist. The effect

causes the journalist to feel the victim's pain and loss. The isolation. The guilt feelings. The separation from family members or friends who have died in the past or the anxiety that family members may be lost in the future. Then comes the loss of sleep and the increased feelings of stress.

Reporters should know their limits and explain to a supervisor if they are not the appropriate people for an assignment. Reporters should take steps to reduce their stress, through talking to someone, enjoying a hobby, or just taking breaks, Hight said.

After the large-scale disaster of the World Trade Center attacks, newsrooms around the country became more attuned to the emotional toll public safety coverage has on journalists. Since 9/11, *New York Daily News* photographer David Handschuh has taken the lead in discussing the effect of disaster coverage on journalists. He covered the Columbine school shootings and the World Trade Center attacks, where he was buried under rubble before firefighters rescued him. He has tried to confront newsroom culture, which tells journalists to suppress the traumatic events they witness and not to discuss them for fear of being seen as weak.

Handschuh realized that silence hurts news personnel, and he set up peer counseling through the National Press Photographers Association. Reporters can talk with one another about any emotional problems resulting from their jobs. Handschuh (2002) explained, "The first step to assistance is for journalists to admit that we are not machines and that it's okay to get some kind of stress debriefing, whether it's talking with a friend, a member of the clergy, a psychologist, a psychiatrist, a counselor, or a peer." From his own experience of being trapped under rubble on 9/11, Handschuh said he learned "life is truly very fragile. I am lucky to be here. . . . Every moment is precious. Journalistically speaking, this reinforces the need for proper preparation and counseling."

ROUTINE BEAT COVERAGE

Not every day on the public safety beat involves tragedy or disaster. Most days few violent crimes or fires occur, and reporters dig into other areas of the beat. Associated Press transportation reporter Leslie Miller (2003) said that when she isn't covering a transportation disaster, she focuses on stories such as aviation security or transportation funding. Because of heightened security in the United States, "I spend most of my time writing about passenger screeners and bomb detection machines, Code Oranges and terrorist threats," Miller said. "Theoretically I'm supposed to be working on security for other modes of transportation, but I think the threats are largely aimed at the aviation system." Her sources tell her which area of transportation is most likely to be a terrorist's target.

Miller also follows funding issues such as whether Congress has given Amtrak enough money to operate. That issue could affect a local reporter in a town on an Amtrak route. Building evacuation plans, for example, have become a significant topic, and part of public safety coverage, since 9/11. Many reporters now know to ask whether building evacuation plans cover people who cannot climb stairs, such as wheelchair users or others with mobility impairments.

Public safety reporters can join with government and housing reporters to discover whether a community's buildings are up to fire or hurricane codes. For example, the *Miami Herald* won a Pulitzer Prize for exposing how weak building codes and bad construction practices greatly added to the extent of damage when Hurricane Andrew hit south Florida in 1992. That hurricane was the costliest natural disaster ever to hit the United States, killing 43 people and costing about $30 billion.

Statistics about fire numbers, crimes, and police behavior also make excellent stories. The *Washington Post* used police statistics to document that the Washington, DC, police force shot and killed more people per resident than did any other large city police force in the United States. The series won an investigative reporting award and caused the district police force to begin a retraining program that doubled the departmental firearms instruction time and taught officers to use alternatives to deadly force (Weil, 1999).

The FBI and local communities release crime statistics annually. Baltimore County police Public Information Officer Toohey (2002) said that local police departments typically post their crime statistics on their Web sites these days, allowing reporters and the public quick and easy access. These reports always make good stories because of the public interest in whether crime is rising or falling. Crime actually might be higher than statistics show because the figures reflect only reported crimes. Victims, particularly in sexual assaults or domestic violence, might not notify police. However, crime statistics have to be studied and reported carefully so reporters—and readers—do not make false assumptions. For example, the *San Jose* (CA) *Mercury-News* (Mowatt, 1996) carefully explained the meaning of increases and decreases to San Jose's crime rate:

> Bucking a nationwide 4 percent decrease in violent crime from 1994 to 1995, San Jose reported a 12 percent increase during that period. It nevertheless remains the safest city of its size—or one of the two safest, depending on how one does the math.

The *Mercury-News* clarified that the rise in violent crime came from rises in robberies and aggravated assaults and that San Jose's overall crime rate dropped by 1 percent because of a large decline in property crimes.

Astute reporters can even catch misreporting of crimes if they have experience in public safety reporting. The *Macon* (Georgia) *Telegraph* discovered that the Macon police, who were claiming one of the lowest crime rates in the South, had incorrectly reported its crime numbers. The newspaper noticed no reports of carjackings in the department's release but knew two had occurred in October and November 2000. The police department said the mistake was unintentional (Associated Press, 2000). The lesson for both police and journalists is to double-check and triple-check crime statistics.

Public safety stories can have poignancy or humor. The *News & Observer* in Raleigh, North Carolina, wrote a short, upbeat story about a Cary, North Carolina, police officer who went to the extra effort to return a bike that had been stolen 10 years before. The bicycle patrol officer said she had "a soft spot for bicycles," so she dug through the community's stolen property database until she found a match with the recently found bike. She then tracked down the owner's current address through the Department of Motor Vehicles database.

The owner, surprised by the return of the 10-speed after 10 years, soon remembered the good times on his bike and vowed to get it into working condition. While not an earth-shattering story, happy-ending stories can balance newspapers' and TV stations' "bad news" (Claycombe, 2003). Good public safety reporters keep their eyes open for fun, lighthearted stories. Figure 10.2 shows a list of public safety story ideas.

SPECIAL CIRCUMSTANCES OF COVERING CAMPUS CRIME

On many college campuses, covering campus crime can be difficult because colleges and universities try hard to give the impression that students are safe there. The university might downplay or even try to cover up major crimes that occur. For example, one small private college on the East Coast discovered several students were dealing drugs on campus. To avoid negative publicity, the college did not turn the lawbreaking students over to county police, but instead suspended them in a closed disciplinary proceeding. The college's actions locked the story away from the city media and the campus media, which eventually heard rumors of what had happened.

Colleges and universities are required to report all campus crime to federal officials. Such reports show that in the late 1990s, college campuses had almost 100,000 crimes, both violent and property crimes. The 100,000 crimes might just be a fraction of the actual crime taking place on college campuses. Several studies have shown that campuses still do not fully report crime statistics, as in the drug-dealing example just cited.

Reporters should also be aware that campus police might have different kinds of relationships with local police. Some are city or county police officers who just happen to work on a college campus; others work for separate campus police departments, which have agreed-upon relationships with local law enforcement, police PIO Toohey said. He added that reporters should be wary of campus public relations officials, who give out crime news. They might not use accurate definitions or terms.

FIGURE 10.2   Story Ideas and Enterprise Tips from *Covering Crime and Justice* by Criminal Justice Journalists

1. **An armament, ordinance, and cop-toy primer.** Does your police agency own a tank? Rocket-launchers? A cache of grenades? Robots? How are they to be used, and under what circumstances? Some agencies might not want to give up these details, but you won't know unless you ask.

2. **Visit the police firing range.** Fire police weapons and ask to go through training exercises. This story idea serves many purposes, including acquainting you with police equipment, usage protocols, and your agency's gun training gurus.

3. **Analyze petty crimes.** You probably know where your city ranks in murders per capita. But what about other crimes, especially the much more prevalent property crimes of theft, burglary, and auto theft?

4. **White-collar crime.** Does your police agency have a specialized unit to investigate corporate crime? Should it?

5. **Take a comprehensive tour.** Ask to visit all police facilities, including both public and private areas. Does your agency have a special operations or command center? That should be part of the visit, as well as remote offices, holding pens and lockups, booking areas, training facilities, even parking garages. The tour may or may not lead to a story, but you might meet new sources on the tour, and you'll understand your agency better.

6. **Review training procedures.** Request a briefing on police training, both for recruits and experienced officers. Ask to sit in on training sessions. Also get a copy of the agency's standard operating procedures, which is a public record in many jurisdictions.

7. **Profile your agency's top cops.** Everyone knows the police chief or sheriff. But what of the next tier of decision makers?

8. **Shadow a cop.** This exercise can offer insight into procedures, attitudes, and the peer culture of your agency. Most agencies offer a ride-along (or walk-along) program, although a 1999 U.S. Supreme Court ruling limited access to private property for tag-along journalists.

9. **Walk through the arrest-to-arraignment process.** Again, this may or may not lead to a story, but it will acquaint you with conditions, bottlenecks, and other potential issues in the system, and those insights will come in handy.

10. **Perp walks.** Does your agency have a history of perp walks? Colorful characters and interesting anecdotes could help you dress up a procedural story about local policy on an issue that many journalists, cops, prosecutors, and defense lawyers are talking about across the country.

11. **Develop a board of directors.** Look outside your agency for expert sources—advocates, academics, even gadflies—in specialized areas. Tap them for fresh research and story ideas. The subjects might include police training, ethics and personnel issues, law enforcement budgets, police use of force and weapons technology, police communications, crime statistics, civil rights and legal process, forensics, crime victims, organized crime and gangs, and fraud and white-collar crime.

(continued)

FIGURE 10.2   Continued

12. **Evaluate your agency.** Consult with outside experts about the reputation of your agency. Is it known for doing something particularly well or poorly? What is the agency's patrol strategy? Is it reactive, depending almost entirely on 911 emergency calls, or has it incorporated proactive policing? How does its response time stack up with other places? Has it embraced community policing, problem-solving policing, the "Broken Windows" paradigm, or some other initiative? Is it working there? What could be improved?

13. **Corruption and rogues.** Police corruption experts say police agencies and the media both do a lousy job of spotting trends in corruption because police bosses convince journalists to view corruption cases as bad-seed aberrations. Yet financial corruption frequently involves a conspiracy among a number of cops. Does anecdotal or statistical evidence indicate increases in law enforcement rogues in your jurisdiction? Has your agency instituted an early-warning system for identifying rogues?

14. **Follow the buck.** Scrutinize the public safety budget in your jurisdiction for leads on new initiatives or patrol strategies—an increase in computerization costs for a new crime-mapping program, for example, or a balloon in equipment costs for a new line of patrol vehicles or a special-use armored truck. Personnel costs and even buildings-and-grounds budget lines can lead to stories.

Source: Reprinted with permission from Criminal Justice Journalists.

Campus Crime Statistics

One gruesome incident precipitated the federal requirements compelling colleges to report campus crimes. In 1986, Jeanne Clery was tortured, raped, and murdered in her dorm room at Lehigh University in Pennsylvania. Her parents became activists for campus security after they found out that Lehigh University officials knew violent crimes had occurred on campus and had not told students. The Clerys reported on their Security on Campus Web site (2001):

> The college, in an ill-conceived attempt to protect its "image," produced a self-serving "report," written by one of its trustees, K. P. Pendleton, which concluded that there was no negligence on the part of the university and that ". . . our present safety policies were complete"; this, despite the administration's knowledge of prior violent crimes on the campus and that there had been 181 reports of propped-open doors in Jeanne's dormitory in the four months prior to her death.

Two years after Jeanne's murder, the Clerys found that only 4 percent of colleges were reporting crime statistics to the FBI. They felt the only way to stop students from being victims of crime was through better awareness. As one student editor at Miami University in Ohio said, when campus crime is unreported or underreported, students "are instilled with a false sense of security," according to the Student Press Law Center (2000).

Through the Clerys' lobbying efforts, President George Bush signed the Crime Awareness and Campus Security Act of 1990, now called the Jeanne Clery Disclosure of Campus Security Policy and Campus Crime Statistics Act. All colleges that receive federal funds must report crime statistics. Under the act, "schools must publish an annual report disclosing campus security policies and three years' worth of selected crime statistics; schools must make timely warnings to the campus community about crimes that pose an ongoing threat to students and employees; each institution with a police or security department must have a public crime log; the U.S. Department of Education centrally collects and disseminates the crime statistics; campus sexual assault victims are assured of certain basic rights; schools that fail to comply can be fined by the U.S. Department of Education," according to Security on Campus (2002).

If schools still try to keep campus crime a secret, the Student Press Law Center reported four methods to get legal access to campus police reports: a state's open records law, the federal open police logs law, a state's open police logs law, and the federal Clery Act. Campus reporters should study their states' laws to see whether college police and security follow their respective open records laws. In addition, "the federal government and seven individual states—California, Kentucky, Massachusetts, Pennsylvania, Tennessee, Virginia, and West Virginia—require public access to the daily logs of college and university police departments," according to the Student Press Law Center (2000). The Center's helpful guidebook, *Covering Campus Crime,* walks reporters through the intricacies of campus crime reporting. It is available free online at www.splc.org.

DISASTERS, BOTH HUMAN-MADE AND NATURAL

Each disaster—airplane crash, nightclub fire, or hurricane—has its characteristics that set it apart or make it different. But reporting on disasters is actually similar to covering any other story: Reporters still have to rely on the sources they have developed on their beats. These sources might be less accessible, however, because they are much busier than usual trying to fight an out-of-control blaze or keep public order. In some cases, officials might set up crisis communication centers with daily or hourly briefings to keep reporters up-to-date.

Similarly, the media often call in many reporters for a team approach to disaster coverage. The police and fire reporters might lead the team in a major fire or natural disaster, and at larger news organizations, transportation reporters might take the lead in plane, train, or multiple car crashes. Each team will have reporters to cover aspects such as the business, health, or social services impact. Along with reporters, editors will assign photographers, videographers, and graphic designers to develop the reporting package.

For example, in 2003 when the *Providence Journal* covered the worst fire in Rhode Island's history—a nightclub fire that killed 100 people—it gathered reporters from all sections of its staff, particularly its online staff. Instead of doing a special print edition, the newspaper created an ongoing special section on its Web site. "The Web site updated the story through the night with information gleaned from print reporters working the story and passing along information to a late-shift online production editor," Steve Outing of the Poynter Institute reported (2003). "Then early Friday, eight of the site's 20 staff members focused solely on the club-fire story, doing some original reporting and gathering information from print *Journal* reporters, wire services, and other sources." The result was a multilayered Digital Extra package that combined all the stories, victim profiles, weblogs, legislation information, TV footage, documents from the National Institute of Standards and Technology investigation, three years of fire inspection reports for the nightclub, and support information for victims' families.

Knowing Who to Call

Leslie Miller, the Associated Press transportation reporter, said after a major transportation crash, the AP's "goal is to be the first to report the news and to get it right" (2003). The AP has deadlines throughout the day and night, and other major media around the country rely on their reports. AP reporters strive to get the facts correct and fast, she said.

> The key is preparation: Knowing the person who will likely have the information, making sure that person knows and trusts me, staying in regular touch, having all his contact numbers, and persuading him that it's in his best interest to tell me first, rather than CNN. My key person for plane crashes is the FAA spokesman, and he knows he'll have to answer a lot fewer questions from a lot fewer reporters if he can get it out on the AP wire first.

Reporting victims' names as well as the cause of a plane or train crash as soon as possible leads the information that reporters want to know. In a big plane crash, the airlines release their passenger lists, but only after families have been notified, Miller said. In small plane crashes, that information comes from the Federal Aviation Administration. In the case of a prominent person, the family or the individual's organization will release the name.

For example, when U.S. Senator Paul Wellstone died in a plane crash in 2002, Miller said the FAA did not report the information until his staff members on Capitol Hill were notified. Then Wellstone's staff members made the announcement themselves. In train crashes, local law enforcement officials usually release the passenger list provided by Amtrak. With the passenger list, reporters can contact local hospitals to get the conditions of the injured.

In terms of information on large-scale crashes or natural disasters, reporters need to find accurate information about numbers of survivors. Journalists should refrain from reporting rumors and speculation because it might either give family members of victims false hope or unnecessarily scare them.

Information about the cause of the crash comes from the National Transportation Safety Board (NTSB). Miller said the NTSB is on the scene quickly to begin investigating the cause of the crash. "They (NTSB officials) arrive on the scene the same day and give regular updates timed before the news cycle," she said (2003). However, two repeating problems surface at this point. With the NTSB on the scene, all other sources generally refuse to speak to reporters. If the other sources do not go silent, they might begin to speculate on what happened without any real knowledge and thus give out incorrect facts. Miller reminded reporters: "You always have to be careful to make sure you're talking to someone with direct knowledge of the situation. The journalistic impulse is to name the cause of the disaster right away and sometimes that just can't be done."

Reporters should have a "stable of sources" with technical expertise who can explain things such as jet propulsion or hurricane science. For example, Miller said, she keeps the telephone numbers of aviation professors at Embry-Riddle University in her Rolodex so they can give her background on any technical aspects that arise during accident investigations. People who know airplanes will not trust the entire story if they read a technical error.

Miller reminded reporters that transportation "accident investigations often take a long time, and it's a good idea to stay in touch with the parties involved in the probe. Pilots, for example, may share what they know about an investigation before an official announcement is made."

During natural or human-made disasters, reporters will also want to track down emergency management services (EMS) personnel. In the event of a hurricane or tornado, information might come from state organizations and be filtered to the media through local EMS staff members. Through warning and watch systems, EMS officials can provide specific details to help residents protect themselves and also know what to do after the storm passes. That information should be part of any reporting.

In disaster reporting, reporters can put themselves in danger trying to get information or visuals. For example, reporters station themselves at the coast when a hurricane approaches. They interview residents who ride out the storm and local law enforcement and EMS officials. Live shots show viewers the storm's progress—and aftermath. If reporters want footage of a forest fire, they might have to work closely with forestry officials to get access and footage safely.

Depending on the size of the disaster and investigators' work, reporters might have to wait for access. For example, when a Delta Airlines plane crashed at the Dallas–Fort Worth Airport in 1985, airport officials allowed reporters within 100 yards of the site because they felt the public needed to know what was going on. But in 1994 when a USAir flight crashed outside of Pittsburgh, three days passed before reporters could visit the crash scene.

Access might also depend on a reporter's relationship with sources. Reporters who have cultivated sources on a beat will have greater access when disaster happens. Miller (2003) said she tried to maintain positive relationships with all her sources: "I take good care of my sources, always sending them copies of stories we've moved that quote them along with a friendly note."

Becoming Part of the Story

In covering public safety, particularly crime stories, journalists have to be careful not to fuel an individual's desire for publicity. The media have been criticized for too much coverage, which critics say produces copycat crimes. Reporters do not want to be pawns of criminals or someone who is unbalanced. Criminal Justice Journalists is a nonprofit organization whose goal is to improve the quality and accuracy of news reporting on crime, law enforcement, and the judicial system. On its Web site former crime reporter David Krajicek (2003) reminds beginning reporters of numerous examples of media manipulation by publicity seekers:

> For example, the two boys who murdered classmates and a teacher at Columbine High School in suburban Denver in 1999 before killing themselves left videotapes anticipating their own media immortality. A failed Atlanta stock-trader who shot up his office made it clear he had decided to exit life in a flash of media fire. The perpetrator of a church shooting in Fort Worth knew he would get TV time. (He had failed to convince local scribes that the government had implanted a chip in his brain, so he climbed to a loftier media pulpit.) The Unabomber was keenly aware of his media image. He made it known he wanted to be called Ted, not Theodore.

Obviously, these crime stories deserved coverage, but reporters had to be careful not to be sucked into the individuals' need to be on the evening news.

Baltimore County police PIO Toohey recounted a situation in 2000 when Joseph Palczynski, who murdered four people and eluded police for 10 days, took his estranged girlfriend's mother, the mother's boyfriend, and their 12-year-old son hostage in a first-floor apartment of a highly populated area. Toohey said police knew Palczynski was watching TV in the house so they had to manage carefully how much information TV reporters received. "We defined goals for dealing with the reporters: deny Palczynski use of the media as an outlet for his demands, and make sure the media did not compromise our operation," Toohey said. However, Toohey said he also had to meet the public demands for getting information about this ongoing dramatic story. Although police limited media to a certain area, Toohey tried to keep reporters as informed as possible, and his relationship with most of them helped the situation. "An established relationship goes a long way during a crisis," he said.

But the media did become part of the story. Palczynski found a cell phone in an empty apartment and called WJZ-TV. At the station a cameraperson videotaped the reporter while he talked to Palczynski. The TV station made a responsible decision and called the Baltimore County police before airing the footage. The police decided that airing the footage might hurt the hostage negotiations so WJZ agreed not to air the tape until after the standoff ended.

Toohey said the media acted responsibly in other ways as well. Most media closely monitored the police scanners and talked to neighbors trapped in nearby apartments. They had access to much unverified information, but never ran it until they checked it out with police officials. "If we did hear them carry something sensitive, they generally responded to our request to pull back from the story," Toohey said. The standoff with Palczynski lasted four days and came to an end when tactical officers broke into the apartment and shot and killed Palczynski as he reached for his gun. The three hostages were unharmed.

Such hostage standoff stories do not occur every day, but during such an event, journalists have to balance their need to report on a dramatic story with the lives in danger during a crisis. Obviously, human lives come first. In addition, journalists have to be wary of sensationalizing crime stories. By overdoing crime coverage, they might unnecessarily scare their news audiences or give them an unrealistic view of the threat of crime. Crime coverage is a paradox among newspaper readers and TV viewers: Although crime stories are popular among news audiences, those same audiences also complain bitterly about too much coverage of the topic.

PRINT VERSUS ELECTRONIC IN REPORTING CRIME NEWS

Television and print reporters have different needs and deadlines in covering public safety stories. Print reporters have the luxury of more time than do TV reporters or online journalists, who have to post their stories quickly. Print reporters at metropolitan newspapers also rely on staff or freelance photographers to take the visuals. Community newspaper reporters at weeklies or small dailies, however, might report the story and take pictures. For larger station news reports, a reporter and videographer might gather the visuals and interviews, whereas in a smaller market a reporter might also shoot video.

Visual elements often determine how—and even if—media cover public safety stories. For example, a murder among known drug dealers in a drug-infested neighborhood might merit only a routine crime story on an inside page of a metropolitan newspaper. A fire at a senior citizen apartment complex typically would not make the front page of a metropolitan newspaper unless multiple deaths occurred. However, local TV stations might lead their news broadcasts with these two stories if news teams captured interesting video and on-camera interviews. The fire story might even warrant a midday TV news-break if firefighting efforts affected traffic in the city.

TV's emphasis on visuals and its instantaneous delivery of information make public safety stories the staple of most local news broadcasts. Local TV news has been criticized for its strong emphasis on crime and disaster reporting. But TV news directors learned long ago that dramatic visuals and riveting footage keep viewers watching.

Gaining Access to Get the Picture

For TV news, the need for live shots makes access to crime, fire, or disaster scenes critical. Sometimes public safety officials cooperate with TV news, and other times, access can be a bitter struggle. Many governmental offices have developed guidelines to govern media coverage of major public safety events. For example, the city of Boston (2002) created a partnership agreement with local broadcast stations to ensure responsible broadcasting in live coverage of public safety incidents. The city reported, "Compelled by increasing competition between media outlets, live coverage during emergency situations has sometimes ventured into dangerous territory, endangering the lives of hostages, bystanders, special teams of officers, and even members of the media."

Boston requires that TV stations appoint one pool camera among themselves and one pool helicopter camera, which will be rotated among TV stations. The stations must agree not to air video until after a hostage situation is resolved. In turn, Boston police will allow the pool camera within the inner perimeter of where the incident happened. The city said it did not intend to limit TV coverage but to make sure everyone's safety was considered.

Other government entities have similar guidelines. The D.C. Metro system requires that anyone wanting to film, photograph, or interview customers on Metro property must get permission from the Metro's media relations office first. If a serious bus or rail accident occurs, media relations officials release their pager numbers so media have easy access to them.

For stories involving seaports, the local or state port authority takes the lead, but reporters might need to gain permission from both the port authority and the companies that are tenants at the seaport. The Port of Miami in Florida notes: "In regards to a breaking news story, jurisdiction for access belongs to the responding federal, state, and local authorities and/or tenant companies. Public information officers or company representatives will provide access to the media and escort media representatives to the site of a breaking story" (Miami–Dade County–Port of Miami, 2002). Because of heightened security at U.S. ports since 9/11, all ports have created stricter media clearance policies.

Visuals versus Individual Rights

A fairly common visual component of crime reporting, the "perp walk," occurs when police walk a suspect through a public area and the media can get video or pictures. A police officer escorts the suspect, usually in handcuffs or leg irons, out of the car and into the jail or courthouse. In many cases, the suspect will cover or avert his or her head to avoid being photographed. In one instance in which police staged a perp walk, the arrested individual sued that his Fourth Amendment right against unreasonable arrest had been violated (2000). The U.S. Court of Appeals for the Second Circuit agreed in this case because the event was staged. The ruling did not address media coverage of the actual transfer of prisoners or whether police can notify the media that a prisoner will be moved.

Police PIO Bill Toohey said that in Baltimore County he releases suspect pictures but not pictures of those arrested or charged. Therefore, reporters should always obtain suspect pictures for their news organization in case that suspect is charged. Although some aspects of police coverage have been altered by U.S. Supreme Court decisions in the late 1990s, the perp walk continues to be legal because reporters watch police activities from a public place.

Reporters who want to go along when police raid a private home or business can no longer do so because of the Supreme Court's 1999 *Wilson v. Layne* decision. The Court ruled that if police allow journalists to accompany them on a raid at a private home, "they are violating the Fourth Amendment privacy rights of the people in the house, namely their right to be free from unreasonable searches and seizures by government," according to *USA Today*'s Supreme Court reporter. Although the police, not the media, would be held liable in such cases, the rulings have made police wary of inviting journalists along on raids.

As noted earlier in the chapter, videos and pictures accompanying public safety stories can include potentially gruesome images. Reporters, photographers, and videographers need to be particularly sensitive to victims and viewers' reactions, as well as assess the emotional toll covering these stories has on everyone involved, including the journalists themselves. For example, most U.S. newspapers and TV stations chose not to show images of people jumping to their deaths from the burning World Trade Center on 9/11, although some foreign and U.S. papers did.

GLOSSARY

Crime Awareness and Campus Security Act of 1990:   Also known as the Jeanne Clery Act; requires colleges that receive federal funds to report crime statistics.

FBI's Uniform Crime Reporting System: Used to report crimes so that comparisons can be made nationally and from state to state.

Log: The record of incidents during a shift within a police or fire department.

National Transportation Safety Board (NTSB):   Federal agency that investigates transportation accidents, primarily airplane and train; usually the official word on the cause of an accident.

Perp walk: When police walk a defendant or person charged with a crime from the police vehicle to jail or to court. The media usually attend to get photos or video.

Public safety: Includes police, fire, and emergency management services.

ACTIVITIES

1. Set up a panel of a public safety reporter and a public safety department public information officer or other individual who provides reports to the media. Have them discuss from each perspective how well the other works in reporting crime news. Are reports easily accessible? Do reporters relate information accurately? What is the most difficult aspect of each person's job?

2. Select a crime and research how the definitions of it might differ between your state and other surrounding states. What is the FBI definition? Can you find out the criminal penalties for the crime?

3. Arrange for your campus security officer or police chief to come to class. Interview him or her about campus crime. Does the office report crime statistics? Are incident reports available? What is the relationship between your campus police and local law enforcement? Write a story about the chief's or director's responses and balance it with quotes from students about how safe they feel on campus.

4. Pick an aspect of public safety other than police or crime, such as disaster preparedness or fire protection. Interview an officer or EMS worker about his or her job and how he or she interacts with others on the public safety beat; for example, how a firefighter works with police and EMS.

5. Go to the Poynter Institute's Web site of front pages from 9/11. Discuss which images were most effective and which were too disturbing.

6. Go to the FBI's Uniform Crime Reports Web site and find the most recent crime statistics for your state, www.fbi.gov/ucr/ucr.htm. Write a story looking at the last five years' statistics. Interview people who can put the figures in context.

RESOURCES AND WEB SITES

Bureau of Justice Statistics: www.ojp.usdoj.gov/bjs
Courts (federal law materials—judicial opinions) (LII): www.law.cornell.edu/federal/opinions. html
Courts (state) (LII): www.law.cornell.edu/opinions.html
Criminal Justice Journalists: www.reporters.net/cjj
Dart Center for Journalism and Trauma: www.dartcenter.org
Department of Justice: www.usdoj.gov
Federal Bureau of Investigation: www.fbi.gov
Firehouse Fashions, Firefighter history and lore Web site: www.firehousefashions.com/ fire-history. html
Firehouse.com, a firefighting, rescue, and EMS community: www.firehouse.com
International Association of Fire Fighters, AFL-CIO: www.iaff.org

Justice Research and Statistics Association: www.jrsainfo.org
National Archive of Criminal Justice Data: www.icpsr.umich.edu/NACJD/index.html
National Criminal Justice Reference Service: www.ncjrs.org
National Interagency Fire Center, Boise, Idaho, primarily about wildland fires: www.nifc.gov
NOAA's Fire Weather Information Center: www.noaa.gov/fireweather
Office for Victims of Crime: www.ojp.usdoj.gov/ovc
Office of Justice Programs: www.ojp.usdoj.gov
Office of Juvenile Justice and Delinquency Prevention: www.ojjdp.ncjrs.org
Officer.com: www.officer.com
Organized Crime: A crime statistics site: www.crime.org/links.html
Poynter Institute's Fighting Wildfire resources page: www.poynter.org/column.asp?id=49&aid=749
Social Statistics Briefing Room: Crime (White House): www.whitehouse.gov/fsbr/crime.html
Sourcebook of Criminal Justice Statistics: www.albany.edu/sourcebook
U.N. Office for Drug Control and Crime Prevention: www.odccp.org/crime_cicp_sitemap.html
USDA Forest Service, Fire and Aviation Management: www.fs.fed.us/fire
U.S. Fire Commission, part of Department of Homeland Security, Hotel and Motel Fire Safety: www.usfa.fema.gov/applications/hotel
Victims and the Media Program (Michigan State University): http://victims.jrn.msu.edu
Wildfire News: www.wildfirenews.com

REFERENCES

Associated Press. (2000, December 25). Reporting errors cause Macon police to re-tally crimes. www.onlineathens.com.
City of Boston. (2002). Partnership agreement for responsible broadcasting. [Press release]. www.cityofboston.gov/police/media.asp.
Claycombe, A. (2003, May 16). Bike surfaces decade after theft. *News & Observer.* www.newsobserver.com/front/v-print/story/2541922p-2360179c.html.
Clery, H., & Clery, C. (2001). What Jeanne didn't know. Security on Campus, Inc. www.securityoncampus.org.
Cochran, B. (2002, December). Access denied. *American Journalism Review, 24*(10), pp. 32–33.
Complying with the Jeanne Clery Act, Clery Act summary. (2002). Security on Campus, Inc. www.securityoncampus.org.
Covering crime: A resource guide (1997). *Columbia Journalism Review.* www.cjr.org/resources/crime.
Cox, C. (2003). Abuse in the Catholic Church, *Boston Globe* team discusses working with victims. www.dartcenter.org/articles/special_features/church_abuse_01.htm.
Handschuh, D. (2002, January 8). Witness wounds. www.poynter.org.
Hight, J. (2000). Covering disasters. www.notrain-nogain.org/Train/Res/RepARC/Disaster.asp.
Krajicek, D. (2003). The crime beat. *Covering Crime and Justice.* www.justicejournalism.org/crimeguide/chapter01/chapter01_pg05.html#crimebeatissues.
Lisheron, M. (2002, December). Stalking a sniper. *American Journalism Review, 24*(10), 20–27.
Mauro, T. (1999, July/August). Another gray area. *Quill,* pp. 30–31.
Miami–Dade County–Port of Miami. (2002). Media access guidelines. www.co.miamidade.fl.us/portofmiami.
Miller, L. (2003, February 24). Associated Press transportation reporter. Email interview.
Mowatt, R. V. (1996, May 6). Violence rose in S. J. during '95. *San Jose Mercury-News,* p. 1A.
Outing, S. (2003, February 21). Projo.com: All day coverage of state's worst fire. Poynter Institute. www.poynter.org/content/content_view.asp?id=21479.

Reporters Committee for Freedom of the Press. (2003, March). *Homefront confidential. How the war on terrorism affects access to information and the public's right to know.* www. rcfp.org/homefrontconfidential.

Reporters Committee for Freedom of the Press. (2002). Access to places: Official permission for access. Retrieved November 25, 2002, from www.rcfp.org/places/officialpermission foraccess.html.

Shapiro, B. (2002, May 8). Dealing with the inner toll. Poynter Institute. www.poynter.org/content/content_view.asp?id=9659.

Shochat, G. (2002, Fall). State agencies pull information from Web sites. *The News Media & the Law, 26*(4), 41.

Silver, K. (2001). *Understanding crime statistics: A reporter's guide.* Columbia, MO: IRE.

Special report: Covering criminal justice, Vol. 2. (2000). *Columbia Journalism Review.* www.cjr.org/resources/crime2k/index.asp.

Special report: Covering criminal justice, Vol. 1. (1999). *Columbia Journalism Review.* www.cjr.org/Resources/crime99.

Staged "Perp Walk" violates suspect's Fourth Amendment rights. (2000, September). Gannett Newswatch. www.gannett.com/go/newswatch/2000/september/nw0929-4.htm.

The Station fire digital extra. (2003). *Providence Journal.* www.projo.com/extra/2003/stationfire.

Sullivan, C. (2003). Police scanners may be headed for the morgue. *Editor & Publisher,* p. 7.

Student Press Law Center. (2000). *Covering campus crime. A handbook for journalists.* Arlington, VA: Student Press Law Center.

Toohey, W. (2002, December 3). Audiotaped interview with public information director of Baltimore County police.

Toohey, W. (2000, August). Media relations during a hostage crisis. *Subject to Debate. A Newsletter of the Police Executive Research Forum, 14*(8), 1, 3–4.

TV news: Covering an airplane crash. (1997). *The Rundown.* www.tvrundown.com.

U.S. Department of Justice. (2001, October 22). *Crime in the United States 2000.* Washington, DC: FBI.

Washington Metro Area Transit Authority. (2002). Media guidelines. Welcome to Metro! www.wmata.com.

Weil, M. (1999, March 2). Police series wins reporting award. *Washington Post,* p. A10.

Wilkinson, A. (2003, June 16/23). This just in dept. Calling all cars. *New Yorker,* p. 74.

Wilson v. Layne (98-83) 526 U.S. 603 (1999) 141 F.3d.111, affirmed.

Wingate, A. (1992). *Scene of the crime: A writer's guide to crime-scene investigations.* Cincinnati, OH: Writer's Digest Books.

Young, J. (2001, May). Law enforcement: Police agencies among worst violators. Retrieved November 25, 2002, from www.pnpa.com/publications/press/may01/police.htm.

CHAPTER 11

COVERING THE COURTS

A local socialite dies in a late-night fall down the back stairs of her mansion in a well-established neighborhood. The police reporter has covered the story from the first accounts through the arrest of her husband, who is charged with first-degree murder. It's been a year since her death, and her husband has been out of jail after he posted bond. His trial starts next week.

The police reporter who has been following the story and reporting its many developments hands the story to the court reporter. The police reporter will still have a role in providing background, but the day-to-day coverage of what happens during the trial will fall to the court reporter. She knows how the system works and how to follow the case. She knows the sources, the documents, and the language. And she knows that once the trial starts, she might be covering it for several weeks or even several months.

While the court reporter must write about the legal aspects of the story, she cannot forget about the personalities. Readers will want to know about the defendant and his demeanor; the attitude of the judge and the prosecutor; the behavior of family members and friends before, during, and after the trial; and even the jury and its makeup. Cameras might not be allowed in the courtroom, so the reporter has to pay attention to detail and include description in stories.

In this chapter you will:

■ Get an overview of the court system, including federal courts,
■ Get tips on how to get started covering the court beat,
■ Learn which documents provide information,
■ Be introduced to key court personnel, and
■ See what types of stories are generated by the court beat.

OVERVIEW OF THE COURT STRUCTURE

Reporters should learn how their respective state's judicial system is set up. While each state has some general jurisdiction courts and then an appeals system, the entry point for cases and the names of courts differ state to state. No textbook can outline every state's court structure. Students can go to the State Court Locator hosted by Villanova University at http://vls.law.vill.edu/Locator/statecourt and click on links to their respective court system as well as court opinions.

Each state has a court system that generally is divided into three general levels: courts of limited jurisdiction, courts of general jurisdiction, and courts of last resort. In some states those translate into district courts, superior courts, and appeals courts. Each level has responsibilities for certain types of cases. Some states have city or municipal courts.

Cases start out in either limited or general jurisdiction courts and then can be appealed to the higher-level courts. Judges and, in some cases, juries can issue verdicts at the lower levels, whereas judges or justices hear cases at the appeals court level. At all levels, judges impose sentencing, although juries might recommend sentences, such as life in prison or death. Some cases can be appealed out of the state court system and into the federal system. The federal system also has three levels and has jurisdiction over specific cases. The federal system will be discussed later in this chapter.

Court reporters must learn how their states' court systems are organized so they know where to look for cases, how to follow their progress, and where to find dispositions of the cases.

Lower-Level Courts

Limited jurisdiction or district courts are often the first point of entry for many cases. Each state's system of lower-level courts varies. In Delaware, cases enter through alderman's court, municipal courts, justice of the peace courts, or court of common pleas. Most of those courts do not have jury trials. Judges, justices of the peace, commissioners, or specially appointed aldermen hear cases and make rulings. For its point of entry, North Carolina has a system of district courts whereby judges hear criminal, juvenile, and civil cases. Among the criminal cases are theft and domestic violence. Other domestic issues, such as divorces and child custody, are also heard in district court. In North Carolina, district courts are not courts of record, which means transcripts or recordings of proceedings are not kept.

Cases are classified as misdemeanors or felonies. A misdemeanor is a crime, such as writing a worthless check or shoplifting, and is less serious than a felony. Often a misdemeanor does not involve injury to a person, and a person convicted would go to jail, pay a fine, do community service, or a combination of all three. A felony criminal case could be murder, rape, or burglary—generally cases whereby an individual harms another person or a person is present during the commission of the crime. Sentences are much more severe, and in capital cases, such as murder, a conviction could mean life in prison or death.

In most states, the largest block of district court cases is misdemeanor traffic cases and civil cases. Traffic charges range from speeding to expired vehicle inspection stickers. Some jurisdictions have special traffic courts just to handle the overwhelming number of traffic violations. Some have specific drug courts to deal with repeat drug offenders. Other types of cases heard in district court might be health commitment cases and probable cause hearings for felony cases to determine whether there is enough evidence to hold a defendant.

Civil cases are brought by a person against another person or an organization or business. The plaintiff or person bringing the case usually is suing for monetary damages. Most states have some lower-level court in which civil cases involving less than $5,000 are heard. In some states, these courts are called small claims courts, and a court employee called a magistrate hears cases. In Delaware, for example, justices of the peace hear civil action cases of less than $1,500. Decisions in these cases are immediate and binding. A party in a small claims case could appeal a magistrate's decision to an upper-level court.

In some states judges can send cases to arbitration, for example, in civil cases whereby an individual is suing for less than $15,000 or in child custody cases. Court-ordered arbitration can save hours of court time and attorneys' fees. Communities often have dispute resolution centers where trained facilitators help resolve conflicts and specific fees are charged. Arbitration agreements go to a judge to be entered as a binding order on all parties in the case.

Juvenile proceedings generally cover youth who are under age 16 and usually are closed to the public and the media. Judges in many states do have the option of allowing someone under age 16 to be tried as an adult in capital cases, such as murder. In states with the death penalty, a teenager could be executed. If found guilty in juvenile court, the youth would be sent to a youthful offenders center for a specific time before being released.

General Jurisdiction Courts

Some cases start in courts of general jurisdiction or upper-level courts and bypass the lower courts, such as civil cases involving more than $10,000 in damages and felony criminal cases. General jurisdiction courts also hear appeals from lower-level courts; for example, a defendant could appeal a judge's sentence for a misdemeanor drug possession. Civil appeals and appeals in domestic and juvenile cases would go directly from the lower-level court to the appeals court and would bypass the general jurisdiction court.

In North Carolina, the general jurisdiction court is called superior court. Delaware also has superior courts and a separate Court of Chancery that hears only equity cases involving suits such as commercial and contractual matters, trusts, estates, and real property disputes.

Appeals Courts

State appeals courts usually have two levels: the lower-level court called the court of appeals and the higher-level or the supreme court. The appeals court

generally hears appeals from felony trials and civil trials from general jurisdiction court and as noted earlier domestic, juvenile, or civil appeals from
lower-level court. At the state appeals courts, judges called justices are assigned cases and sit in panels of three to render decisions. Justices do not look
at the facts of the case but rather determine whether any legal errors occurred
at the lower level. For example, a justice could determine that a lower court
judge's instructions to the jury did not include all verdict options.

State supreme courts hear appeals from the state court of appeals and in
most states hear appeals on death penalty cases. The latter do not go through
the appeals court but move directly from general jurisdiction court to the
supreme court. Judges at this level are also called justices. They select the cases
they will review and sit as an entire body to hear the cases, rather than in panels as the appeals court does. Lawyers from each side argue their cases before
the justices, who can ask questions. The justices hand down written opinions
often weeks after the hearing, and the majority rules. In many cases, any dis-
senting opinions are included.

In some states the supreme court is not the highest court. In New York,
the Supreme Court is a trial court. The highest court is the Court of Appeals.
Again, as a court reporter, you need to know how your state's court system is
organized. Also, who follows the appeals varies. In some states the prosecutor at the lower-level court follows the case up the appeals ladder. In other
states, lawyers who work for the state attorneys general are assigned to represent the state on appeal.

Cameras in Courtrooms

Cameras in courtrooms are a fairly recent phenomenon. Judges and court administrators have been reluctant to admit cameras. They felt that witnesses
often played to the cameras and were more self-conscious in their testimony
if they knew their actions and words were being filmed. They also worried
about jurors and their ability to pay attention if camera lighting or sounds dis-
tracted them.

Although reporters were allowed to take notes and record any aspect of
court, still and video cameras were considered more intrusive and disruptive
to the legal process. In *Chandler v. Florida* (1980), the Supreme Court overturned a 1960 ruling barring cameras in courtrooms. The ruling allows states
to determine whether cameras are in, but they must ensure that defendants
are not denied due process or the right to a speedy trial.

Since the early 1990s, cameras have slipped more and more into courtrooms. Judges have the discretion to allow cameras into courtrooms. Some
states' press associations, such as the Idaho Press Association (2003), have
guidelines for reporters in using cameras in courtrooms, whether still cameras or television cameras. Most prohibit photos of jurors and require that
cameras be set up well before court starts. In many cases, reporters have to
pool or share cameras when a judge allows only one photographer and one

videographer into a court session. The visual benefit of cameras allows viewers to watch the actual trial and see the players' actions and reactions. Cameras document events that are public record.

GETTING STARTED ON THE BEAT

A reporter assigned to the court beat must first learn his particular local and state court structure, as noted earlier in this chapter. The state constitution can be found online and is a starting point. Another quick resource is the state administrative office of the courts or a similar agency that serves as the support and records organization for the state court system. To find their states' administrative offices, reporters can go to the State Court Locator at http://vls.law.vill.edu/Locator/statecourt.

The Basic Knowledge

Reporters must also know the players: judges, district attorneys and their assistants, court clerks, public defenders, to name a few. Reporters should learn judges' reputations and how long they have been in office. Reporters should also know how judges apply sentencing guidelines, that is, whether they are inclined to give the maximum sentence for certain offenses. If judges in the state are elected, the local and state elections boards can provide data on when they were elected, how many times they have sought political office, and the vote counts. In some states, clerks of courts and district attorneys are also elected. Closely tied to each state's court system is an attorney general, who is charged with upholding the laws of the state and protecting citizens.

In addition, a reporter must learn the terminology, the types of documents that will give information, where the documents can be found, and the individuals who work in the court system. Most court stories are not accounts of flashy trials but are the result of reporters reading court calendars and determining which cases are worthy of coverage. Just as the police reporter does not write a story on every traffic accident or arrest, the court reporter does not follow every court case. The story might be a summary based on court documents and an interview with an assistant district attorney. Only for the most high-profile cases do court reporters sit through court sessions.

Knowing how to get information and determine the newsworthiness of court actions is key to being a successful court reporter. One assistant district attorney advised student reporters to know who was charged and the charges before calling and asking for details about a case. A reporter might not have the docket number for a case, but prosecutors need some place to start if they are going to provide any information.

Most court proceedings involving adults are open to the public and the media. Some courtrooms have specific press tables or areas for the media. Often those locations put reporters close to attorneys, prosecutors, and juries so they can hear questions and testimony. As noted earlier, however, juvenile cases are closed. A judge can also choose to close a proceeding if he has adequate cause. For example, a judge could close a hearing on a child sex abuse case.

Gagging Information from the Media

Judges can also issue gag orders that bar trial participants from speaking to news media about anything related to a lawsuit. The judge might determine that pretrial publicity could hinder a defendant's right to a fair trial under the Sixth Amendment of the Constitution. Too much information could also hinder efforts to get a jury if community members have read or heard extensive details or comments about the case. Judges should have a compelling reason to issue gag orders and should feel that they have no other recourse to ensure a fair trial, such as a change of venue or location of the trial.

Gag orders can be imposed before or during court proceedings. For example, a judge could issue a gag order if attorneys can show that publication of the information would cause irreparable harm. A plaintiff in a case could seek a gag order to prevent a defendant from talking, such as a husband versus a wife in a high-profile divorce case. Or the judge could rule during a trial that defense attorneys cannot talk to the media about the case.

Gag orders typically apply to prosecutors, attorneys, defendants, jurors, and other parties to a suit. When basketball player Kobe Bryant was charged with sexual assault in 2003, a Colorado judge issued a gag order preventing law enforcement officials from leaking information, such as the victim's name, to the media. The gag order came after some media had already revealed the woman's identity, but the judge aimed to prevent other leaks prior to Bryant's trial.

Media will appeal gag orders, generally contending that barring the information is unconstitutional. Media consider gag orders to be prior restraint on their First Amendment right of free speech. Judges, and eventually higher courts, have to determine whether an individual's right to a fair trial is more important than the media's right of free speech. Many gag orders are stopped early or are overturned on appeal.

In November 2002, the city of Colorado Springs tried to get a gag order against an alternative newspaper, the *Colorado Springs Independent*. When two reporters requested the job file of a town police officer, a temporary clerk mistakenly gave the reporters the detective's complete file. A supervisor requested the file be returned, but the reporters had already made notes and refused to return the notes. The city threatened to seek a gag order to prevent the newspaper from publishing any material from the personnel file. The state chapter of the American Civil Liberties Union said its lawyers would represent the paper, and the city withdrew its suit.

Some judges have issued orders limiting media interviews of jurors after cases have been decided. According to the *First Amendment Handbook* of the

Reporters Committee for Freedom of the Press (2003), courts have upheld decisions to restrict jurors' comments about the actual deliberations in a trial. The courts did not restrict, however, access to the jurors, jurors' comments about the verdict, or comments from jurors' relatives about the case.

Information through Documents

The Internet has brought court record keeping into the electronic age. Anyone can go online, access a particular court system, and find out the status of a defendant's case. Before the Internet, those records were filed away in courthouses and required a personal visit to get them.

Reporters still have to go to courthouses to find some records that are not available online. For example, warrants and motions related to a specific case will not be online. They will be in the case file kept in the courthouse. Some smaller jurisdictions' records might not yet be computerized.

In addition, some court records might not be public under a state's open records laws. Reporters need to know which documents their states' laws exempt. For example, adoption records or grand jury indictments are not available to reporters. Neither are juvenile files, unless the juvenile has been legally declared an adult. Other areas that clerks can protect from public view are expunged records, involuntary commitments, and unserved arrest or search warrants. Remember: If a court official denies access to a record, it is the official's responsibility to show the reporter or private citizen the section of law that keeps the record private.

Judges can also seal records. For example, the specific amounts of alimony or child support in a high-profile divorce or the monetary damages awarded in a class action suit against a company could be sealed. Reporters can be held in contempt of court if they find and print information from the sealed record. They could be fined, along with their employer, and even sent to jail. Reporters can talk with people familiar with a case, however, and perhaps find someone who is willing to talk about the settlement in general. But publication of specific details could have profound effects. Some settlements have nonpublication clauses in which parties agree not to reveal the terms. If the terms become public, a judge could set the settlement aside, that is, declare it void.

Among the specific documents a court reporter would seek are the following:

■ **Dockets.** Dockets are the listings of cases that will be heard in a particular court on a given day. The docket will list the defendant, the charge, and the arresting officer. A docket for one morning session of district court could have 500 traffic cases. Some individuals will have multiple charges. For example, a teenager might be pulled over for failing to stop at a stop sign and be charged with that offense along with an expired vehicle inspection, underage possession of alcohol if the officer saw an opened beer can, and resisting arrest. Dockets are generally available at least 24 hours in advance. Often clerks will post the docket publicly but will not provide numerous copies. Good reporters establish a rapport with the clerk so they can get copies of the dockets.

■ **Warrants that have been served.** Warrants list plaintiff and defendant, unless police determine that revealing a plaintiff's name jeopardizes his or her safety. They tell the charges, addresses, and a summary of the information that led to issuing the warrant, be it a search warrant or an arrest warrant. Warrants are issued by magistrates, who will keep them unless they are being served by law enforcement officers. If officers fail to serve a warrant, it will be returned to the magistrate.

■ **Complaints.** Complaints are the documents that start a civil lawsuit. An individual brings a complaint against another individual or a company.

■ **Motions.** Attorneys on both sides of a case can file a motion to dismiss the case, to suppress evidence, or to respond to a motion filed by the other side. These motions are filed in the case record. Often, in a well-publicized case, attorneys will make their motions available to the media because they want their side or their latest charge aired.

■ **Disposition.** The disposition or settlement of a case will also be included in the case record. Unless it is sealed, as noted earlier, it is part of the case record and, therefore, public.

■ **Court reporter's transcript.** In trials, courts hire reporters or stenographers to take down word for word the proceedings and the testimony of witnesses. Court reporters usually sit near the judge and the jury box so they can hear clearly. They are required to produce a transcript within a specified time after the trial because a verbatim account is necessary if the case is appealed.

■ **Sentencing guidelines.** The U.S. Sentencing Commission at www.ussc.gov is an independent agency created in the 1970s resulting from concern about the disparity in sentences that judges could hand down. After more than a decade of debate and research, the commission and national sentencing guidelines went into effect in November 1987. Their constitutionality was challenged but upheld by the U.S. Supreme Court, and the guidelines were implementated by January 1989.

According to its Web site, the commission can submit guideline amendments to Congress each year. The guidelines give judges fair and consistent sentence ranges based on the severity of the crime and the individual's criminal record. Sentences that are not within the guidelines' range are subject to review. More information is available at www.ussc.gov/general/ovrvuweb.PDF.

Reporters can also get information about sentences from the National Association of Sentencing Commissions at www.ussc.gov/STATES.HTM.

Available are federal sentencing statistics by circuit for type of sentence, mode of conviction, and length of imprisonment for all federally sentenced individuals as well as from each circuit or district.

People as Sources

Although some states have city or municipal courts, most court systems are administered by the state. Lower-level courts are housed in counties or districts, usually in county or city courthouses. Employees are state employees, rather than employees of the local government. Knowing who employs court employees is important. If state employees are not getting a pay raise because of a budget shortfall, local court workers will be affected and could be sources. When a controversy arises at the local level, such as a backlog of cases, a reporter might need to look at the state level for information or even background, such as the allocation of judges that could relieve the backlog.

People at all levels of power and responsibility make the court system operate: magistrates, clerks, bailiffs, judges, public defenders, and others. Reporters must know the sources and each source's responsibilities and expertise so they can follow cases through the system. Those sources can translate legal proceedings and put them in context. People, whether the judge or the defendant, also add the human element and often the drama to any court story. Court reporters must include color and quotes for a story to be complete and compelling.

At the same time, reporters must be aware that prosecutors should not comment on cases before they are tried. Prosecutors should tell reporters only what's in the record. They should not discuss evidence, a prior record, or what they think will happen in the case. After the trial, they can comment. Prosecutors also cannot tell reporters in advance of a trial if a plea bargain—whereby a defendant pleads guilty to a lesser charge and accepts a sentence—has been worked out. Defense lawyers, however, can say whatever they want, but they might be circumspect so that no prejudicial or unfair comments are made about clients prior to trial. Sometimes a reporter needs a national source to provide reaction or background. A good resource is the associations link on the National Center for State Courts' Web site at www.ncsconline.org/Associations/index.html.

Among the people most commonly found in the courthouse are the following:

■ **Bailiff.** The bailiff sits in the courtroom, keeps order, stands, and announces the judge's entrance. The bailiff also is responsible for making sure that defendants get to court on time and that all people behave appropriately.

■ **Clerk of court.** Each court has a clerk who is responsible for keeping track of who has been arrested, the trial calendar, and the disposition of case.

The clerk posts a docket or schedule of upcoming court cases on a particular day. The court calendar lists which days court will be in session. The clerk also catalogs exhibits and evidence submitted in conjunction with a case and handles estates filed in the county, special proceedings such as adoptions, and even foreclosures.

■ **Magistrates.** Magistrates sit as judges in small claims court, as noted earlier. But they are also responsible for issuing arrest and search warrants and overseeing bond hearings. At a bond hearing, a magistrate decides what bond—cash, property, or other collateral—must be posted to secure a person's release from jail.

■ **District or state's attorneys.** A district or state attorney serves as the prosecutor for the state or government at the local level. The prosecutor will have a staff of assistant prosecutors who are assigned to cases in some manner, such as by type of case (assault, rape, traffic) or by court level (upper or lower). Or they might be assigned to prosecute all the cases that appear on a court docket on a given day. Prosecutors who are elected might opt to take the high-profile cases that can aid their reelection bids. Knowing how prosecutors are assigned to cases can help reporters seeking information.

■ **Public defenders.** Some states have a system of public defenders who are appointed by the courts to represent people who cannot afford to hire attorneys. A judge must make a determination of financial need. Those districts that do not have public defenders appoint private attorneys to represent financially needy people. The state pays expenses and fees, but if the person is found guilty, he or she might have to repay the state.

■ **Judges.** Judges in many states are elected. Often they are appointed by the governor of the state to fill a vacancy, then they run for that office. Judges can rule in some cases without a jury. Many states have set sentencing guidelines that dictate prison terms based on the crime. Judges cannot rule outside those parameters.

Judges must also follow strict ethical guidelines that extend to political campaigns. A judge could not campaign on a platform related to judicial decrees he or she might hand down. While judges still run on party lines, some critics have launched efforts to make judicial elections nonpartisan. Although the candidate has a party affiliation, the political party would not be listed on the ballot.

In some states, judges are not allowed to advertise for campaign funds. Individuals might give to judges' campaigns, but those judges cannot actively seek donations. Judges are elected to varying terms, some serving four years and others eight years.

■ **Plaintiffs and defendants.** The plaintiff is the individual or organization bringing the suit, whereas the defendant is the person or organization charged with some violation. Each has a story to tell and can add a human element.

■ **Jury members.** Once a verdict has been determined and a sentence handed down, jury members can give insight into deliberations and considerations about a defendant's guilt or innocence.

THE FEDERAL COURT SYSTEM

The federal court system is overseen by the Judicial Conference of the United States, which supervises the director of the Administrative Office of the United States Courts. The presiding officer is the chief justice of the U.S. Supreme Court. Members are the chief judge of each judicial circuit, the chief judge of the court of International Trade, and a district judge from each regional judicial circuit. Members serve three to five years. The conference addresses issues such as personnel, probation, sentencing, and judicial salaries, among others.

The Structure

The Associated Press Stylebook (2003) notes that the "federal court system that exists today as the outgrowth of Article 3 of the Constitution is composed of the Supreme Court of the United States, the U.S. Court of Appeals, U.S. District Courts and the U.S. Customs Courts." Four district judges are appointed to cover U.S. territories, such as Puerto Rico.

■ **The U.S. District Court.** Each state has one or more regions for district court where most cases are heard. There are 94 U.S. District Courts. Some states such as Alaska are a single district, whereas others, such as North Carolina with three, have multiple districts. Judges hear cases. Reporters can link to the federal district court system through www.uscourts.gov/links.html.

■ **U.S. Court of Appeals.** The United States is divided into 11 circuits or geographical districts. The smallest is the 1st with six judgeships to hear cases, and the largest is the 9th with 28 judgeships. Judges hear cases. The 11 districts plus the District of Columbia and Federal Circuits are noted in Figure 11.1.

■ **U.S. Supreme Court.** The highest court in the country is based in Washington, DC. The Court selects cases it will hear. The chief justice is the reigning judge, and the other eight members of the Court are called associate justices. All nine justices hear cases from the first Monday in October through

FIGURE 11.1   U.S. Court of Appeals Districts

District of Columbia Circuit;

Federal Circuit;

1st Circuit based in Boston and covering Maine, Massachusetts, New Hampshire, Rhode Island, Puerto Rico;

2nd Circuit based in New York and covering Connecticut, New York, Vermont;

3rd Circuit in Philadelphia: Delaware, New Jersey, Pennsylvania, Virgin Islands;

4th Circuit in Richmond, Virginia: Maryland, North Carolina, South Carolina, Virginia, West Virginia;

5th Circuit in New Orleans: Louisiana, Mississippi, Texas;

6th Circuit in Cincinnati: Kentucky, Michigan, Ohio, Tennessee;

7th Circuit in Chicago: Illinois, Indiana, Wisconsin;

8th Circuit in St. Louis: Arkansas, Iowa, Minnesota, Missouri, Nebraska, North Dakota, South Dakota;

9th Circuit in San Francisco: Alaska, Arizona, California, Hawaii, Idaho, Montana, Nevada, Oregon, Washington, Guam;

10th Circuit in Denver: Colorado, Kansas, New Mexico, Oklahoma, Utah, Wyoming;

11th Circuit in Atlanta: Alabama, Florida, Georgia.

the summer. Decisions typically begin to be released in late spring. The bulk of the decisions are released at the end of the session. A local reporter might follow a case through the state courts, appeals courts, and Supreme Court, but the entire process might take years.

How Cases Progress in U.S. Courts

Cases regarding federal issues generally start at the lower-level U.S. District Court. Those cases involve matters that cross state lines, such as criminal cases, tax, or antitrust cases. U.S. district attorneys are the prosecutors in U.S. District Court.

Individuals cannot file criminal cases in federal courts. The government brings proceedings through the U.S. attorney's office and a law enforcement agency, such as the Federal Bureau of Investigation (FBI). Civil actions begin when an individual files a complaint and pays a $150 filing fee.

Bankruptcy cases are heard in federal court. An individual files a petition along with a statement of assets and liabilities. People can file different types of bankruptcy, but the most common is Chapter 7. The person is required to liquidate certain assets to pay debts and to keep exempt property, such as a house or car for business. Under Chapter 11, a business can continue to operate while it develops a plan to repay its creditors. Chapter 12 applies to family farmers who have financial problems. Under Chapter 13 bankruptcy, a person repays creditors over a three- to five-year period. A bankruptcy judge, who is appointed by a majority of judges on the appeals court within that district, hears such cases. The Association of Bankruptcy Judicial Assistants has links to helpful Web sites at www.abja.org/links.htm. Bankruptcy as a business story is discussed in Chapter 9.

Cases from district court can be appealed through the appeals court and on to the supreme court. As noted earlier, some cases from the states can be appealed directly from the state court system to the U.S. Court of Appeals and even to the U.S. Supreme Court.

When the U.S. Supreme Court determines which cases it will hear, that case list makes news. For example, in fall 2002, many in higher education paid attention when the Supreme Court decided to hear a Michigan case regarding the use of race in admissions decisions. Media around the country ran stories because the Supreme Court's ruling would affect every institution of higher education.

The progress of cases can be monitored through the PACER Service Center, described as "the Federal Judiciary's centralized registration, billing, and technical support center for electronic access to U.S. District, Bankruptcy, and Appellate court records." Not all courts participate, but reporters or anyone willing to pay the user fee can get information about a particular individual or case.

Federal Court Personnel

The sitting U.S. president nominates people to be district and appeals court judges and Supreme Court justices. The Senate Judiciary Committee is responsible for holding hearings on the nominees before the U.S. Senate confirms them. The president selects from individuals named by congressional members or members of the president's political party. Getting an appointment to a federal judgeship is a coup. Once appointed, the judge holds the post for life.

People who are confirmed as U.S. Supreme Court justices can have an extraordinary role in the direction of case law in the country. Whether members are conservative or liberal can determine the legality of such contentious issues as abortion, search and seizure, and affirmative action.

More information on the federal court system can be found at www.uscourts.gov/index.html. Historical and other material can be found through the Federal Judicial Center at www.fjc.gov. Reporters can access landmark legislation and biographies of federal judges since 1789. Reporters can also learn what judges and court administrators are learning through special education programs listed on the Judicial Center Web site. Some events are designed to help media better understand court workings and give them access to judges.

Beyond Trials on the Federal Court Beat

Most media do not have reporters who are assigned to cover the federal courts full time. Often a reporter's contact with federal courts and judges occurs if a case she is following is appealed to federal courts or if someone tips her that a case has been filed in federal court, such as a bankruptcy filing.

Reporters can find stories in federal courts, however. The U.S. Courts Web site has a newsroom that contains recent news releases. It is worth an occasional visit. For example, a story in December 2002 noted that bankruptcy filings hit a historic high in fiscal year 2001–2002, but no new bankruptcy judgeships had been created and no additional funds had been allocated. As a result, the current judges struggled to keep up with cases. You can also find out where vacancies exist, why, and who has been nominated to fill the positions by accessing www.uscourts.gov/vacancies/01.html.

Reporters can get other story ideas by accessing the U.S. Courts news archives at www.uscourts.gov/nrarchive.html. Those stories might have relevance in any community and might warrant a local angle or look.

A DAY IN COURT

Many reporters write court stories without ever going to court. They know that a case is scheduled, and after the fact, they call clerks or assistant district attorneys to find out what happened. The information might show up as a short article or it might be in a wrap-up of many court actions in one day.

But sometimes a case has attracted enough attention at the arrest and initial stages that the reporter and his or her editors decide that it is worth covering day after day. Covering a court case requires a major time commitment. A trial, from jury selection to jury decision, can take a few days or months. When a reporter makes the decision to cover a trial, he or she has to settle into the courthouse for the long haul.

A visible example of a lengthy pretrial and trial process is the kidnapping case of Elizabeth Smart, the Utah teen who disappeared from her Salt Lake City home and was discovered nine months later. Pretrial meetings, motions, and orders on behalf of the two charged with her kidnapping, Brian David Mitchell and Wanda Ilene Barzee, occupied days of media coverage. Mitchell even appeared in court on a lesser shoplifting charge before being arraigned on the kidnapping charges. The *Salt Lake Tribune* (2003, March 15) reported that day:

> In his first public appearance since his Wednesday arrest for allegedly kidnapping Elizabeth Smart, Brian David Mitchell was arraigned in Salt Lake City's justice court on a shoplifting charge from September 2002.

In a later story, the *Salt Lake Tribune* (2003, April 2) reported:

> Third District Judge Judith Atherton—assigned as the trial judge in the Elizabeth Smart kidnapping case—on Tuesday held a private 40-minute discussion with a dozen members of the prosecution and defense teams.

Covering the Mitchell charges and trials would occupy months of any reporter's time, and the reporter would need to have good sources.

In covering any court case, reporters should consider the following tips:

- Get description. How are people dressed? What are their reactions to testimony or verdicts?
- Make sure you state the charges in the story. Give background leading up to the trial. Sometimes months or even years pass between the actual crime and the trial.
- Be careful about language. Until the person is actually convicted, you should not call him or her a murderer. *The Associated Press Stylebook* (2003) cautions not to say someone was murdered "until someone has been convicted in court" or "authorities say premeditation was obvious."
- Get plenty of comments. Interview defendants, defense attorneys, prosecutors, plaintiffs, judges.
- Use testimony. Remember that whatever a witness said under oath in court is protected, that is, if you print it, you cannot be successfully sued for libel. Testimony is protected under the defense of qualified privilege.
- In jury cases include comments from jury members after the verdict is given. Have jurors explain their reasoning. Include how long the jury deliberated.

TYPES OF STORIES COURT REPORTERS COVER

As a court case progresses, a reporter writes a succession of stories. After the arrest story, usually written by the police reporter, will be a first appearance. At that time, a defendant is read the charges and confirms that he or she understands the charges. The judge makes sure the warrant is sufficient, determines probable cause, and sets the conditions of release, such as posting bail.

A Watersbury plumbing contractor made his first court appearance Tuesday on charges of assaulting the 15-year-old boyfriend of his daughter. He posted $15,000 bail and was released until his trial next month.

Deferred prosecution can occur if a defendant agrees to certain conditions to have his record expunged.

Three teenagers who set fire to cages at a local turkey farm were ordered Wednesday to perform 100 hours of community service each at a local animal protection agency. In exchange, they will have the charges wiped from their records.

If the case is a high-profile one, a reporter might write stories in advance of the trial.

The trial of a former Watersbury Elementary School teacher who was charged with child endangerment in punishing a 7-year-old boy by locking him in a closet will begin in Superior Court on Monday.

The story will be reported when the trial begins and will continue each day with the latest information leading the story.

Jury selection in the trial of a former Watersbury Elementary School teacher who was charged with child endangerment after punishing a 7-year-old boy by locking him in a closet began in Superior Court on Monday.

The defense certified six jurors, but the assistant district attorney denied one of those because she knew the defendant. Jury selection will continue Tuesday.

Mary Jane Sinclair, 37, of 423 State Road was charged in December with locking a 7-year-old boy in a closet in her elementary school classroom. She contended that the youngster repeatedly hit other children. The parents who brought the charges claim their son suffered psychological damage from sitting in the dark closet for an hour. Sinclair was suspended when she was charged.

When testimony begins, court stories can become quite dramatic.

A child psychologist testified Thursday that a 7-year-old boy has suffered "irreparable harm and damage to his trust in adults as a result of his encounter with the defendant and may suffer for years to come."

Dr. David Langford of Watersbury testified in the fourth day of the trial of Mary Jane Sinclair, 37, of 423 State Road. She was charged in December with child endangerment after she locked a 7-year-old boy in her elementary school classroom closet. Sinclair was suspended from her teaching duties.

Jury selection took the first two days of the trial, which started Monday. Witnesses for the prosecution began testifying Wednesday.

When a jury determines the guilt of a defendant, the reporter has another lead.

A jury deliberated only two hours on Tuesday before finding Mary Jane Sinclair guilty of child endangerment after locking a 7-year-old boy in her elementary school classroom closet for an hour last year.

The jury had listened to four days of testimony from psychologists, the child's parents and other relatives, and law enforcement officials as well as character witnesses for Sinclair. Neither the child nor Sinclair testified. The trial began last Monday with two days of jury selection before testimony began on Wednesday. Testimony resumed Tuesday after courts were closed for Memorial Day. Judge Michael Warner gave the jury its instruction Tuesday early afternoon after testimony ended that morning.

"We were just convinced from what we heard from the child's parents and police that the incident had occurred and that the child was affected. The fact that Sinclair did not testify hurt her case," said juror Helene Brantham.

Sinclair will be sentenced by Warner Wednesday.

In some cases, a reporter will write another story from the sentencing hearing. At that hearing, the defense can present evidence that might influence a judge to give a lesser sentence.

> Family of Mary Jane Sinclair pleaded with the court Wednesday to give her the least possible sentence and also recommend psychiatric help after the former teacher was found guilty Tuesday of locking a 7-year-old boy in the classroom closet as a disciplinary measure.
>
> "She's got family of her own," said Sinclair's sister, Natalie Crisp. "This whole incident has torn her apart and us apart. She needs help not jail time."

Then the actual sentencing leads to still another story.

> Judge Michael Warner has sentenced former school teacher Mary Jane Sinclair to two years in jail but suspended the sentence and attached a recommendation for psychiatric services after she was found guilty Tuesday of locking a 7-year-old boy in her classroom closet as a disciplinary measure last December.
>
> Warner said he gave the lightest sentence he could while still recognizing the seriousness of the offense. He noted that Sinclair had no prior charges and none had come forth as a result of the trial.
>
> Sinclair had no comment and left the courtroom immediately with her attorney.
>
> The child's parents said they had hoped for a stronger sentence, although the mother admitted that putting Sinclair in jail wouldn't help her child.

You will notice from the previous examples that while the latest information starts the stories, background information is essential to let readers know what trial the reporter is covering and a summary of what has happened before.

Quotes from witnesses as they testify—jurors, prosecutors, defense attorneys, and even judges, if you can get to them—are essential elements. Disruptions, testimony, the behavior of defendants, and their dress add color and detail to the story.

In the following story about a complicated murder trial, note how reporter Jeff Scullin (2003) sets up the latest information in the lead but also gives readers a twist: If the defendant had accepted a plea bargain, he would have served less time in jail. Within the first six paragraphs, readers know who was convicted, who died, the charges and the sentence, and an explanation of the more serious charge.

From there the reporter unfolds the story. Scullin uses time elements such as "on Friday" in graph 2, "Monday" in graph 11, "the night of April 26, 1998" in graph 17, and "in September" in graph 41 to keep readers straight on what happened when. He writes short paragraphs with one event, one development, and one new piece of information in each paragraph. He quotes sources such as the defense attorney and assistant state attorneys. Testimony, court records, and police reports provide the information that pieces together the chain of events from the shootings to the jury verdict and judge's sentencing. All the elements of a good court story are included: conviction, sentencing, testimony, quotes, sequence of events, and description.

SARASOTA—Curtis Shuler gambled this week on the sympathy of a jury, rejecting a plea deal for his part in a 1998 Haines City shooting spree that would have freed the 21-year-old well before his 30th birthday.

On Friday, Shuler lost the bet. And he'll likely pay for it with the rest of his life.

After deliberating more than eight hours Thursday afternoon and Friday morning, jurors convicted the Haines City man of first-degree felony murder for the killing of 32-year-old Larry Steven Tyler.

Circuit Judge Michael McCarthy promptly sentenced Shuler to a mandatory life sentence for first-degree murder.

Under felony murder statutes, a defendant can be convicted of first-degree murder for taking part in a felony that leads to someone's death. The defendant need not take an active role in the actual killing.

The jury also convicted Shuler on a charge of attempted burglary, but found him not guilty of shooting into an occupied vehicle.

The verdicts suggest that jurors rejected the theories of both the prosecution and the defense in the trial.

Prosecutors argued that Shuler, though aided by accomplices, was the one who shot Tyler during an attempted carjacking.

The defense claimed that Shuler was not present when the murder took place. "It's a little puzzling because the jury, on their own, rejected everyone's theory," said Shuler's lawyer, Gil Colon Jr. "They obviously did not believe he was the shooter," but thought he was there.

Even more puzzling is why Shuler, facing a mandatory life sentence if convicted of first-degree murder, would refuse to make a plea agreement with prosecutors, who offered him a 15-year deal as late as Tuesday.

Monday, the day jury selection began, prosecutors made him a seemingly irresistible offer of 12 years in prison. According to Colon, Shuler would have had to serve about five years of that sentence, based on the amount of time he already has spent in jail and state sentencing guidelines.

But Shuler continues to maintain he did not shoot Tyler and refused to plead guilty to his murder, Colon said.

"This young man gambled a life sentence for what was a few years," Colon said. "(But) he says he's not guilty. . . . Obviously, he's not happy with the verdict. He's not happy with the sentence.

"Now, if the appeal fails, he's going to die in prison."

If it stands, Shuler's conviction would mark the final trial of those accused in a 1998 4-day shooting spree that terrorized Northeast Polk County.

Two people, including Tyler, were killed and seven others wounded.

Prosecutors argued that Shuler shot Tyler the night of April 26, 1998, as the Davenport man and a friend, Steve Green, were driving near the Grenelefe Resort, east of Haines City.

Shuler and two accomplices, Victor Lester, 22, and Sylathum Streeter, 21, had parked their car in the woods and were waiting for someone to stop so they could rob them, prosecutors said.

As Green and Tyler approached a stop sign, a man flung open the passenger-side door of Green's Ford Explorer and fired three shots before Green sped away. Tyler, who was in the passenger seat, was hit and later died from his injuries.

Lester and Streeter also were convicted in the shooting. Both received multiple life sentences in 2000 for first-degree murder and other charges related to the Haines City shootings, which took place between April 26 and April 30, 1998.

All three of the former Haines City High School students were teenagers at the time and, therefore, could not be sentenced to death.

Four days after Tyler was shot, Shuler shot Cathy Boyd of Davenport as she stood in front of her mailbox. He was convicted on a felony charge of causing bodily injury in 1999.

However, the 2nd District Court of Appeals in Lakeland voided Shuler's 12-year sentence in June and ordered the trial court to re-sentence him. Officials with the Bartow-based 10th Judicial Circuit have been waiting for Shuler's murder trial to conclude before re-sentencing him in the Boyd case.

Lester and Streeter were convicted of shooting several people on the same day Shuler ambushed Boyd outside her home.

Minutes after Boyd was shot, Kristina Large, 20, of Haines City was shot and killed during another botched carjacking near Dundee. Large's cousin, James Aaron Jackson, who was in the car with her, was injured but drove away.

The two teens also burst into a Haines City hotel room and shot a family of five visiting from Georgia, including a 10-year-old girl and her 14-year-old sister.

The sometimes shaky accounts Streeter and Lester have given of Tyler's murder figured prominently in Shuler's 5-day trial.

Originally, Streeter said Shuler shot Tyler, but testified this week that Lester did. Lester, who previously identified Shuler as the shooter, refused to testify during the trial.

Friends and relatives of Shuler testified that he had worked on his car through the night of April 26, 1998—the same day he attended a church celebration honoring his grandfather—and could not have killed Tyler.

Assistant State Attorney John Aguero asked jurors to look beyond the testimony of people he said were, above all else, interested in saving Shuler from a life behind bars.

He asked jurors to see what he described as a simple truth.

"Curtis Shuler . . . he's the murderer," Aguero said. "He shot Larry Tyler."

Based on their verdicts, however, jurors saw something less clear.

While concluding that Shuler participated in a crime that led to Tyler's death, they remained unconvinced he had pulled the trigger.

Nevertheless, prosecutors hailed the hard-won verdict.

"It's a gratifying win both for the office and John Aguero given the difficulties that had developed for him in re-trying the case," Administrative Assistant State Attorney Chip Thullbery said.

The trial was the fourth time prosecutors tried Shuler for Tyler's murder.

Shuler received a life sentence after a jury convicted him of first-degree murder in 1999.

But the Lakeland appeals court threw out his conviction in May because then–Circuit Judge Robert Young allowed prosecutors to remove a black woman from the jury pool. An all-white jury eventually convicted Shuler, who is black. Two other attempts to convict Shuler ended in mistrials.

In September, McCarthy declared a mistrial three days into jury selection after several potential jurors saw a photo of Shuler in *The Ledger* and discussed the fact that the trial was his second on the murder charge.

Shuler's November trial was moved to Sarasota to avoid pretrial publicity. But McCarthy again declared a mistrial after jurors split 10-2 on a verdict after deliberating more than six hours. (Reprinted with permission of *The Ledger*.)

GLOSSARY

Alternative dispute resolution: Outside of court, a mediator helps two parties in dispute resolve their differences mutually or with an arbitrator who listens to the parties and makes a nonbinding decision.

Appeal: A legal action that seeks review by a court of a lower court decision.

Appellant: The side that lost in the trial court and has filed an appeal. Sometimes called the petitioner.

Appellee: Generally, the side that won in the trial court and whose victory is being appealed by the losing side. Sometimes called the respondent.

Civil: Not criminal. In a civil action, one person or entity is suing another, usually for monetary damages.

Clerks of court: The clerks of superior court exercise the judicial power of the state in the probate of wills, administration of estates, and the handling of special proceedings such as adoptions and foreclosures. Clerks also keep the county court records. Clerks of court might be elected.

Complaint: The document which, when filed with the court, initiates a lawsuit. It sets forth the plaintiff's claims against the defendant.

Court of appeals: An intermediate appellate court. Judges sit in rotating panels of three and hear appeals from trial courts in all civil cases and all criminal cases except death penalty cases. They also hear appeals from certain state administrative agencies. Judges are elected to eight-year terms.

Court reporters: Official court reporters record word-for-word trial proceedings. If the case is appealed, the verbatim record must be transcribed promptly for the appellate court.

Court-ordered arbitration: Most civil cases involving claims totaling $15,000 or less are subject to court-ordered arbitration. A trained and approved arbitrator conducts arbitration hearings.

Defendant: A person accused of a crime or a person being sued in a civil action.

District or state's attorneys: Also known as prosecutors or state attorneys. They represent the state in all criminal actions brought in superior and district courts and in juvenile delinquency cases in which an attorney represents the child. In many states they are elected.

District court: In civil cases, district court judges hear cases for all actions involving $10,000 or less. The court has preliminary jurisdiction over felony cases and over the trial of all misdemeanors and infractions. It has exclusive jurisdiction over all juvenile proceedings, mental health hospital commitments, and domestic relations cases. District court judges might be elected.

Docket: A published list of court cases scheduled to be heard on a specific day in a particular court.

Felony: Any of a number of serious crimes such as murder, rape, or burglary.

Judge or justice: A public official who hears and decides cases brought before a court of law.

Judgment: The decision of a judge or jury resolving a dispute and determining the rights and obligations of the parties.

Jurisdiction: The power and authority of the court to hear certain cases, for example, the jurisdiction for divorce cases is in civil court.

Magistrates: In some states, magistrates issue warrants of arrest, preside over trials of small claims, and perform marriages. Their offices are usually located in or near the courthouse.

Misdemeanor: An offense of lesser gravity than a felony.

Plaintiff: The one who initially brings a suit.

Pool camera: The photographer or videographer selected to be in the courtroom and take photos or video that will be shared by all media covering the proceedings.

Prosecutors: Same as district or state attorneys.

Public defender: Legal counsel for defendants who have been determined by a judge as financially unable to hire their own attorneys.

Warrant: Court authorization that allows most often law enforcement officers to search a property or arrest an individual.

ACTIVITIES

1. Go to statelocator.com and find sites that relate to your state's court system. Develop a chart that shows how a misdemeanor case and a felony case move through the court system.

2. Find a court story, preferably a court issue, that has extended over several days. Clip the stories and analyze how the reporter has written the lead, included background, and developed the rest of the story.

3. Check the stories you clipped. See how many sources you can list. Develop a local source list for the court beat.

4. Have a district or state attorney talk to the class about cases and issues pertinent to your community. Have him or her describe the layout in the courtroom.

5. Get a copy of a court docket. Figure out a case you could cover. Where would you go to get additional background before actually going to court?

6. After the discussion from the local court official and reviewing the docket, go to court. Sit in a session and take notes. Make arrangements to talk with a district attorney or other prosecutor to get additional information about the story. Outline the basic facts and write a story.

7. Send your court story to the court official and ask for an evaluation of your story's completeness and accuracy.

RESOURCES AND WEB SITES

Courts.net: www.courts.net.com. Links to several unusual court sites, focuses on trial-level courts.

Federal Judicial Center: www.fjc.gov. Historical and other information, including biographies of federal judges.

Findlaw: www.findlaw.com. Links to all U.S. codes and statutes, as well as federal court decisions.

Legal Information Institute: www.law.cornell.edu. Links to court decisions "in the news," good source of basic legal information.

Lexis: www.lexisone.com. Links to research tools. Users must register for free.

The National Center for State Courts: www.ncsconline.org. Links to educational programs and a unique courts search engine.

PACER Service Center of the Administrative Office of the U.S. Courts: http://pacer.psc.uscourts.gov

State Court Locator: http://vls.law.vill.edu/locator/statecourt

Thomas: http://thomas.loc.gov. The congressional information site including links to laws and bills passed by Congress.

U.S. Courts: www.uscourts.gov. Links to all three of the main levels of the federal judiciary, as well as bankruptcy court.

Writing a legal research paper or brief: www.ibiblio.org/medialaw/264LegalResearchPrimer.htm. An outline for both a legal research paper and a sample case brief.

REFERENCES

American Civil Liberties Union. (2003, July 1). Web site. www.acluco.org/news/casesummary/summary__csindependent.htm.

Basic Courtroom Rules for Broadcast Reporters and News Photographers. (2002). North Carolina Administrative Office of the Courts. Raleigh, NC.

Chandler v. Florida (79-1260) 449 U.S. 560 (1980).

Cook, S. (Ed.) North Carolina Judicial Branch. (2002, August). Newspapers in Education. Chapel Hill, NC.

Deniston, Lyle. (1992). *The reporter and the law: Techniques of covering the courts.* New York: Columbia University Press.

Facts about the U.S. courts. (2003). www.uscourts.gov/faq.html.

Glossary of court terms. (2003, April). North Carolina Administrative Office of the Courts. Raleigh, NC.

Goldstein, N. (2003). *Associated Press Stylebook and Briefing on Media Law.* New York: Associated Press.

Idaho Press Club. (2003). Cameras in the courtroom. www.idahopressclub.org/iccam.htm.

Meeting held with Smart-case teams. (2003, April 2). *Salt Lake Tribune.*

Mitchell arraigned on theft charge. (2003, March 15). *Salt Lake Tribune.*

Presentation by Assistant District Attorney James Woodall. (2003, February 10). UNC–Chapel Hill.

Reporters Committee for Freedom of the Press. (2003). Gag orders in the *First Amendment Handbook.* www.rcfp.org/handbook/viewpage.cgo?0601.

Scullin, J. (2003, March 29). Jury finds Shuler guilty of murder. *The Ledger.* www.theledger.com.

CHAPTER 12

COVERING SPECIALTY BEATS

When faced with small staffs or limited resources, news media organizations have to stretch to cover all that happens in their communities. While readers say they are interested in local government, news audiences also have a keen interest in other topics, such as science, medicine, health, the environment, and religion, according to the Pew Center for Research on the Public and the Press (1998).

"The public expresses considerably less interest in news about political figures and events in Washington and international affairs—topics which often lead network newscasts," according to the Center in a report on its Web site. Health issues generally top the list of subjects that interest audiences. Remember how long the SARS outbreak remained in the news as the disease showed up in China, then Canada, and then the United States. And events such as 9/11 have made audiences more aware of religious faiths' impact on world and even local events.

As a beginning reporter at a smaller media organization, you might be asked to write such special-interest stories occasionally. Or one of these beats might be combined with your regular government beat, such as county government and health.

Larger publications or news stations see these beats as a given and might devote specific space in each day's edition or a regular weekly section to them. For example, the *New York Times* has a highly regarded science section every Tuesday, and in summer 2003, the *Baltimore Sun* began a two-page science and medicine section each Monday. Other publications combine health topics with daily living sections, such as the *Southern Illinoisan*'s Our Time section, which covers healthy living, leisure, and money issues. At larger TV stations, health segments air almost daily.

Reporters need special skills to cover these beats. Generally reporters are assigned to a specialty beat after several years on another beat, such as police or local government, or general assignment on which they cover anything that comes up. More and more specialty beat reporters have taken extra classes or have advanced degrees, such as a master's in public health or science communication. Many journalism professors advise their students to take courses in a specific area, such as biology, so they will have some expertise if they decide to specialize later on.

Without advanced study, reporters new to a specialty beat have to train themselves. That can take time if they choose to enroll in classes or pursue another degree. Beginning specialty reporters can find numerous resources and lots of information from journalism organizations that support specialty reporters, such as the National Association of Science Writers (NASW), Society of Environmental Journalists, Religion Newswriters Association, and the American Medical Writers Association. All have Web sites.

Sometimes reporters take on a specialty beat because it represents an area of particular interest. For example, a reporter who has survived a heart attack might decide to become a health reporter. Or a reporter who lives in a city with continually high ozone levels might opt for an environmental beat. Whatever the case, beat reporters must be careful not to appear as zealots through the topics they choose to write about, the sources they choose to interview, and the ways they position their stories. If they become too involved with the topics they cover, they need to switch beats. Their credibility and that of their news organizations can suffer if they use their beat as a platform or appear in any way biased in their coverage.

In this chapter, you will:

- Learn general issues in covering science, medicine, and health,
- Get lists of science, medicine, and health sources,
- Review environmental issues,
- See the local angle on national stories,
- Cover potential pitfalls in science, medicine, and the environment beats, and
- Learn the basics of covering religion stories.

COVERING SCIENCE, MEDICINE, AND HEALTH

Because of the technical nature of science, medicine, or health news, reporters on these beats have to translate complex topics in a way that the average reader can understand. Their role is crucial because "the most important single information source for the public about science and technology is the media," according to *Communicating Science News* (2000), a National Association of Science Writers (NASW) publication. The average person looks to the mainstream media for information from the latest cancer treatment to the newest findings in astronomy.

Mainstream U.S. media have paid attention to science and medicine coverage since the early twentieth century, said Dorothy Nelkin in her book *Selling Science* (1995), which looks at how the media cover science and technology.

In 1919, the American Chemical Society, a professional organization for chemists, set up the first science-related news service. In 1921, the Scripps Science Service was founded to distribute science news to hundreds of periodicals. The service still exists, publishing the weekly magazine *Science News Online* and conducting science education programs. The NASW formed in 1934 to promote good science writing. It publishes *ScienceWriter,* a quarterly that focuses on issues related to science journalism and public information.

Nelkin (1995) explained that coverage of science and medicine can have an enormous effect on people's lives, so journalists have to be particularly careful in their reporting.

> Bad news about science and technology can influence consumer behavior, especially if alternative products are available. Thus, following the ozone controversy, people bought fewer aerosol sprays. . . . After extensive media reports on dietary studies relating cholesterol-producing foods with heart disease, consumption of beef, eggs, and fatty milk products declined.

Good news equally influences people. For example, when the media started writing about the promise of the antidepressant Prozac in the early 1990s, sales of the drug hit the billion-dollar mark quickly. Even when negative stories about its side effects arose, consumer demand continued, Nelkin said. It had already been framed as a "wonder drug" and was in wide use, so the backlash had little influence. "The media coverage of Prozac had a major influence on its rapid rise as a drug of choice," she said.

Media coverage of science and medicine also can affect public policy and influence future generations of scientists. "Coverage of science and technology attracts more public and private support for research and attracts interested, talented students to careers in science and engineering," NASW pointed out on its Web site.

Media stories on scientific findings even tell other scientists what their colleagues are working on. "Experience has shown that after a piece of research is publicized, a scientist usually receives a significant number of requests for further information from fellow researchers, many of whom might have missed the published scientific paper or meeting talk," the NASW reported (2000).

Initial Sources for Science and Medical Stories

Science or medical writers—if they want to be good at their beats—have to keep up with voluminous amounts of information. Consider how many branches of science exist, from biology and physics to chemistry and geology, and the number of medical specialties. One science writer at a publication has to keep up with advancements and developments in literally hundreds of scientific and medical fields.

A beginning science writer's first stop should be EurekAlert.org, a Web site run by the American Association for the Advancement of Science. The site covers all the sciences, which can be searched by topic. All the news releases are archived on its site so they are searchable. EurekAlert! also provides news releases, journal articles, and information from scientific conferences. "The primary goal of EurekAlert! is to provide a forum where research institutions, universities, government agencies, corporations and the like can distribute science-related news to reporters and news media," the site states. Anyone can access the information.

Another excellent resource, Newswise, is limited to full-time journalists or freelancers. Basically an online news service for research news, it has research from "universities, colleges, laboratories, professional organizations, governmental agencies, and private research groups active in the fields of medicine, science, business, and the humanities," the site noted.

Federal government-funded institutes are another important group of sources, especially for medical and health information. The National Institutes of Health (NIH) is composed of more than 20 institutes, centers, and divisions, including the National Cancer Institute, National Institute on Aging, and the National Institute of Nursing Research. In addition, the National Library of Medicine runs an online database called DIRLINE, dirline.nlm.nih.gov, which gives anyone access to health organizations online.

For nongovernment types of medical resources, reporters should contact organizations specific to a disease, disability, or condition such as the United Cerebral Palsy Association or the National Kidney Foundation. The organizations also help reporters track down people with the specific medical conditions if they need to interview them for their stories.

Using Published Research

The publication of research in scientific and medical journals spawns many stories. To be accepted, research has gone through a process called peer review, whereby other scientists or doctors in the specific field have evaluated anonymously the quality and findings of the research. Although such journal articles can be a valuable source, reporters new to the beat need to understand some peculiarities about peer-reviewed research.

Most scientists generally will not discuss their research until it appears as a peer-reviewed conference paper or in a peer-reviewed journal because they want it to be evaluated by other experts in their field. Journalists should remember that peer review does not mean the research is without flaws, only that it has been evaluated. The peer-review process helps journalists because it tells them the research is credible.

"Peer review and formal publication do give journalists a comfort zone by guaranteeing that the work presented is accurate to the best of the experts' knowledge," the First Amendment Center report on science journalism

(Hartz, 1998) explained. According to the Center report, peer evaluation looks at several factors: "Is the discovery really new? Is it significant? Was proper care taken to ensure the integrity of the experiment and analysis of the data?" After positive reviews, the article might be published in the journal.

Almost every academic discipline has a journal for publication of research in that field. Journalists might subscribe to find interesting research that will make good stories. Most scientific and medical journals send out news releases about what significant findings will be announced in their next issues. Many news releases are sent to journalists ahead of the journal's publication date, so the writers will have time to understand and gather information about any complex topic. Such releases are "embargoed," that is, the information is not to be released until the date given. Embargoed releases are especially prevalent in science and medicine. Some news organizations refuse to honor embargoed material, and if so, the scientific organization might stop sending them embargoed information.

Once the reporter has the research or study finding, he or she must find expert sources who were not authors of the research to discuss it. Experts should be able to comment on the application of the findings in "the real world."

Sigma Xi, the Scientific Research Society, provides science and technology sources for journalists through its Media Resource Center. At no charge, "Media Resource maintains a database of thousands of (primarily American) scientists, engineers, physicians, and policy-makers who have agreed to provide information on short notice to print and broadcast journalists," Sigma Xi stated on its Web site.

As journalists cover the science or medical beat over time, they have the opportunity to meet experts in a particular field at annual conventions or other large group meetings throughout the year. Researchers present their findings, and science or medical writers cover most of the major conferences of organizations such as the American Medical Association or the American Chemical Society annual meetings.

The NASW (2000) reminded: "Research presented at a meeting is considered in the public domain, and all presented data, whether in press or not, are fair game for journalistic coverage." Most breaking news in science, technology, and medicine comes from scientific publications or papers delivered at professional meetings and conferences, NASW added.

Finding the Local Angle

While research findings might be widely reported national stories, they might have local angles that interest audiences of smaller publications and in smaller broadcast markets. That's when an editor might assign such a topic to a local reporter. A newspaper or television station in smaller markets is more likely to have a health or medical writer than a science writer—or one person might cover all three areas. Audiences can relate to topics on medicine or health, which more directly affect lives, than to topics about geology or astronomy, which can have less tangible effects. For example, when researchers discovered they could identify which women might have a genetic predisposition for breast cancer, many women rushed to clinics to get genetic testing. The local story quoted local gynecologists, genetic counselors, and women to explain the implications of the discovery.

Newer diseases arise every few years—and might find their way into your community. Every summer, most local media do stories about the first case of the mosquito-born West Nile virus that year. In 2003 an affliction called monkeypox infected several people in the Midwest. The disease had first occurred in Africa, and the cases were the first incidence of monkeypox in the United States. In the smallpox family, the disease caused some panic for several weeks until doctors discovered its transmission source: pet prairie dogs.

After the initial stories, reporters continued to report the ongoing story. Here's how the health reporter at the *Wisconsin State Journal* (Simms, 2003) in Madison handled the introduction of one follow-up story:

> In the aftermath of the monkeypox outbreak last month, Wisconsin agriculture officials are developing new rules to govern the sale and transport of all exotic pets.
>
> State Veterinarian Robert Ehlenfeldt said Tuesday the state may eventually require that all exotic pets be checked by a veterinarian and registered with the state when they enter Wisconsin.
>
> There is currently no way of keeping track of exotic pets like the Gambian rat that was shipped from Ghana to Texas on April 9, Ehlenfeldt said.
>
> The rat, three dormice and two rope squirrels infected a batch of prairie dogs with the rare West African disease, according to the Centers for Disease Control and Prevention. (Reprinted with permission of the *Wisconsin State Journal*.)

In addition to stories on diseases, a health reporter will cover hospital-related topics, such as new equipment or technology, the birth of quintuplets, or hospital expansion. Some of these stories might overlap with government beats if a county or city runs a hospital. Also, many states run hospitals for people with mental illnesses, and the federal government operates Veterans Administration Hospitals, hospitals for federal inmates, and specialty hospitals.

Local medical stories also might overlap the business beat if pharmaceutical or medical technology companies locate nearby. For example, the *Wall Street Journal* covered the business angle of the medical study that recommended less-invasive coils instead of surgery for ruptured brain aneurysms (Zimmerman, 2002). The story discussed the economic impact of the recommendations on the Massachusetts-based corporation that is the number one manufacturer of the coils.

Sometimes general medical studies can have a local angle as well. One scientific study on autism published in 2002 found that the incidence of autism tripled in California from 1987 to 1998 (Blakeslee, 2002). A medical reporter there could write a story using health sources plus education experts, people from local advocacy groups, and parents of autistic children.

COVERING ENVIRONMENTAL ISSUES

Many of the recommendations for covering science, medicine, and health apply to covering the environment. Because this beat literally covers the land, animals, sea, and air of planet Earth, it connects to all other beats. And environmental issues cross state lines. For example, in 2003 the governor of South Dakota called on governors in five other states through which the Missouri River flows to discuss the effect on downstream states when upstream states release water from reservoirs in the spring and summer. Environmental reporters in several states followed the Missouri River Summit, its findings, and subsequent fallout (Associated Press, 2003).

"The environmental beat is the most significant beat one can cover right now," said Dale Willman, an environmental reporter who has covered the beat for National Public Radio (NPR). "That's because it deals with the very fundamentals of the existence of life—clean air, water, and land." Major topics on the beat are water pollution, air pollution, land use, endangered animals, hazardous waste, recycling, and wildlife, according to a survey of environmental reporters by the Society of Environmental Journalists.

Other more specific topics are loss of biodiversity, global warming, fishery collapse, and toxic waste or chemical generation, Willman (2003) said. For example, in the area of toxic waste, he stated:

> As many as 70,000 different chemicals are manufactured each year in this country. Perhaps 3,000 are produced in large quantities. Yet, complete safety studies have been done on just a handful, perhaps 500. And those safety studies generally do not look at what is known as synergistic effects—the problems created when two or more chemicals are mixed. And yet, everyone is exposed to dozens of chemicals every day, even though we don't know exactly what harm they may be causing.

Government and politics affect environmental issues and coverage at all levels, and sometimes government officials' and environmentalists' views conflict. For example, on the topic of global warming, although politicians say it is not clear-cut, almost all scientists agree global warming is occurring. Therein lies the conflict. The Environmental Protection Agency (EPA) tries to enforce laws and to fine polluters who do not clean up toxic dump sites, while lobbyists vie for exceptions for their industries.

Documents Lead the Way

From federal to state to local laws, the environment endures much regulation. EPA revisions, such as in the federal Clean Air Act, have produced much coverage, not only of the EPA changes but of states' reactions. According to a news release from one New York attorney general, several states brought lawsuits against the agency in 2003 for revisions that they say allowed older power plants, particularly coal plants, to upgrade without installing modern pollution control equipment. The EPA requirements come into conflict with states' permit regulations, so northeastern states such as New Hampshire, Connecticut, and New York sued so that they could retain some control (Leavens, 2003). Reporters will have to follow a documents trail along with the actual trials in reporting those stories.

Reporters also need to learn the requirements of local, state, and federal environmental laws as to record keeping, such as the pollutants an industry produces and discharges. State laws, for example, might require businesses that produce or use hazardous chemicals to register with local offices. The record keeping results in reports and files that document which businesses comply with environmental laws, which do not, which have been fined and how much, and much more information for curious environmental reporters. Jim Detjen, director of the Knight Center for Environmental Journalism at Michigan State University, explained (2003):

> If you learn to comb these files on a regular basis, you'll soon be breaking stories that few other reporters in your area have reported about or written. If the Alpha Manufacturing Company has been fined $50,000 by the state environmental agency for violating clean water laws, go to the agency and ask to review all their files. Check their permits, inspection reports, notices of violations of agency regulations, and other documents. Become friends with the secretaries and clerks who maintain these files, and they'll often become valuable sources of tips for future stories.

Detjen added that reporters might find that a company has a poor record of complying with environmental laws, but no government agency has intervened to force it to comply. Why? An understaffed agency doesn't have the manpower to force compliance. Or perhaps politics caused the agency to ignore the company in noncompliance. Either way, the information can become a good story. Detjen said if local officials try to block access to environmental records, reporters should file a Freedom of Information Act request.

Withholding information might not always be standard operating procedure. "Many state and federal environmental agencies are filled with altruistic people who genuinely care about improving the environment," Detjen (2003) said. "You may discover inspectors or enforcement officials who are disgusted with the politics they see in their agency and who are willing and even eager to talk to you about the political pressures they see and experience."

Bringing the Story Closer to Home

While many environmental stories start as national news, issues such as pollution make for significant local stories. Detjen and Willman both recommended that reporters find local sources in addition to the "usual suspects," that is, government officials and scientists. "Make sure you are constantly searching for more people who can bring new perspectives to the stories you are writing or producing," Willman (2003) said.

Consumers and people affected by an environmental crisis add a significant and human aspect to a story. "'Citizen scientists' are those people who might not have academic credentials in a particular field, but who have gained a great deal of knowledge from living close to the land. These people are often ignored in environmental coverage, and yet they can be some of the best sources," Willman said (2003).

Sometimes the best sources are those who are not as obvious, Detjen (2003) said. "When I've written about water pollution being discharged into a river by a chemical company, I've sometimes found it useful to interview anglers, swimmers, or water skiers who utilize the river to get their views on the situation," he said. "When I've written about air pollution, I've interviewed window washers, city foresters, and pilots." One of the best sources on river pollution for environmental reporters in North Carolina proved to be a local resident who became the self-appointed "keeper" or monitor of conditions on the Neuse River.

CHALLENGES OF COVERING SCIENCE, MEDICINE, AND THE ENVIRONMENT

Science, medical, and environmental writers cover complex, complicated topics. They have the challenge of making stories readable to audiences, and sometimes they struggle to make audiences just pay attention. Renowned science writer Jon Franklin, who won two Pulitzer Prizes on medical and science topics, said science writers were caught in the middle between the fascinating research of scientists and the general public who might not understand or care about that research. He explained the disconnect this way (1997):

> Biochemistry was deconstructing life, and people wanted to know if fluoride was really a poison. They still do, many of them. Science writers mentioned life in the universe, and the public thought UFO. We wanted to talk about cancer science. What they wanted was hope and miracle cures.

Jargon as a Roadblock for Audiences

Scientists and doctors truly speak their own language, so reporters have to understand complex jargon to cover these topics and make them relevant to readers. They have to translate technical jargon into words their audiences can understand. The National Association of Science Writers explained (2000):

Of the many kinds of specialized writers, the science writer has a unique responsibility to the reader. Unlike the sportswriter, for example, whose reader already knows, often in extraordinary detail, the rules of the game and who the players are, science writers must often introduce readers to a new "game" with every article. Imagine if a sportswriter had to assume readers had no knowledge of football every time he or she had to write about the latest NFL game.

Science writers also have a sometimes difficult job of teasing out details and anecdotes to produce an evocative article, video, or radio segment that will draw a casual reader or viewer into a topic they might not at first care much about.

The science writer must first understand the science, often the toughest part of the job. Then the writer must write it—frequently within the hour—translating it accurately into a form that is both interesting and intelligible to the layman.

In translating, scientists and journalists might define the same words in different ways, which could lead to misunderstandings and possibly inaccurate stories. "Scientists and journalists are quite literally 'divided by a common language,' " Dr. David Goodstein told a science reporting institute (Murray, 2001). "The two groups mean different things when they use words such as 'force,' 'theory,' 'error,' and 'energy.' Force as used in journalism and law implies imposition of one person's will over another. In science, force is a technical word relating to the magnitude of velocity and carries no other baggage," Goodstein said.

In addition to jargon, science, health, and environmental stories encompass more than one field. "Unlike many other stories, environmental issues are quite multi-disciplinary," Willman (2003) said. "Just one story may cut across the fields of biology, botany, zoology, and climatology, for example. So reporters need to have a basic grounding in many areas. That's not to say they need to be experts in all these areas. However, they need to have a great enough understanding of the basic science that they can become translators, able to convey complex information to a lay audience."

Finding and Keeping Sources

In covering these technical fields, reporters need good source relationships. That can be difficult. As noted earlier, scientists might be reluctant to talk too soon about their research. Bruce Murray, the managing editor of the Foundation for American Communication (FACS), explained that journalists and scientists view the world differently. First, Murray (2001) noted, they have different understandings of the rules of evidence. Journalists try to get several sources in a story so it will be credible and have a believable thesis. Scientists have to be much more rigorous and test a theory over and over to confirm its validity. Second, the two groups have different tolerance levels for uncertainty. Scientists can tolerate uncertainty; journalists cannot.

FACS Senior Vice President Randy Reddick explained that aspect. "The idea [in science] is not necessarily to resolve uncertainty but measure the uncertainty. Most scientists are very reluctant to show cause and effect. Journalists often like to see issues in black and white: there has to be a good side, and there has to be a bad side."

Third, journalists might be slow or unwilling to understand the influence of variables in scientific studies. Scientists realize that more than one variable can influence research findings. Journalists want to know definitively which variable is causing the results.

For these reasons, many scientists are hesitant to talk to journalists. "A scientist often approaches an interview or news conference with trepidation," according to the National Association of Science Writers' Web site (2000). "He or she may worry about hostile media, misquotation, or appearing to be a self-promoter, particularly in the eyes of colleagues."

In addition, scientists worry when journalists start focusing on them as people, rather than solely on the research. Many times reporters try to make dry, research-oriented stories more interesting by adding human or personal details. The scientist or doctor might become "a character" in an in-depth feature story on the topic.

Although scientists might object to that approach, NASW applauds the more feature-type science and medicine stories. As long as the stories were accurate and fair, the added dimension and perspective could help the audience understand the topic. "Also, such human-interest stories make science and technology more accessible to young people who might be interested in scientific careers," the association noted on its Web site (2000).

COVERING RELIGION

Although not as prevalent as science, medicine, or health sections, religion sections do appear in a number of newspapers. For example, the *Kansas City Star* has a Saturday religion section that runs a variety of stories, such as a dialogue between Israeli Jews and Palestinians, fate versus freedom in open theism, and whether Muslims, Jews, and Christians worship the same God.

Most religion sections focus on features, rather than breaking news. Important religion news will make it onto the front page or to the top of the news hour. But beginning reporters should remember that in covering religion, all the same good reporting rules apply.

"(Religion reporting) requires the same rigorous adherence to journalistic standards as other beats," said Kathi Wolfe (2003), a news correspondent with the Religion News Service. "It also requires the reporter to be well-informed (though not an expert in) subjects ranging from bioethics to medicine to psychology to science to theology to ethics to the arts."

Religion news has grown in visibility and importance because 9/11 illustrated to the U.S. news media just how much they—and their audiences—

did not know about different forms of Islam. Because religions are the backbone of many cultures, religion writers say that they must cover the beat effectively. Gayle White, a religion writer with the *Atlanta Journal–Constitution*, explained (2001): "Religion provides the 'why' in the equation of a story. Faith motivates people, groups, and, at times, nations. Religion plays a significant role in world events from war in the Middle East to tension in Northern Ireland to terrorism in the United States." The threads of religion can be found in politics, education, legal issues, disaster relief, poverty reduction, and even art and music, she added.

Local Angles on National Stories

Religion stories can have connections at the local and national level. At the local level, reporters can look at significant issues that affect local congregations, Wolfe said. For example, plagiarism of sermons became an issue in Washington, DC, in summer 2003. The *Washington Post* focused a page one story on how the minister of Washington's National City Christian Church, a leading, flagship church of the Disciples of Christ denomination, "borrowed" without credit or attribution the sermons of other churches' ministers (Wilogren, 2003). The story had the local angle for Washington and also a national angle: The minister had served a two-year term as a moderator of the Disciples of Christ, an elected position, Wolfe said.

Religion reporters also bring home the impact of denomination politics on the faith groups or congregations in their coverage area. A religion reporter in Des Moines, Iowa, could take the *Post* story and forge a local angle by interviewing ministers to get their reactions. The reporter could expand to another topic, such as how ministers find and research sermon topics.

Many organized denominations have national meetings every few years or even yearly, Wolfe noted. At these policy meetings, denominations confirm their stance on issues ranging from marriage to cloning to gun control to abortion. Their decisions affect people in local congregations, Wolfe (2003) said.

If the religion reporters' news organizations cannot afford to send them to the national meetings, reporters can still write a local story by interviewing people who attended as delegates. Information would also be posted on the denomination's Web site. For example, Wolfe said, some stories that might have local angles include a historic church closing; churches performing same-sex unions; a new synagogue, mosque, or temple; new forms of worship; or liturgy issues.

At the national level, bioethics has become one of the top religion issues, Wolfe (2002) said. She noted:

> It deals with issues from abortion, stem cell debate, cloning to genetic discrimination, to the ethics of caring for severely disabled infants, to the debate over assisted suicide and euthanasia. . . . how these issues play out will determine in the upcoming century how we are born and how we will die.

Reporters might have to find theologians or ethicists as sources because many clergy were not trained about these issues when they were in seminary, Wolfe said. She wove the intersection of religion with bioethics into a story she did about Leon Kass, the head of President Bush's new bioethics council. The story moved on the Religion News Service and appeared in the *Washington Post*. Wolfe first described Kass's background in her story:

> Kass grew up in Chicago. His parents were Yiddish-speaking, Eastern European Jews.
> "It wasn't a religious household," he said. "But there was reverence—if not for God, for human life. My parents were socialists. I learned later that their socialism was in the moral spirit of the Jewish prophet—not Marxism."
> Kass adds, ruefully: "I didn't realize how much moral passion there is in the Jewish tradition. I'd have been a rabbi if I'd lived during the time of the czars."

Then she moved into his bioethics interest, which made him the choice for the president's council.

> His interest in bioethics developed "indirectly," Kass said, when he was a graduate student and he and his wife, Amy, returned to Harvard after spending the summer of 1965 doing civil rights work in Mississippi.
> "I was puzzled," he said. "Why did I find more decency in the black farmers there than in the privileged graduate students? If the teaching of the Enlightenment was correct—if you removed poverty and superstition, you would give people the opportunity to be moral human beings. But the graduate students around me were self-promoting." (2002 Religion News Service. Used with permission.)

The place of gay and lesbian people within different denominations continues to be a national religion story. Gay people as clergy and gay marriage have engendered much debate. Any story on marriage in general can be a wonderful religion story, Wolfe noted. "What does marriage mean to different religions? In different cultures?" she questioned. The interaction of religion and popular culture forms a basis for intriguing stories. For example, a number of religion reporters have covered the controversy over the popular Harry Potter children's books because critics call them anti-Christian and say they promote witchcraft.

Sources for Religion Stories

Local religious leaders, both clergy and lay, should be the first on the religion reporter's contact list. Reporters should add ministers, rabbis, priests, and others at the national level as well when getting the religion perspective on issues such as grief, holiday observances, liturgy, theology, same-sex marriage, war and peace, or other topical issues, Wolfe said.

In developing source lists, reporters might have to add ethicists and bioethicists, especially for topics such as cloning, stem cell research, family values, or the right to die. Religion blends with other topics, and reporters might also want mental health professionals as sources for stories on suicide, assisted suicide, or how mental illness affects churches and temples. For popular culture stories about religion, reporters need to get access to historians or pop culture experts, such as university professors who do research on such topics. Religion sources can also be valuable to other beat reporters who need an ethical or moral perspective on a story.

Religion reporters should also know leaders of advocacy groups not affiliated with religion, such as the National Association for the Advancement of Colored People (NAACP), the Disability Rights Education & Defense Fund (DREDF), the Gay and Lesbian Alliance Against Defamation (GLAAD), the John Locke Foundation, or general human rights organizations. "These are people who can be sources on stories that involve social issues like racism, homophobia, disability issues," Wolfe (2003) said.

As for organizational sources, Wolfe said most faiths and even individual churches have Web sites, where reporters can gain a quick introduction to the religion or denomination. There, reporters can find background on the denomination, beliefs and practices of the religion, and stances on social, cultural, political, and ethical issues in the United States and around the world. Web sites also will provide contact information on how to reach staff leaders within the denominations.

Sites will likely list or have links to complementary national, regional, and state agencies. Reporters also can use Web resources to gain understanding of religious texts. For example, a site from the University of Michigan has a completely searchable English translation of the Koran (2000). Certain groups' Web sites could suggest topics or guide reporters to stories. For example, a Web site called ChristianLesbians.com has links to "gay-welcoming congregations" listed by state.

Most religions and even individual congregations have publications. From the Dallas-based *Baptist Standard* to the *National Catholic Reporter* to *Hinduism Today*, reporters can glean story ideas as well as keep up-to-date on a specific religion's perspective on issues. If they are not familiar with such publications, reporters should check out which ones clergy and others read. They might be able to get copies when they go for interviews.

Apart from people, documents, and the Internet as sources, reporters should make informational visits to local temples, mosques, churches, synagogues, or other places of worship, Wolfe said. They can observe the service and meet leaders or congregants of the faith, who could be sources later. For an even deeper understanding of a faith, reporters could visit a seminary, particularly if one is nearby. For example, one seminary for the Presbyterian U.S.A. church—Presbyterian Theological Seminary—has been in Louisville, Kentucky, since 1853.

Religion reporters also might have to cover what some consider "cults" and others just consider the beginning of a new religion. A helpful resource is ReligiousTolerance.org, which tries to define the differences among actual cults, such as the suicidal Heaven's Gate group and groups such as Wicca, which is considered to be a non-Christian faith group. When looking for information to evaluate these groups, the typical search term "new religious movements" yields academic research on the topic.

Obviously, defining a group as a cult rather than as a non-Christian religion could be considered biased reporting. A reporter must be careful that sources do the defining and that any controversial story is complete and balanced. Bias and preconceived notions about religions can be a particularly vexing problem for those reporters who cover religion.

Challenges in Covering Religion

The intricacies and differences among religions make the beat challenging and fascinating. Within one week a reporter might write about a church's financial struggles, another's efforts to attract teenagers to services, religious leaders' efforts to unite a neighborhood, and a temple of a faith new to the community. Reporters must be open to new religions and to story ideas. They might be reporting on ethics and values along with religion, noted Kathi Wolfe.

From a practical standpoint, covering religion as a business can be a challenge. Churches and "religious institutions are exempt from property taxes, provided the property is used for religious purposes," explained Charles Austin, a former religion reporter for the Hackensack, New Jersey, *Record.* "But clergy pay income taxes and 'non-religious' income received by faith groups is taxable" (2000). So some records might be available if a religion reporter and possibly a business reporter team to do a story on a denomination's or church's finances. In addition, although the United States was founded in part on the tenet of freedom of religion, religious groups still must live within the laws of the country or state. Churches must be built within zoning law requirements, and the state can license clergy to perform marriages, for instance.

Some other challenges might not be as clear-cut as looking at a building permit. Because the United States is dominated by Judeo-Christian traditions, many reporters might be unaware of non-Christian faiths. They might think they know all about Christian faiths because they grew up in one. Denominations might have a number of wings, such as the Southern Baptists who will have liberal, conservative, and moderate churches. Southern Baptists differ from American Baptists; each is a denomination within Christianity. Religion reporters must keep the differences clear. Having the name *Baptist* does not mean they share the same practices or beliefs.

Whether a reporter is reared within a religious tradition, he or she probably has some general beliefs about certain religions. Reporters need to be wary of their beliefs because they might be wrong or connected to stereotypes. Wolfe said reporters have to be aware of their biases and ensure that these biases don't influence their reporting. Sources on the religion beat might have specific attitudes toward religion and might suspect the reporter has biases. Wolfe (2003) explained:

> People on the "religious right," conservative sources, may feel either that the reporter is devoutly religious or not religious enough. These sources may think that the "liberal" press is biased against religion. People on the left, liberals, may feel that religion reporters are "too religious" or have a conservative view of religion.

In addition, Wolfe advised new religion reporters not to categorize issues in terms of liberal versus conservative. On some issues, liberals and conservatives might work together to support or oppose an issue. For example, on the topic of therapeutic or research cloning, disparate groups such as social conservatives, some feminists, environmentalists, Southern Baptists, and the Roman Catholic Church oppose therapeutic cloning. In another case, liberals and conservatives have worked together to fight against genetically engineered food.

As with any beat, Wolfe said, some sources on the religion beat will expect the reporter to endorse their specific beliefs, not merely to report them. Other sources might believe that only someone who is a member of their faith can report on their faith. Reporters will have to be clear with their sources about the focus of stories, so sources will know that the stories will be balanced. Reporters, particularly reporters new to the religion beat, might have difficulty keeping sources on track during interviews. Some sources might move into proselytizing, and reporters must be able to direct the interview politely and firmly back to the topic.

A reporter relatively new to the beat might wonder whether he or she should reveal his or her own religious affiliation. Julia Lieblich, a religion writer for the *Chicago Tribune,* said most religion writers come up with their own informal guidelines about when and why to tell their religion. She said in talking with some sources, revealing her religious background might be appropriate. Most times she just tries to figure out why the sources want to know; that is, do they want to convert her to their religion? At these instances here's the advice Lieblich (2001) said a religion writer once gave her:

> When asked, "Are you a Christian?" the writer replied: "I don't like to talk about my religion when I am working. But if you are wondering whether I will be sensitive to the beliefs of Christians, the answer is yes."
> I like that response because it helps ease the fears of a source who may feel the press tends to be dismissive of fundamentalist and evangelical Christians, and that it conveys the message that this may not be a good time to evangelize.
> This kind of response is particularly valuable for reporters whose atheist or agnostic beliefs would elicit a strong reaction from some believers.

Because religion reporters often cover complex and unfamiliar religions or ethics topics, Wolfe recommended making religion stories sparkle by including intriguing personal stories from sources. "These personal stories will hook the reader into your story," she said. "They will make people in an unfamiliar faith real to the reader—turn the faith from being an abstraction into a real life entity." For example, she wrote a story on a secular humanism conference and interviewed former *Saturday Night Live* comedian Julia Sweeney. She had just "come out" as an atheist after a bout with cancer. "By telling her story, I was able to tell the reader in human terms why someone would leave her church to become an atheist or secular humanist," Wolfe (2003) explained.

Finally, religion reporters might have to put up with bias against their beat in their newsrooms. "Some journalists in other beats still regard religion reporting as 'soft' journalism," Wolfe said. Reporters might need to educate their editors and colleagues about religion reporting. David Gibson, a religion reporter at the *Star-Ledger* in New Jersey, said some editors are beginning to see the significance of religion coverage because they have learned that readers are interested in the topic. Good stories prove the importance of the religion beat. Gibson (2001) said:

> You do that by tackling tough, controversial, and complex topics head-on. You research, interview, research some more, and write insightful pieces that will get the editor reading and thinking, and will do the same for your readers. Make it so balanced and so fair and so true that people will have no chink in the armor. They'll have to love you. And your stuff.
>
> Do that and your editor will find himself or herself realizing religion is a great beat—interesting, challenging, provocative.

OTHER ASPECTS OF SPECIALTY REPORTING

Obviously any media organization can come up with additional specialty beats, and many community newspapers and local broadcast stations will not have these specialty beats at all. Some choose to assign reporters to areas, such as children and youth issues, women's issues, the military, or technology.

A community's makeup of residents and businesses will influence beat structure. A newspaper close to a military base will assign a reporter to cover crime, lifestyles, recruitment, construction, or promotions on the base. That reporter might travel if troops are deployed overseas, such as the invasion of Iraq in 2003. Some states with high-technology or research parks might warrant the attention of one reporter on that beat.

Covering the Specialty Beat as a Freelancer

Some publications or media might use freelance writers to cover stories on specialty topics. While most beginning reporters do not become freelancers, they might find a story idea that would not be covered in depth in their newspapers but could be expanded for a longer feature story in a specialty publication.

Being a freelancer on a specialty beat can present a specific set of challenges. First, a freelancer works for numerous publications, from newspapers to magazines focused on a specific niche. (It should be noted that except for weekly news magazines, most magazines rarely have many staff writers and rely heavily on freelancers.) Magazines have a more creative and flexible writing style than newspapers do. Readers go to specialty magazines to get definitive answers about whatever topic the magazine is focused on. For example, someone who subscribes to *Audubon* magazine is interested in nature, the environment, and wildlife, but he or she also has a higher level of interest, and possibly knowledge, than someone who reads about environmental issues only in the local newspaper.

The magazine reader will want not only the facts but also an analysis of the issue and even the perspective of the writer. Some magazines even practice what is known as advocacy journalism, in which a publication's stories take an editorial stance to make readers aware of a social issue and advise them to act on it. Most of the magazines you see on your local newsstand are called consumer magazines, which typically contain advertising and are sold as a consumer "product." Many magazines are published by trade organizations, professional associations, or advocacy groups or are sponsored by a corporation, such as the magazine in your seat pocket on a commercial airplane.

Most magazines are written far in advance of when they are published, which means their stories have to be timeless and anticipate trends and topics that would interest their audiences. That type of deadline differs greatly for the freelancer who writes for a newspaper and has more pressing deadlines.

Magazine stories tend to be more feature-oriented, more analytical, and longer and may allow the writer's "voice" in stories. For example, in an *Audubon* story about wolves thriving in the northern Midwest and Canada, writer Ted Williams wrote in first person about his quest to find wolves living in the wild.

Maintaining Professional Distance

Because specialty beat writers amass much knowledge and expertise on a topic, they might find themselves identifying with their sources or developing deeper relationships with sources than with editors. The latter especially can happen with freelance writers, who are dependent on sources for the stories that produce income. They return to excellent expert sources over and over when writing about complex subjects. A freelance journalist might become overly dependent on sources and try to please them. All writers can avoid such problems by being clear with sources about how stories will be written and maintaining some distance. Sources should not become social companions or friends.

On the other hand, while covering specialty beats, reporters might encounter people who believe that they carry favorable bias toward the topic they cover. Some pro-business sources might see some environmental beat reporters as pro-environment just because they cover environmental issues, according to environmental journalist Dale Willman (2003). "Environmental journalists have to fight charges of bias, simply because they are covering environmental issues," he said. "Religion reporters are not attacked for going to church, nor are business reporters accused of bias for being capitalists. Yet environmental reporters are regularly labeled as zealots simply because of the field they have chosen."

Specialty beat reporters have to be aware of how they can be perceived, particularly if they have covered a beat for many years. Some publications will rotate beat reporters just to avoid reporters' becoming too close to sources or too familiar with the issues. If beat reporters want to retain a specialty beat, they must guard against becoming too involved. Like any beat reporter who wants to be good on the job, specialty reporters have to be fair, accurate, complete, and balanced in reporting every story.

GLOSSARY

Advocacy journalism: A publication whose stories take editorial stances that make readers aware of a social issue and advise them to act on it.

Bioethics: Study of scientific, ethical, and social concerns about the effect of biotechnology on life and society.

Consumer magazine: Typically has advertising and is sold as a consumer "product" by subscription or at a newsstand.

Embargoed news releases: When a public information officer hands out the news release days or weeks before the information can be made public. Has a release date on which it can officially be released; common in science and medical reporting so writers will have time to gather information and sources on complex stories. Reporters should be aware that if they violate a news release embargo, the public information officer might not give them access to an embargoed release again.

Global warming: The trend whereby damage to the protective ozone layer in the Earth's atmosphere is allowing gradual warming, which among other aspects is melting glaciers and ice at the poles and raising the ocean level. Scientists have debated the existence of global warming.

Noncompliance: Failure to meet a deadline; for example, industries that do not install equipment so they can meet EPA emissions requirements by a certain date are considered noncompliant after that date.

Peer-reviewed: An academic journal article or conference paper has been judged by experts in that field to be valid research.

ACTIVITIES

1. Find a national medical or environmental story and develop a local angle for your county. For example, what is your county doing to prevent West Nile virus? Are

hospitals using expensive diagnostic equipment? Which businesses use toxic materials and might be on an Environmental Protection Agency cleanup list?

2. Go to the Web sites of your local hospitals and check out their news releases. What new programs or procedures are they offering? Select one that might make an interesting story and write about it. Start with the hospital public information officer as a source, but expand to consumers and professionals outside the hospital setting. If the procedure or equipment required state approval, get a comment from the state agency.

3. Research the religions and congregations in your community. How much diversity did you find? Do a feature on religion in your community that is not Judeo-Christian-based. For example, find the mosques or Hindu temples in your community and profile the congregation.

4. Do a local angle on a national religious issue by talking to a range of community religion sources. Be sure to include background on the national issue. Look for a topic that has not been widely covered.

5. Put together a panel of health, science, or environmental reporters in your community. Have them talk about how their beats overlap.

RESOURCES AND WEB SITES

Religion Resources

Religion Newswriters Association: www.religionwriters.com. Complete list of most religions' and even congregations' publications or Web sites.

ReligiousTolerance.org: www.religioustolerance.org/cultmenu.htm. Cults, a.k.a. new religious movements.

Science and Environment Writing Resources

Chemical Health & Safety Data: http://ntpserver.niehs.nih.gov/Main_Pages/Chem-HS.html. Information on more than 2,000 chemicals studied by the National Toxicology Program.

EnviroLink News Service: www.envirolink.org/environews. Links to environmental stories from around the world.

Environment News Service: http://ens.lycos.com. An international environmental news wire.

Environmental Defense Fund: www.environmentaldefense.org. A nonprofit organization charged with protecting environmental rights.

Environmental Health Perspectives: http://ehis.niehs.nih.gov. The Web site of *Environmental Health Perspectives (EHP),* a peer-reviewed journal dedicated to the discussion of the effect of the environment on human health.

EurekAlert!: www.eurekalert.org. From the American Association for the Advancement of Science (AAAS).

FACS: www.facsnet.org. Numerous reporting tools on science, technology, the environment, biotechnology, and risk.

Food science and agriculture links from Junkscience.com: www.junkscience.com/links/foodlink.htm.

Global warming FAQ: www.ncdc.noaa.gov/ol/climate/globalwarming.html. From the U.S. National Oceanic and Atmospheric Administration.

HazDat Database: http://atsdr1.atsdr.cdc.gov:8080/hazdat.html. Information on hazardous substances and U.S. Superfund sites and emergencies. From the Agency for Toxic Substances and Disease Registry.

Journalist's Toolbox: www.journaliststoolbox.com/newswriting/science.html. The American Press Institute page on science. Provides links to thousands of sites.

National Association of Science Writers: www.nasw.org

National Audubon Society: www.audubon.org

National Earthquake Information Center: http://gldss7.cr.usgs.gov/neis/data_services/data_services.html. From the U.S. Geological Survey. Its Bigquake service will send out a message whenever a large earthquake occurs.

Natural Resources Defense Council: www.nrdcaction.org/join/join.asp. An environmental action organization.

National Science Foundation: www.nsf.gov/home/cns/start.htm. An independent agency of the U.S. government, established by the National Science Foundation Act of 1950.

NewsWise: www.newswise.com. News from thousands of research institutions.

NTIS Database: http://grc.ntis.gov/ntisdb.htm. From the U.S. Department of Commerce's National Technical Information Service (NTIS); provides full summaries of more than 2 million publications NTIS has received from government agencies since 1964.

Pesticide database: www.panna.org/resources/pestis.html. Pesticide information from the Pesticide Action Network North America (PANNA).

PowerReporting: http://powerreporting.com/category/Beat_by_beat/Science. A long list of links for the science beat.

Poynter Institute's tip sheet on writing a good science story: www.poynter.org/content/content_view.asp?id=10457.

Right-to-Know Network: www.rtknet.org. A service from OMB Watch that has searchable databases, documents, and conferences on the environment, sustainable development, and the Toxic Release Inventory.

Scripps Research Institute: www.scripps.edu. Biomedical research.

Sierra Club: www.sierraclub.org. The country's oldest grassroots environmental organization.

Sigma Xi, Media Resource Center: www.mediaresource.org

Society of Environmental Journalists: www.sej.org/resource/index.htm. A links database that contains more than 1,500 entries of useful Web sites for environmental reporters.

U.S. Environmental Protection Agency: www.epa.gov. Environmental information from the U.S. government.

USGS national map: http://nationalmap.usgs.gov/index.html. An online interactive map of U.S. topography from the U.S. Geological Survey.

U.S. Nuclear Regulatory Commission: www.nrc.gov. The government agency that oversees nuclear power.

Woods Hole Oceanographic Institution: www.whoi.edu. Nonprofit research facility dedicated to the study of marine science.

Yahoo! Science: www.yahoo.com/Science. Listing of scientific resources by field.

Medical Writing Resources

Achoo Internet Healthcare Directory: www.achoo.com/main.asp. A health care search site.

American Cancer Society site: www.acs.org

American Medical Association: www.ama-assn.org. Links to research, current issues, and so on. Comprehensive.

American Medical Writers Association (AMWA): www.amwa.org. Many helpful links.

Association of Health Care Journalists: www.ahcj.umn.edu. Extensive references and essays.

BioMedNet: www.bmn.com. A portal to life sciences information.

Cancer Web On-line Medical Dictionary: http://cancerweb.ncl.ac.uk/omd. Online medical dictionary from the University of Newcastle, UK.

Columbia Journalism Review article on how to cover managed care: www.cjr.org/year/99/2/hmo/index.asp

Free Medical Journals: www.freemedicaljournals.com. Promotes free access to medical journals.

Galaxy: http://galaxy.einet.net/galaxy/Health. A directory of sites on health topics.
Gannett's list of resources for covering health care: www.gannett.com/go/newswatch/ nwwebtips/healthmed.html
Healthfinder: www.healthfinder.gov. Health information from the U.S. Department of Health and Human Services.
Healthweb: www.healthweb.org. Health issues Web site.
MedBioWorld: www.medbioworld.com. 25,000 links to journals, associations, and databases.
MEDLINEplus: http://medlineplus.gov. A service of NIH and the National Library of Medicine.
MedWeb at Emory University: www.medweb.emory.edu/MedWeb. A service of the Woodruff Health Sciences Center Library.
National Institutes of Health: www.nih.gov
National Library of Medicine. DIRLINE: http://dirline.nlm.nih.gov
National Library of Medicine Online Databases: www.nlm.nih.gov/databases/databases. html. Databases and online information.
New England Journal of Medicine: http://content.nejm.org. Possibly the most respected health care/medicine journal.
Online Medical Dictionary: www.online-medical-dictionary.org. A free online medical dictionary search engine for definitions of medical terminology, pharmaceutical drugs, health care equipment, health conditions, medical devices, specialty terms, and medical abbreviations.
A Poynter guide to covering the health beat: http://iml.jou.ufl.edu/rxcellence/index.html
Toolkit for New Medical Writers: http://www.amwa-dvc.org/toolkit/index.shtml. From American Medical Writers Association's Delaware Valley Chapter.
U.S. Centers for Disease Control: www.cdc.gov. Data and statistics from CDC.
Welch Medical Library: www.welch.jhu.edu. The Welch Medical Library at Johns Hopkins University.
Yale Medical Library: http://info.med.yale.edu/library/reference/publications

REFERENCES

Associated Press. (2003, September 4). Nebraska, other states committed to Missouri River Summit. Pierre, South Dakota, *Journal-Star.* www.journalstar.com/latest_reg.php?story _id=77644h.
Austin, C. (2001). What are the laws regarding how churches and religious institutions comply with government guidelines? Religion Writers Association. www.religionwriters. com/public/faq/faq7.shtml.
Blakeslee, S. (2002, October 18). Increase in autism baffles scientists. *New York Times,* p. A1.
Broadway, B. (2003, August 16). Borrowed sermons roil downtown congregation. *Washington Post,* p. A1.
Burkett, W. (1986). *News reporting: Science, medicine, & high technology.* Ames, IA: Iowa State University Press.
Detjen, J. (2003, Summer). The beat's basics. A primer on taking over the environment beat. *SEJournal* Excerpts. www.sej.org/pub/SEJournal_Excerpts.htm.
Faith section. (2003, August 2). *Kansas City Star,* section G.
Franklin, J. (1997, March 17). The end of science writing. The Alfred and Julia Hill Lecture at the University of Tennessee. National Association of Science Writers. www.nasw.org/ endsci.htm.
Gastel, B. (1998). *Health writer's handbook.* Ames, IA: Iowa State University Press.
Gastel, B. (1983). *Presenting science to the public.* Philadelphia: ISI Press.

Gibson, D. (2001). Do editors care about religion coverage? www.religionwriters.com/public/faq/faq3.shtml.

Hartz, J., & Chappell, R. (1998). *World apart. How the distance between science and journalism threatens America's future.* Nashville, TN: First Amendment Center.

Knight Center for Environmental Journalism. (1996). Findings: Coverage. Reduced environmental coverage by TV and newspapers. http://Environmental.jrn.msu.edu/survey_coverage.html.

The Koran. (2000). http://www.hti.umich.edu/k/koran.

Leavens, S. B. (2003, September 4). State suing EPA over Clean Air; New York, Connecticut also challenging recent revision. *Concord Online Monitor.* www.cmonitor.com/cgi-bin/clicks/mbb.cgi.

Lieblich, J. (2001). When do you reveal your religion to sources? Religion Writers Association. www.religionwriters.com/ public/faq/faq6.shtml.

Murray, B. (2001, July). The methods of science and journalism. Foundation for American Communication. www.facsnet.org/tools/sci_tech/methods.php3.

Nelkin, D. (1995). *Selling Science.* New York: W. H. Freeman.

Pew Center for Research on the Public and the Press. (1998, June 8). Internet news takes off. http://people-press.org/reports/display.php3?PageID=564.

Simms, P. (2003, July 16). Monkeypox may affect future laws. *Wisconsin State Journal,* p. B3.

States Sue Federal Government to Protect Clean Air Act. (2003, October 27). News release. Office of New York State Attorney General Eliot Spitzer. http//www.oag.state.ny.us/press/2003/oct/oct27b_03.html

White, G. (2001). Why should the secular media cover religion? Religion Writers Association. www.religionwriters.com/public/faq/faq1.shtml.

Willman, D. (2003, August 28). Email interview with freelance environmental reporter who worked for NPR.

Wilogren, D. (2003, August 18). Pastor asks congregants to forgive "borrowing." *Washington Post,* p. B1.

Wolfe, K. (2003, August 18). Email interview with news correspondent for the Religion News Service.

Wolfe, K. (2002, March 6). Bush's bioethics chief a "Renaissance man." Religion News Service.

Zimmerman, R. (2002, October 25). Aneurysm treatment is less risky. *Wall Street Journal,* p. B5.

■ ■ ■ ■ ■

CHAPTER 13

ELECTIONS AND POLLS

When actor Arnold Schwarzenegger announced as a candidate for governor of California in 2003, media swarmed over the story. Within a week, questions about his character surfaced after he reportedly admitted in an interview 25 years earlier that he had smoked marijuana and participated in what some called an orgy. Mr. Universe-turned-politician said he did not recall the interview.

Elections happen in communities every year as politicians—and people not yet politicians—seek state and federal offices. Elections themselves generate reams and reams of copy and generate scores of media stories. Even when an election is not pending, elections and election fallout produce dozens of articles as reporters determine whether officials are following through on campaign promises and if they are carrying out their duties ethically and responsibly.

In covering elections, reporters have a responsibility to present candidates and their views so that voters can make informed decisions. Reporters must focus on issues as well as the candidates' personalities, their voting records if they have held public office, and how they financed their campaigns. That means reporters must know candidates inside and out. They must also know how their states' elections are set up, the agencies and organizations that control and monitor elections, voting patterns, and which party dominates.

Across the country, county boards of elections handle the administration of elections, such as registering voters, maintaining voting records, setting up precincts for voting, and counting ballots on Election Day. State boards have the overall responsibility for administering the election process, including campaign finance expense reporting. Reporters should know who sits on their state elections boards as well as on their local elections boards and each board's responsibilities.

Today, reporters can access election and voting information quickly via the Internet, but covering elections still requires hitting the campaign trail and watching the candidates interact with voters. Covering elections also means monitoring the polls to see how candidates are faring with voters. While a multitude of organizations conduct polls year-round, election cycles draw out even more pollsters to tell candidates and voters who's ahead and why.

In this chapter you will:

- Get an overview of the elections process,
- Find out the primary contacts in covering elections,
- Review types of election stories,
- Learn who conducts polls and why,
- See how to translate poll data to audiences, and
- Learn how to write the poll story.

AN OVERVIEW OF THE ELECTIONS PROCESS

Much information on elections can be found initially on the Federal Elections Commission Web site for both federal and state elections. State and federal laws dictate election cycles, from filing deadlines to dates for primary and general elections. Laws outline the rules for runoff elections, or when one candidate does not receive a plurality of votes. Reporters should consult the laws or their state elections boards to develop a calendar of upcoming elections.

Some states have initiated what is called one-stop voting where specific sites in each county are open before Election Day. People who will be out of town on Election Day or otherwise unable to vote can stop at these sites and cast their ballots early. Usually these one-stop sites are open for a set time period and close prior to Election Day. The sites save voters from the more cumbersome process of having to get absentee ballots.

Voters who will not be near their precincts for whatever reason or who cannot use one-stop voting can vote by absentee ballots. Each county has a process for casting an absentee vote, such as the deadline for submitting in person or mailing in the ballot. If an individual votes by absentee ballot but happens to be home on Election Day, he or she cannot vote again.

Voter registration drives are conducted each year. Many counties have made it easier for individuals to register to vote by allowing them to register at libraries and even when they update their driver licenses. In handling voter registrations, staff members of those agencies are not allowed to influence an applicant's political preference or party registration, to make any statements or take any action to discourage an applicant from registering to vote, or to imply that whether a person registers will affect getting services.

WHO'S ON THE BEAT

The most obvious sources in an election are the *candidates for office*. Candidates for public office might declare their intentions to seek seats on the local school board or in the U.S. Congress any time prior to an election. Often a person will put out feelers to determine support—what some people call "floating a trial balloon"—before actually becoming a candidate. In this try-it-out period, the person wants to get a sense of whether people would actually vote for him or her and support his or her campaign financially.

Prior to any election is a filing period, when candidates for public office pay a fee and officially declare their candidacy. State and federal laws set filing deadlines. A candidate can withdraw prior to election, but after a certain date, his or her name will still appear on the ballot. In some cases, candidates who have withdrawn—and even died—have received considerable votes or even been elected.

Reporters must be aware of a candidate's experience in politics and with the media. Some candidates might not be used to media coverage. For newcomers to politics, a reporter covering a campaign should sit down with the candidates and just get to know them, explain the types of stories that will be written, and note the opportunities the candidates will have to get their views and points covered. The reporter can also explain the newspaper's or television station's policies regarding coverage, such as whether the newspaper endorses candidates. Candidates might want to know whether you as the reporter have any say in such endorsements.

Reporters also have to watch out for people who have become almost professional candidates, that is, those who have years and years of running for public office. They seem to have the same answer to the same questions, almost as though the answers were prerecorded. They also might try to dictate the stories they want covered around a campaign and in an election year.

Along with the candidate in any campaign are the aides, press secretaries, speechwriters, volunteers, and others on the *candidates' staffs*. The candidate might lay out certain rules or policies governing what staff members can say to the media. In most cases, a press secretary is the designated representative for handling media inquiries. Getting to know other staff members can help the reporter throughout the campaign and particularly on Election Day and Night when emotions and activity hit a high as results become known.

Reporters on the election beat must also be in contact with people who oversee the voting process, particularly *local elections board staff members* and perhaps *state elections board members*. A state elections board might also have a press secretary, who issues information about upgrades in voting machines, changes on ballots if a candidate drops out, and other statewide issues. Throughout the campaign, reporters should visit the state elections board Web site periodically—and particularly when candidates file campaign expense reports.

If a reporter covers a race involving congressional or federal elections, he or she will also have to monitor the *Federal Elections Commission* (FEC) and any information related to federal campaigns. The FEC on its Web site has a "Guide for Members of the Media," which includes a calendar, news releases, information on campaign finance, and additional references. For example, the FEC maintains information on the almost 4,000 political action committees (PACs) registered in the country. The Web site also has a guide to accessing the

FEC's database and campaign expense information on candidates in federal and state races.

Members of PACs can also be a source, but reporters should remember each has a particular bias. The list of registered PACs, known as Pacronyms, can be downloaded from the FEC Web site. Corporate PACs make up the largest group, such as American Airlines (AAPAC) and Philip Morris Companies (PHILPAC). Labor unions, such as the Ironworkers Political Action League (IPAL), nonprofit organizations, such as the American Diabetic Association (ADAPAC), and folks with political interests such as Re-Elect Freshman of the Republican Majority PAC (REFORM PAC) have created committees to lobby Congress. Reporters can even find BUBBA's List, which represents Brothers United for Building a Better America based in Austin, Texas.

On Election Day, reporters will want to track down *poll workers,* those who work for the candidate and hand out literature outside polling sites and those who work for the county elections board. The latter, called registrars, can give reporters the latest figures on the numbers of people who have voted at a particular time and assess their moods.

STORIES ON THE CAMPAIGN TRAIL

Stories occur at every point in a campaign. Reporters will cover the following:

■ **Prefiling stories.** These stories cover people who might be candidates. For example, long before Schwarzenegger made his announcement that he would be a candidate for governor of California, political observers and reporters bandied his name as a potential contender. Once he announced, dozens of stories focused on topics ranging from his political savviness to his physique.

■ **Filing stories.** Each day prior to the filing deadline, reporters check with local, state, and federal elections officials to see who has filed for each office. Usually a flurry of filings occurs the last day.

■ **Profile stories.** Prior to each Election Day, media will run profiles or in-depth personality stories examining the candidates, their backgrounds professionally and politically, family ties, behavior, and on and on. Anything in a candidate's life is considered fair game if the person wants to be a public official. People who choose to be in the public eye know they will be the subject of media scrutiny that will look into their actions and statements years earlier. Reporters new to the beat who wonder what to ask candidates can consult political reporter Robert Niles's Web site (2003) at www.robertniles.com/data/questions. He has a list of questions to ask political candidates based on his professional experience, including having been senior producer at latimes.com.

■ **Campaign spending stories.** Campaign finance has been a huge issue in recent years as candidates have conducted multimillion-dollar efforts to get elected. North Carolina's 2002 U.S. Senate race was one of the most expensive in the United States. Elizabeth Dole's campaign raised more than $12 million and Democratic challenger Erskine Bowles's political machine more than $10 million. Candidates often spend more than they raise and will personally finance their campaigns. Many campaigns end up in debt and spend years after the election is over trying to raise funds. Between 1992 and 2000, campaign spending just in U.S. Senate races went from $37.8 million to $66.4 million. One of the most expensive campaigns was Democrat Jon Corzine's race in New Jersey for U.S. Senate in 2000. He raised $63 million and won with just 51 percent of the vote. Former first lady Hillary Clinton raised almost $30 million to win a Senate seat from New York in 2000.

■ **Voter registration stories.** Prior to each election, local boards of elections will conduct voter registration drives to sign up new voters and to make sure that people who have moved have also switched their precinct registration. Legally, people cannot vote in a precinct where they no longer live. In the voter registration stories, reporters can note the percentage of voters by party affiliation, such as Democratic, Republican, or Independent; by race and ethnicity; and by gender. Over time, reporters can do analyses of how the voter profile in precincts, certain sections of a city, or even the state has changed. For example, an area of town might have an increased Hispanic population, an important factor if the town's first Hispanic candidate appears on the ballot. Having such statistics helps report election results and voting trends.

■ **Issues stories.** Usually media set the issues stories, although other topics might surface during the campaign. Editors and reporters will determine what the major issues are and set a schedule for getting candidates' opinions on those issues. Those stories might be overall wrap-up stories by issues, quoting each candidate. Sometimes media will put forth the question and then include candidates' responses in a question-and-answer format. As a campaign progresses, issues might change. Reporters need to pay attention to what voters are saying about issues as well as about the candidates.

■ **Special-interest-group stories.** In any campaign, certain organizations come out in support of candidates who they think will push for their interests if elected. Those groups range from companies, such as utilities to financial institutions, to politically charged organizations, such as Nature Conservancy, the National Rifle Association, and the National Abortion Rights League.

■ **Endorsement stories.** Everyone endorses candidates, including candidates who lose in early or primary elections to special-interest groups to the media. Some groups' endorsements carry substantial leverage. Each endorsement might be a story.

■ **On the campaign trail.** Reporters often travel with candidates. For national offices, such as president, a reporter or team of reporters might be assigned to the campaign and parceled out to particular candidates. The reporters file stories daily on what the candidates say in their stops around the country. On the local level, reporters cover candidates' forums and rallies. They might even follow a candidate for a day as he or she crisscrosses the county or the state.

■ **Political advertising stories.** In the mid-1970s, negative advertising particularly on television brought a new angle to political campaigns. The news media covered the issue of negative ads for the first few decades, but in the last 10 years, the media have begun to critique the content of political ads. Some newspapers, for example, will take apart political ads for the language and the facts. Readers can get a handle on whether the ad has any truth to it. Media also write stories on where candidates are placing their advertising dollars: television, Web sites, direct mail, print, or radio, for example.

■ **Ballots and polling sites.** Just prior to an election, news media, particularly print and online sites, will post polling sites and sample ballots for voters. Voters can also find the information on local election boards' Web sites.

WHO'S GOT THE MONEY

Reporters write hundreds of stories each year on how candidates raise and spend money—and whom they owe after the votes are counted. Reporters should be familiar with recent changes in federal campaign expense reporting laws and how that reporting affects local elections. Across the country, individual organizations and even politicians are working to change campaign finance laws.

State and federal laws require candidates, political parties, and political action committees (PACs) to file campaign finance reports. Reporters need to look at the Federal Elections Commission's as well as their respective states' campaign expense reporting requirements. Many of those reports are filed electronically, which makes them easily accessible via the Internet. A good resource for reporters following the money trail in politics is Peter Overby's article, "Covering Money and Politics," in *Columbia Journalism Review* in 1999.

Political Payback

Donors come in all sizes and expect different levels of payback. For example, Overby noted donors who gave large sums to the Democratic and Republican parties got access to candidates and legislative leaders. They weren't the only ones. PACs fund candidates, and each has its agenda to put before a candidate. Any organization can create a PAC, raise money from its membership, and give it away. PACs are limited to the amount of money they can give to one candidate during a primary and subsequent election, however.

Interesting stories develop from who is giving how much to campaigns. Out of that information can come later stories on patronage, that is, who gets which job in an administration. Whom does the candidate owe and how much? Often people who have given money to the politician's campaign coffers expect favors in return. If the candidate is elected, handing out favors could affect governmental policies and even the official's reelection.

Much campaign revenue, however, comes from donors who give $100 or less to a campaign. Their names might not be as important to a reporter as the names of donors who hand over larger sums. In local elections, a reporter should check out all the donors' names, addresses, and business affiliations. Stories have been uncovered when employees of a business gave the maximum individual amount to a certain candidate—but the funds actually came from their employer who asked them in turn to make the contribution.

More and more candidates are funding their own campaigns through personal fortunes, loans, or second mortgages on their homes. Overby reported in the *Columbia Journalism Review* article (1999) that another trend is contributions through tax-exempt committees. "Some organizations create them to run media campaigns, including so-called issue ads. . . . Tax-exempt committees don't register with the Federal Elections Commission, so their finances—even their identities—often go largely unreported," he said. Political reporters can enlist business reporters to help them identify these groups through records, such as IRS 990 forms, which tax-exempt organizations must file and which are public documents.

In following the money trail, reporters will hear about "hard" money and "soft" money. Hard money, according to Overby's definition, is "money raised and spent by candidates, party committees, and political action committees under the limits and rules of federal campaign finance laws." Soft money has no restrictions and is "raised without restrictions by party committees (from corporations, unions, and wealthy individuals) but supposedly not used directly to benefit specific candidates," Overby wrote in the *CJR* piece. That means the Republican Party or any other organization with a political agenda can run issue ads or even partisan ads paid with so-called soft money. In theory the ads are not supposed to attack a specific candidate but rather an issue. In reality the issue and candidate might be too entwined to be separated.

Reporters can track throughout a campaign how well a candidate is doing financially. Are debts surpassing cash on hand? Where is money being spent, particularly closer to Election Day? When all the votes are cast and funds are in, reporters can calculate just how much each vote cost the candidate. Reporters should also determine the campaign's debt after the election and what fund-raisers are planned to wipe out that debt. Overby noted that nonincumbents were more likely to go into debt than were politicians seeking reelection.

As an aside, Overby also pointed out that reporters should pay some attention to lobbyists. While lobbyists do not make donations to campaigns (unless the donation is personal), whoever paid their salaries might. In looking at campaign finance reports, a reporter might make note of a company president who gave the maximum allowable to a specific candidate or political party.

Lobbyists are required to register within the state where they operate, usually at the state secretary of state's office. Lobbyists who work congressional halls or anywhere in the federal executive offices are required to register under the Lobbying Disclosure Act of 1995. In following the trail from company president to company lobbyist, reporters might find interesting figures on how much a company is wooing and subsidizing a senator and representative who also benefited from corporate executives' campaign contributions.

ELECTION DAY, NIGHT, AND AFTER

All the months of campaigning, schmoozing, and just plain old hard work ends on Election Day. Voters cast ballots, and media cover aspects ranging from voter turnout to predictions of who will win to the emotions of the final day. Here's where the excitement comes in, for the reporter as well as the candidate and his or her staff.

On Election Day, reporters generally go along on last-minute campaigning with the candidate they have covered, including following the candidate to vote. They will look at the weather, assess people's moods, do exit polling to try to calculate who's ahead, analyze previous elections, recap the campaign, and on and on. They might stop in at precincts to talk with poll workers.

By the time the polls close, reporters will be stationed wherever the candidate plans to await election results. Sometimes candidates reserve ballrooms at local hotels, or they join other party candidates at Republican or Democratic offices. Television stations will broadcast results as they are fed in from local elections boards and precincts.

Reporting the Results

Mood, color, reaction, tension, and joy become part of election night reporting, particularly for television stations that can capture immediately the emotions. Reporters must always remember that campaign staffs and candidates will be smiling but tense, optimistic but guarded until the final tallies come in. Throughout the night, reporters will seek out candidates for the latest comment—a fact that might try some candidates' patience in the final hours.

How fast those results come in from the precincts that are the most likely predictors of winners will determine when an election can be called or assigned a winner. Media monitor precincts that traditionally have reflected who will win races. Broadcast media have been criticized for calling races when less than one-fifth of the precincts has reported results. To offset the criticism, national networks in national elections have blocked reports from the East Coast before polls closed on the West Coast. In prior election years, voters in California could hear who had won key eastern states before they had even voted. Some people feared that knowledge prevented some voters from bothering to cast ballots.

If a race is close, the candidate who is behind might be reluctant to concede, and the night might drag on past midnight. In some cases, voting machines malfunction, further delaying results. Once a candidate is ready to concede, broadcast media go on air. They cover the speech, then move to the winning candidates' quarters. With today's technology, viewers can see both candidates juxtaposed or viewed at the same time, having the advantage of seeing each person's actions and reactions simultaneously.

For print reporters, their versions of Election Day will not appear until hours after election results are known. In some cases, however, a reporter might have to meet a deadline without knowing who won. Just remember the 2000 presidential election and how many times the race moved between George W. Bush and Al Gore during the night. Some newspapers called a winner, only to discover hours after the paper was printed that no clear winner had been determined.

Election night bounces between excitement and exhaustion for candidates, their staffs, and reporters. Coverage does not end with the next day's story announcing the winners, assessing why one candidate won over another, and recapping the issues. Depending on the election and the outcome, a reporter might be writing follow-up stories for days—or weeks. If a candidate does not have a plurality, he or she can call for a recount, further delaying official results. One school board incumbent asked for a recount when she lost by fewer than 40 votes. The recount confirmed that she did indeed lose by three dozen votes.

After the Election

Bridget Hall Grumet, a reporter for the *St. Petersburg Times,* wrote the following story after an incumbent commissioner won reelection in fall 2002. The story is a good example of how a reporter can recap a campaign, cover new material, and leave readers with something to think about.

> INVERNESS—It seems the County Commission District 4 race came down to two issues:
>
> "Character and judgment," said Jim Fowler, a Republican who handily won his third commission term Tuesday with 58.56 percent of the vote.
>
> "A hundred thousand dollars and the dirtiest campaign I've ever seen in my entire life," said nonparty challenger Scott Adams, who said he lost the race because he lacked the time and money to respond to Fowler's negative ads.
>
> Okay, make that four issues.
>
> Although Fowler and Adams discussed everything on the campaign trail from water quality and taxes to mandatory garbage collection, character became a decisive factor in this highly watched commission race.
>
> Fowler came under fire early in the campaign for his vote to approve the Halls River Retreat condominiums. Critics said he didn't listen to residents who opposed the controversial time share complex and other developments.

As hefty campaign contributions rolled in from builders and businessmen, a perception grew—inaccurately, Fowler says—that the commissioner was beholden to the development community.

"There are some who would believe I'd sacrifice the environment for property rights, which I deeply believe in, but I would never do that," Fowler said Tuesday evening.

Having amassed an unprecedented $94,960 campaign war chest—half of which he had spent in the tight Republican primary—Fowler put his money toward mailings to combat the character issue. One brochure showed a smiling Fowler, "Willing to Listen, Ready to Work."

Two more slick mailers, which arrived in voters' mailboxes the week before the election, hammered on Adams' colorful past.

"Scott Adams wants to be a Citrus County Commissioner because. . . . He spends so much time at the Courthouse already," reads one mailer, which lists Adams' decade-old arrests and more recent civil court battles.

Adding to Adams' image problems, Sheriff Jeff Dawsy called a press conference last week to brand Adams "delusional" and a "liar" for telling people the Sheriff's Office is under investigation. (Dawsy and other officials say it's not.)

And then there was the e-mail Commissioner Josh Wooten sent fellow Democrats, urging them to support Fowler over Adams.

"Please think long and hard before you cast your ballot in this race, as I'm the one who has to sit there with the winner," Wooten wrote. "Who would you want to sit next to if you were making decisions affecting the safety, health and welfare of one hundred and twenty thousand citizens?"

Adams said the cumulative effect of those attacks was too much, especially coming late in the campaign for a low-budget candidate. Of Adams' $13,922 campaign fund, $9,190 came out of his own pocket.

"What they did after (Fowler's) phone surveys showed they were behind, they came out with a plan of attack that you couldn't recover from," Adams said. "You've got a sheriff, you've got a commissioner writing e-mails, you've got mailers bombarding you like B-52s."

"I'm just proud there's 42 percent of the people that's been following everything that's happening," Adams added, alluding to the voters who landed in his column Tuesday.

Adams won four precincts—two in Homosassa and one apiece in Chassahowitzka and Inverness—and picked up votes elsewhere from residents who rejected Fowler's negative ads.

"I think Adams had a raw deal," said Floral City resident Patricia Holmes. "I don't believe in dragging up dirt like that."

Others said Adams' past was all they needed to know.

"He didn't seem like somebody that should even be running, let alone win," said David Talarico, a Floral City voter.

Even with the election behind him, Fowler said Tuesday night he has his own image problem to fix.

"I think over the past year a perception has been created that I'm not a good listener and that I'm arrogant," Fowler said. "Nothing could be further from the truth."

Fowler said he will try to project a more approachable image. (Copyright *St. Petersburg Times* 2002. Used with permission.)

The story incorporates all the aspects of covering elections: knowing the candidates and following the campaign; having contacts that can give an assessment of the race, including voters; campaign finance spending; and the character and tone of the campaign. In the last graph she left an angle to cover in a few months: Has commissioner Fowler started projecting a more approachable image? That angle also could be used when the next election rolls around.

Once candidates become officeholders, reporters still must cover them. Reporters must let the public, that is, the voters, know whether the candidates are fulfilling campaign promises. Or did the candidates support legislation introduced by the lobbyists whose political action committees made contributions? Politicians' behavior will be fodder for stories should they seek office again.

POLLING: ELECTIONS AND OTHER ISSUES

On any day in any newspaper, a reader most likely could find a story that includes poll results. Who is leading whom in the Fourth District congressional race? How well is the president doing his job? What do residents think about U.S. immigration policies? How do residents spend their leisure time? How much money do they spend a year on vacations? Do college students vote? How much ice cream do they eat?

Polling costs money. Candidates fork out huge amounts for polls to know where they stand, as do businesses from car manufacturers to cosmetic companies. Even media companies have in-house poll directors who oversee periodic surveys on a broad menu of issues.

Most polls phrase questions to get yes–no, approve–disapprove, agree–disagree responses that can be quantified. Simply put, the results make it easy to add up results. For example, 600 out of 1,000 respondents say the president will be reelected and 350 say he will not. In any poll some respondents will say they don't know or will refuse to give an answer. On occasion, pollsters will try to get respondents' reasons, such as why they would not vote for a candidate. They can give respondents a list of choices along with a "don't know" category. Or they can ask open-ended questions to allow respondents to state their reasons. Those types of questions give qualitative responses.

At the end of the survey, pollsters will ask demographic information about the respondents: race or ethnicity, level of education completed, whether they voted in the last general election, if they use the Internet, if they are married, and even more personal questions such as age or income range. Generally pollsters do not ask gender and indicate gender based on the respondent's voice. Demographics provide valuable information, particularly if the same questions are asked over time. With demographics, for example, surveys can tell over time if women vote more often for Democratic candidates, how people of a certain age or income traditionally vote, or how many people with less than a college education use the Internet.

Who Conducts Polls?

Just about everyone does polls. Many organizations want to know how they are viewed, who buys their services or products and why, or what people think about a host of topics. A household name for polling organizations is Gallup, one of the world's largest management consulting businesses. It has more than 2,000 employees and conducts polls almost daily on what people are thinking about issues from support for trade unions to the president's performance to how people grade public schools.

Media organizations, such as *USA Today*, NBC News, *Los Angeles Times*, *Star-Tribune*, ABC News, and CBS News, have their own polling organizations. They might team up to conduct polls during elections or to assess the national mood on issues.

The Roper Center at www.ropercenter.uconn.edu/links.html has links to commercial firms, associations, and academic research institutes that do polls. The Pew Research Center on the People and the Press has conducted a number of surveys and has links to other polls on its Web site. A list of professional polling organizations and trade groups can be found at www.startribune.com/stories/784/700412.html. Among them are the American Association for Public Opinion Research (AAPOR), World Association for Public Opinion Research (WAPOR), and the National Council on Public Polls (NCPP).

Some local governments will poll citizens to find out what they think of services and town performance, like officials did in Kalamazoo, Michigan. The results appear in stories such as Ed Finnerty's article in the *Kalamazoo Gazette* (2003).

> Kalamazoo residents are pleased with public safety, recycling, and many other city services but not too happy with the shape of its streets, a survey suggests.
>
> They are fairly divided on whether the city should ban public nudity or adopt an income tax.
>
> The city's first extensive citizen survey in several years drew 538 responses out of 2,500 queries mailed to residences across Kalamazoo in May. The response was adequate to represent Kalamazoo households with a confidence level of 95 percent, according to a report by the Kercher Center for Social Research at Western Michigan University, which conducted the survey.
>
> Curbside recycling, street snow removal and fall leaf pickup were the three services with which 80 percent or more of respondents said they were somewhat or very satisfied. Only about half of respondents were satisfied with the condition of neighborhood streets and city recreation programs, while just under one-third who responded were somewhat or very satisfied with the building inspections department.
>
> When asked what services or areas they have "no problem" with, a mere 8 percent said they have no problem with the condition of city roads and streets. At the opposite end of the spectrum, 77 percent saw no problem with the level of fire protection and 61 percent saw none with police protection.

"Overall, respondents seem satisfied with the majority of services offered by the city of Kalamazoo," a report on the survey presented Monday to the City Commission said.

Sixty percent of respondents said they think they are getting good services for their tax dollar. Thirty-six percent said they would support implementation of a city income tax coupled with a property-tax decrease, while 41 percent said they oppose an income tax and 22 percent were undecided or skipped the question.

When asked to pick services that should be cut first in light of city budget deficits, 40 percent chose downtown-revitalization efforts. Next closest was parks and recreation, at a distant 17 percent.

Nearly twice as many respondents said there are too many adult-entertainment businesses in Kalamazoo than those who said there are enough, yet 44 percent said they do not support adoption of a public-nudity ban, compared to 47 [percent] who support such a ban.

As for quality of life in Kalamazoo, 33 percent of respondents said it has improved over the last five years, while 27 percent said it has declined.

The City Commission received a report on the survey at the start of a work session on budget priorities for 2004. (© 2003 Kalamazoo Gazette. All rights reserved. Used with permission of *Kalamazoo Gazette.*)

What Do the Numbers Mean?

After pollsters evaluate the survey's results, they release numerical data, that is, what number and what percentage of respondents have which opinions. Several professional organizations such as the National Council on Public Polls (NCCP) and the American Association for Public Opinion Research (AAPOR) publish guidelines for reporting polls. The list typically includes sponsor, question wording, population represented in the sample and sample size (or who was polled and how many were polled), dates, and the method of polling. These points should be included in the story.

Here is the lead from a poll story during the first week of the war in Iraq in 2003:

> A large majority of North Carolinians support the war in Iraq and remain optimistic about its outcome, according to the latest Carolina Poll, a statewide survey conducted twice a year by the UNC-CH School of Journalism and Mass Communication.
>
> In a telephone survey of 613 adults carried out March 23–27, two-thirds (69 percent) agreed the war was a good idea, while one in five (21 percent) said it was a bad idea. Ten percent had no opinion. In a related question, three-quarters (79 percent) said they were optimistic about the outcome of the war, while 15 percent said they were *not* optimistic.

Editors might not want all the technical details of how a survey was conducted, but reporters must know how to evaluate a poll's reliability. Professor Robert L. Stevenson, who for many years has directed the Carolina Poll at

UNC–Chapel Hill, suggests that reporters use NCCP and AAPOR guidelines to determine whether they should accept the poll as reliable. A simple test: Look at the demographic characteristics of the sample (age, gender, race, for example) to see if the sample matches, more or less, the larger population it is supposed to represent, such as all adult North Carolinians. For example, if 55 percent of the state's residents are women, then close to 55 percent of the poll's respondents should be women.

Respondents should be selected in such a way that everyone in the population had an equal chance of being interviewed, the simple definition of a "random sample," Stevenson noted. If the poll overrepresents people who are easy to find or easy to interview, then reporters should question the poll's accuracy.

Stevenson notes that the first—and often the only—question reporters ask is about sampling error. It is a question you never need to ask because its calculation applies to a sample of anything. See Figure 13.1 on how to calculate sampling error. A survey specialist can also help you determine what inferences you can draw from a poll and how much bias or deviation from the population can occur before the survey is not considered "good enough."

Survey researchers know that polling a certain number of residents will give a specific level of accuracy or what is called the confidence level. That's why a media organization can poll 1,200 people and apply those results to the entire U.S. population of 292 million residents. With that number of respondents, researchers say a poll has a margin of error of plus or minus 4 percent. In a poll that interviewed only 650 out of 2.5 million state residents, the margin of error might be plus or minus 5 percent. If a survey has a margin of error of plus or minus 4 points, that means that if the survey were conducted again, 95 times out of 100, the answers would be within 4 percent of figures that would be expected if all adults in the population were interviewed.

Understanding margin of error can be extremely important in analyzing results, particularly in election polls. *The Associated Press Stylebook* (2003) cautions that "if the difference between the candidates is more than twice the sampling error margin, then the poll says one candidate is leading. If the dif-

FIGURE 13.1 Calculating Sampling Error

The simple "error" associated with any random sample is:

$$1.96 * \frac{p * q}{n}$$

Where p = a percentage, $q = 100 - p$, and n = the sample size. If you do some calculations, note that the "error" increases as the percentage approaches 50 and that it varies by the square root of the sample size. Thus, the "error" associated with a poll finding of 25 percent is different from a finding of 50 percent in the same sample, and doubling the sample size does not cut the error in half.

---

ference is less than the sampling error margin, the poll says that the race is close, that the candidates are dead even."

That means if a poll with a margin of error of plus or minus 4 percent showed that 42 percent of respondents supported Candidate Jones and 48 percent supported Candidate Smith, one candidate could not say he was leading. The difference between the candidates is six percentage points, not twice the margin of error, or eight percentage points. Support for Candidate Jones could be anywhere from 38 percent to 46 percent of voters and for Candidate Smith 44 percent to 52 percent. So Candidate Smith could actually lose 44 percent to Jones's 46 percent. An easy way to keep the numbers correct: The original 42 and 48 percent add up to 90 percent (remember the respondents who were undecided and make up the remaining 10 percent). The other combinations could be 38 and 52 or 44 and 46, each combination adding up to 90 percent.

Writing the Poll Story

When reporters look solely at the numbers, they have little more to report than "Eighty percent of state residents believe that campaign finance spending requirements should be changed and limits placed on how much a candidate can spend." Expanding a bit more, the reporter could write that "Four out of five of state residents believe that campaign finance spending requirements should be changed and limits placed on how much a candidate can spend."

The lead of the poll story, as noted in the Carolina Poll story cited earlier, should summarize the most important findings and attribute the source. Subsequent graphs will elaborate on findings and give the technical details. Reporters need to dig deeper into why people responded as they did. If the question had been asked in an earlier poll, the reporter could compare responses in the latest poll with previous results. Readers then could see a trend in residents' thinking. If a major event related to campaign expense reporting had occurred, say a candidate accepted illegal contributions, then the issue might be more visible to residents, who in turn might have thought more about the cost of campaigns. That could affect responses in the later poll.

Reporters can also ask political observers to comment on the poll results. Those interviews put a qualitative context on the numbers and give some explanation of why residents might respond in a certain way. Candidates or politicians who have been outspoken for or against campaign expense reform would also be good sources.

To recap the technical details that should be in a poll story, see Figure 13.2. When writing poll stories, reporters should also:

- Include findings that would be of most interest to readers.
- Translate statistics clearly, as in one out of two respondents said . . . .
- Organize the story so readers can comprehend the most significant findings. Use bullets to outline key statistics.

FIGURE 13.2   What to Include in Poll Stories

- **Who sponsored the survey.** Readers should know if a private organization with a vested interest paid for the poll. That could affect the outcome.
- **The dates of polling.** A major news event could change the way respondents would answer if asked the same questions again.
- **The method of polling** (telephone, face to face, mail survey). Telephone polls are the fastest and cheapest way to conduct a poll.
- **The population polled.** Who was polled can also affect results. Surveys are more credible if respondents are chosen by some random selection method, such as a computer picking every eighth name on a telephone number list. If a political action committee surveyed only Democrats, the results could be different than if only Republicans or if members of both parties were polled.
- **The size of the sample.** How many people were polled will determine the margin of error, which affects the reliability of the results.

- Include relevant details about the sample and the method used for gathering the information.
- Remain neutral in writing.

Polls as Sources

Reporters should treat polls as just another source, despite pressure to base a story on a particular poll's results. Nonprofit organizations or corporations will push to get coverage of poll findings that advance their vested interests or agendas. Both want to prove that the public favors their products or services. As Election Day approaches, poll results often lead the news. People treat election poll findings almost like a crystal ball, predicting who the next senator or president will be, and the candidate who is leading the polls will want those results known.

Poll information should be reported in context. Reporters need to include major news events that could affect public sentiment along with when and how the poll was conducted. They should note reaction from supporters and opponents. Just as with any story, poll coverage should be complete and balanced. The bottom line remains the reporter's and the media's reputation and credibility.

GLOSSARY

Confidence level: A poll's believability. The assurance that the same poll results would be obtained every 95 out of 100 times the question(s) are asked.

Demographics: Background information on people polled, such as their age, gender, race or ethnicity, income, education level, and so on.

Federal Elections Commission: Created in 1975 to administer and enforce the Federal Election Campaign Act. Oversees campaign finance regulations, among other duties.

Gallup: One of the best-known management consulting businesses, particularly for polling. More than 70 years old.

Hard money: Money that candidates, party committees, and political action committees raise and spend under the limits and rules of federal campaign finance laws.

Incumbent: The person holding the office.

Margin of error: Also known as sampling error, it predicts the accuracy of poll results. Given in a plus or minus X percentage points, not percent, figure. The more people polled, the smaller the margin of error.

Patronage: When a candidate returns contributors' favors (in this case, a substantial donation) such as naming them or family members to boards; often the boards have power, such as a highway transportation board that determines where road repair dollars will go.

Political action committees: Known as PACs. Usually formed by corporations and labor organizations to funnel money into political campaigns.

Precinct: The geographic unit where voters are assigned to cast ballots. Generally determined by population size.

Sample size: The number of people polled in a poll or survey.

Soft money: Money raised for candidates without restrictions by party committees. Funds are not be used to benefit directly candidates.

ACTIVITIES

1.   Go online and find a news story published within the last two months that uses poll data *as the basis for the story.* Check the story and determine whether it includes the following information essential in any poll story.

    - Who sponsored the survey.
    - Who conducted (if different from sponsor).
    - The dates of polling.
    - The method of polling (telephone, face to face, mail, Internet).
    - The population polled.
    - The size of the sample.
    - The margin of error.

2.   Looking at the story you selected in Activity 1, evaluate the story for completeness by considering the following questions:

    - What findings are of most interest to you as a reader?
    - Are statistics interpreted clearly, as in one out of two respondents said . . . ?
    - Is the story organized so readers can comprehend the most significant findings?
    - Did the author remain neutral in writing?
    - Are the statistics enhanced by open-ended questions; that is, are individuals, such as experts, government officials, or people in the sample, interviewed? Be sure the story is more than just the results.

3. Find the Web site of a major polling organization, such as Gallup, or poll results of a media organization, such as CBS or *USA Today*. What types of questions are being asked? Are these questions asked over time? Can you find out how respondents' opinions have changed over time? What national events have occurred that could have changed those opinions?

4. You are a city hall reporter. The town is planning to start rollout garbage service, but many residents have opposed the plan when it was proposed in earlier years. The town decided to do a survey of residents to determine overall feelings about the rollout service, which the town has projected will save $250,000 a year in collection costs. Under the rollout plan, residents will purchase heavy-duty plastic trash cans that can hold at least a week's worth of garbage for the average family. They will roll out garbage once a week instead of sanitation workers emptying cans, often located in residents' side or backyards. You have the following information. Write a story.

    ■ 76.7 percent of those polled had a college degree and 13 percent had some college.
    ■ 50 percent were working full time, 17 percent were going to school, and 14 percent retired.
    ■ 52 percent were women, 48 percent men.
    ■ 40 percent had lived in town more than 10 years, 17 percent for 1 to 5 years, and 18 percent for 6 to 10 years.
    ■ 9 percent of respondents were minority.
    ■ Half the respondents were 25 to 44 years old; 10 percent were 18 to 24; 27 percent 45 to 64; and 16 percent were 65 or older.
    ■ 62 percent of the people polled said they would favor rollout garbage collection; 24 percent disapproved; and 13.5 percent had no opinion.
    ■ Most who disapproved were 45 years of age or older.

    Mayor Bart Simmons said in an interview: "We have been considering rollout collection for several years. We estimate it will save us $250,000 a year in workers' time because we would pick up garbage once a week instead of twice a week. Now sanitation workers must go behind people's houses and into their yards to collect garbage. Centerville has used rollout garbage cans for five years, and there seems to be no complaint. We would give waivers to individuals who are not physically able to roll the cans to the street. The cans would be large enough to hold a week's garbage. With this positive response, I feel confident that town council members will vote to begin rollout service within the next three months. I am pleased with the results of the survey."

5. Check Ed Finnerty's story on pages 276–277 to see whether it included what should be in every poll story.

RESOURCES AND WEB SITES

Elections Coverage
BallotWatch: www.ballotwatch.org. Information on every referendum up for statewide election.
Center for Responsive Politics: www.crp.org. Campaign finance data and links to other campaign finance–related sites.

Election Resources on the Internet: http://electionresources.org. Links to election resources worldwide.

Federal Elections Commission: www.fec.gov. Good source for campaign finance–related information, including information on party fund-raising and expenditures.

Federal Voting Assistance Program: www.fvap.gov/index.html. Information for voters; provides information on how, when, and where to vote.

Individual state board of elections sites: Links to information on all state elections as well as voter registration statistics.

Investigative Reporters and Editors: www.ire.org. Dozens of links to political and other sites that monitor candidates and elections. Site has additional link at www.campaignfinance.org. Tip sheets on elections and campaign finance reporting.

National Institute on Money in State Politics: www.followthemoney.org. Tracks data on state legislative candidates.

Poynter's Election Coverage site: www.poynter.org/subject.asp?id=50. Helpful criticism of journalists' coverage of elections and links to election coverage resources.

Project Vote Smart: www.vote-smart.org. Database of elections and elected officials; aimed at providing information to voters.

Voter Information Services: www.vis.org. Detailed information about the U.S. Congress and votes within the House and Senate.

Resources for Polling

The Gallup Organization: www.gallup.com. Links to recent polls and reports; helpful information for understanding polling.

National Council on Public Polls: www-rci.rutgers.edu/~ncppolls. Check out the "20 Questions a Journalist Should Ask Before Reporting on a Poll" section.

Pew Research Center on the People and the Press: http://people-press.org. Results of its Global Attitudes Project surveys and links to other polls. Surveys and commentary on U.S. politics, values, and the media.

PollingReport.com: www.pollingreport.com. Quick links to recent polls.

The Roper Center for Public Opinion Research: www.ropercenter.uconn.edu. Links to reports and poll data on recent topics. Also has "Polling 101," an introduction to the basics of polling.

Public opinion polls on the Internet: www.library.miami.edu/netguides/socopin.html. Links to many of these same sites as well as hundreds more.

The Pulse: www.epinet.org/pulse/pulse.html. Links to many polling sites; useful search tools.

Washington Post Poll Vault: www.washingtonpost.com/wp-srv/politics/polls/polls.htm. Links to *Post* polls and stories; good examples of stories about polls.

Zogby International: www.zogby.com. A competitor to Gallup, provides even more access to polling data; heavily commercial site.

REFERENCES

Finnerty, E. (2003, July 1). Survey: Public services adequate. *Kalamazoo Gazette.* www.mlive.com/news/kzgazette/index.ssf?/xml/story.ssf/html_standard.xsl?/base/news-6/1057073146304620.xml.

Goldstein, N. (2003). *Associated Press Stylebook and Briefing on Media Law.* New York: Associated Press.

Grumet, B. H. (2002, November 7). Character focus gives Fowler edge. *St. Petersburg Times.* www.sptimes.com/2002/11/07/Citrus/Character_focus_gives.shtml.

Niles, R. (2003, September 7). Questions to ask political candidates. www.robertniles.com/data/questions.

Overby, P. (1999, September/October). Covering money and politics. *Columbia Journalism Review.* http://archives.cjr.org/year/99/5/money-main.asp.

CHAPTER 14

FINDING RESOURCES

When reporters and even student journalists want information these days, their first resource is to go to the Internet. That's fine as long as anyone who uses the Internet recognizes its limitations and dangers. Journalists must remember that the Internet is just a starting place for getting data, leads on additional sources, background, perspective, or supporting evidence. Search engines have to be specific to the task. A search may yield thousands of hits, many of which are useless. Web sites may be outdated, inaccurate, or incomplete.

With the downside clearly in mind, journalists can rely on the Web as one step in information gathering. Throughout this text, resources for each type of beat reporting and references for material used in the chapters have been included. This chapter gives journalists additional Web sites. But note: By the time this book is published, some of these sites may have disappeared or become less valuable, or new ones will have emerged.

DEVELOPING LOCAL SOURCES

Every journalist needs to develop his or her Web catalog with notes about which sites are the most helpful and what each contains. Here's a start to developing that resource file. The first section is an example of how a Baltimore County reporter for the *Baltimore Sun* might compile a list of useful Web sites. The list shows how broad a Web site list can be to cover all pertinent areas of a local government beat. The second section shows a list that would help a reporter covering Maryland and Maryland state government. Subsequent sections focus on broader topic areas.

GENERAL BALTIMORE COUNTY WEB SITES

Baltimore County: www.baltimorecounty.com/baltimore

Baltimore County Bar Association: www.bcba.org

Baltimore County Conference and Visitors Bureau: www.visitbacomd.com

Baltimore County Council: www.baltimorecountycouncil.org

Baltimore County Department of Health: www.co.ba.md.us/ p.cfm/agencies/health/index.cfm

Baltimore County Department of Economic Development: www.bcinfobank.com

Baltimore County Environmental Protection & Resource Management: www.co.ba.md.us/p.cfm/agencies/deprm/index.cfm

Baltimore County Fire Department: www.co.ba.md.us/bacoweb/ services/fire/html/firedept.htm

Baltimore County Government: www.co.ba.md.us

Baltimore County Historical Society: www.bcplonline.org/ branchpgs/bchs/bchshome.html

Baltimore County Permits & Development Management Department: www.co.ba.md.us/p.cfm/agencies/permits/index.cfm

Baltimore County Planning Office: www.co.ba.md.us/p.cfm/ agenices/planning/index.cfm

Baltimore County Police Department: www.co.ba.md.us/bacoweb/ services/police/html/police.htm

Baltimore County Public Library: www.bcpl.lib.md.us

Baltimore County Public Schools: www.bcps.org

Baltimore County Public Works Department: www.co.ba.md.us/ p.cfm/agencies/pubwks/index.cfm

Baltimore County Recreation and Parks: www.co.ba.md.us/bacoweb/ services/recpark/html/rechome.htm

Baltimore County Social Services Department: www.co.ba.md.us/ p.cfm/agencies/socserv/index.cfm; www.dhr.state.md.us/ baltocounty.htm

Baltimore County Technology Council: www.bctech.org

Marine Trades Association of Baltimore County: www.mtabc.org

Towson University: www.towson.edu

Baltimore general search: www.WebGuideBaltimore.com. Rated the fastest search engine. The starting point to Baltimore's best sites on the Web. Newspapers, sports, weather, airport, map, hotels, restaurants, and jobs.

MARYLAND SITES

Maryland county governments: www.mec.state.md.us/mec/ meccount.html

Maryland Electronic Capital: www.mec.state.md.us

Maryland General Assembly: http://mlis.state.md.us. Has full text of bills, legislative status, hearing schedules, legislator information, and so forth.

Maryland Department of Health & Mental Hygiene: www.mdpublichealth.org; www.dhmh.state.md.us

Maryland's governor: www.gov.state.md.us

Maryland Judiciary: www.courts.state.md.us

Maryland lobbyists: www.op.state.md.us/ethics/listing.htm. Includes all lobbyists registered in Maryland. Maryland's Most Wanted.com: www.inform.umd.edu/UMS+State/MD_Resources/MDSP/mmw.html

Maryland property records: www.dat.state.md.us/sdat/CICS. The Maryland Department of Assessments and Taxation database of property records, which is searchable by address.

Maryland public records: www.pac-info.com. A searchable site of state public records available on the Internet, including Maryland.

Maryland state government: www.mdarchives.state.md.us/msa/mdmanual/html/mmtoc.html. Includes the Maryland Manual Online.

Maryland state government phone directory: http://archive2.mdarchives.state.md.us/scripts/qpweb20fe/qntwfe20.dll/frame. Lists state government agencies and employees.

GOING TO NATIONAL SITES

Additional Education Sites

American Council on Education: www.acenet.edu. The membership organization of colleges and universities.

American universities list: www.clas.ufl.edu/CLAS/american-universities.html. Links to home pages of U.S. universities.

Argus on Education: www.clearinghouse.net/cgi-bin/chadmin/viewcat/Education?kywd++. Online research library links to resources on topics ranging from education to science and mathematics.

Ask ERIC: http://ericir.syr.edu. A wealth of resources on education. Funded by the U.S. government.

ChildStats: http://childstats.gov. Federal and state statistics and reports on children and their families from several U.S. government agencies.

Chronicle of Higher Education: www.chronicle.merit.edu. Weekly news publication about colleges and universities and their issues.

College and university home pages: www.mit.edu:8001/people/cdemello/univ.html. Alphabetical list of more than 3,000 college sites.

Digest of Education Statistics: http://nces.ed.gov/pubs99/digest98. An annual compilation that serves as a snapshot of education in the United States.

ERIC (Educational Resources Information Center): www.accesseric. org. National information system providing access to education-related literature. Supported by the U.S. Department of Education, Office of Educational Research and Improvement, and the National Library of Education.

Federal Resources for Education Excellence: www.ed.gov/free. Information on educational excellence from several U.S. government agencies.

Integrated Postsecondary Education Data System: http://nces.ed.gov/ ipeds. Data on college enrollment by race, ethnicity, and sex; salaries; tuition; revenue and expenditures; and so on. From the National Center for Education Statistics.

School District Data Book: http://govinfo.kerr.orst.edu/sddb-stateis. html. Information on enrollment, graduation rates, and so forth, for each U.S. school district.

U.S. Department of Education: www.ed.gov

Federal Government Sources and Databases

Centers for Disease Control and Prevention: www.cdc.gov

Central Intelligence Agency: www.odci.gov. Home of the CIA World Fact Book, containing basic information on every country in the world.

Defense Link: www.dtic.mil/defenselink/locator. A searchable database of documents on the Web within the Defense Department.

Edgar: www.sec.gov/edaux/searches.htm. Beginning in 1997, all public companies were required to file their documents to the Securities and Exchange Commission electronically. They are stored at the Edgar archives at the SEC's site.

Federal Deposit Insurance Corporation: www.fdic.gov. A searchable database of financial facts about banks or locations of bank branches.

FedStats: www.fedstats.gov. This is the megastatistics site for the federal government. Index listings and links to federal agencies with statistical programs.

GPO Gateways: www.gpo.ucop.edu/search/default.html; or www.gpo.gov/su_docs/aces/aaces001.html; or Purdue University's GPO Web site: http://thorplus.lib.purdue.edu/gpo. They're basically the same, with full-text searching of documents ranging from GAO reports and the Congressional Record to the Joint Economic Committee's latest compendium of economic indicators and the Federal Register.

Social Security statistics: www.ssa.gov/statistics/ores_home.html. A wealth of searchable information.

Thomas: Congress Online: http://thomas.loc.gov. The online gateway to Capitol Hill and Congress. Named for Thomas Jefferson, it includes the status of bills in Congress by topic, bill number, and short title. It also has an updated calendar of events.

U.S. Census: www.census.gov. Gigabytes of demographic and economic information that is easy to use and to search.

U.S. Department of Justice: www.usdoj.gov

White House: www.whitehouse.gov. The administration site has a good set of links to important government agencies. Its "briefing rooms" are a good way to keep tabs on basic economic and social indicators.

PEOPLE SEARCHES

Ancestry.com: www.ancestry.com. Find heirs or see if someone has died. Updated every six months.

WhoWhere? PeopleSearch: www.whowhere.com. Another people locating service, including email addresses.

Yahoo! People Search: www.yahoo.com/search/people. Another phone and email search engine.

TELEPHONE DIRECTORIES

Four11 Directory Services: www.Four11.com. Email addresses and reverse directories to trace someone when you have only an address.

Phonebook Gateway: www.uiuc.edu/cgi-bin/ph/lookup?Query=. More than 300 university telephone books with phone, address, and email, especially for college professors.

Search.Com: www.search.com

Click on Person Search for a list of some of the biggest directories. Clicking on Yellow Pages gives you access to a series of business listings, including an 800 number directory.

Switchboard: www.switchboard.com. Find phone numbers nationwide.

EMAIL AND WEB ADDRESS TRACERS

Big Foot: http://bigfoot.com. Another email address finder (in both directions).

Internet Address Finder: www.iaf.net. An email address finder.

WhoIs: http://rs.internic.net/cgi-bin/whois. Tells who owns a site, including the city and phone number of the person who signed up for a site's Web address.

PUBLIC RECORDS ON THE INTERNET

Military City Online Web Outpost: www.militarycity.com. The latest military news. If you subscribe to the sponsors, you can search for military personnel in a four-million-record database and get details on military installations. Sponsored by the publisher of *Space News*, *Federal Times*, *Defense News*, and *Army Times*.

All military sites together: www.maingate.com

Prospect Research Center (property tax records online): www.people.virginia.edu/~dev-pros/Realestate.html. Regularly updated site from the University of Virginia; links to searchable property tax records throughout the country. Some are searchable by name, others just by address.

Social Security Death Index: www.ancestry.com/SSDI/main.htm. A genealogy company that keeps publicly accessible information on people who have died while collecting Social Security. If you find someone there, you can find his or her Social Security number.

Surname trace: www.wdia.com/forms/sur_nm-s.html. A pay service (usually $15 to $25 per request) to list people in cities using only a last name. Reporters can get dossiers on people, but the Web version is much more limited.

Vital records: www.medaccess.com/address/vital_toc.htm. Information on how to find birth and death certificates from every state.

FINDING EXPERTS

Kitty Bennett's Experts List: http://sunsite.unc.edu/slanews/internet/experts.html. The *St. Petersburg Times*'s news researcher shares her list of expert sites.

FACSNet: www.facsnet.org. Run by and for journalists, FACSNet offers resources and workshops for journalists. The site has experts, valuable for journalists working on deadline.

Hot news from the Poynter Institute: www.poynter.org

National Press Club's News Sources: http://npc.press.org/library/reporter.htm. Click on "News sources" to access the National Press Club's searchable database of nonprofit and corporate sources.

Policy.com: www.policy.com. Policy statements and research papers compiled for Microsoft Network and Intellectual Capital.

ProfNet: www.profnet.com. An intermediary to find experts at more than 1,000 universities, think tanks, and corporations. Not for deadline; takes a few days.

West's Legal Directory (WLD): www.wld.com. Westlaw's searchable directory of more than 675,000 lawyers and law firms.

MISCELLANEOUS DATABASES

FECInfo: www.tray.com/fecinfo. Maintained by a former FEC official and designed to give up-to-date information on electronically available federal campaign contributions. Similar information is available on its sister organization, the Center for Responsive Politics at www.crp.org.

Internet Law Library: www.pls.com:8001. Includes U.S. Code and Code of Federal Regulations, plus links to state, federal, and international laws, treaties, regulations, and other information.

"Landings" aviation site: www.landings.com. Searchable database on aviation and aircraft. Note: Information may be incomplete. Similar information can be found on the FAA's site of service difficulty reports or the National Institute of Computer-Assisted Reporting's CD-ROMs.

National Library of Medicine—MEDLINE: www.ncbi.nlm.nih.gov/PubMed. Publicly available resource to medical journals; links to participating journal sites.

Patent and Trademark Office: www.uspto.gov. The U.S. Patent and Trademark Office database. An alternative with more history: IBM's Patent Server at http://patent.womplex.ibm.com.

Securities Clearinghouse: http://securities.stanford.edu. Created by Stanford University's Law School. Examples of full text of securities class action lawsuits on the Web.

BACKGROUNDING BUSINESS

D&B Credit reports: www.dnb.com. For a fee, you can get a credit rating and other summary information on a business.

Hoovers: www.hoovers.com. Profiles of large companies.

Nonprofits from Guidestar: www2.guidestar.org. Lists basic information from 500,000 nonprofits' 990 reports in a searchable database. A good place to begin if all you need is one company at a time.

Non Profits Org: www.nonprofits.org/library/gov/irs/search_irs .shtml. Check on the nonprofit status of a company.

PR Newswire: www.prnewswire.com. Searchable database of news releases.

CITIES, COUNTIES, AND STATES

City Net: www.city.net. Links to hundreds of cities on the Web.

Regional Economic Information System: www.lib.virginia.edu/ socsci/reis. A searchable database of income and other data produced by state or city. Useful for regional economic reporters.

Standard state home pages: www.globalcomputing.com/states.html. Links to every state's home page. Or guess, using this url structure: www.state.xx.us, replacing "xx" with the 2-letter postal designation, such as MD for Maryland.

MAPS AND GEOGRAPHY

Association of American Geographers: www.aag.org

Consortium for International Earth Science Information Network (CIESIN): www.gateway.ciesin.org

CrimeMap: www.ojp.usdoj.gov/cmrc/faq/welcome.html. Sponsored by the National Institute of Justice's Crime Mapping Research.

General maps and directions: www.mapquest.com

The Geographer's Craft: www.utexas.edu/depts/grg/gcraft/ contents.html

U.S. Geological Survey: www.mapping.usgs.gov

JOURNALISM SITES

AJR NewsLink, *American Journalism Review:* http://ajr.newslink.org/ menu.html

American Press Institute: www.newspaper.org

American Society of Newspaper Editors: www.asne.org

Casey Journalism Center for Children and Families: http://casey.umd.edu

Center for Community Journalism: www.oswego.edu/~ccj

Center for Integration and Improvement of Journalism:
www.journalism.sfsu.edu/www/ciij/ciij.htm

Center for Investigative Reporting: www.muckraker.org

Center for Media and Public Affairs: www.cmpa.com

College Newspapers Online: www.bowdoin.edu/~sgershey/papers

Editor & Publisher: www.mediainfo.com

FACSNET, resources and education for journalists: www.facsnet.org

Freedom Forum: www.freedomforum.org

Investigative Reporters and Editors: www.ire.org

Media Studies Center: www.mediastudies.org

NewsCentral: www.all-links.com/newscentral

NewsDirectory.com: www.newsdirectory.com

NICAR, National Institute for Computer-Assisted Reporting:
www.nicar.org

No-Train, No-Gain: www.notrainnogain.org. Links to how-to articles
for reporters.

PowerReporting, resources for journalists: www.powerreporting.com

Poynter Institute for Media Studies: www.poynter.org

Project for Excellence in Journalism: www.journalism.org

Society of Professional Journalists: www.spj.org

SEARCH ENGINES

Altavista: www.altavista.com

Dogpile: www.dogpile.com. This search engine compiles 10 or more of
the biggest search engines.

Excite Netsearch: www.excite.com

Google: www.google.com

Inference: www.inference.com/ifind. A search engine that searches
lots of the biggest others. Results organized by the kinds of site found,
such as government, foreign, and so on.

Yahoo!: www.yahoo.com

REFERENCES

Haller, B. (2000). Web site. www.towson.edu/~bhalle/web-rep.html.

INDEX

■ ■ ■ ■ ■ ▬▬▬▬▬▬▬▬▬▬▬▬▬▬▬▬▬▬▬▬▬▬▬

Reporter's religious background, 257
Secular humanism, 258
September 11, 2001, 252
Sexual orientation, 253, 254
ReligiousTolerance.org, 256, 260
Reporting skills (general), 17
Research, 20–21, 25–37, 40–42
  Academic sources, 26
  Computer-assisted reporting, 30–35, 36
  For interviews, 36, 40–42
  Online, 20–21, 27–30
  Organization, 35–36
  Pitfalls, 27
  Profnet, 25
  Search engines, 28, 37
  Trade publications, 25–26
  Trade and industry groups, 26
  Web site credibility, 28–29
Retail beat, 178
Revenue bonds, 147–148, 151
Revenue sources for businesses, 180–182
Revenue sources for local government, 138–146
Rhode Island nightclub fire, 210
Rolodex interviews, 80, 91
Roper Center, 276

S

Sales tax, 140–141, 151
Sample size, 281
Sampling error, 278–279
SARS, 242
Scanners (*see also* Public safety), 201
Science reporting, 242–252
  American Chemical Society, 244, 246
  Embargoed news releases, 246
  First Amendment Center report, 245

Foundation for American Communication (FACS), 251–252 , 261
Jargon, 250–251
National Association of Science Writers, 243–244, 246, 250, 252, 262
National Institutes of Health, 245
Peer reviewed research, 245
Scripps Science Service, 244
Sigma Xi, 246, 262
Science sections, 242
Search engines, 28, 37, 292
  AllTheWeb, 28
  Dogpile, 28, 292
  Google, 28, 292
  How they work, 28
Secular humanism, 258
Securities and Exchange Commission (SEC), 113, 179, 180, 182, 185
Sentencing (*see also* Court coverage), 226–227
September 11, 2001, 2, 12, 85, 86, 164, 189, 194, 200, 201, 204, 205, 215, 242, 252
Sexual orientation, 71, 87, 253, 254
Shield laws, 73, 74, 75
Sigma Xi, 246, 262
Sixth Amendment, 72–73, 75
Smart, Elizabeth, 232
Sniper attacks in Washington, DC, area, 30, 195–196, 200
Society of Environmental Journalists (SEJ), 243
Society of Professional Journalists (SPJ), 18, 61–62, 79–80, 85, 292
  Diversity Toolbox, 79–80
Socioeconomic class, 88–90
Soft money, 271, 281
SOT, 55–56, 57